To Awaken
My Afflicted
Brethren

Peter P. Hinks

To Awaken
My Afflicted
Brethren

*David Walker and the
Problem of Antebellum
Slave Resistance*

The Pennsylvania State University Press
University Park, Pennsylvania

Library of Congress Cataloging-in-Publication Data

Hinks, Peter P.
  To awaken my afflicted brethren : David Walker and the problem of
antebellum slave resistance / Peter P. Hinks.

        p.   cm.
  Includes bibliographical references and index.
  ISBN 0-271-01578-0 (cloth : alk. paper).
  ISBN 0-271-01579-9 (pbk. : alk. paper)
  1. Walker, David, 1785–1830.   2. Abolitionists–United States—Biography.
3. Free Afro-Americans—Biography.   4. Antislavery movements—United States.
5. Slavery—United States—Insurrections, etc.   I. Title.
E446.W178H56   1997
326′.0973—dc20   96–28090
                                                                      CIP

It is the policy of The Pennsylvania State University Press to use acid-free paper
for the first printing of all clothbound books. Publications on uncoated stock satisfy the minimum requirements of American National Standard for Information
Sciences—Permanence of Paper for Printed Library Materials, ANSI Z39.48-1992.

In memory of my friend and teacher, Charlotte Lambek

SETH: Nigger, you crazy!

LOOMIS: How much big you want?

SETH: You done plumb lost your mind!

BERTHA: Leave him alone, Seth. He ain't in his right mind.

LOOMIS: You all don't know nothing about me. You don't know what I done seen. Herald Loomis done seen some things he ain't got words to tell you.

BYNUM: What you done seen, Herald Loomis?

LOOMIS: I done seen bones rise up out the water. Rise up and walk across the water. Bones walking on top of the water.

BYNUM: Tell me about them bones, Herald Loomis. Tell me what you seen.

—from August Wilson, *Joe Turner's Come and Gone*

Contents

Acknowledgments

My research, analyses, and prose have been enhanced by numerous colleagues. One of my longest and largest debts is to Peter Wood and Lil Fenn. Both friends heartily encouraged me in late 1986 to undertake the risky work of investigating so seemingly inaccessible a person as David Walker. Their support was invaluable to me as I was watching my former dissertation topic wither and I sought some security for a new focus on Walker. They also helped this unscrubbed Yankee navigate what were for me the uncharted channels of Southern archives and protocol. I will never forget their kind hospitality and wisdom as I winnowed the North Carolina Piedmont for Walker. Peter's unsparing criticisms of one of my key conclusions on Walker also saved me from committing what would have been a blunder.

If there is any merit whatsoever to my prose or argument, it is due mainly to the trenchant and patient intervention of my dissertation adviser, David Brion Davis. In a schedule encumbered with manuscripts to be read and students to be counseled, David somehow managed to find time to fill my margins with literary guidance and historical coaching that was always appropriate and never failed to energize me. Without his championing my topic from conception, David Walker likely would continue undisturbed.

I well remember the long, congenial discussions about Walker I had with John Blassingame, and how following them I often realized that John had quietly prodded me into looking at Walker and his world from some novel and significant angle. I hope I was able to translate some of that insight into this book.

I have benefited from the wise comments of many scholars who took time from their busy schedules to read my manuscript: Douglas Egerton,

Roy Finkenbine, Julie Winch, Marc Lendler, Cornel West, Jim Turner, and Jack McKivigan. I owe special thanks to Jack, whose counsel so often proved invaluable and who introduced me to Merton Dillon in 1988. Merton generously and closely reviewed my chapters and unreservedly shared his own research in the field of slave resistance with me.

One of the greatest boons of my work on Walker has been coming to know Bob Paquette. Bob's zealotry for thorough research challenged me on many occasions to push further into matters I glibly imagined exhausted. His detailed excavations of the networks of confederates in Cuba's La Escalera conspiracy stood as a paradigm for my own unearthing of the distribution network for Walker's *Appeal*. While my efforts pale in the face of his meticulousness, I thank him for all the generous assistance he gave me and apologize for any doors on Walker I left unopened.

I have been fortunate to be under the editorial care of Peter Potter, who has been shepherding this book through various stages over the last seven years or so. My book is improved by his counsel, and my life is enhanced by his friendship. Peggy Hoover, who minutely copyedited this book, has spared me from many gaffs, imprecisions, and verbosities.

I also gratefully acknowledge the assistance of the following fellowships in helping me meet the costs of my research and writing: Charlotte W. Newcombe Doctoral Dissertation Fellowship; John F. Enders Fellowship of Yale University; and Albert J. Beveridge Grant for Research in the History of the Western Hemisphere.

My daughter, Aoife Eileen, has, I am sure, learned far more about David Walker and antebellum slave resistance than she ever bargained for. She was my sharp-eyed companion on tramps through Talbot County and Maryland's Eastern Shore in search of Frederick Douglass and has listened patiently to her father expound far too many times. Yet her own fierce commitment to indict the outrages and injustices of the world helped me see into the passionate heart of David Walker probably far more often than my own words illuminated him for her. My life is immeasurably enriched by all she has brought into it, and I thank her for having helped sustain me over the long road of this book.

Introduction:
"Strange to ever keep in mind"
The World of David Walker

> *How we could be so submissive to a gang of men, whom we*
> *cannot tell whether they are as good as ourselves or not, I*
> *never could conceive.*
>
> —David Walker's *Appeal*

"Everything must be transacted through the medium of negroes," complained Scottish naturalist Alexander Wilson in 1809 upon visiting a tavern in Washington, North Carolina, a town near the center of the state's coast. Later in the same year, while discussing Charleston in a letter, Wilson characterized this dependence much more graphically: "Everything must be done through the agency of these slovenly blacks and a gentleman here can hardly perform the services of Cloacina without half a dozen negroes to assist him." Wilson's ridicule was not far off the mark. In the same letter, he observed more soberly: "The superabundance of negroes in the Southern States has destroyed the activity of the whites. The carpenter, bricklayer, and even the blacksmith, stand with their hands in their pockets, over looking their negroes."[1] Although concerned for the enervation of free white labor, Wilson also revealed that while the white craftsmen loitered their black charges were actually performing the skilled trades. Wherever he looked along the southeastern coast of the United States, Wilson found blacks overwhelming whites demographically and performing virtually every task required to keep the region alive and growing.[2]

Similar dynamics prevailed in Wilmington, North Carolina. Lying near the southern corner of the North Carolina coast in New Hanover County,

---

1. Clark Hunter, ed., *The Life and Letters of Alexander Wilson* (Philadelphia: American Philosophical Society, 1983), 299, 310–11.

2. For an excellent description of the various tasks and skills performed by black labor in late-eighteenth-century Charleston and an analysis of the significant economic influence slave laborers wielded in the town, see Philip Morgan, "Black Life in Eighteenth-Century Charleston," *Perspectives in American History*, n.s., 1 (1984), 185–222.

and equidistant from Washington and Charleston, Wilmington had a black demographic majority from the first federal census in 1790 through at least 1820. The town and the surrounding Lower Cape Fear region—named for the large southern branch of the Cape Fear River, which passed through the region—relied heavily on black labor and artisanry. The production of naval stores, rice cultivation, river and coastal pilotage, cooperage, metalworking, and vending at the marketplace were only some of the essential local enterprises that were largely dependent on black workers.

No industry in the town of Wilmington so clearly evinced its reliance on black labor as the building trades. White contractors often assembled whole teams of black masons, carpenters, plasterers, and other craftsmen to work on large projects and they were not uncommonly supervised by a black foreman.[3] Despite pressure from local white craftsmen to prevent it, several blacks—such as Anthony Howe and James Sampson—became prominent contractors in their own right and marshaled the forces of a number of slave and free black builders. Indeed, many young free black males were virtually forced into apprenticeships in the building trades and thus provided a steady stream of carpenters and masons. A large part of the town's most elegant houses still standing from the antebellum era are the result of slave and free black labor.[4] Wilmington's most famous mansion from that age—the Bellamy Mansion on Market Street—was built exclusively by black labor in 1860. Rufus Bunnell of Vermont, architect of the house, offered a striking picture of that situation:

> I found the negro mechanics quite docile and I took pleasure showing the foremen how to carry out my drawings; it however seemed strange to ever keep in mind, that almost to a man these mechanics (however seemingly intelligent,) *were nothing but slaves* and capable as they might be, all the earnings that came from their work, was regularly paid over to their masters or mistresses.[5]

3. Such work arrangements were not unusual in antebellum Wilmington. For example, in an 1802 petition to the North Carolina legislature, white mechanics in Wilmington complained: "Most of those Negroes whose time is hired to themselves, employ on work to their own benefit and advantage, gangs of from eight to twelve negroes; [and] that those gangs are consequently entirely dependent on, and at the disposal of their employers." Note that "their employers" were also black. These arrangements are discussed further in Chapter 1. General Assembly Session Records November–December, 1802, Box 3, File "Petitions" (folder 4), North Carolina State Archives, Raleigh.

4. Catherine W. Bishir, "Black Builders in Antebellum North Carolina," *North Carolina Historical Review* 61 (October 1984), 422–61.

5. "The Autobiography of Rufus William Bunnell" (typescript), 136 in Bunnell Family Papers, Box 20, file 360, Manuscripts and Archives, Yale University, New Haven, Connecticut.

The paradox Alexander Wilson disparaged in 1809 still puzzled Bunnell in the Wilmington of 1860: while whites observed at a distance, African Americans actually built and sustained the material foundation of Southern towns. Indeed, the very symbol of planter dominance—the elegant and capacious residence—was executed and maintained by the African Americans that the planter subordinated. This was a society dependent not only on black skills but also, despite its best efforts to obscure that reality, on black initiative and guidance. Yet this was also a society ruled by the fact "strange to ever keep in mind, that almost to a man these mechanics (however seemingly intelligent,) *were nothing but slaves* and capable as they might be . . . regularly paid over [their earnings] to their masters or mistresses." This was the world in which David Walker grew into young manhood and first encountered the tough paradox: How could such a powerful people be also so powerless?

David Walker was born a free black in late-eighteenth-century Wilmington, and his memories of that world would deeply color the work for which he is best remembered, a pamphlet entitled *Appeal to the Colored Citizens of the World,* one of antebellum America's most powerful political documents. My book is about David Walker's life in that world and the many other worlds he entered into and fathomed in his short, passionate life. While numerous historians have acknowledged Walker's significance, only a handful have investigated and treated him at any length, and their emphases have been overwhelmingly on the more accessible years he spent in Boston and on summaries and critiques of the *Appeal.*[6] Little is known about his years in the South, and we still do not know much about his life in Boston and the North, or about the full significance of the *Appeal.* His perambulations in early-nineteenth-century America—ranging from Wilmington and Charleston in the South to Boston in the North—surveyed the troubled map of race in the nation and endowed his young and vivid voice with an authority far surpassing his years. This book strives to give flesh to that experience.

This book is also about how David Walker compressed all that expe-

6. See Herbert Aptheker, *"One Continual Cry": David Walker's Appeal to the Colored Citizens of the World (1829–1830)—Its Setting and Its Meaning* (New York: Humanities Press for AIMS, 1965); Merton Dillon, *Slavery Attacked: Southern Slaves and Their Allies, 1619–1865* (Baton Rouge: Louisiana State University Press, 1990), 145–50; Vincent Harding, *There Is a River: The Black Struggle for Freedom in America* (New York: Vintage Books, 1983), 75–100; Donald Jacobs, "A History of the Boston Negro from the Revolution to the Civil War" (Ph.D. diss., Boston University, 1968), 55–79; Donald Jacobs, "David Walker: Boston Race Leader, 1825–1830," *Essex Institute Historical Collections* 107 (1971), 94–107; Sterling Stuckey, *Slave Culture: Nationalist Theory and the Foundations of Black America* (New York: Oxford University Press, 1987), 98–137; and Wilson Jeremiah Moses, *Black Messiahs and Uncle Toms: Social and Literary Manipulations of a Religious Myth* (University Park: The Pennsylvania State University Press, 1982), 38–46.

rience and knowledge into one great and unprecedented effort to goad an exploited people into uplifting their understanding of themselves and smashing the slavery that was blighting their lives. His *Appeal* was the instrument of that uplift and his cultivation of a covert communication network in the South, the vehicle for delivering it. The *Appeal* is a masterpiece of exhortatory writing whose impact—psychological and social—on contemporary African Americans can be compared only to the impact that Thomas Paine's *Common Sense* had on the white patriots of revolutionary America. This book excavates Walker's neglected text and the buried fibrils of the fine net he cast to distribute it. Only recently have historians begun careful efforts to reconstruct those covert networks, which are hidden but critical components of the slaves' political and intellectual culture.[7] Digging into Walker allows us to uncover more.

Not only a biography and an exegesis, this book is also a study of the nature, frequency, and impact of slave resistance in early antebellum America and how these forces may have influenced Walker. The years 1800–1831 comprised the period of the most active and carefully planned slave conspiring and rebelling in American history. Gabriel's conspiracy in 1800, the Easter Plot of 1801–2, the uprisings in Louisiana in 1811–12, the Vesey conspiracy of 1822, Walker's disseminations in 1829–30, and Nat Turner's famous march in Southampton in 1831 are only the more celebrated incidents in an era of unprecedented slave restlessness and organizing.

Why were those thirty years so volatile? This is far from the first time a historian has raised that question. Herbert Aptheker posed it and many others for all of us fifty years ago with his pioneering *American Negro Slave Revolts,* and in recent years Merton Dillon has advanced the investigation in *Slavery Attacked: Slaves and Their Allies, 1619–1865.* The intention of the present book is neither to attempt exhaustive inquiries into these various incidents of revolt and conspiring nor to answer the above question with any conclusiveness. Rather, after reading relevant primary sources and the findings of other historians, I chose here to discern in these events patterns and influences that will help us understand what relationship they had to Walker, a son of this era and region and the

7. For some of the best work currently being done, see David Cecelski, "The Shores of Freedom: The Maritime Underground Railroad in North Carolina, 1800–1861," *North Carolina Historical Review* 71 (April 1994), 174–206; Douglas R. Egerton, " 'Fly Across the River': The Easter Slave Conspiracy of 1802," *North Carolina Historical Review* 67 (April 1991), 87–110; and Egerton, *Gabriel's Rebellion: The Virginia Slave Conspiracies of 1800 and 1802* (Chapel Hill: University of North Carolina Press, 1993).

architect of one of its boldest and most innovative plans for slave empowerment and organization.

Situating Walker in the context of the South and its tremors of 1800–1831 allows us to begin to answer certain key questions and to understand far more sharply Walker's great significance in the black struggle against slavery. Why was planning for revolt so intense during these decades? Why was so much of this activism concentrated along the eastern seaboard of the South, from Richmond to Charleston and especially in the region of southeastern Virginia and northeastern North Carolina? Why did evangelical Christianity play such a central role ideologically and organizationally for Walker and most of his predecessors? What force did America's revolution and its birth of republicanism and democracy have on the rebels' aspirations and plans? How did the varied conspirators communicate among themselves, extend their plots geographically, and recruit new members? How were these acolytes brought to endorse rebellion and steeled against fearing its terrible risks? How did Walker's broad geographical mobility and deep exposure to Northern culture shape his thinking and stratagems?

David Walker opens a window through which we can view more closely the problems of antebellum black resistance. Walker's *Appeal*, and his efforts to circulate it among the slave population, was one of the boldest and most innovative plans for slave empowerment and resistance ever executed in America. Shocked white Southern authorities reacted against its arrival in their communities swiftly with new and sterner prohibitions against slave literacy, against distribution of antislavery literature, and against contact between blacks living in port towns and black sailors from Northern vessels passing through. Yet, despite the novelty of the effort, the resolve of Walker and his few associates, and the braying of Southerners about the damage the *Appeal* had caused, the quick reaction of the authorities readily stopped the work from ever threatening the fundamental security of any Southern locale.

The obstacles confronting any attempt at conspiracy and rebellion were huge: a vigilant and resident white population that was demographically dominant throughout most of the South and well-organized in local militias and patrols; a terrain that did not have any place for large groups of rebels to safely retire and protect themselves against white attacks; and a legal and extralegal system that brought swift and brutal retribution on conspirators and made the risks of resistance terrible. These daunting forces only made all the more remarkable and courageous the actions that were taken against slavery between 1800 and 1831. Even with these odds, some slaves in the South opted to resist and created a tradition of resistance. Yet this tradition must not obscure the reality that raising rebellion of the sort that could truly threaten the slave regime in the South by 1830 was immensely difficult if not impossible, even with a plan as resourceful as Walker's. There is much sad truth to Eugene Genovese's pronouncement "In the United States those prospects [for successful slave rebellion], minimal during the eighteenth century, declined toward zero during the nineteenth."[8] One of Walker's great challenges, therefore, was to persuade his audience of their imperative and their ability to defy their enslavement against the seemingly overwhelming arguments urging quiescence.

But Walker feared the likelihood of an even more pressing problem in any accommodation of African Americans to white supremacy: some significant degree of internal assent within black individuals to the supposed naturalness of white dominion over blacks. The biggest problem Walker addressed was the one of the individual psyche: how to transform the consciousness of individual blacks mired in the paradox of powerlessness amid power into personalities unified around an awareness of their own strength, integrity, and freedom. Walker's work is far from a simple harangue against slavery and whites intended to fire blacks to overwhelming acts of destruction against that institution and the racism justifying it. Truly directed, persevering, and effective rebellion could not occur until the individual participants had begun to possess for themselves the self-knowledge, self-definition, and awareness of entitlement from which the lords of slavery had labored to keep them.

Walker ascertained that the planters demoralized and confused the slaves by constantly assailing them with their own self-serving definitions of who African Americans were. For Walker, the first act of resistance occurred when the black individual began to doubt these prescriptions. Only then could the individual begin to shake free of the grip of the paradox, and only then could the individual begin to move toward the responsible self-knowledge and self-ownership that Walker and numerous other contemporary reformers—white and black—believed would be the foundation of a regenerated America where whites and blacks would live in a productive and respectful equality. The *Appeal* was to be the device to spark this transformation. It was a huge and daunting task Walker assigned himself and his handful of colleagues, and one that they would only begin, let alone fulfill. But he was certain that without this internal regeneration America would have nothing on which to rebuild itself, that acts of resistance would become mere vagrant flailing, venting only rage without direction, understanding, or any success.

8. Eugene Genovese, *Roll, Jordan, Roll: The World the Slaves Made* (New York: Random House, 1974), 594.

How can the powerless and the demoralized be helped to recognize their power and dignity and embrace those attributes as theirs? How can they be emboldened to take deliberate collective action against the system that cultivated their degradation? These were the questions David Walker put to himself at an early age and to which his life's work was a long response. Walker commenced his disseminations at a time when hopes for black empowerment and positive change in race relations were actually rising among many blacks in the North in the late 1820s. Free black communities with increasingly confident leaders were coalescing throughout the North. A religious enthusiasm that stressed the ability of individuals to remake themselves under God and banish sin from their lives was sweeping the North. And the first signs of some willingness on the part of whites to consider other ways for the races to live together was becoming apparent as a handful of thoughtful whites began to reject the popular colonization movement to return American blacks to Africa. Walker believed that African Americans not only could but must change themselves: their traditions, prospects, and power were all available to them. Through their change, America would have to change as well. This study strives to explain why by 1829, against so many odds, David Walker beieved all this must come to pass.

1

Born Free into Slavery

David Walker's Early Years

"Those who are rich can't get hands to assist them until they can buy Slaves, and teach them handicraft Trades," exclaimed the English author of an early-eighteenth-century report outlining the essentials of North Carolina colonization.[1] "If you intend to do any business here a Cooper and a Craft that will carry about 100 barrels will be absolutely necessary. I have suffered much for want of them, and that want of Craft and negroes will be a great obstruction in securing the Quantity of Naval Stores at this time that otherwise I might do," complained James Murray in 1741 about developing his large tract of land along the northwest branch of the Cape Fear River.[2] From the beginning of white settlement in the Lower Cape

---

1. William Saunders, ed., *Colonial Records of North Carolina,* 10 vols. (Raleigh, N.C., 1886–90), 6:1026. (Hereafter cited as Saunders, *Colonial Records.*)
2. From *Letters of James Murray, Loyalist,* ed. Nina M. Tiffany (Boston, 1901), quoted in

Fear region in the 1730s, most prospective colonists realized that there were two absolute requirements to settling there successfully: owning many slaves and owning as much land as possible along the Cape Fear and its tributaries. Once white colonization of the area began in earnest in the 1730s under the initiative of Maurice Moore, the question of land distribution was settled, and several of the early settlers, especially those friendly with the royal governor, George Burrington, were allowed to engross up to 5,000 acres of the choicest land.[3]

The introduction of slaves into the region was equally dominated by the wealthiest and best-connected settlers. The whole coastal region of the province of North Carolina lacked sufficient white labor to exploit the colony's rich potential for producing tobacco, naval stores, and other commodities.[4] While most white colonists in North Carolina did not have enough cash to purchase slaves, a few settlers arrived not only with money but also with a large number of slaves. Maurice Moore and his brothers, Roger and Nathaniel, and twelve other men from the Charleston district, acquired more than 80,000 acres of prime land and introduced over 1,000 slaves into the region by the early 1730s. In 1742 James Moir of the Society for the Propagation of the Gospel estimated that there were 3,000 souls in the Wilmington district, 2,000 of whom were black.[5] In the decades to come, these and other large planters would be overwhelmingly responsible for the spiraling presence of Africans in the region.

The opportunities for exploitation of the land and its products in North Carolina were numerous. The prospect of tapping the vast pine barrens of the Lower Cape Fear region for naval stores and lumber attracted many white immigrants. Parliament's restoration of bounty payments on pitch, tar, turpentine, and rosin in 1729, and Charleston's steady move away from naval stores production and to large-scale rice cultivation, only encouraged the settlers' hopes. From the beginning of Cape Fear colonization, the processing of pine products flourished in the region and quickly became the principal item of foreign trade. By 1772 the British Empire centered its essential naval stores industry in the Lower Cape Fear re-

---

Lawrence Lee, *The Lower Cape Fear in Colonial Days* (Chapel Hill: University of North Carolina Press, 1965), 152.

3. For further discussion of these matters of settlement, see Lee, *The Lower Cape Fear*, 152.

4. A passage in a report sent to the Lords' Proprietors of the colony in 1764 makes this scarcity of white labor quite clear. See Saunders, *Colonial Records*, 6:1026.

5. Ibid., 4:605.

gion, where as much as 32 percent of the American colonies' pine derivatives were produced and exported.[6]

Blacks performed virtually all the labor related to this industry. They "boxed" the trees by carefully cutting cavities in them to receive the sap and then distilled it into turpentine. Enslaved coopers made the barrels to hold the fluid. Slaves supervised the kilns used in the dangerous process of turning decayed pine into tar and pitch and were equally skilled at converting turpentine into rosin. Once these products were ready to be moved to the wharves of Wilmington or Brunswick, black pilots floated them down the Cape Fear River on rafts built by black carpenters. From turpentine orchard to shipside, black slaves drove the naval stores industry.[7]

Blacks likewise dominated in the lumber industry. From first settlement, the Lower Cape Fear region had a ready market for lumber in the wood-hungry islands of the West Indies, especially Barbados. By the time of the Revolution the region had no less than fifty sawmills in full operation, generating wealth that was second only to pine products. One of the largest plantations along the Cape Fear, "Hunthill," had a "grand" sawmill capable of producing up to 3,000 sawed planks a day. It was worked almost exclusively by blacks. Throughout North Carolina and the Southeast, blacks regularly worked in the woods, not only at felling trees but also at squaring them for market, moving them from the forest, and conducting them down rivers to ports. Large-scale exploitation of the woods would have been impossible without these skilled blacks to execute it.[8]

While blacks in the Cape Fear region regularly served as teamsters, their role in river transport—North Carolina's main mode of transportation in the colonial era—was even more critical. Pervasive as boatmen in the lumber and naval stores industry, they also guided the heavy mercantile traffic between Wilmington and Fayetteville along the northwest branch of the Cape Fear. Fayetteville was an important entrepôt for the products of the state's interior, and its merchant class had close political and economic ties with that of Wilmington. Successful navigation of this

6. Lee, *The Lower Cape Fear,* 155.

7. Janet Schaw, *Journal of a Lady of Quality,* ed. Evangeline Walker Andrews and Charles McLean Andrews (New Haven: Yale University Press, 1939), 184–85; John Brickell, *The Natural History of North Carolina* (1737; reprint, Raleigh, 1910), 265–67; James H. Brewer, "An Account of Negro Slavery in the Cape Fear Region Prior to 1860" (Ph.D. diss., University of Pittsburgh, 1949); Lee, *The Lower Cape Fear,* 150–53.

8. Charles William Janson, *The Stranger in America, 1793–1806,* ed. Carl S. Driver (New York: Press of the Pioneers, 1935), 380–81; Mark Van Doren, ed., *Travels of William Bartram* (New York: Dover Publications, 1955), 256–57; Schaw, *Journal of a Lady,* 184–85; Lee, *The Lower Cape Fear,* 149–50.

tricky river solidified this bond. James Sprunt, a local historian and ra-
conteur, remembered how "the pilots [of the northwest branch], many of
whom were negroes, knew every crook and eddy of the stream. Dan Bux-
ton, an esteemed colored man of this city, has a record of fifty years
faithful service as a pilot on the Cape Fear." In a 1765 law written to
prevent slaves from gathering on the streets of Wilmington after 10:00
P.M., black boatmen were specifically exempted because their "journies,
or . . . Emergent business" might require their late arrival or activity.
Despite the best efforts of local white pilots to outlaw black pilots, Fayetteville and Wilmington mercantile interests in the state legislature combined to quash any measures excluding this cheap, reliable labor.[9]

Gaining access to the state's several ports could be quite dangerous
because its coastline was very irregular and riddled with shifting bars
and shoals; ships often ran aground and were lost. Although the entrance to the Cape Fear River was the least treacherous, even its Frying
Pan Shoals jeopardized many ships. The health of the state's ports depended on the ready availability of competent pilots, without which
they would lose coastal and foreign traffic to the more accessible ports
of Norfolk and Charleston. Vessels entering the Cape Fear regularly
hired black pilots to conduct them through the treacherous flats. In
1762 a black pilot who conducted a party of Moravians into the river
misled them on the navigability of a certain inlet for fear the Spanish or
French might come into possession of it. To the north, black pilots
brought many ships through the even more challenging Ocracoke Inlet
into the Pamlico Sound. Francisco de Miranda, a widely traveled Span-
iard who visited the United States in 1783–84, characterized Pamlico as
"this very dangerous sound" through which he was conducted by pilots
who "are to my mind the most careful and capable I have seen." White
pilots there complained bitterly in 1773 about the use of slave and free
black pilots, but they met a fate similar to that of their colleagues in
Wilmington and Fayetteville: in 1783, the state legislature enacted a
law allowing for any examined and certified black to serve as a pilot
into any of the state's several ports. One can be certain that many
more than the certified were employed.[10]

9. James H. Brewer, "Legislation Designed to Control Slavery in Wilmington and Fayetteville," *North Carolina Historical Review* 30 (April 1953), 163–64; James Sprunt, *Chronicles of
the Cape Fear River, 1660–1916,* 2nd ed. (Raleigh, N.C.: Edwards & Broughton Printing Co.,
1916), 206; Donald R. Lennon and Ida Brooks Kellam, eds., *The Wilmington Town Book,
1743–1778* (Raleigh: North Carolina Division of Archives and History, 1973), 168.

10. Adelaide Lisetta Fries, ed., *Records of the Moravians in North Carolina,* 7 vols.
(Raleigh, N.C.: Edwards & Broughton Co., 1922–70), 1:259; John S. Ezell, ed., *The New Democracy in America: Travels of Francisco de Miranda in the United States, 1783–1784* (Nor-

Because of the scale on which naval stores and lumber dominated the region's economy by the revolutionary era, farming and animal husbandry were relatively minor commercial preoccupations. Small-scale rice cultivation did exist from the beginning of white settlement in the area and was centered largely in neighboring Brunswick County. With the collapse of the British market for naval stores after the Revolution, however, planters increasingly turned to rice production, until by the first decades of the nineteenth century rice replaced naval stores as the leading product of the Lower Cape Fear region. As was the case in the districts of Charleston and Savannah, blacks exclusively performed the tasks of rice cultivation. Whites who could fled the stench and disease of the rice swamps and liked to characterize blacks as peculiarly fitted for such demanding work.[11] From planting to threshing, blacks managed the rice crop. Slave carpenters, coopers, blacksmiths, bricklayers, and other craftsmen also resided on the rice plantations, where they built and maintained floodgates, constructed barrels, erected buildings, shaped iron, cut tools, and met almost all the other material needs of a rice-growing community. The variety of black laborers made the rice plantations nearly self-sufficient.[12]

Most slaves on the rice estates worked under a task system where a certain job was allotted them for the day. When that job was complete, they were free to follow other pursuits. Many chose to work the little plot of land the owners often allotted them, where they produced important supplements to their diet and perhaps a surplus for the local market. From the beginning of settlement in North Carolina, self-interested planters had recognized that blacks were often excellent farmers and that they could virtually meet their own dietary requirements. The keen-eyed Janet Schaw particularly noted this capacity in blacks:

> The Negroes are the only people who seem to pay any attention to the various uses that the wild vegetables may be put to. For example, I have sent you a paper of their vegetable pins made from the prickly pear, also molds for buttons made from the calabash,

---

man: University of Oklahoma Press, 1963), 4–5; Saunders, *Colonial Records,* 9:803–4; Walter Clark, ed., *The State Records of North Carolina,* 20 vols., numbered 11–30 (Goldsboro, N.C.: Nash Bros., 1895–1914), 24:503.

11. One of numerous examples is Janet Schaw's exclamation "There is no living near it [the rice swamps] with the putrid water that must lie on it, and the labour required for it is only fit for slaves, and I think the hardest work I have seen them engaged in" (Schaw, *Journal of a Lady,* 194).

12. James M. Clifton, "Golden Grains of White: Rice Planting on the Lower Cape Fear," *North Carolina Historical Review* 50 (October 1973), 365–93.

which likewise serves to hold their victuals. The allowance for a Negro is a quart of Indian corn pr day, and a little piece of land which they cultivate much better than their Master. There they rear hogs and poultry, sow calabashes, etc. and are better provided for in every thing than the poorer white people with us.

Other commentators also observed the facility with which blacks in North Carolina made things grow and how they often profited from them commercially.[13] There are strong indications, in fact, that slaves were too good at agriculture and animal husbandry. For example, in 1774 the state passed a law prohibiting any slave in the northeastern tobacco-growing counties from raising any of that plant "for his own benefit," and in 1779 an act providing for the poor stated "No slave shall be permitted, on any pretence whatsoever, to raise any horses, cattle, hogs or sheep," on penalty of seizure and sale of the animals, with half the proceeds going to the poor whites of the local county. These laws clearly suggest that blacks had to be forced to stop competing effectively with small-scale farmers and merchants. Such laws to minimize the slaves' independent economic activity and increase their dependence on their owners did not have a high success rate in the Lower Cape Fear region.[14]

Wilmington's old market house was located on Market Street between Front Street and the river, just beyond the wharves. Here many slaves brought their own produce and wares, or what they had produced for their owners to sell or barter. They were a formidable presence in the marketplace, and laws at both the local and the state level were regularly written and rewritten to try to rein in these numerous black merchants. At least as early as 1765 the Wilmington Town Council attempted to regulate the presence and activity of blacks in the marketplace. In that year the town's first comprehensive slave code was written, and one of its leading provisions limited selling in the market only to slaves who could produce a ticket issued by their owner authorizing them to vend. This provision, however, does not seem to have been enforced. In 1772 an updated slave code reiterated that no person—white or black—was to have any transaction with a slave who lacked a ticket from his owner or

---

13. Schaw, *Journal of a Lady,* 176–77. For further descriptions of blacks' agricultural skills, see "Informations Concerning the Province of North Carolina, Addressed to Emigrants from the Highlands and Western Isles of Scotland," in William K. Boyd, ed., *Some Eighteenth Century Tracts Concerning North Carolina* (Raleigh, N.C.: Edwards & Broughton Co., 1927), 445; Brickell, *Natural History of North Carolina,* 275–76.
   14. Clark, *State Records,* 23:952, 24:260.

overseer. This same code went so far as to order: "No Slave or Slaves shall Trade or Traffic (even with the leave of their Master, Mistress, or Overseer) at Stands in the Public Streets of the said Town." Again, the laws intended to minimize the competition blacks offered whites. Yet in 1778 the town council issued another directive forbidding any white person "to deal, trade or traffick with any slave or slaves for any matter or thing whatever without a Ticket or Tickets." In 1785 the North Carolina state legislature, in a series of acts intended "to Regulate and Restrain the Conduct of Slaves and Others" in Wilmington, Washington, Edenton, and Fayetteville, lent its own voice to this matter and repeated that no one was to barter or trade with any slave whose owner had not permitted him or her to do so.[15]

As late as 1816, despite this impressive battery of restrictions, slaves in Wilmington were actively engaged in public trade without tickets. On December 7, 1816, a notice in the *Cape Fear Recorder* requested the "store keepers of Wilmington, and the owners of slaves in general . . . to meet at the Court House . . . [in order] to enter into an arrangement for trading with negro slaves, as a custom has prevailed for negroes to sell many species of produce without permits."[16] Once again a more rigorous checking of tickets was proclaimed as the solution. It is significant that no proposal was made to remove slaves engaged in trade from the marketplace, for the reliance of both white merchants and planters on them is evident. Planters needed slaves not only to move their merchandise to town for them, but also, upon arrival, to market it. The produce from slave plots was also an important contribution to the available food supply in a town that was so focused on the production of naval stores and, by 1816, rice. A vigorous market for produce and other goods from owners existed in Wilmington, as it did in numerous Southern towns, and many whites—either knowingly or unwittingly—relied on slaves to sell these items to them. Indeed, a certain collusion appears to have existed between black slaves and the poorer whites around this traffic. Yet those whites were actually dependent on the plantation laborers to supply the items, for only the slaves had any regular access to the possessions.[17]

15. Donald R. Lennon and Ida Brooks Kellam, eds., *The Wilmington Town Book, 1743–1778* (Raleigh: North Carolina Division of Archives and History, 1973), 165, 204–5, 233; Clark, *State Records,* 24:729. The efforts of white authorities to control slaves in the marketplace had been ongoing since the town's creation. In 1745, in an act intended "for the better regulating the said Markets," all citizens were forbidden from "buying or dealing with Negroes bringing Provisions or other Goods without proper Tickets from their Masters, Mistresses or Overseers" (ibid., 23:235).

16. *Cape Fear Recorder,* December 7, 1816.

17. For example, a former-slave author, William Grimes, discussing one of his overseers in Georgia, wrote: "This Bennet, and his mother, had lived on land rented to them by my

Many slaves in Wilmington were involved in another form of commercial transaction: the sale or, as it was commonly called, the hiring-out of their own labor. Right up to the Civil War the annual hiring-out day—usually occurring on January 1—was a seasonal institution that marked the end of Christmas festivities and the beginning of a new year of work arrangements.[18] The town's economy hinged on the skilled black laborers hired on that day, and because of this fact many owners allowed their slaves to contract independently with that year's employer—even permitting some to secure their own room and board—so long as they turned over to the owner a stipulated weekly or monthly sum of money. The regular petitions by white mechanics against this practice only clarified its extent.[19] But as with other white skilled laborers whose employment was restricted by the use of cheaper skilled black labor, the powerful merchants and planters of eastern North Carolina secured legislative sanction for the hiring-out system in Wilmington, Fayetteville, Edenton, and Washington, while the practice was forbidden in the balance of the state.[20] The observation of Francis Asbury, the first bishop of the American Methodist Church, in 1803 that "the Africans [of Wilmington] hire their time of their masters, labour and grow wealthy," probably continued to hold some truth throughout the antebellum era.[21]

Not only were blacks dominant in many of the trades and labors of the Lower Cape Fear region, but by 1790 they were also the demographic majority in the region. The first national census determined that blacks made up 56 percent of the population of New Hanover County, which had Wilmington as its seat: 3,026 whites to 3,738 black slaves and 67 free

---

former master, Colonel Thornton. They were then very poor, and secretly bot' things from the negroes which they had stolen from my master" (William Grimes, *Life of William Grimes, the Runaway Slave* [New York, 1825], 19). Once he became overseer, however, Bennet was horribly severe.

18. For interesting descriptions of the hiring-out day, see, for the year 1840, Sprunt, *Chronicles of the Cape Fear River,* 179–80, and for the year 1860, "The Autobiography of Rufus William Bunnell" (typescript), 132–33, in Bunnell Family Papers, Box 20, file 360, Manuscripts and Archives, Yale University.

19. For example, see "House Bills (November 29)," Box 1, and "Petitions," Box 3, both in General Assembly Session Records November–December 1802, North Carolina State Archives; *Wilmington Gazette,* November 22, 1808; Brewer, "Legislation Designed to Control Slavery," 164–65. For the Edenton area, where a similar practice prevailed, see mechanics' complaint significantly reprinted in *Cape Fear Recorder,* November 20, 1816.

20. Clark, *State Records,* 24:726–27; Brewer, "Legislation Designed to Control Slavery," 165–66. See also the useful discussion of the hiring-out system in Brewer, "Account of Negro Slavery," chap. 6.

21. Elmer T. Clark, ed., *The Journal and Letters of Francis Asbury,* 3 vols. (London: Epworth Press, 1958), 2:380.

blacks.[22] By 1800 the percentage of blacks in the total population in New Hanover had actually increased to 59 percent: 2,908 whites to 4,058 slaves and 94 free blacks. In Wilmington, blacks had an even greater presence, with 68 percent of the inhabitants: 545 whites to 1,125 slaves and 19 free blacks.[23] The census of 1810 documented only a small decrease in the black portion of the population (57 percent), while their actual numbers continued to increase dramatically: there were 4,891 white inhabitants of the county, and 6,574 blacks, 132 of whom were free blacks.[24] Wilmington had a significant fraction of this overall figure. Throughout the first decades of the postrevolutionary era, Wilmington and its county had an indisputable predominance of black residents.

This was David Walker's black world—skilled, prolific, and enslaved. While Walker's origin in the Lower Cape Fear region cannot be proven conclusively, several indicators point to this area as the seat of his youth. Internal evidence within his *Appeal* indicates a direct familiarity with slavery, and probably an environment where slaves predominated demographically. Walker was particularly disturbed by black servility in settings where blacks decisively outnumbered whites, as in Jamaica or in regions of the southern United States.[25] Referring to America, he wrote:

> Here now, in the Southern and Western sections of this country, there are at least three coloured persons for one white, why is it, that those few weak, good-for-nothing whites, are able to keep so many able men, one of whom, can put to flight a dozen whites, in wretchedness and misery?

While Walker's ratio is wholly inaccurate for almost any area of the South, it bears a relationship—albeit a somewhat inflated one—to actual figures for such districts as Charleston and Wilmington in the early decades of the nineteenth century. Moreover, he continues to emphasize—as in the passage that opened the Introduction—that the level of competency of the blacks is as high as, if not perhaps higher than, that of the whites. One needed to spend little time in Wilmington or Charleston to confirm that fact. The intensity of Walker's puzzlement over this juxta-

22. *Heads of Families at the First Census, 1790: North Carolina* (Washington, D.C.: Government Printing Office, 1908).
23. 1800 Federal Census, North Carolina, New Hanover County.
24. 1810 Federal Census, North Carolina, New Hanover County.
25. David Walker, *Appeal to the Colored Citizens of the World, But in Particular, and Very Expressly, to Those of the United States of America*, rev. ed., ed. Sean Wilentz (New York: Hill & Wang, 1965), 23–25, 62–64. (Hereafter cited as *Appeal*.)

position of power and skill with submissiveness suggests his lengthy exposure to the slavery of those or similar towns.

The only evidence from his era stating that Wilmington was the birthplace of David Walker is a short biography contained in Henry Highland Garnet's 1848 reprint of the third edition of the *Appeal*.[26] In this brief but important sketch, Garnet wrote: "Mr. Walker was born in Wilmington, North Carolina, Sept. 28, 1785. His mother was a free woman, and his father was a slave." The source of this information, however, is not completely clear. In his preface, Garnet stated that he had "procured permission from his [Walker's] widow, Mrs. Dewson" to reprint the *Appeal* as well as "a brief notice of his life." Along with placing her imprimatur on the work, she also presumably supplied Garnet with information about Walker's history. Despite her likely assistance, Garnet cautions: "In regard to his life, but a few materials can be gathered." Nevertheless, they are probably correct on something so basic as his birthplace.

Unfortunately, no free black David Walker is to be found in the relevant records of New Hanover County or in the neighboring counties of Brunswick or Duplin. A thorough search through tax lists, censuses, county court minutes, wills, deeds, and assorted miscellaneous records related to slaves and free people of color yielded no David Walker.[27] Yet there is nothing unusual about a free black not appearing on official records, especially at the turn of the nineteenth century. Moreover, the transplantation of hundreds of Scotch Presbyterians into the Lower Cape Fear region in the eighteenth century led to a profusion of Walkers there, both white and black, and increases the likelihood that he originated there.

Another possible explanation for Walker's absence from county and municipal records concerns his date of birth. Speculation surrounds this event as well. Historians and commentators have exclusively listed Walker's birthdate as 1785, drawing on the figure in Garnet's work. Yet some significant problems exist with this date. First, within the Garnet sketch itself, he is said to have died at the age of thirty-four. Perhaps this number was a typographical error and the numbers should be reversed,

26. Henry Highland Garnet, *Walker's Appeal, With a Brief Sketch of His Life. By Henry Highland Garnet. And Also Garnet's Address to the Slaves of the United States of America* (New York, 1848), v–vii.

27. The critical census schedule for 1810, listing heads of households and numbers and age-groupings of household members, is missing for North Carolina, presumably either lost or destroyed. Thus this source, which may have listed David Walker, cannot be checked. Tax records for antebellum New Hanover County are also incomplete, with only the years 1815–19 reliably documented. See New Hanover County Tax List, 1815–19; New Hanover County Tax List, 1816, 1836, 1838; New Hanover County Tax Records, 1779–1869 (broken series), all in North Carolina State Archives.

giving the age of forty-three. But this figure still does not square with a death in 1830. A possibility remains that the age was correct and the birthdate wrong, and this possibility is increased by the fact that his death record in Boston lists his age in 1830 as thirty-three, although, unfortunately, it does not also offer a birthdate or birthplace.[28] That information could place his birth as early as September 1796—given an August 1830 death—making the age of thirty-four much more viable, especially if one considers that Dewson could have misremembered his age from a distance of eighteen years.

The point of this examination is not simply to identify Walker's birthdate; it is to propose that an adjustment of that date might make his absence from official records in North Carolina more understandable. If Walker left Wilmington in the latter years of the 1810s—as I argue later in this chapter—or absolutely no later than 1824, which is very unlikely, and was born in 1796 or 1797, that would make his absence more plausible, because he would be too young to appear on all but a few tax lists and could not have been listed on the 1810 census as head of a household. Likewise, if he was born in 1785 this gap becomes comparatively more difficult to explain, for the probability that he would appear on official records increases significantly. Although records are spotty for several years, and free blacks especially could miss state reckoning, the chances that Walker could elude it for more than thirty years are small. All free black males and females of sixteen years and older were subject to annual poll taxes and, as with most municipal tax records, a relatively faithful accounting of payments was kept. Walker's absence from these lists and others tends to support the later birth date of 1796/97.[29]

A final way to locate David Walker in Wilmington is by searching for his parents. This inquest produced, at best, some possibilities. Black Walkers of reproductive age—both male and female—did live in New Hanover County at the two suggested times for his birth, and a correlation with the later date, particularly, seems to exist. Although not the free woman usually designated as his mother, a Charity Walker, owned by Major John Walker of Wilmington, bore seven children between January 1781 and

28. *Index of Deaths, 1801–1848*, 300, in Registry of Births, Marriages, and Deaths, City of Boston.

29. One further possibility is that Walker and his parent(s) lived on the land of a white person as laboring tenants and were therefore listed as members of that household. There are many such unnamed free blacks in North Carolina census schedules. It would not be unlikely for free black tenants to make arrangements with planters to cover their poll taxes, especially because such a relationship became formalized in state law in 1827. See John Hope Franklin, *The Free Negro in North Carolina, 1790–1860* (Chapel Hill: University of North Carolina Press, 1943), 103–5. Yet the names of taxables still should have appeared on the appropriate lists, at least up until 1827.

February 1799. While her dates of fertility span the time of David's birth and their surnames agree, she probably was not his mother, unless she was able for nine months to escape the watchful eye of her owner, who kept a strict accounting of the birthdates of each of her offspring.[30]

A more likely but by no means definite parent of David Walker was the interesting Anthony Walker—an Ibo of Nigeria who was owned by the Revolutionary War hero Major General Robert Howe.[31] Apparently taken at an early age from Africa with "his playmates," Anthony (known as "Oboto" or "Umboto" in Africa) was purchased by John Walker of Brunswick County upon arriving in America. But as his grandson John Thomas Howe, recounted, "he barely remembered the Walker Plantation, as the stay was short." John Walker died in early 1775 and, according to Anthony's biographer, his plantation was sold to Robert Howe to cover John's debts.[32] Thus, by approximately 1775–76 Anthony Walker was transferred to the Howe plantation in Brunswick County.

Determining Anthony's age with some accuracy at this time is not easy, but is necessary to gain some idea of his chronological relationship to the birth of David Walker. There is some conflict in Anthony's biography. While one report says he was lured onto a slave ship with his playmates—suggesting an age roughly no more than ten years or so—another report has him leading a number of slaves in rebuilding their hurricane-damaged cabins only a few months after he moved to Howe's estate, seeming to indicate a much older person, especially considering that he was supposed to have learned these building skills in Africa. Yet if he was

30. "Day Book," John Walker Papers, 1735–1909. In August 1812, approximately a year before his death, John Walker (also known as "Major Jack") had a deed of emancipation executed for Charity and her daughter, Appalina. Evidence strongly suggests that this young woman was the mistress of the unmarried John Walker. They were the only slaves emancipated before his death in an estate that by 1800 already comprised sixty-four slaves. (See "Census—Return of John Walker's Family made to Saml. Bloodworth esq. 1st Oct 1800," John Walker Papers.) The daughter's namesake was probably John's sister, Appalina, who resided in Berwick-upon-Tweed in England. See Sallie McLaurin, "Walker Family," typescript, Lower Cape Fear Historical Society, Wilmington. Appalina's delivery of a baby girl, Betsey, on September 11, 1806, is especially noted in the "Day Book." Finally, John Walker deeded a lot in town to Appalina in September 1812. See Deed Book, Q, 173, John Walker to Appalina S. Walker, New Hanover County.

31. I am indebted to Beverly Tetterton, curator of the Local History Room at the New Hanover County Public Library in Wilmington, for alerting me to the existence of this intriguing biography of Anthony Walker and his offspring. All of the following information is drawn from it. See Nada R. McDonald Cotton, "The Walker-Howe Family of Wilmington, North Carolina in New Hanover County," typescript, file "Family History and Biography," in Local History Room, New Hanover County Public Library.

32. John Walker's will was proved in March 1775, while the will itself was signed by John on February 10, 1775. See Real Estate Conveyances, Book B, page 55, Brunswick County, North Carolina State Archives.

roughly twelve when taken from Africa, he may have been old enough to have learned some of his tribal building practices. Perhaps he had some unique skills, which—despite his relative youth—drew the attention of older, less adept slaves during a crisis.[33] If he arrived at the Howe plantation by 1776, his age could have been in the range of thirteen to fourteen years. Thus, by 1785 he would have been approximately twenty-two or twenty-three—certainly old enough to be the father of David Walker.

Yet problems also exist with Anthony. By 1785 he was married to a very young Tuscarora Indian girl adopted by the Howes several years earlier. In the same year, Robert Howe had manumitted Anthony through his executed will. Moreover, Walker lived a long life, not dying until May 13, 1837. Garnet's biography indicates that Walker's father was a slave who died a few months before his birth. Whether the father and mother were married or not is not mentioned. Records exist for all the offspring of Anthony and Tena—who all bore the surname Howe—and none of them is named David. The possibility remains that the date of David's father's death is wrong and that Anthony could have fathered him out of wedlock. Anthony's direct African lineage could also support this possibility, for David's "complexion was dark," according to Garnet. At this point, however, these possibilities stand only as hypotheses that are difficult to prove, and David Walker's parentage continues to be hidden.

Other aspects of David Walker's early life in the Lower Cape Fear region remain equally obscure. So far, there is no evidence of where he may have lived in the area, who the people were in and around his family, or what his upbringing was like. The type of employment he had is also unknown. It was not uncommon for a young free black male to be apprenticed to someone in the building trades in Wilmington. A search for a deed of apprenticeship in Walker's name to someone in that field or in any other trade proved futile.[34]

Because of the degree of learning evident in the *Appeal,* especially with regard to biblical and historical texts, many questions have arisen about Walker's educational background. The fluidity of his writing style strongly suggests someone who was comfortable with writing and had been doing it for quite some time. Public schools in North Carolina, however, were closed to free blacks, so Walker would have had to acquire learning elsewhere. Up until 1838 every master in North Carolina was required by law to teach an apprentice—black or white—how to read and write.[35] This

33. By the early decades of the nineteenth century, he was directing one of the most successful construction companies in the Wilmington area.

34. The fact that Walker did not pursue any building trade could argue against Anthony, a leading local builder, as his father.

35. Franklin, *The Free Negro in North Carolina,* 165.

avenue may have been one way Walker gained literacy, but without a deed of apprenticeship we do not know for certain. Walker's commitment to black education was deep: he particularly stressed the need for educated blacks to teach their untutored fellows the basics of reading, writing, and grammar, as well as uplifting ideas of freedom and dignity. Walker himself, as a youth, could have learned from just such a teacher.

While by no means easy for a slave or a free black to acquire in either the colonial era or the antebellum era, literacy was not unattainable, especially in the Lower Cape Fear region. Moravians, Quakers, Baptists, Methodists, Episcopalians, and other Protestant faiths all acted in one form or another to extend religious education to blacks in North Carolina. In a number of cases this instruction included teaching reading so the student could study the Bible.[36] Methodists and Episcopalians in particular provided educational resources for blacks in the Wilmington region.

In the late colonial era, an organization known as "Associates of Dr. Bray" may have laid the foundation for a limited tradition of a more independent instruction among blacks in and about Wilmington. Created in 1723 by Anglican clergyman Dr. Thomas Bray to concentrate attention on converting blacks and Native Americans to Christianity, the Associates labored in the colonies, especially after 1750, to open Negro schools at various sites. Although successful only in Philadelphia, where a school opened in 1758 persisted beyond the Revolution, schools were also attempted in North Carolina at Bath, Edenton, and Wilmington. Planter opposition and lack of funding and teachers doomed them, but by the 1760s Dr. Bray's Associates had established a rudimentary structure for the education of slaves in the Lower Cape Fear area, employing the slaves themselves as teachers. Local Associates either identified slaves who already had some reading skills, or tutored others in reading and then sent them back into the slave community with books, both to read religious matter to the slaves and to teach them reading fundamentals. After noting the number of blacks he had recently baptized in 1767, the Reverend John Barnett, an Associate in Brunswick, just fifteen miles south of Wilmington on the Cape Fear River, added: "Several among them can read and having promised me to take pains to instruct such of their fellow Slaves as are desirous to learn I have given them many of the Associates books."[37]

36. Guion Griffis Johnson, *Ante-Bellum North Carolina: A Social History* (Chapel Hill: University of North Carolina Press, 1937), 541–50; Franklin, *The Free Negro in North Carolina,* 164–68.

37. John Barnett to John Waring, August 17, 1767, in John C. Van Horne, ed., *Religious Philanthropy and Colonial Slavery: The American Correspondence of the Associates of Dr. Bray, 1717–1777* (Urbana: University of Illinois Press, 1985), 262. This method of fostering slave education was by no means limited to the Lower Cape Fear region and North Carolina.

Barnett continued this strategy at least through 1770, when he mentioned in another letter, regarding a parcel of books sent to Cape Fear, that he had "given directions to a Friend there to distribute them among those Negroes who can read a little."[38] Some success must have come from his efforts, for in 1768 he asked for many books that "may be most easily understood" because "upwards of 150 Slaves have applied to me for books."[39] These letters indicate the existence of some base of literacy among slaves in late colonial Lower Cape Fear, but they also suggest that an educational network of sorts—complete with teachers and books— was created, with the capacity to sustain itself independent of any Associate. Such a structure could have continued undetected among the slaves in their communities and fostered a tradition of some literacy among them. It is not unreasonable to speculate that Walker's education could have begun under such a program, or under some free black who had already profited from it. The great weight Walker's *Appeal* places on the duty of literate blacks to educate and uplift their illiterate companions could have a connection with an experience of learning under blacks in Wilmington. Moreover, David Walker's later zeal to circulate printed material among the slaves may point to his awareness that more literacy existed among them than whites were aware of.

While Walker's education probably commenced under an autonomous black organization, there is no question that his religious life was initiated through the inspiration of a black-led church. "In Piedmont and Western North Carolina, Methodism at first made its greatest appeal to the yeomanry; in the East, especially in Fayetteville and Wilmington, the Negroes were the first to accept the faith," asserted Guion Johnson in her classic work on antebellum North Carolina.[40] Although visited during and after the Revolutionary War by a few Methodist preachers who helped create a fleeting society there, Wilmington throughout the balance of the eighteenth century remained almost completely outside the administration of the Methodist episcopacy. Indeed, interest in Methodism appeared so low in the town that the Wilmington Circuit was abolished in 1786 and replaced in 1787 by the Bladen Circuit, which bordered the town. Not only did Wilmington lack a stationed preacher; it also had only irregular visits from itinerant circuit riders. Francis Asbury, commenting on Wilmington

Dr. Bray's Associates had been employing it at least since 1746 and in areas ranging from Virginia, Delaware, and Philadelphia to Braintree, Massachusetts. This scope points to a need to reconsider our understanding of slave literacy. See letters in ibid., 97, 98–99, 206, 225, 255.

38. John Barnett to John Waring, June 9, 1770, in ibid., 273.
39. Barnett to Waring, June 11, 1768, ibid., 273.
40. Johnson, *Ante-Bellum North Carolina*, 344.

in 1785, observed: "I felt the power of the devil here," and left the town to its own devices.[41]

Yet some constructive Methodist activity must have been going on in Wilmington at the same time. No later than 1795, William Meredith, formerly a Methodist missionary in the British West Indies, settled in Wilmington and began preaching to and working with local black Methodists. Brought to America in 1793 as an adherent of William Hammett and his schismatic Primitive Methodist Church of Charleston, Meredith soon broke with Hammett, although not then joining forces with Asbury's Methodist Episcopal Church, and moved north along the coast in search of a site for missionary activity.[42] The Reverend James Jenkins, probably the only contemporary to have noted a conversation with Meredith, recorded the missionary's initial experience in Wilmington:

> Before leaving, I [Jenkins] took occasion [in 1798] to visit Wilmington, where there was a small society of coloured people, with Meredith (once with Hammett) at their head. He said that as he was passing, he found these "sheep without a shepherd," and consented to serve them as pastor.[43]

This statement clearly indicates that some sort of religious association among blacks already existed in Wilmington, and that it was organized enough to seek the consent of Meredith to remain among them. Several

41. Clark, *Journal and Letters of Francis Asbury*, 1:486; W. L. Grissom, *History of Methodism in North Carolina from 1772 to the Present Time*, 2 vols. (Nashville, Tenn.: Smith & Lamar, 1905), 216–22.

42. On Meredith, see William M. Wightman, *Life of William Capers*, . . . *Including an Autobiography* (Nashville, Tenn., 1858), 161–63; and D. A. Reily, "William Hammett: Missionary and Founder of the Primitive Methodist Connection," *Methodist History* 10 (October 1971), 39–40. Hammett, an Irish Methodist preacher, was himself a fiery and courageous missionary to St. Kitts and other British West Indies islands in the late 1780s. In 1791 Hammett broke with Bishop Francis Asbury and his Methodist Episcopal Church after Asbury failed to appoint him the exclusive head of the church in Charleston, South Carolina. Hammett took a large number of the established church's congregation in Charleston to form the Primitive Methodist Church and return to original Wesleyan concepts of church organization. Disowned by the British Methodists, Hammett nonetheless built a church in Charleston and had some influence over others in Savannah, Georgetown, and Wilmington. These churches appear to have been particularly keen to bring Methodism to blacks. Hammett died in 1803, by which time most of his denomination's organization had collapsed. Reily, "William Hammett"; Emory Stevens Bucke, ed., *The History of American Methodism*, 3 vols. (Nashville, Tenn.: Abingdon Press, 1964), 1:617–22; and F. A. Mood, *Methodism in Charleston* (Nashville, Tenn., 1856), 47–60.

43. James Jenkins, *Experience, Labours, and Sufferings of Rev. James Jenkins* (n.p., 1842), 86.

sources could have contributed to the creation of this association: earlier work among the slaves by the Society for the Propagation of the Gospel or by Dr. Bray's Associates, previous Methodist missionary activity, or some other unknown Christian organization. The initial influence was not necessarily solely Methodist; any Christian activity could have laid the groundwork for the group's assent to a variety of Christian creeds, especially a faith preached as emotionally as Meredith's.

That Meredith helped to solidify this religious community is unquestionable. Despite harassment and persecution, Meredith persisted in his work among Wilmington's blacks. At one point he was imprisoned, but soon released because he refused to stop preaching through the grate in his cell. With the penny offerings he received from his congregation, he purchased a parcel of land on the outskirts of town, where a meetinghouse was built; surrounding lots were rented to free blacks. Soon, however, a number of local whites burned the meetinghouse down, but the undaunted Meredith called his flock together in the marketplace and chastised the local whites, exclaiming, "As they loved fire so well, God had given them enough of it," referring to the several serious fires in town between 1795 and 1799. By his death in 1799 a second meetinghouse was completed. In four or five years, William Meredith had helped put Methodism among the town's blacks on a stable foundation.[44]

Yet the church he had worked to establish remained outside the official Methodist Episcopal organization. Although Meredith willed the church and its property to Francis Asbury, it was several years before Bishop Asbury and his appointed preachers would be able to bring it within their control. As early as 1796, Asbury exclaimed in his journal: "If we had men and money, it would be well to station a preacher in such places as Wilmington."[45] While the town was reinstated in the Minutes of the Annual Conference for 1800 as a site having a stationed preacher, the extent to which one was there is not clear. Bennett Kendrick, appointed for 1801 and 1802 and then again in 1806, appears to have spent some time there, but Asbury never mentioned him in his journal for 1801–02, although the bishop stayed there at least twice during those years. The first reference Asbury made to a preacher in Wilmington was in a letter to Kendrick of February 20, 1804, where he mentioned that the people of Wilmington "are pleased with brother [Jeremiah] Russell," who was stationed there that year. Yet by January 1805, Asbury was again decrying the fact that

44. Clark, *Journal and Letters of Francis Asbury,* 2:186; Grissom, *History of Methodism in North Carolina,* 1:223; Jenkins, *Experience, Labours, and Sufferings,* 86; Wightman, *Life of Bishop Capers,* 162–63.
45. Clark, *Journal and Letters of Francis Asbury,* 2:109.

Wilmington lacked a preacher. Not until 1806, when Kendrick returned to the town and work had progressed on enlarging and finishing the church, did the official Methodist ministry there appear to have become settled.[46]

During these years of inconsistent white ministerial presence, however, the African or black wing of the Methodist church in Wilmington thrived, and apparently with a good deal of autonomy. It had a much more solid foundation than the white church, which according to Jesse Lee, had formed its first class only in December 1797 under the tutelage of William Meredith and still suffered from the antipathy of the majority of local whites.[47] In February 1803, blacks in fellowship with the church numbered 878 while only a "few whites" were so enrolled. While whites and blacks participated together in church functions, the black church also operated separately. In January 1802 Asbury noted that he had appointed African stewards to watch over the African church. In February 1803 he mentioned, "I met the people of colour, leaders and stewards," and as late as January 1810 he was still having meetings with "the African elders" and discussing the African church's upcoming fast day. These positions of authority were the most consistent ones for the Methodists in Wilmington, at least through the first half of the decade, and indicate that on a day-to-day basis blacks were administering their own church, if not the white one as well.[48] By 1813, when quotidian authority had shifted more clearly to whites, William Capers, the town's stationed preacher for that year, remarked with unabashed frankness: "The negro meeting-house was become the Methodist church."[49]

46. *Minutes of the Annual Conferences of the Methodist Episcopal Church for the Years 1773–1828* (New York, 1840), 93; Grissom, *History of Methodism in North Carolina,* 224; Clark, *Journal and Letters of Francis Asbury,* 2:284, 325; 3:281, 306, 339–40.

47. Jesse Lee, *A Short History of the Methodists in the United States* (Baltimore, 1810), 209.

48. Clark, *Journal and Letters of Francis Asbury,* 2:325, 380, 628.

49. Wightman, *Life of William Capers,* 174. This was quite literally true. The church building that Meredith and local blacks built had by Capers's time become the seat of the established Methodist church in Wilmington and named the Front Street Methodist Episcopal Church. Blacks had been moved from the lower floor and sat in the galleries, the construction of which Asbury's African stewards largely oversaw.

The case of Fayetteville is even more clear-cut. There, a black itinerant shoemaker and licensed Methodist preacher from Virginia by the name of Henry Evans stopped on his way to Charleston to preach to the local blacks, probably sometime in the 1790s. Inspired by his preaching and example, his local audience prevailed on him to settle among them and help build a church. He consented and, despite years of persecution and a forced evacuation of the congregation to neighboring desolate sandhills, held the overwhelmingly black church together and was eventually invited back into the town through the intervention of a growing number of white supporters. As church membership expanded, especially with whites, Evans, "as an humble, good Christian, transferred church, congregation, and all, over to the

David Walker was likely exposed to this church in his childhood. Wilmington had only the Methodist church and an Episcopal church until a Presbyterian congregation was created in 1818.[50] Moreover, the Methodists directly appealed to blacks—unlike the Episcopalians, who only later opened their facilities for some form of black participation. Walker's later deep devotion to the African Methodist Episcopal faith could surely argue for an earlier exposure to a black-dominated church. Indeed, Walker's education could have begun here; Asbury made clear his interest in erecting a school for blacks in Wilmington. In the Wilmington Methodist church, Walker would have seen blacks administering their own affairs, leading classes, and preaching—founding a church that would then be co-opted by whites as their attitudes toward Methodism changed. Once again the power of blacks amid exploitation would have been apparent to Walker.

The *Appeal* also indicates that Walker had experience with religious gatherings of blacks in the South. One vivid description merits quoting at length:

> I have known tyrants or usurpers of human liberty in different parts of this country to take their fellow creatures, the coloured people, and beat them until they would scarcely leave life in them; what for? Why they say "The black devils had the audacity to be found *making prayers and supplications to the God who made them!!!!*" Yes, I have known small collections of coloured people to have convened together, for no other purpose than to worship God Almighty, in spirit and in truth, to the best of their knowledge; when tyrants, calling themselves *patrols,* would also convene and wait almost in breathless silence for the poor coloured people to commence singing and praying to the Lord our God, as soon as they had commenced, the wretches would burst in upon them and drag them out and commence beating them as they would rattlesnakes—many of whom, they would beat so unmercifully, that they would hardly be able to crawl for weeks and sometimes for months.[51]

---

white Methodist preachers." He died in 1810 in a shack attached to the church he helped to build. J. S. Bassett, "North Carolina Methodism and Slavery," *Historical Society of Trinity College,* 4th ser. (Durham, N.C., 1900); Wightman, *Life of William Capers,* 124–29; Jenkins, *Experience, Labours, and Sufferings,* 120–21; Thomas O. Summers, ed., *Autobiography of the Rev. Joseph Travis, A.M.* (Nashville, Tenn., 1856), 101–2.

50. See the interesting section entitled "Wilmington Churches" in Sprunt, *Chronicles of the Cape Fear River,* 603–47.

51. *Appeal,* 37.

Such incidents could easily have occurred at the Wilmington African church, which was regularly subject to persecution from local whites even as late as the early 1810s.[52] Burning the church was only one form that persecution took.

As a member of this church, Walker would also have acquired familiarity with the lives, culture, and abilities of Wilmington's slaves, because virtually all the blacks in the congregation were enslaved. One cannot be certain, however, whether the black leaders of the church were enslaved or free. Neither Asbury nor any of the preachers who commented on the African church indicate one way or the other. Although free blacks rented lots surrounding the church, there is no sign that they were there for administrative reasons. Slaves could have just as easily been among the leadership of the African church, and thus given Walker one more opportunity to witness their resourcefulness.

In Wilmington such an ecclesiastical arrangement would not be unusual. By 1800, blacks numbered well over two-thirds of the town's 1,700 inhabitants, and only 19 of those blacks were free. Blacks were predominant demographically in early-nineteenth-century Wilmington, and in those years to be black in that town essentially meant one was a slave.

Free blacks in Wilmington then necessarily lived in relatively close contact with slaves and were grouped with them. But Walker, being free, might also have reacted with particular intensity against being grouped with the unfree—not, however, because he rejected slaves but because he reviled the condition that degraded his race and made the life of a free black so difficult in Wilmington. The fact that slaves performed so much of the labor in the town damaged employment prospects not only for working-class whites but for free blacks as well. The only trades clearly open to free blacks were in the building industry, and it appears that Walker did not pursue this line of work. While free blacks in Wilmington lived socially almost solely in the context of slaves, their economic opportunities were also sharply curtailed. Walker probably concluded that the possibilities for him were so restricted that leaving town would profit him more than remaining. Such a decision would especially have suited a young man of approximately eighteen to twenty years who was intelligent and for the first time seriously assessing his prospects in an exploitative world.[53] Somewhere between 1815 and 1820, David Walker chose to leave

52. Both Asbury and the numerous preachers cited above refer to these problems. See, for example, Asbury's journal entries for January 28, 1807, where he wrote: "We took our flight from Wilmington: what I felt and suffered there, from preachers and people, is known to God" (Clark, *Journal and Letters of Francis Asbury,* 2:530).

53. Thus I argue again for adjusting Walker's birthdate to 1796/97. I find it difficult to believe that a free black of Walker's particular passion and perspicacity would have re-

Wilmington and make the short journey south to Charleston, South Carolina, not only with the plan of improving his employment prospects in a city with hundreds more free blacks, but also with the desire to clarify the meaning of his blackness and freedom in a world dominated by slavery.

---

mained in Wilmington for upward of forty years and then arrived in Boston and produced what he did.

2

"There is a great work for you to do"

Coming of Age in Vesey's Charleston

They think that we do not feel for our brethren, whom they are murdering by the inches, but they are dreadfully deceived.
—David Walker's *Appeal*

Visitors to Charleston, especially those from the North and from Europe, frequently commented on the large numbers of blacks in the city's streets and environs. From the end of the American Revolution onward, a significant percentage of these blacks were free. Between 1790 and 1820 the free black population in Charleston District nearly quadrupled, moving from 950 in 1790 to 3,615 in 1820.[1] Other than Baltimore and New Orleans, no city in the South could boast of a larger population. The most spectacular increase occurred between 1810 and 1820, when more than 1,800 new free blacks came to reside in Charleston District, more than doubling the population

1. Charleston District comprised not only the city of Charleston but also Charleston Neck, a long, thin stretch of land commencing immediately west of the city boundary and running between the Ashley and Cooper Rivers. It also contained several parishes to the north and west. The Neck was famous for its high concentrations of free blacks and self-employed slaves.

from 1,783 to 3,615. While natural increase accounted for a portion of this rise, a large proportion was the result of immigration. The wave of refugee free blacks from St. Domingue accounted for much of the growth in the 1790s, but after 1800—and particularly from 1810 to 1820—most of the immigrants were from surrounding Southern States.[2]

The prospect of employment was one of the principal reasons free blacks came to Charleston.[3] No city on the eastern seaboard south of Baltimore could compare with Charleston for the opportunity it offered free blacks. A sampling of the skilled occupations of free blacks in Charleston in 1823 lists no less than thirty-five trades, ranging from carpenters and tailors to fishermen, hairdressers, and bricklayers. The possibilities for work were numerous and diverse in Charleston, but there was also a good deal of tolerance among local whites for the existence of a broad free black artisanal and laboring class, both out of necessity and out of economic expediency. While they provided an indispensable labor supply, free blacks were also, at all levels, less expensive to hire than whites. The petitions of white mechanics seeking to restrict black artisans were regularly denied by the cost-conscious Charleston City Council. The city's economy offered options for a free black that were inconceivable in the slave-dominated environment of Wilmington.[4]

Charleston had another resource that Wilmington lacked: a population of free blacks large enough to organize themselves into associations for mutual assistance. In 1790, light-skinned refugees from St. Domingue joined together to create the Brown Fellowship Society, which provided

2. Marina Wikramanayake, *A World in Shadow: The Free Black in Antebellum South Carolina* (Columbia: University of South Carolina Press, 1973), 17–22. For an example of white Charlestonians' complaints against the influx of free black immigrants from neighboring states, see the petition of October 16, 1820, in General Assembly, Petitions, 1820, no. 143, South Carolina Department of Archives and History, Columbia.

3. For instance, Bishop Capers, writing of the itinerant free black shoemaker Henry Evans, who came from Virginia and brought Methodism to Fayetteville, North Carolina, remarked: "While yet a young man, he determined to remove to Charleston, S.C., thinking he might succeed best there at his trade." Wightman, *Life of William Capers,* 125.

4. Wikramanayake, *World in Shadow,* 100–105; Ulrich B. Phillips, "The Slave Labor Problem in the Charleston District," *Political Science Quarterly* 22 (September 1907), 427–28. See in Phillips's article the excerpted "Memorial of the Citizens of Charleston . . ." (1822), in which it is stated: "Every winter, considerable number of Germans, Swiss, and Scotch arrive in Charleston, with the avowed intention of settling amongst us, but are soon induced to emigrate towards the West by perceiving most of their mechanical arts performed by free persons of color" (431). See also Leonard P. Curry, *The Free Black in Urban America, 1800–1850: The Shadow of the Dreams* (Chicago: University of Chicago Press, 1981), chap. 2, Curry argues that within antebellum America occupational opportunity was greatest for free blacks in the lower South, especially in Charleston and New Orleans. As one progressed northward, prospects were increasingly curtailed.

benefits for financially distressed members as well as education for children. Close on its heels in 1791 was the Society of the Free Dark Men of Color, formed with both educational and mutual-aid objectives. By 1813 at least three more organizations with similar premises existed among Charleston's free blacks: the Humane and Friendly Society, the Minors Moralist Society, and the Friendly Union. While each of these associations usually restricted their membership to the upper echelons of free black society—and even to complexional distinctions within that caste, as was the case with the societies of the Brown Fellowship and Free Dark Men of Color—they nevertheless offered financial and educational assistance to impoverished and orphaned free black children and showed some concern for the situation of free blacks in general. Burial and mutual-aid societies almost certainly existed among free blacks of lesser means but are not nearly so identifiable.[5]

Implicit in the formation of these benevolent associations was the growing awareness among a significant number of free blacks that they were a socially distinct group with their own specific needs. Cut off from any participatory role in white institutions and from the mobility open to whites at the same time that they were struggling to define their relationship to the slaves, free blacks in Charleston occupied a tenuous position. Their greatest security was in the invaluable labor they supplied. While some—mainly from the light-skinned upper classes—opted to define themselves as a third caste separate from both whites and black slaves and worked to justify and extend that distinction, others, often from the artisanal classes, did not deny their distinctiveness as free blacks in a slave society, but also did not segregate themselves so sharply from the slaves. Indeed, they probably socialized with slaves—especially with those who had similar skills—married among them, and thus saw themselves as very close to the enslaved. A third layer of free blacks lived in such poverty that their condition resembled that of the slaves in whose midst they lived in Charleston Neck or elsewhere, and fostered a strong identification with them despite their nominal freedom. The varieties of group consciousness that existed among the free blacks of Charleston attested to that caste's relative strength in that immediate region.[6]

5. Curry, *The Free Black in Urban America,* 197–98, 199, 203; Wikramanayake, *World in Shadow,* 80–87; James B. Browning, "The Beginnings of Insurance Enterprise Among Negroes," *Journal of Negro History* 22 (October 1937), 422–28; E. Horace Fitchett, "The Traditions of the Free Negro in Charleston, South Carolina," *Journal of Negro History* 25 (April 1940), 144–45.

6. Michael Johnson and James Roark, "'A Middle Ground': Free Mulattoes and the Friendly Moralist Society of Antebellum Charleston," *Southern Studies* 21 (Fall 1982), 246–65. See also the important discussions of the forms of and the material conditions surrounding

By 1817, however, free blacks from all these strata had joined together to help form an African Methodist Episcopal (AME) church. Before 1815, black Methodists in Charleston, both slave and free, had conducted their affairs with a good deal of autonomy. Although formally under the control of the stationed preacher, black stewards, exhorters, and class leaders actually preached, taught classes, oversaw love feasts, and collected and disbursed funds. Bishop Capers described his oversight of the black wing of his Methodist church in Charleston in 1811. Led by "men of intelligence and piety, who read the Scriptures and understood them, and were zealous for religion among the negroes, . . . these colored men were permitted to hold meetings with the negroes pretty freely" and did so not only in Charleston proper but also in such widely scattered places as Goose Creek, Cooper River, Wando, Wadmalaw Islands, Pon-Pon River, and the parishes of St. Paul, St. James, and St. John. Capers goes on to discuss the power granted these men: "We authorized them to admit and exclude members; kept regular lists of their classes as belonging to our charge in Charleston; (for there was no other to which they could belong); and they reported to us minutely on Monday what had been done on Sunday. They were the only persons who for Christ's sake were zealous enough to undertake such a service, and who, at the same time, could get access to the people that that service might be rendered." Capers stressed their allegiance to the church and Christ's cause. These men, almost all of whom were skilled artisans, were fervent evangelicals. When actions were taken to curtail their independence, no less than three of the eight mentioned men—Smart Simpson, Harry Bull, and Alexander Harleston—put their names on the petition requesting the right to form an AME church.[7]

In 1815 a newly stationed preacher, the Reverend Anthony Senter, sought to remove this independence and bring the blacks more directly under white supervision. That was no surprise at the time. As Methodism made itself more palatable to white slaveholders and they began joining the church, they also maneuvered to gain complete hegemony over what had been originally overwhelmingly black congregations. By 1815 Wilmington and Fayetteville had already undergone this transformation. Rev-

---

free black self-consciousness in Ira Berlin, *Slaves Without Masters: The Free Negro in the Antebellum South* (New York: Pantheon Books, 1974), 250–315. On the extensive degree to which free blacks and slaves socialized and intermarried in Charleston, see the observations in "Memorial of the Citizens of Charleston to the Senate and House of Representatives of the State of South Carolina" (1822), in Ulrich B. Philips, ed., *Plantation and Frontier*, vol. 2 of John R. Commons et al., eds., *A Documentary History of American Industrial Society* (Cleveland: Arthur H. Clark Co., 1910), 109.

7. See Wightman, *Life of William Capers,* 138–40.

erend Senter commenced it in Charleston by abolishing separate black Quarterly Conferences, placing black collections under white steward-ship, and requiring all trials of black members to be before a white minis-ter.[8] While blacks in Charleston responded to these events with shock, they did not do so publicly. Instead, over the next two years, Morris Brown, Henry Drayton, Charles Corr, Amos Cruckshanks, and others who were prominent leaders and teachers of the black Methodists secretly organized support among their followers for a break with the white Meth-odist church. Morris Brown and perhaps Henry Drayton went so far as to slip away to Philadelphia, where in 1816 they met Richard Allen, the first bishop of the AME Church, were ordained by him, and planned for the creation of an AME congregation in Charleston.

In 1817, soon after their return from the North, a dramatic moment in the history of Methodism in Charleston occurred. With the surrender of the black class-leaders' papers to church authorities, 4,367 black mem-bers left the church. "The galleries, hitherto crowded, were almost com-pletely deserted, and it was a vacancy that could be *felt*," recalled F. A. Mood in 1856.[9] From this point on, Morris Brown and his adherents fo-cused on building a wholly separate AME church in Charleston and they were vigorously challenged every step of the way.

As early as January 27, 1817, a group of free blacks calling themselves the Independent Religious Congregation successfully petitioned the Charleston City Council to purchase a burying ground adjacent to the Methodist churchyard for their exclusive use. This action had probably been taken preparatory to seceding from the white Methodist church, for a building had been erected on the lot by December 1817, when 469 blacks were arrested for "disorderly conduct" while worshiping in it. Hav-ing next decided to abandon the burial lot, Brown, Henry Drayton, and others petitioned the South Carolina House of Representatives for permis-sion to erect an AME church in the Hampstead section of Charleston Neck. Despite the petitioners' willingness to have whites regularly inspect the church and attend services, the legislature denied their request. Nev-ertheless, a structure was erected again and one Sunday in June 1818 some 140 members—including Brown and four other ministers—were seized for unlawful assembly. Making clear his commitment to serving the

8. There was some suspicion that Senter wanted to wrest control of finances from the black stewards, for along with using these funds for charitable purposes they were also secretly purchasing the freedom of some slaves with them. Albert Deems Betts, *History of South Carolina Methodism* (Columbia, S.C.: Advocate Press, 1952), 237.

9. Wikramanayake, *World in Shadow,* 123–28; Mood, *Methodism in Charleston* (1856), 130–33; James O. Andrew, "Rise and Progress of Methodism in Charleston, South Carolina," *Methodist Magazine and Quarterly Review* 12 (1830), 22–24.

blacks of Charleston, Brown went to prison for one month rather than choose the other punishment of banishment from the state.

An 1820 petition to the South Carolina legislature complaining about "a spacious building . . . lately . . . erected in the immediate neighbourhood of Charleston for the *exclusive* worship of Negroes and coloured people, from means supplied them by Abolition Societies in the Eastern and Northern States" makes it clear that, regardless of the harassment to which they were subject, African Methodists continued to hold their church together. Even though this petition led to more-stringent measures against free black immigration and a reiteration of laws prohibiting unsupervised black assembly, authorities in Charleston were unable to eliminate the church until the uncovering of the Denmark Vesey conspiracy in 1822 gave them the justification for razing it. For seven years, the black congregation struggled successfully to prevent a much more powerful opponent from wresting control of their church from them.[10]

Free blacks were essential to the creation and preservation of this church. They provided the leadership. The status of free blacks entitled them to greater mobility and breadth of action than slaves, and thus made it more difficult for the authorities to shut down the facilities summarily. As with Morris Brown and a few others, their wealth helped fund the church. By no means did all free blacks join in the AME effort; a number remained with the white Methodist church, while many from the upper echelon continued at St. Philip's Episcopal Church, the city's oldest church and a bastion of Charleston's elite. Nevertheless, the African church drew support from all layers of local free black society, from the lightest skinned to the darkest, from the wealthiest to the poorest. However, the artisanal strata of free black society clearly supplied most of the leadership in the building of the church. Of the 26 free blacks who signed the petition sent to the South Carolina legislature in about 1818 for the incorporation of the AME church, 10 are identifiable as artisans and 2 were ministers in the church.[11] It was in this stratum that the heart of political and religious activism among free blacks in Charleston was located.

But the creation of the AME church in Charleston was by no means solely the effort of free blacks. Slaves figured significantly in the work too.

10. *Charleston City Gazette,* December 4, 1817; *Charleston Courier,* January 29, 1817, and June 9 and 11, 1818; General Assembly, Petitions, n.d., no. 1893 and 1820 no. 143, South Carolina Department of Archives and History, Columbia.

11. Four were shoemakers, three were tailors, one was a drayman, another a carpenter, and the tenth was a painter-porter. The other sixteen signers were also probably artisans, but their trades were not discernible. *Charleston Directory and Stranger's Guide for the Year 1816; The Directory and Stranger's Guide for the City of Charleston . . . for the Year 1819; The Directory and Stranger's Guide for the City of Charleston . . . for the Year 1822.* See Appendix A.

While it is difficult to estimate just how many were involved, of the 4,367 members who left the church in 1817 well over half must have been slaves. Reports from both whites and blacks pertaining to the church between 1817 and 1822 indicate that the slave presence was prominent. The transcript from the trials of those involved in the Denmark Vesey conspiracy also gives some insight into slave membership in the AME church. Of the 131 individuals who were arrested and tried for complicity, 36 were clearly current or former members of the African church, 5 having also been class leaders. The incidence of attachment to the church was probably much higher among the conspirators, for of that 131 only 71 had their trial transcripts reprinted in the record, and of those recordings many were very short, sometimes only a sentence or two and with no biographical information whatsoever.[12] Most of the men brought to trial were also artisans who hired out their time. The magistrates of the court astutely noted:

> The enlistments appear to have been principally confined to Negroes hired or working out, such as carters, draymen, sawyers, porters, laborers, stevedores, mechanics, those employed in lumber yards, and in short to those who had certain allotted hours at their own disposal, and to the neighboring country Negroes.[13]

Charleston's AME church, especially, was the product of a particular stratum within the free black and slave classes: that of artisans and small merchants. Those most committed to building the church and those most often leading it were from this layer. Both slaves and free blacks from this stratum served as class leaders and as other important figures in the church. Their joint commitment is no surprise—they had trades and economic concerns in common, lived in the same neighborhoods, socialized together, and intermarried. Their association heightened not only the awareness of many artisanal free blacks regarding the conditions of slaves, but also their commitment to assist them. The building of Charleston's African church evinced that commitment. A glaring symbol of black resistance to white hegemony, the church also stood as a constant reminder to all blacks of how they might seek out freedom together.

12. Some of those tried also appear to have been associated with the church—having knowledge of Morris Brown and other ministers, knowing of proceedings and other members—but because they were not definitely indicated as being members, I did not include them in my figure. A complete list of those who were associated with the church is in Appendix B. For source of names, see John Oliver Killens, ed., *The Trial Record of Denmark Vesey* (Boston: Beacon Press, 1970).

13. Killens, *Trial Record of Denmark Vesey,* 17.

The presence of large numbers of free blacks, numerous employment prospects, and the development of a church with black leadership all probably served to draw David Walker to Charleston in the late 1810s. Other evidence also places him in Charleston at this time. In the *Appeal* he stated:

> I remember a Camp Meeting in South Carolina, for which I embarked in a Steam Boat at Charleston, and having been five or six hours on the water, we at last arrived at the place of hearing, where was a very great concourse of people, who were no doubt, collected together to hear the word of God.[14]

This event could not have occurred any earlier than 1816–17, because steamboats were not employed on the Cooper, Ashley, or any other regional river or waterway prior to then.[15] In fact, this particular meeting probably transpired in 1821, for in that year on April 17 and 21 a number of advertisements in the *Charleston City Gazette* announced, for the first time ever, passage by packet, schooner, or steamboat to two sites where camp meetings were currently taking place: Sullivan's Island and Goose Creek.[16] Goose Creek was probably the site Walker visited, because the first Methodist camp meetings in Charleston took place there in 1814. Moreover, the steamboat would have required roughly the five hours he mentioned to arrive there, for Goose Creek was seventeen to eighteen miles upriver from Charleston and steamboats often went four miles an hour or less going against the current, especially with the numerous hazards that cluttered the Cooper River. Transport to Sullivan's Island, which was in the bay, would not have required as long a journey.[17]

Another reference Walker made in the *Appeal* points to time spent in Charleston. In the first article, he observed: "I saw a paragraph, a few years since, in a South Carolina paper, which, speaking of the barbarity of the Turks, it said: 'The Turks are the most barbarous people in the

14. *Appeal,* 39.

15. See reference to the launching of a new steamboat in Charleston in *Charleston Courier,* March 3, 1817. The article suggests that this was the first such launching. By 1818–19, talk of steamboats and of forming steamboat companies was constant in the *Courier.* And as of 1816, steamboats had also just appeared in Savannah, a town that was developing this mode of transportation in close conjunction with Charleston. See also Ulrich Bonnell Phillips, *The History of Transportation in the Eastern Cotton Belt to 1860* (New York: Columbia University Press, 1908).

16. Similar advertisements in the *Charleston Courier* at an earlier date were never noted.

17. *Charleston City Gazette & Commercial Daily Advertiser,* April 17 and 21, 1821; Mood, *Methodism in Charleston,* 125–30. For the site of Goose Creek Campground, see the map in John B. Irving, *A Day on the Cooper River,* reprinted with notes by Samuel Gaillard Stoney, 3rd ed. (Columbia, S.C.: R. L. Bryan Co., 1969).

world—they treat the Greeks more like *brutes* than human beings.'"[18] A thorough search through the *Charleston Courier* and the *City Gazette* for the years 1817–23 did not yield this exact quotation, but nearly every approximation of it was produced from about the middle of 1821 onward. In early 1821 a twenty-nine-year-old Greek rebel, Alexander Ypsilanti, led a band of followers out of Russia into Romania with the intention of rallying Greeks and pro-Greek elements in the Turkish empire to revolt. Although this maneuver failed, it touched off among Greeks in the Ottoman realm a rebellion that continued to flare through 1829. These revolts received much coverage in American newspapers, especially in the early years, and highly colored commentary on Turkish barbarity was frequent.[19] The quoted sentence places Walker in Charleston at least as late as the second half of 1821, for it could not have appeared earlier. The fact that he specifically cited a South Carolina newspaper rather than any number of other papers from that time, which would have contained similar information, strongly argues for his having seen the newspaper in that state and then retained the relevant portion of it, from which he quotes directly.[20] This quotation and the reference to the camp meeting make it highly likely that David Walker not only spent time in Charleston but also was there at least through 1821.

By late June 1822 the Denmark Vesey conspiracy—in planning, some speculate, for up to four years[21]—had been uncovered, and executions of its leaders were well under way by early July. David Walker may have had his first experience with organizing for revolt during the germination of this famous American slave plot. There is a remarkable similarity between the rhetoric and ideas expressed by Walker in his *Appeal* and those expressed by Vesey in the trial transcripts pertaining to him. Regarding the foundations of Vesey's thinking, one witness to his discussions stressed:

> His general conversation was about religion which he would apply to slavery, as for instance, he would speak of the creation of the world, in which he would say all men had equal rights, blacks as well as whites,—all his religious remarks were mingled with slavery.[22]

18. *Appeal,* 12.

19. For example, the *Charleston Courier* for September 20, 1821, exclaimed: "The Turks were prominent in giving proofs of the most inhuman barbarity." Such characterizations were common.

20. Otherwise, why not have used much more readily obtainable newspapers, both past and current, in Boston?

21. Peter Poyas, the ferociously dedicated co-leader of the 1822 conspiracy, remarked at one of the rebels' meetings regarding the plot: "God has a hand in it, we have been meeting for four years and are not yet betrayed" (Killens, *Trial Record of Denmark Vesey,* 52).

22. Ibid., 64. All statements attributed to Vesey issue from witnesses who heard him di-

Walker's use of religion to attack slavery and to defend black rights pervades the *Appeal*. Here is one of numerous examples:

> Do they believe, because they are whites and we blacks, that God will have respect to them? Did not God make us all as it seemed best to himself? What right, then, has one of us, to despise another, and to treat him cruel, on account of his colour, which none, but the God who made it can alter? Can there be a greater absurdity in nature, and particularly in a free republican country?[23]

What links the sentiments of the above two passages so forcefully is not only their yoking of religion with slavery but also, and more specifically, their clear belief that God was the creator of natural rights and of the fundamental equality of all human beings. For both Walker and Vesey, evangelical notions not only happened to correspond with a theory of natural rights but were in fact integrally bound together, working always to exalt their ultimate source, the Christian Deity. Republicanism was divinely ordained.

Both men were also unrestrained in describing the current situation of blacks as intolerable. Vesey's indictment is succinct and revealing. Frank Ferguson, a slave, recounted:

> Vesey said the Negroes were living such an abominable life, they ought to rise. I said I was living well—he said though I was, others were not and that 'twas such fools as I, that were in the way and would not help them, and that after all things were well he would mark me.[24]

Walker similarly joined a stark assessment of the condition of black people with an unsparing attack on anyone refusing to recognize the reality of that condition and their need to right it. In a key passage Walker wrote:

> I met a coloured man in the street a short time since, with a string of boots on his shoulders; we fell into conversation, and in course of which, I said to him, what a miserable set of people we are! He asked, why? —Said I, we are so subjected under the whites, that

---

rectly and who corroborate one another. Vesey himself remained silent throughout the trial. The court also attested to leaving evidence "as it was originally taken, without even changing the phraseology, which was generally in the very words used by the witnesses" (ibid., 1). Although some overstatement probably exists here, the court's claims on evidence suggest the relative accuracy of the transcriptions.

23. *Appeal,* 42–43.
24. Killens, *Trial Record of Denmark Vesey,* 63.

we cannot obtain the comforts of life, but by cleaning their boots and shoes, old clothes, waiting on them, shaving them &c. Said he, (with the boots on his shoulders) "I am completely happy!!! I never want to live any better or happier than when I can get a plenty of boots and shoes to clean!!!" Oh! how can those who are actuated by avarice only, but think, that our Creator made us to be an inheritance to them for ever, when they see that our greatest glory is centered in such mean and low objects?[25]

Here again in this powerful description Walker is grappling with how to help blacks change some of their most fundamental perceptions of themselves. The information in both these passages is conveyed in the context of an exchange with a fellow black. Vesey's and Walker's statements on the status of blacks are made publicly for two reasons: to inquire into the degree of support for their position and plan of action, and to make blacks who might be deluding themselves confront the reality of their condition. Their condemnation was not isolated in bitter moaning, but rather had an intensely educational purpose behind it and was often conducted as a kind of informal social inquiry into being black in America.

Their remarkably similar pronouncements on individual and group exertion were also always directed at the public forum. The unnamed slave who divulged the plot to the authorities just days before the intended uprising stated:

I know Denmark Vesey—I was one day on horseback going to market when I met him on foot; he asked me if I was satisfied in my present situation; if I remembered the fable of Hercules and the Waggoner whose wagon was stalled, and he began to pray, and Hercules said, you fool put your shoulder to the wheel, whip up your horses and your wagon will be pulled out; that if we did not put our hand to the work and deliver ourselves, we should never come out of slavery.[26]

Walker supported this position fully. In his third edition of the *Appeal,* he exhorted:

25. *Appeal,* 29. In another passage, with an outraged tone almost identical to Vesey's, Walker said: "Can our condition be any worse?—Can it be more mean and abject? If there are any changes, will they not be for the better, though they may appear for the worst at first? Can they get us any lower? Where can they get us? They are afraid to treat us worse, for they know well, the day they do it they are gone" (ibid., 2).
26. Killens, *Trial Record of Denmark Vesey,* 43.

> It is not to be understood here, that I mean for us to wait until God shall take us by the hair of our heads and drag us out of abject wretchedness and slavery, nor do I mean to convey the idea for us to wait until our enemies shall make preparations, and call us to seize those preparations, take it away from them, and put everything before us to death, in order to gain our freedom which God has given us. For you must remember that we are men as well as they. God has been pleased to give us two eyes, two hands, two feet, and some sense in our heads as well as they.[27]

Faith would help lead one to freedom, but not without exertion and courage. Walker's exhortation especially embodied the positive activism required by the evangelicalism fueling the Second Great Awakening of the 1830s: the individual must enthusiastically assent to receiving God's free offer of grace and must make that receipt manifest through acts of goodwill in the world. The faith of those who only wait was really no faith at all. God had actually done nothing for those who refused to recognize and use the power he had implanted within them.

Both Vesey and Walker agreed that the oppressed's pursuit of holy righteousness might have to take on terrible forms: massacres of whites could be justified. Rolla Bennett, one of the chief conspirators who was broken under solitary confinement, probably torture, and a sentence of death finally confessed that Vesey, while again speaking to a group, had counseled that

> the best way . . . for us to conquer the whites, is to set the town on fire in several places . . . and for every servant in the yards to be ready with axes, knives, and clubs, to kill every man as he came out when the bells began to ring. He then read in the Bible where God commanded, that all should be cut off, both men, women and children, and said, he believed, it was no sin for us to do so, for the Lord had commanded us to do it.[28]

Walker would have found such a strategy, while certainly unfortunate and to be avoided if at all possible, nevertheless intelligible. In excoriating a black female slave who reported to whites the murder of several slave

27. *Appeal,* 11n; see also the preamble in the 3rd edition and p. 62.
28. Killens, *Trial Record of Denmark Vesey,* 46. See also the letter of Benjamin Elliott reprinted in [Edwin Clifford Holland], *A Refutation of the Calumnies Circulated Against the Southern and Western States, Respecting the Institution and Existence of Slavery Among Them . . .* (Charleston, S.C., 1822), 79, for further and more specific uses of the Bible by the conspirators to legitimize massacre.

dealers by men who had freed themselves of their coffle and thus led to their recapture, he exclaimed:

> We must remember that humanity, kindness and the fear of the Lord, does not consist in protecting devils. . . . What has the Lord to do with a gang of desperate wretches, who go sneaking about the country like robbers—light upon his people wherever they can get a chance, binding them with chains and handcuffs, beat and murder them as they would rattle-snakes? Are they not the Lord's enemies? Ought they not to be destroyed? Any person who will save such wretches from destruction, is fighting against the Lord, and will receive his just recompense.[29]

The fact that Walker publicly took on this dangerous position that almost all contemporary black reformers shunned espousing so openly suggests the influence of Vesey, especially because both grounded their use of violence in Scripture. Walker's threat that anyone not helping "will receive his just recompense" has a startling resemblance to Vesey's threat that "he would mark" someone unwilling to perceive his oppression. Neither was averse to applying biblical pressure on the hesitant. Walker, like Vesey, had no illusions about what would be required to throw off their immensely powerful and ruthless opponent.

They likewise had a ferocious intolerance for informants. Vesey and his associates always made clear how they would deal with marplots. One witness testified that Rolla Bennett had threatened that

> if any black person is found out giving information or evidence against them, they would be watched for day and night and be certainly killed. Even now the friends of those in prison are trying about the streets to find out who has given information—If my name was known I would certainly be killed.[30]

Walker particularly vilified informants and those who turned against the best interests of their race. Speaking about the serious problem black communities throughout the North faced from their own members who sold runaways back into slavery, Walker warned:

29. *Appeal,* 25; see also p. 26.
30. Killens, *Trial Record of Denmark Vesey,* 44; see also p. 52. Vesey was also careful of who was informed of the arrangements (ibid., 135). One person was not to be told because he was once "seen in a state of intoxication" and another was cut off because he "was a babbling fellow" (p. 135).

[One] may see some of those ignorant and treacherous creatures (coloured people) sneaking about in the large cities, endeavouring to find out all strange coloured people, where they work and where they reside, asking them questions, and trying to ascertain whether they are runaways or not, telling them, at the same time, that they always have been, are, and always will be, friends to their brethren; and, perhaps, that they themselves are absconders, and a thousand such treacherous lies to get the better information of the more ignorant . . . whom they [then] scandalously delivered into the hands of our natural enemies.

He posed the solution to this plague rhetorically before a large group of blacks in Boston: "Brethren and fellow sufferers, I ask you in the name of God, and of Jesus Christ, shall we suffer such notorious villains to rest peaceably among us?"[31]

Informants threatened the unity that was essential to the success of any resistance and that both men believed had eluded African Americans. Walker, in one of numerous examples, exhorted: "Unless you are united, keeping your tongues within your teeth, you will be afraid to trust your secrets to each other, and thus perpetuate our miseries under the Christians!!!!"[32] Vesey was equally adamant about unity and the absolute need for faith in each other:

We must unite together as the Santo Domingo people did, never to betray one another, and to die before we would tell upon one another. . . . We were fully able to conquer the whites, if we were only unanimous and courageous, as the Santo Domingo people were.[33]

Walker's statement to the General Colored Association in December 1829 reflected this conviction:

The primary object of this institution, is, to unite the colored population, so far, through the United States of America, as may be practicable and expedient; forming societies, opening, extending, and keeping up correspondences, and not withholding anything

31. *Appeal*, 22–23; David Walker, "Address Delivered Before the General Colored Association at Boston," reprinted in John Bracey et al., eds., *Black Nationalism in America* (Indianapolis: Bobbs-Merrill, 1970), 33.

32. *Appeal*, 11.

33. Killens, *Trial Record of Denmark Vesey*, 46, 58.

which may have the least tendency to meliorate our miserable condition.[34]

The overriding preoccupation of Walker and Vesey was identical: how to make each individual black pointedly aware of his or her oppression, and then how to move them to reject it and join together in a firm struggle against it. For each of them, this task acquired the scale of an all-consuming mission that was both sacred and secular. William Paul, a slave who testified against Vesey, recounted:

> He studied all he could to put it into the heads of the blacks to have a rising against the whites, and tried to induce me to join. He tried to induce all his acquaintances—this has been his chief study and delight for a considerable time. . . . He studied the Bible a great deal and tried to prove from it that slavery and bondage is against the Bible.

As the conspiracy coalesced and the date for action approached, Vesey devoted himself constantly to his ideological and organizational efforts. One witness recalled that Vesey "even ceased working himself at his trade, and employed himself exclusively in enlisting men, and continued to do so until he was apprehended." Vesey also often displayed himself publicly as an embodiment of strength and will to resist. A white youth deposed:

> Denmark Vesey frequently came into our shop which is near his house, and always complained of the hardships of the blacks. He said the laws were very rigid and strict and that the blacks had not their rights—that everyone had his time, and that his would come round too.

Vesey calculated that such bold acts, made before an audience of blacks and whites, would clearly show that a black could challenge whites and walk away from it.[35]

A mission of equal vigor animated Walker:

> Men of colour, who are also of sense, for you particularly is my *Appeal* designed. Our more ignorant brethren are not able to penetrate its value. I call upon you therefore to cast your eyes upon the wretchedness of your brethren, and to do your utmost to enlighten

34. Walker, "Address Before the General Colored Association," 30.
35. Killens, *Trial Record of Denmark Vesey,* 61, 64, 70.

them—*go to work and enlighten your brethren!*—Let the Lord see
you doing what you can to rescue them and yourselves from degradation.[36]

Walker presented this mission first to a cadre of courageous and enlightened African Americans, who he believed would be most capable of understanding its dimensions and urgency. They were then to organize to
deliver secular education and the word of God to the mass of blacks
demoralized by their privations and ignorance, and commence the personal and social transformation of this vast populace. At the same time,
this core would be a shining counterweight to the pervasive indictment of
blacks as inferior. As more were brought to an awareness of who they
were and what the scale of their strength actually was, they in turn would
reach out to still others and geometrically increase the number of soldiers in the holy army.

The church was a key inspirational and organizational tool for both
men. "Gullah" Jack Pritchard, an African-born conjurer who was a leading
conspirator, proposed rebellion as early as 1818, "when the Negroes of
the African Church were taken up." It is no surprise that Peter Poyas
traced the planning for the 1822 revolt back four years to the time of
these arrests. Indeed, Vesey proclaimed that the fact that "our Church
was shut up so that we could not use it" necessitated resistance and
revolt as much as did the whites' depriving the blacks of their rights and
dignity. Whites' efforts to suppress the AME church played a central role
in the genesis of the Vesey affair.[37]

Planning for the revolt and preparing the minds of numerous blacks for
justifying it certainly occurred in one form or another within the several
African congregations and their associated classes.[38] While any local
white assessment of the plot and its development must be judged carefully because the evidence available to them was limited, it was also to
their advantage to evaluate the conspiracy and its machinery as accurately as possible in order to prevent such events in the future. The best-
informed whites all concluded that the existence of the African church
was essential to the development of the plot, both ideologically and orga-

36. *Appeal*, 28.
37. Killens, *Trial Record of Denmark Vesey*, 52, 58, 89.
38. Preaching and organizing among blacks in the outlying regions around Charleston
that were also drawn into Vesey's conspiratorial network could have been done by black
Methodists who had been serving the parishes of St. Paul, St. James, St. John, and others at
least since 1811. Several of these preachers became closely affiliated with the African
church. Their noted zeal suggests that they would not have easily abandoned their missions
to the slaves in the countryside.

nizationally. One observer remarked that the blacks "had been allowed to assemble for *religious* instruction."

> The designing leaders in the scheme of villainy, availed themselves of these occasions to instill sentiments of ferocity, by *falsifying the Bible*. All the severe penal laws of the Israelites were quoted to mislead them, and the denunciations in the prophecies, which were intended to deter men *from* evil, were declared to be divine commands which they were to *execute*.

The magistrates of the trial likewise concluded that "inflammatory and insurrectionary doctrines, without any direct proposal for such an attempt, were inculcated" at class meetings that were also "to be used as places of rendezvous and rallying points for communicating to all, the exact night and hour, on which the first blow was to be struck." The relationship of the leaders of the conspiracy to the AME Church lends credence to these findings. Three of the five principal conspirators—Denmark Vesey, Peter Poyas, and Ned Bennett—were class leaders in the church. Of the thirty-five men found guilty and executed and generally considered the most heavily involved in the affair, twenty-one (60 percent) were clearly members of the church, and there was a strong possibility that many of the others were members as well (see Appendix B). One of the executed, Jack Glenn, was described by the local white Baptist minister, Richard Furman, as "a Preacher among them, & for one of his Oportunities [*sic*], of extraordinary Talents." And neither Morris Brown, Henry Drayton, nor Amos Cruckshanks was by any means fully absolved of complicity in the plot. While black revolt in the Charleston of 1822 would have been possible without the AME Church, its organizational potential would have been severely curtailed. One can legitimately call the Charleston AME Church the center of the Vesey conspiracy.[39]

David Walker could have been directly acquainted with this use of the church. If, as is likely, he was in Charleston at the time of the plot, Walker was also probably a member of an African congregation there. A passage in the *Appeal* suggests direct familiarity with events related to the AME Church in Charleston. After referring to Richard Allen and his proselytizing successes in the Middle Atlantic states, Walker added:

39. Holland, *Refutation of the Calumnies*, 79; Killens, *Trial Record of Denmark Vesey*, 15–16, 140–41; Wikramanayake, *World in Shadow*, 60, 125; Richard Furman Papers, letter to Governor Thomas Bennett, c. 1822 (incomplete), South Caroliniana Library, University of South Carolina, Columbia.

Tyrants and false Christians however, would not allow him to penetrate far into the South, for fear that he would awaken some of his
ignorant brethren, whom they held in wretchedness and misery—
for fear, I say it, that he would awaken and bring them to a knowledge of their Maker.[40]

Walker was probably exposed to autonomous black churches in both
Wilmington and Charleston. He knew that the church and Christianity
could be a powerful amalgam to bind slaves and free blacks together. In
Charleston, Walker may have concluded that an independent black
church with its own system of biblical interpretation was the single greatest threat to white authority because of the degree to which it upheld a
vision of black autonomy, solidarity, and mission. He, along with Vesey,
was convinced that the Bible and Christianity were antislavery and that
they justified racial solidarity and aggressive actions against enslavement
and oppression.

Your full glory and happiness, as well as [those of] all other coloured people under Heaven, shall never be fully consummated, but
with the *entire emancipation of your enslaved brethren all over the
world*. . . . For I believe it is the will of the Lord that our greatest
happiness shall consist in working for the salvation of our whole
body. When this is accomplished a burst of glory will shine upon
you, which will indeed astonish you and the world. . . . There is a
great work for you to do, as trifling as some of you may think of it.[41]

For Walker, as for Allen, Vesey, and other black leaders, Christianity and
the church could be the keys to resolving the painful paradox of vigorous
independence and degrading submission that he observed in African
American society.

If David Walker was not directly acquainted with Denmark Vesey, there
are numerous signs that suggest he knew about the Vesey affair and perhaps was involved in it.[42] The strong possibility that Walker interacted

40. *Appeal,* 59.
41. *Appeal,* 29–30.
42. A few other passages from the transcripts and the *Appeal* also closely resemble each
other. At one point Walker stated, "'Every dog must have its day,' the American's is coming
to an end," while Vesey proclaimed "that everyone had his time, and that his would come
round too." Perhaps Vesey regularly used this characterization. Vesey also frequently referred to the fact that Santo Domingo and in some statements Africa "will assist us to get
our liberty if we will only make the motion first." He evinced a great respect for the Haitians,

largely with members of the artisanal stratum of free black and slave society—the source of significant support for the AME Church and the 1822 plot—increases the likelihood that he was exposed to these events.[43] Walker's experiences in Charleston helped him to recognize that his freedom was bound up with the slaves' freedom, and that any modicum of liberty he already possessed in no way validated his abandoning this struggle. If anything, it only mandated greater effort on his part. By the early 1820s David Walker seems to have become the radical evangelical activist he would remain for the rest of his life.

The Denmark Vesey conspiracy, however, was by no means Walker's first exposure to black resistance and revolt. Walker grew up in a region of the South that had a long tradition of slave resistance, conspiracies, and marronage. Ever since the establishment of the Lower Cape Fear's first colonies, whites had feared slave revolt. As early as 1721 an attempted insurrection had nearly resulted in the decimation of the southeastern coast's white population. Fear of revolt in 1745 led local magistrates to restrict black gatherings and, in 1747, ships filled with "Mulattoes and Negroes" terrorized settlements along the Cape Fear River.[44]

The dense swamps and forests of the Lower Cape Fear region provided habitats favorable to runaways and maroon camps, and from these haunts outliers regularly marauded against nearby white farms and settlements. In 1767 the magistrates of New Hanover County were "inform'd that upwards of Twenty run away Slaves in abody Arm'd" were threatening the area and that more than thirty men were sent out to kill them on sight if they refused to surrender.[45] Immediately before and during the Revolution, rebellious slaves, taking advantage of the war's social disruptions and of their owners' democratic rhetoric, used their superior knowl-

---

and faith in their sense of responsibility to blacks oppressed in America. Walker too had a high regard for the Haitians and a faith very similar to Vesey's. In mentioning sites other than Africa to which black Americans might emigrate, Walker proposed: "Go to our brethren, the Haytians, who, according to their word, are bound to protect and comfort us." *Appeal,* 15, 56, 62; Killens, *Trial Record of Denmark Vesey,* 42, 43, 46, 64, 93.

43. In Boston, Walker owned a used-clothing shop and a home, signs of genuine success in that city's black community. He also lived nearby and regularly socialized with members of Boston's black artisanal/shopkeeper class (see later chapters). The ease with which he mixed with this class soon after his arrival in Boston in 1825 suggests that he had previously lived among people with similar economic concerns and political orientations.

44. Brewer, "Account of Negro Slavery in the Cape Fear Region," 70–71; Saunders, *Colonial Records,* 2:421, 4:922.

45. *New Hanover Court Minutes,* September 1767, quoted in Alan D. Watson, "Impulse Toward Independence: Resistance and Rebellion Among North Carolina Slaves, 1750–1775," *Journal of Negro History* 63 (1978), 324.

edge of these swampy fastnesses periodically to mass in intimidating numbers near Wilmington. Arriving in town in July 1775, Janet Schaw wrote: "There had been a great number of them [blacks] discovered in the adjoining woods the night before, most of them with arms." After the Revolution, the outlying and marauding continued unabated. In July 1788 a maroon camp discovered on a creek near Wilmington "was the repository for the goods which have been stolen in this town for some time past." The site included more than an acre of cleared ground planted with corn, as well as numerous tools, cooking utensils, and other manufactured items.[46]

In July 1795, runaways posed a serious threat to the security of Wilmington and neighboring plantations. Led by a man called "The General of the Swamps," they hid by day and at night descended on vulnerable farms, taking livestock, clothing, and grain and, in two cases, killing a hated overseer and wounding another. A 1796 petition summarized the depth of the local residents' alarm:

> The outrages committed by a number of runaway Negroes in the County of New Hanover, became so enormous, that the safety of the people made it necessary that vigorous and speedy measures should be taken to suppress the various depredations committed by them[.] Your petitioners well knowing unless decisive measures were adopted and pursued, consequences immediately fatal to that part of the country would happen, & the State in a great measure endangered.

A force of local whites was gathered, and this particular band was eventually subdued—but not without at least one white being shot.[47]

Marronage, however, continued unabated in the region. At the turn of the century, famous naturalist William Bartram was traveling north along the coast at the border of South and North Carolina. Remarking a distant party of blacks moving toward him on the road, Bartram immediately panicked, fearing "a predatory band of Negroes; people being frequently attacked, robbed, and sometimes murdered by them at this place." He was fortunate that the exchange was friendly. As late as 1841, armed

46. Schaw, *Journal of a Lady,* 199; Jeffrey J. Crow, "Slave Rebelliousness and Social Conflict in North Carolina, 1775–1802," *William and Mary Quarterly,* 3rd ser., 37 (1980), 83–84.

47. *Wilmington Centinel,* July 2, 1788; *Wilmington Chronicle,* July 3, 10, and 17, 1795; General Assembly, *Session Records,* November–December 1795, Box 3 "Miscellaneous Concerning Claims" file, North Carolina Department of Archives and History, Raleigh; General Assembly, *Session Records,* 1796, Box 3, file 1, "Petitions (folder 1)."

outliers continued to harass Wilmington with pillaging and occasional killing.[48]

Before and during the years Walker spent in the South, the entire coastal plain running from Norfolk through Wilmington, Georgetown, Charleston, Savannah, and farther south was riddled with the camps and communities of runaways and maroons, causing constant problems for local and state authorities. The Charleston region, with its numerous islands, intricate waterways, and swamps, had always had problems with outliers. In the 1760s the growing number of runaways led to fears of general rebellion; in 1765 the militia was sent to destroy a large camp of maroons, and in 1768 another battle occurred, with "a numerous collection of outcast mullattoes, mustees, and free negroes." Savannah, which had a geography similar to that of Charleston, also had many camps. One maroon stockade—which occupied "[a] space of ground, about half a mile long and less than four hundred feet wide, [and] had been surrounded by a kind of breastwork, four feet high, . . ." made of logs and cane—was located twenty miles north of Savannah and inhabited by blacks who were trained by the British during the siege of Savannah and "still called themselves the King of England's soldiers." So entrenched were these maroons that in 1786 the militias of Georgia and South Carolina, supported by Catawba and Creek warriors, were required to disperse them. Nevertheless, troops were back in the vicinity five months later, attempting once again to rout a large and well-established maroon camp.[49]

Far to the north the Great Dismal Swamp, just south of Norfolk and running into the northeastern counties of North Carolina, had served as a refuge for runaways for as long as slavery had existed in the region. A late-eighteenth-century traveler, J. F. D. Smyth, noted that some slaves disappeared into the swamp for years, settling on elevated pieces of land where they built cottages, planted gardens, kept livestock, and sustained themselves well, in spite of the unfavorable conditions. In 1818 a tutor from Connecticut, Samuel Huntington Perkins, wrote: "Travelling here without pistols is considered very dangerous owing to the great number of runaway negroes" who hid away by day and plundered at night. African

48. Mark Van Doren, ed., *Travels of William Bartram* (New York: Dover Publications, 1955), 373; Herbert Aptheker, *American Negro Slave Revolts,* 5th ed. (New York: International Publishers, 1983), 335.

49. Herbert Aptheker, "Maroons Within the Present Limits of the United States," *Journal of Negro History* 24 (1939), 167–84; William Bacon Stevens, *A History of Georgia,* 2 vols. (1859; reprint, Savannah, Ga.: Beehive Press, 1972), 2:376–78; Philip D. Morgan, "Black Society in the Lowcountry, 1760–1810," in Ira Berlin and Ronald Hoffman, *Slavery and Freedom in the Age of the American Revolution* (Charlottesville, Va.: U.S. Capitol Historical Society, 1983), 139n; Aptheker, *American Negro Slave Revolts,* 208; Ulrich Bonnell Phillips, *American Negro Slavery* (New York: D. Appleton & Co., 1918), 510.

Americans labored exclusively and deep in the swamps as lumberers and diggers of the Great Dismal Canal. Once this key channel was complete, they became the sole boatmen working it. It was no surprise that the British relied so heavily on blacks to guide them through this watery terrain during their siege of Norfolk in 1814. Some of these outliers near Elizabeth City and on the southerly edge of the Great Dismal Swamp were undoubtedly involved in the plotting of the slave insurrection scare that swept Virginia and North Carolina during 1802.[50]

The first decades of the nineteenth century witnessed no subsidence of maroons or of their marauding. A string of runaway camps appears to have run from near Savannah north to the Georgetown / Pee Dee River area. In the swamps between the Ashepoo and Combahee Rivers, a maroon encampment had existed "for a long time," but by 1816 it had grown by such proportions and so markedly increased its depredations that a large military force was sent in to suppress it. This militia was not as successful as people thought, for by the summer of 1822 at least twelve armed outliers in the nearby Coosawatchie area regularly harassed mail-deliverers shuttling between Savannah and Charleston. The outliers had so far proved untrackable in the swamps. Henry Ravenel of Charleston District noted "a regular chain" of runaway camps along the Santee River with at least thirty armed blacks in them, all of whom, save two, had eluded capture. Four years later several outliers were captured near Pineville in the vicinity of these camps. One rebel was notorious enough to have his decapitated head exposed publicly on a stake. The numerous coastal rivers and swamps between Charleston and Georgetown sheltered many runaway camps. Some were settled enough to plant gardens, keep livestock, and even tan hides. One in the Georgetown vicinity was so well established that it had a "large quantity of beef . . . drying on scaffolds, four hides, a fine fat cow, . . . hamstrung, pots, clothes, a hog pen, wells dug, and every necessary preparation for a long residence."[51]

50. J. F. D. Smyth, *Tour in the United States of America,* 2 vols. (London, 1784), 2:101–2; Robert C. McLean, ed., "A Yankee Tutor in the Old South," *North Carolina Historical Review* 47 (January 1970), 56–58; William Palmer, ed., *Calendar of Virginia State Papers,* 11 vols. (Richmond, Va., 1875–93), 10:368.

51. Aptheker, "Maroons Within the United States," 156, 159; *Washington (D.C.) Daily National Intelligencer,* August 24, 1822; Phillips, *Plantation and Frontier,* 2:91; *Charleston Courier,* February 10 and 14, 1820; *Boston Courier,* June 29, 1826.

Further evidence for the existence of extensive runaway communities in this region and for communication between them and numerous supportive slaves remaining on plantations is provided by Jacob Stroyer who was a slave near Columbia, South Carolina, in the late antebellum era. He recounted that "runaway slaves, of eight, ten and even twenty, belonging to different owners, got together in the woods" and that they "were mostly armed, and when attacked in the forests they would fight." Many stayed out for a very long time and some-

Less than fifty miles northeast of Wilmington, in the region of Carteret and Onslow Counties, a serious uprising of some eighty armed outliers—slaves and free blacks—occurred in August 1821. Their strength so alarmed the magistracy that more than seventy men were arrayed against them for almost four weeks. This force, however, still failed to apprehend many of the outlaws and was satisfied instead with "arresting some, and driving others off, and suppressing the spirit of insurrection." That spirit rarely laid low for long in the volatile coastal plain of North Carolina and Virginia. In March 1820 the county militia was called out against "a gang of runaway Negroes, who at present infest" Gates County, adjacent to the Great Dismal Swamp, who had already shot and killed one white resident. In the southern part of Virginia's Norfolk County in the spring of 1823, a large group of armed maroons had put the citizens "in a state of mind peculiarly harassing and painful"—they had already killed several white men, and more deaths were expected. In 1824 a large gang of maroons, fortified with seventeen slaves they had rescued from a coffle passing south, plundered farms along the eastern border of Virginia and North Carolina and were accused of murdering a white man in Gates County. Their leader, Bob Ricks, formerly a slave of Southampton County, was apparently never captured and continued to live in the swamps of the Tidewater. All these incidents of rebellious marronage were only the ones that reached the newspapers and the attention of legislators. The majority went unrecorded in a region inured to outliers and their subversive settlements.[52]

There must have been some connection between these seemingly disparate groups of outliers, at least at the regional level. At the turn of the century and from approximately 1820 to 1824, a high incidence of outlying activity from numerous groups occurred in the counties of Virginia and North Carolina surrounding the Great Dismal Swamp, as well as in the vicinity of Wilmington from roughly 1790 into the early years of 1800.

---

times never returned, preferring to live in the woods. Close connections between outliers and slaves on the plantation benefited both: runaways had greater access to beef and swine than did plantation slaves, and they traded it with these slaves for the bread, corn flour, salt, and other items they lacked. These runaway communities—because they comprised slaves from numerous plantations—provided an essential communication nexus for otherwise separate and distant plantations. See Jacob Stroyer, *My Life in the South* (Salem, Mass., 1898), 61–64, as reprinted in William Katz, ed., *Five Slave Narratives: A Compendium* (New York: Arno Press, 1968).

52. *Charleston Courier,* March 29, 1820, and September 3, 1821; General Assembly, *Session Records,* November 1825–January 1826, Box 4, "House Committee Reports (Claims)" file, North Carolina Department of Archives and History; Johnson, *Ante-Bellum North Carolina,* 514–15; Aptheker, *American Negro Slave Revolts,* 267, 276–77; Thomas C. Parramore, *Southampton County, Virginia* (Charlottesville: University Press of Virginia, 1978), 70–71.

More such activity took place in the region of Charleston and Georgetown from the late 1810s through the middle of the 1820s. Although clear evidence of communication among these groups is not readily forthcoming, their proximity to each other in terms of time and locale at least suggests the possibility of correspondence, especially since large-scale slave conspiracies were planned in two of the areas during the times indicated.[53] Slaves often knew of the whereabouts of maroon camps; some assisted in supplying them, and recent runaways might use them as refuges. One commentator on outliers in northeastern North Carolina observed in 1817 that "a constant intercourse is maintained between runaways and those who remain" and that they were regularly supplied with provisions by many on neighboring farms who would never betray them despite "the most extravagant rewards."[54] It is not unlikely that some camps knew of the existence of others and that there was some contact between them, however rudimentary. These loose networks of runaways and mobile slaves, which are discussed in Chapter 5, were probably involved in moving the *Appeal* in some states, especially North Carolina. And even if we cannot determine in some places whether they were involved or not, Walker likely hoped that they would be.

By the late eighteenth century, much more deliberate and rigorous efforts to create communication networks characterized the work of certain slave rebels. Indeed, the organization and orientation of slave resistance changed with the onslaught of the American Revolution, and particularly after the conflict was over. While resistance became more ideologically grounded, rebels strove to organize greater numbers of participants over a broader geographical expanse. In September 1775 John Adams fretted over the risks of enlisting the support of Georgia and South Carolina in the Revolution because of their huge and problematic black population. Any word of a British emancipation would move quickly among them, because "the negroes have a wonderful art of communicating intelligence among themselves; it will run several hundreds of miles in a week or fortnight." Despite the efforts of whites to delimit the revolutionary fervor to themselves alone, many blacks shared fully, if not as publicly, in assenting to the era's pervasive anticolonial and democratic ideology. From

---

53. For example, outliers in Bertie County, North Carolina, were implicated in the planning and arming of slaves in that region during the 1802 slave conspiracy that swept the state and Virginia. The defendant Tom stated: "The runaways from the other side of the [Albemarle] sound had brought over a case of Guns and 20 lb of powder which wem [torn] d in the swamp." *State v. Tom,* Slave Collection 1787–1856, "Transcripts, Conspiracy 1802" file, North Carolina State Archives.

54. McLean, "A Yankee Tutor in the Old South," 62–64.

1775 onward, taking advantage of the Revolution's social disruptions to pursue their own agenda of freedom, blacks from Georgia to Maryland stepped up the extent of their resistance to slavery and forced white revolutionaries to adjust their strategy to reckon with the threat posed by the slaves. The slogan "Liberty to Slaves" emblazoned across the uniforms of Lord Dunmore's Virginia regiment of runaways in late 1775 heralded the shift in orientation of slave resistance from the local and precipitate to the regional, deliberate, and ideological.[55]

This shift was even more apparent in the resistance orchestrated by slaves in the postrevolutionary era. Some of these changes could be detected in the turbulent region south of Richmond where North Carolina meets Virginia. In 1794 in Carolina's Granville County, the slave Quillo showed his allegiance to electoral politics and democratic principles by intending to sponsor an election "treat" where slaves might select burgesses, justices of the peace, and sheriffs from among their own, "in order to have equal Justice distributed so that a weak person might collect his debts, as well as a Strong one." Plans were also made with slaves in neighboring Person County to rise and march toward Granville "and to murder all who stood in their way."[56] During the summer of 1792 in New Bern, a notice was issued stating, "The negroes in this town and neighbourhood, have stirred a rumour of their having in contemplation to rise against their masters and to procure themselves their liberty."[57] In Bertie County in May 1798, a force of 150 slaves armed with "Guns, Clubs, Swords, & Knives" threatened "to overturn & Revolutionize the good and wholesome government of the State." They initially scattered the pa-

---

55. For extensive discussions of slave activities during the era of the American Revolution, see Aptheker, *American Negro Slave Revolts,* 197–243; Jeffrey J. Crow, *The Black Experience in Revolutionary North Carolina* (Raleigh, N.C.: Department of Cultural Resources, 1977); Benjamin Quarles, *The Negro in the American Revolution* (Chapel Hill: University of North Carolina Press, 1961); and Peter H. Wood, "'The Dream Deferred': Black Freedom Struggles on the Eve of Independence," in Gary Y. Okihiro, ed., *In Resistance: Studies in African, Caribbean, and Afro-American History* (Amherst: University of Massachusetts Press, 1986), 166–187. For works focusing more specifically on shifts in the organization and ideology of slave resistance, see Crow, "Slave Rebelliousness and Social Conflict," 79–102; Eugene D. Genovese, *From Rebellion to Revolution: Afro-American Slave Revolts in the Making of the Modern World* (Baton Rouge: Louisiana State University Press, 1979); Gerald W. Mullin, *Flight and Rebellion: Slave Resistance in Eighteenth-Century Virginia* (New York: Oxford University Press, 1972); Sylvia Frey, *Water from the Rock: Black Resistance in a Revolutionary Age* (Princeton: Princeton University Press, 1991). The quotation from John Adams's diary is quoted in Wood, "'The Dream Deferred,'" 176.

56. As quoted in Crow, *The Black Experience,* 86–87.

57. As quoted in Aptheker, *American Negro Slave Revolts,* 213.

trollers sent to subdue them and killed one of them. By the end of the month, however, they were dispersed and brought to trial.[58]

One of the decade's most dramatic events—the St. Domingue revolution—was only now beginning to inspire a new fervor for resistance among the slaves. In Richmond in 1793, conspiring slaves noted: "You see how the blacks has killed the whites in the French Island and took it a while ago."[59] Dreading the exposure of their slaves to the example of St. Domingue, and blaming slave rebelliousness on the news from the island, slaveholders all along the eastern coast struggled unsuccessfully from 1792 onward to keep the slaves of white émigrés and free persons of color fleeing the island from either disembarking on their shores or, when they did, from contaminating their slaves.[60]

The two events most indicative of the new mode of slave resistance were Gabriel's conspiracy of 1800 and the 1802 slave conspiracy in Virginia and North Carolina. Gabriel's conspiracy was one of the most complex expressions of slave rebelliousness ever witnessed in America. Inspired by the revolutions in America and St. Domingue and by the partial message of egalitarianism still adhering to the republicanism and revivals blazing through Virginia in 1800, Gabriel and his chief associates—centered in and about Richmond—conspired to end not only their own enslavement but also slavery everywhere in Virginia. They intended to strike against the institution in concert with slaves far-distant in the countryside and in other Tidewater towns. One conspirator proclaimed, "We have as much right to fight for our liberty as any men."[61] Slavery was no longer something to be ignored or tolerated if one personally could avoid its chains. An evil corrupting the whole of society, slavery had to be eliminated so that society could mature into a just, democratic, and economically progressive one. But this bold, new aspiration also mandated popular organization at an unparalleled scale.

As Gerald Mullin and, more recently, Douglas Egerton have argued with great force, Gabriel and his chief conspirators represented a new breed of

58. "Slave Papers, 1796–1800," Bertie County, North Carolina State Archives.

59. As quoted in Aptheker, *American Negro Slave Revolts*, 214.

60. For an excellent example of these fears in Norfolk, see the anxious letter of Norfolk's mayor, John Cowper, to Governor Monroe on March 11, 1802 (Palmer, *Calendar of Virginia State Papers,* 9:287). North Carolina also shared in the panic. See, for example, R. H. Taylor, "Slave Conspiracies in North Carolina," *North Carolina Historical Review* 5 (January 1928), 25–26. The most thorough examination of the repercussions of the St. Domingue revolution on African Americans is Julius Scott, "The Common Wind: Currents of Afro-American Communication in the Era of the Haitian Revolution" (Ph.D. diss., Duke University, 1986). For a review of its impact on Virginia, see ibid., 291–92.

61. Palmer, *Calendar of Virginia State Papers,* 9:160.

slave rebels. They were highly skilled artisans who were literate, mobile, and comfortable with town life and selling their labor in urban marketplaces; they were conversant with contemporary political events and had especially imbibed the ideology of urban republicanism; and their hatred of slavery and any restraints on their liberty ran deep.[62] They were the beneficiaries of the deep disruptions—social, economic, and ideological—wrought by the Revolution, of the ever-mounting demand for the labor of black artisans in the commercially expanding Tidewater, and of the greatly increased opportunities for mobility and autonomy all this created for them.

At no time before the revolutionary era in Virginia had slaves ever been allowed so much independence of movement and employment, and this independence provided them with an unprecedented opportunity for collective organizing over a wide expanse of territory. Their objective of smashing slavery within the state mandated such a scale of organization. Gabriel concentrated his efforts in Richmond and the surrounding countryside. He began by revealing his plan to a select few at his blacksmith's shop on the plantation of his owner, Thomas Prosser. They included his brother Solomon and Ben, another slave at Prosser's. Repeating the structure employed by Quillo, he next used barbecues and treats at the nearby Brook Bridge and revival encampments as the nexus of his initial recruiting strategy. At these meetings, Gabriel, Solomon, and Ben enlisted such key figures as Sam Byrd, Jack Ditcher, and Ben Woolfolk. At one meeting a bitterly contested election was held in which Gabriel was chosen as the general of the rebels and Jack Ditcher was voted head of the cavalry. These meetings were also ideological workshops where passages from the Bible legitimating resistance were quoted by such religiously inspired conspirators as Gabriel's older brother Martin and where nerves were steeled against fears of the terrible risks of insurrection. A core group of perhaps 200 men ultimately attended these meetings and joined the ranks.[63]

But the organizing did not stop there. Gabriel, Sam Byrd, and Ben Woolfolk all recruited actively among blacks working in tobacco warehouses in Richmond and on the James River docks. Their numerous jobs in the town and freedom of movement there facilitated this effort. Gabriel

62. Mullin, *Flight and Rebellion;* Douglas R. Egerton, "Gabriel's Conspiracy and the Election of 1800," *Journal of Southern History* 56 (May 1990), 191–214, and *Gabriel's Rebellion: The Virginia Slave Conspiracies of 1800 and 1802.* My discussion of the organizational efforts of Gabriel and his comrades relies heavily on Egerton's painstakingly detailed reconstruction of Gabriel's conspiracy, esp. 50–68.

63. Palmer, *Calendar of Virginia State Papers,* 9:141.

often spent Sundays trying to procure arms and ammunition and to determine where the town's military stores were located. The energetic Sam Byrd also intentionally hired his time during the summer of 1800 in Petersburg, another rapidly growing Tidewater town just to the south of Richmond, where he could recruit among the large number of free blacks and slaves who lived there. He had some success and secured the significant support of several black boatmen who shuttled between Norfolk, counties to the south and west, and even as far away as North Carolina. They were key links in the communication grid, and one local militia leader later recounted that the chief danger was expected "from the batteaux men."[64] Some conspirators sought to extend the network as far east as Norfolk, but that town was too distant from Richmond to be fully integrated into the plot.

Organizing in the more rural counties to the north and west of Richmond moved apace as well; the force of hundreds of armed slaves from there was deemed critical for the taking of Richmond. Ben Woolfolk brought the word to Caroline and Hanover Counties. Sam Byrd visited Hanover as well as Louisa and Albemarle Counties to the west, even recruiting in Thomas Jefferson's Charlottesville. Another compatriot worked Goochland. Yet this rural recruiting never produced the level of forces the core conspirators knew they needed. As Egerton has noted, the conspiracy remained largely urban. Nevertheless, these remarkable westward grasps revealed the vastness of Gabriel's vision of rebellion and the degree to which they needed to rely on extensive and covert communication networks made possible by the greatly increased opportunities for slave mobility. While Gabriel's finely crafted conspiracy was ultimately doomed by informants and torrential rain on the night of attack, his vast organizational strategy and ideological foundations set the pattern for all of the most significant acts of slave resistance to come.

The slave conspiracy of 1802 was the first to follow and issued in part from the momentum built up in 1800. Soon after the suppression of Gabriel's Conspiracy, signs arose that it was persisting, or at least that slaves attracted by the plot and drawn into the existing communication networks carried on the impulse to rebellion. In the last week of December 1800 in Norfolk, a general insurrection of the blacks was expected

---

64. Ibid., 152. In Petersburg, free blacks were concentrated in a community called Pocohantas along the Appomattox River and consequently many of them made their living in fishing and in the river-carrying trade. Indeed, blacks completely dominated those trades on the river, and could move as much information in southeastern Virginia as they did tobacco. See Luther P. Jackson, "Free Negroes of Petersburg, Virginia," *Journal of Negro History* 12 (July 1927), 368–69.

almost daily. A white man had overheard a number of blacks discussing an imminent uprising with such words as "cowards and liberty."[65] While a rapid marshaling of whites may have discouraged the rebels from further acts, slave conspirators were simultaneously planning an even larger insurrection in the town of Petersburg and counties just to the west of it. White officials in Petersburg during the first days of January 1801 learned through a black informant that several hundred blacks in Nottoway County, under the direction of their own officers, were to commence killing whites while marching toward Petersburg. Meanwhile, other rebels were to array themselves at strategic points around Petersburg, to enter it suddenly, and to spare no one in the taking of it. Although this plot also was never activated, it employed a strategy almost identical to that of Gabriel and his comrades and was geographically within the scope of his original conspiracy. Giving even more credence to the probable communication of rebels over a relatively large expanse of land was the fact that white authorities were initially unable to question one leader of the latter plot because he was then in Richmond, having conducted one of the authorities' wives there in a carriage.[66]

By the fall of 1801 the spirit of rebellion seemed to be sweeping this entire region of Virginia and North Carolina. Egerton argues that this turbulence swirled around the black boatmen who worked the rivers of southeastern and southwestern Virginia—the Roanoke, the Appomattox, the James, and the Meherrin, as well as their numerous tributaries.[67] Black

65. Palmer, *Calendar of Virginia State Papers,* 9:173.

66. Ibid., 263–66. Commenting on Gabriel's plot and its aftermath, the shrewd observer George Tucker wrote: "We have hitherto placed much reliance on the difficulty of their acting in concert. Late experience has shewn us . . . they have maintained a correspondence, which, whether we consider its extent, or duration, is truly astonishing" ([George Tucker], *Letter to a Member of the General Assembly of Virginia on the Subject of the Late Conspiracy of the Slaves, with a Proposal for Their Colonization* [Richmond, Va., 1801], 10). Mullin argues that the loss of Gabriel's leadership led to the collapse of organization among the slaves and that they therefore returned to isolated, individualized acts of resistance, such as running away. Without their head man, they could no longer orchestrate insurrection (*Flight and Rebellion,* 154–55). However, the persisting effort to organize rebellion over a large area never subsided, as events in Southside, Nottoway County, and northeastern North Carolina in late 1800 and 1801 made clear. Although later acts of resistance may have lacked the discipline of Gabriel's organization and focus, rebellious slaves did find more collective alternatives than running away. Mullin's conclusion also ignores the fact that Gabriel helped shape a machinery of communication that did not cease with his death. Mobile members of the slave and free black community continued to exchange information among themselves and broadcast it over a wide area. While Gabriel was certainly a powerful leader, black rebelliousness was not contingent on his presence. Gabriel himself was as much a product of that tradition as he was an innovator of it.

67. See Douglas Egerton's carefully detailed discussions in "'Fly Across the River,'" 87–110, and *Gabriel's Rebellion,* 119–46. My description and understanding of these events has

rivermen were overwhelmingly relied on to move the agricultural products of rural southern Virginia to ports at Norfolk or in North Carolina's Albemarle Sound. They often labored without any white supervision, were gone for many days at a time, and had wide geographical mobility. They came about as close to independence as a slave might come. During the tumultuous postrevolutionary era in Virginia, some of them wanted to realize it in full.

Egerton points to one of these boatmen, Sancho, who worked the Roanoke and was involved in Gabriel's plot, as the key instigator of the conspiracies in 1801 and 1802. Sancho and the few around him began in the fall of 1801 to plan an uprising for Easter 1802 in the Virginia and North Carolina counties through which the Roanoke passed. Their strategy was to recruit among a select group of other boatmen who traveled the river and have them raise a few more slaves in their locality. On the day of revolt, they would commence marching at the various points and presumably draw many more slaves at that time into each one of the actions.

While this novel decentralized organization allowed for much local flexibility, it also made it difficult to control the extension of the plot, its schedule, and who was drawn into it. Soon the plotting became diffuse and stretched far beyond the purview of the original cadre. It also came to involve many more people than boatmen and testified to the breadth of unrest among the region's African American population. By December 1801 it had spread from the Roanoke to more eastern counties like Nottoway. There Joe, one of the principal agents for "advising, consulting and conspiring a rebellion and insurrection of the slaves of this State," went about proclaiming just before Christmas that "the white people had so much more liberty than they had, that they could not do as they pleased unless the white people were destroyed." Joe's forces chose officers and were "to kill and cripple all the white people" as they marched to Petersburg where they would secure more arms.[68]

---

been informed by Egerton's. Thomas Parramore has criticized many of these findings in "Aborted Takeoff: A Critique of 'Fly Across the River,'" *North Carolina Historical Review* 67 (April 1991), 111–21. Parramore marshals an array of evidence to argue that black boatmen played no key role in either formulating or promoting this conspiracy and that no organized slave plot existed beyond the overheated imaginations of anxious whites. Parramore suggests that Egerton overemphasized the scale and form of the boatmen's involvement, noting that only one boatman is referred to in the relevant documents and that conspiratorial talk happened as often away from rivers as it did near them. Yet Parramore too readily dismisses the fact that the plot did generally move along the lines of these key commercial rivers.

68. Palmer, *Calendar of Virginia State Papers*, 9:271–73. Governor James Monroe endorsed the execution of Joe and one of his comrades on January 16, 1802, but had no doubt that one of the conspirators' leading motives was "the growing sentiment of liberty existing

By early 1802 there came word of slave conspiracies flaring up through-out southeastern Virginia. Signs of approaching uprisings surfaced in Powhatan County, near Richmond—possibly, as Egerton suggests, moving out of the Appomattox and into the James. In Williamsburg one reporter claimed there was "not even the smallest grounds for doubting that an insurrection was in agitation."[69] In Brunswick County, Virginia, for which one of the boundaries is the Roanoke, two men were tried and quickly hung for attempting to raise several companies of men in their county and in North Carolina "to kill the white people." In March, reports circulated in Norfolk:

> Frequent meetings are held in the neighborhood of this place; that those meetings have consisted of from one to three and four hundred; that a correspondence is held by these meetings with similar ones in North Carolina; that an emissary is now in this town shortly to take his leave to that State with communications.

Although the reporter placed little weight on these statements, and his efforts to apprehend the emissary were "frustrated by the interference of the civil magistrate," the public's fears did not abate, and by April a new and more clear-cut plot against Norfolk was uncovered. At basically the same time yet another plot to fire Richmond was discovered—this time with the support of slaves in neighboring Hanover County—and authorities were now concluding that the conspiracy was "spreading over every county in the State."[70] While these plots certainly had a mixture of unfounded rumor and exaggeration (such as the claim that there were "ten thousand in readiness" in Powhatan County in January), they should not be used to discount the widespread existence of profound discontent, plotting, and preparedness to rebel among the slaves of this region.

Events were unfolding simultaneously with a similar speed in northeastern North Carolina. The plot seemed to follow rivers like the Roanoke

---

in the minds of the [slaves]." Stanislaus Murray Hamilton, ed., *The Writings of James Monroe,* 7 vols. (New York: AMS Press, 1898–1903), 3:328–29.

69. The objective of the Powhatan forces—garnered from a written communication taken from the conspirators—was to march along the James River killing every man until they reached Richmond, which they would destroy "when joined to the army that will meet us there." Gabriel's tactic of country forces meeting urban forces is repeated here. Palmer, *Calendar of Virginia State Papers,* 9:274–75.

70. Ibid., 286–87, 288–89, 293–94, 296–301. Further evidence of communication between town blacks and country blacks was found in papers carried by an Irishman traveling in the vessel of a free black near Petersburg (ibid., 300).

and Chowan and to move toward Albemarle Sound. In May a conspiracy directed by Tom Copper, "General to command this county in a plot to kill the white people," was revealed, but not before Copper and "six stout negroes" raided the jail in Elizabeth City from their camp in the swamps surrounding the town. He was undoubtedly connected with the far grander plan that had been developed in Hertford, Bertie, and surrounding counties to launch an uprising on June 10, 1802. The existence of a communication network—one stretching throughout northeastern North Carolina and reaching into Virginia—connected with this conspiracy is unquestionable. An anonymous but knowledgeable black informant warned white authorities in Virginia and North Carolina just before June 10: "There has been expresses going In Every direction for some days to see all the negroes they could this holladay, to make the arrangements and conclud what time it is to commence and at what plasis they are to assemble."

Because some of the leading conspirators were literate, correspondence could be through letters. One rebel, Ashbourn's Davy, wrote a letter to Virginia requesting assistance and noted to his Carolina comrades that "they could get encouragement from Virginia. The head negroes in Virginia lives about Richmond." A remarkable letter recovered from the conspirators summarized a meeting of a "great number of our Representitives" and exclaimed: "We had intelligence from almost all parts that our intentions have successfully spread with the greatest secrecy." The author unabashedly proclaimed their revolutionary intentions:

> I dont doubt but the great Conflagration . . . will strike such a damp on there [the whites'] Spirets that they will be not only willing to Acknowledge, liberty & Equallity. but purchase their lives at any price. . . . They shall know the birth of liberty is as free for us as for themselves.

The rebels of 1801 and 1802, while not as disciplined in their organization as those in Gabriel's were, still showed the same concern for ideology and networks of communication that strove to incorporate large numbers of people over broad territories into revolt.[71]

While the experience of the American Revolution and the example and organizational work of Gabriel set the background for the 1802 conspiracy, the religious revivals sweeping the region in 1801–3 added a further

71. Aptheker, *American Negro Slave Revolts,* 231–32; Crow, *The Black Experience,* 87–94; Johnson, *Ante-Bellum North Carolina,* 510–13; Palmer, *Calendar of Virginia State Papers,* 9:306–9; various documents from Slave Collection 1787–1856, "Transcripts, Conspiracy 1802" file, North Carolina State Archives.

web linking the localities together. In May 1802 one Dr. Joe, an itinerant Baptist preacher, was found guilty of assisting Tom Copper in raising a revolt; he got off easy with a directive to cease preaching or exhorting to any assembly of slaves. The slave, who had gone from Virginia to raise men in North Carolina, enlisted them while "doctering," a term probably referring to exhorting and praying. Jeremiah Cornick, a Norfolk slave condemned to die in May 1802 for conspiratorial activities, stated that on the day in question he was at "a baptizing"—a near certain reference to a revival or one of the revival-inspired mass baptisms that had become weekly events as church membership soared in this religiously enthused region of Virginia and North Carolina.[72] A reference to meetings of blacks "of from one to three and four hundred" in Norfolk, and to their communication with similar meetings in North Carolina, was likely to revival meetings, the number of participants (black and white) at which often exceeded 1,000 or more.[73] A gathering of blacks of this size for any other even vaguely autonomous purpose would have been extremely difficult to achieve. In northeast North Carolina in early 1802, where revival activity was particularly intense, blacks were clearly using religious gatherings to plan for revolt.[74] Itinerancy, concentrations of many blacks in one place over several days, the autonomous and semi-autonomous black churches, and even Baptist Association meetings all provided forums for

72. Robert M. Calhoon, *Religion and the American Revolution in North Carolina* (Raleigh: North Carolina Department of Cultural Resources, 1976), 66–68; Palmer, *Calendar of Virginia State Papers,* 9:279, 297–98.

73. Palmer, *Calendar of Virginia State Papers,* 9:173. On the strength and breadth of the revivals of 1802–3 among Baptists in this region of Virginia and North Carolina, see various references in Lemuel Burkitt and Jesse Read, *A Concise History of the Kehukee Baptist Association from Its Original Rise Down to 1803* (Halifax, N.C., 1803), 141–313. Presbyterian revivals in the nearby counties of north-central North Carolina that also drew large numbers of blacks are described in the chapter on revivalist James McGready in William Henry Foote, *Sketches of North Carolina* (New York, 1846), 367–413.

Large numbers of church-affiliated black Baptists existed in southeastern Virginia. It is significant that the church in Norfolk "had a number of blacks" and chose a black preacher from Northampton County to be their minister from 1796 through at least the next several years (Burkitt and Read, *Concise History,* 263–65). These opportunities for blacks in the Baptist church unquestionably fueled their response to the revivals of 1802. Both W. Harrison Daniel and Carter G. Woodson emphasize the degree to which independent black preachers and a number of black congregations existed in this area at the turn of the century. Some racially mixed churches even used black members to represent them at Association meetings. See W. Harrison Daniel, "Virginia Baptists and the Negro in the Early Republic," *Virginia Magazine of History and Biography* 80 (January 1972), 60–63; Carter G. Woodson, *The History of the Negro Church* (Washington, D.C.: Associated Publishers, 1921), 53–56. See also Luther P. Jackson, "Religious Development of the Negro in Virginia from 1760 to 1860," *Journal of Negro History* 16 (April 1931).

74. Crow, *The Black Experience,* 88–89.

the exchange of subversive information and its distribution to other areas. It was religious networks such as these, further extended by the networks existing among runaways and black mariners, rivermen, teamsters, and other mobile laborers, that Walker attempted to use in distributing the *Appeal.*

The potentially subversive message of the revivals' evangelicalism was equal in significance to the networks they fostered. If not presented with restraint and countering biblical examples, its strong undercurrent of egalitarianism always threatened the existing hierarchies at the same time that it provided rebellious blacks with ideological ammunition. The white Baptists in Virginia, from their prerevolutionary struggles with the Anglicans and beyond, had stressed the equality of all before God and witnessed especially to those outside the channels of power until they themselves became more settled in them. Their fierce commitment to proselytizing led them to bring this message to hundreds of Virginia and northeastern North Carolina blacks, many of whom joined churches as full members, some in positions of authority as preachers and deacons.[75] The Baptists and Methodists were perhaps too successful in reaching out to blacks. By 1800 a broad enough number of them adhered to or were familiar with the tenets and visions of these denominations to warrant placing a preacher, Martin, and his "preachments" at the heart of his brother Gabriel's efforts to organize the slaves. Like any evangelical touched with millennial hopes, Martin could exclaim: "If we will worship Him [God] we should have peace in all our land," and then follow it immediately, like the radical Christian he also was, with the divine charge "Five of you shall conquer an hundred, and a hundred a thousand of our enemies."[76] Blacks became the unintended and dangerous beneficiaries of Protestant America's remarkably successful combination of democratic ideology with evangelicalism's emphasis on liberty and equality before God.[77]

This subversive message of equality was only reinforced by the joint participation of blacks and whites in the turn-of-the-century revivals.

75. Rhys Isaac, "Evangelical Revolt: The Nature of the Baptists' Challenge to the Traditional Order in Virginia, 1765 to 1775," *William and Mary Quarterly,* 3rd ser., 31 (1974), 345–68; Daniel, "Virginia Baptists and the Negro," 60–63. In northeastern North Carolina the Baptists were the dominant evangelical sect. While Methodists existed in the region along with a few stationed preachers, Asbury observed in Pasquotank County in March 1804: "These people [the Baptists] carry the day here in respectability and numbers." Their success was fueled by the recent revivals. Clark, *Journal and Letters of Francis Asbury,* 2:428. See also similar comments for Roanoke River region (ibid., 426).

76. Palmer, *Calendar of Virginia State Papers,* 9:151.

77. Burkitt and Read, *Concise History,* lauded the religious tolerance in Virginia with the exclamation "But blessed be God, all scruples now are removed by the glorious Revolution, which gives all, under its auspicious government, equal and impartial liberty" (270).

However, a scene from a Presbyterian-led revival that often included Baptist and Methodist ministers reveals the degree of black-white interaction and physical proximity at these events. The Reverend Samuel McCorkle, surveying the scene at a revival with more than 2,000 people in Iredell County, North Carolina, wrote:

> The first particular object that arrested my attention was a poor black man with his hands raised over the heads of the crowd, and shouting, "Glory, glory to God on high." I hasted towards him from the preaching-tent; but was stopt to see another black man prostrate on the ground, and his aged mother on her knees at his feet in all the agony of prayer for her son. Near him was a black woman, grasping her mistress' hand, and crying, "O, mistress, you prayed for me when I wanted a heart to pray for myself. Now thank God, he has given me a heart to pray for you and everybody else." I then passed to a little white girl. . . .

Church membership for both blacks and whites skyrocketed in the Baptist counties of northeastern North Carolina between 1801 and 1803, especially in Bertie, Northampton, and Hertford Counties, the main seats of the insurrectionary plots of 1802.[78] At the height of the revivals, the fundamental boundary between master and slave seemed to be disintegrating.

The two leading historians of Gabriel's conspiracy both downplay the role of religion in the plot. Gerald Mullin argues that "the insurrectionists' goals were essentially political." He views religion and "preachments" simply as devices that the totally secular Gabriel and others used to get less-acculturated country blacks together to talk war, but there is no evidence that the strong sentiments, like those expressed by Martin Prosser, were simply tactical and not heartfelt convictions. Mullin equates a zealous pursuit of secular objectives with an irreligious or antireligious perspective, which accords with his understanding of the democratic ideologue in the Age of Revolution. Yet there is nothing unusual about a ferocious Protestant attentiveness to worldly objectives and the unfolding of secular events, certainly in America. The leaders of the plot could have

---

78. Foote, *Sketches of North Carolina,* 392; Burkitt and Read, *Concise History,* 146–47; John Scott Strickland, "The Great Revival and Insurrectionary Fears in North Carolina: An Examination of Antebellum Southern Society and Slave Revolt Panics," in Orville Vernon Burton and Robert C. McMath Jr., eds., *Class, Conflict, and Consensus: Antebellum Southern Community Studies* (Westport, Conn.: Greenwood Press, 1982), 92 n. 53. Methodist-inspired meetings in Southside Virginia and just north of it in 1776 and 1789 drew, in one case, "hundreds of Negroes," as well as large numbers of whites. Jackson also emphasizes the inherent leveling tendencies in the early revivals of Virginia (Luther P. Jackson, "Religious Development of the Negro," 172–73, 179).

tough political savvy and democratic objectives while still being inspired by fervent millennial hopes. Indeed, given the religious enthusiasm spreading there among all races and classes at the time, it is more logical to conclude that religion did drive Gabriel and his cohort than that it did not.[79]

Douglas Egerton too insists that religion was not significant: "There is not a *single* extant primary document that supports the contention that Gabriel was a deeply religious slave or that Martin was a slave preacher."[80] Yet there is no documentation for Egerton's contention that Gabriel spent a good deal of time with other white and black artisans in Richmond grog shops listening and contributing to political discussions.[81] While Egerton's careful reconstruction of the social context in which Gabriel moved might lead us to believe that he passed time in such shops, there is far more evidence that he did have some relationship to evangelical religion that Egerton gives no weight at all. Why around the issue of religion does Egerton become so much more exacting about the use of evidence? References to critical recruiting and strategy meetings occurring at "preachments" abound.[82] Although that is no guarantee of Gabriel's support for evangelical religion, when compounded with other factors it likely indicates favorable regard.

And other factors there are. Not only Gabriel's older brother, Martin, but also the key organizer, Ben Woolfolk, had a pointed and well-informed discussion in front of many of their compatriots about the character of Moses' leadership of the Israelites out of Egypt.[83] Gabriel had in fact precipitated this dialogue because he had conceded to Martin the right "to decide upon" when the revolt should begin, a decision both Martin and Ben clearly believed had to be justified biblically. Why is Egerton unwilling to consider that Gabriel's according this remarkable power to the religious Martin might suggest that Gabriel recognized that religion had an important role to play in the revolt? While its precise function will probably never be fully understood, religion was nevertheless a vital part of Gabriel's conspiracy.

Other related forces had also contributed to Virginia's social instability. Antislavery sentiment among whites in the region was by no means dead. David Barrow's antislavery circular had just passed through Southampton County's Baptist churches in 1798; the antislavery pronouncements of the

79. Mullin, *Flight and Rebellion,* 157–60.

80. Egerton, *Gabriel's Rebellion,* 197.

81. Ibid., 30, 33.

82. See, for example, Palmer, *Calendar of Virginia State Papers,* 9:141, 150, 151, 153, 158, 166–68.

83. Ibid., 151.

Methodists' Conference of 1800 had been widely circulated in this region despite much white opposition; Virginia intellectuals such as George Tucker continued to doubt the viability of slavery; and pockets of opposition to slavery remained among some resident white Baptists, Methodists, and Quakers.[84] A scattering of whites clearly sympathized with the rebellious slaves, and some even participated in plotting. Two Frenchmen apparently helped to instigate Gabriel's revolt, and the rebels made clear that "the Quakers, the Methodists, and the Frenchmen . . . were to be spared on account as they conceived of their being friendly to liberty";[85] numerous reports of white involvement surfaced during the 1802 conspiracy, prompted by a sense of common class interests that could have been fostered in part by joint participation in revivals.[86] Amid this confusion over the parameters of racial interaction and servitude, news about unfolding events in St. Domingue spread rapidly, inspiring great fear in whites while sustaining hope in rebellious blacks.[87] Brought to a head by the great revivals, a sense of new possibilities for freedom existed with unusual vigor among blacks during this era and made the cage of slavery a nearly insupportable confinement for many of them. That this region witnessed then a level of slave agitation, plotting, and actual resistance never before seen is not at all surprising.

84. See the excellent discussion of antislavery's losing battle in the early national upper South in David B. Davis, *The Problem of Slavery in the Age of Revolution, 1770–1823* (Ithaca, N.Y.: Cornell University Press, 1975), 196–212. Davis, however, adds: "Though recent scholarship has correctly emphasized the weakness of antislavery in the South, the persistence of any antislavery activity is a remarkable social fact. The very diversity of southern society for a time made slavery a more vulnerable institution than in any other plantation regime" (p. 211). This vulnerability was particularly pronounced at the turn of the century. See also Daniel's discussion of Baptist antislavery in "Virginia Baptists and the Negro," 63–69.

85. Egerton's painstaking archival work has established that the two Frenchmen probably did exist, likely having come to Virginia with French regiments during the American Revolution. See *Gabriel's Rebellion,* 182–85.

86. The slave Arthur said in 1802 that "he had long had this plan [of insurrection] on his mind, and had joined with both black and white, that is, the 'common men of poor white people,' and with mulattoes" (Palmer, *Calendar of Virginia State Papers,* 9:299; see also 9:141, 152, 294, 298, 301). George Tucker again sensed the subversive potential of evangelicalism: "Fanaticism is spreading fast among the Negroes of this country, and may form in time the connecting link between the black religionists and the white. Do you not already, sir, discover something like a sympathy between them?" (*Letter to a Member,* 11).

87. For example, John Cowper wrote to Governor James Monroe from Norfolk on March 11, 1802: "There are now a considerable number of [slaves from Haiti] in this place, whose dispositions, I apprehend, will be influenced by the accounts which are daily arriving and published concerning the horrid scenes of St. Domingo. . . . The situation of this place is such as a few hours would reduce it to ashes" (Palmer, *Calendar of Virginia State Papers,* 9:287).

A high incidence of slave conspiring and resistance seems to correlate with the presence of four factors: (1) a high density of slave population, at least at the level of a black-white ratio of 2 : 1; (2) fairly consistent, regional marronage and outlying, from which issue regular marauding and resistance; (3) a mobile slave population facilitated by the wide-scale use of slaves as boatmen, pilots, teamsters, mariners, lumberers / forest workers, couriers, and other traveling laborers; and (4) evangelical enthusiasm, especially—although not exclusively—when communicated through itinerant or local black preachers and/or an established, independent black church.

The religious factor appears to be central to organizing any large-scale insurrection. While high density offered numerical strength, the communities of outliers provided both refuges for new runaways and a regular example of subversion and alternatives to slavery. A mobile slave labor force laid out the grid for the essential communication network. Evangelical gatherings supplied both the ideological foundation and the forums for communication and the experience of solidarity. All these factors were present in the relevant, turbulent region of Virginia and North Carolina at the turn of the century and in the volatile Charleston/Georgetown area from roughly 1816 to 1822.

Yet slavery remained, and those benefiting from it were intent on keeping it that way. Evangelicalism and the large, enthusiastic revivals were quickly spotted as potential threats. George Tucker wrote in 1801: "It certainly would not be a novelty, in the history of the world, if Religion were made to sanctify plots and conspiracies." John Scott Strickland, in a brilliant analysis of the 1802 slave plot in North Carolina, argued that the revivals were central to fostering some sense of equality between whites and blacks, but that the white elite also recognized this new spirit, however dimly, and used the hysteria generated by the discovery of the slave plots to reinforce the traditional racial boundaries that the revivals had eroded.[88] In 1807 Jacob Read, a prominent Federalist of Charleston, voiced sentiments regarding evangelicals that were common among the ruling elite of the South's eastern seaboard:

> For tis in vain to conceal from ourselves the fact that there spread everywhere through the state religious and other enthusiasts who are preaching very dangerous Doctrines and exciting in our black populations—Sentiments that must lead to fatal results which

88. Tucker, *Letter to a Member,* 11; Strickland, "The Great Revival and Insurrectionary Fears," 57–95.

nothing but their want of a common head and some one daring
enough to make the attempt.[89]

After Gabriel, the plots of 1801 and 1802, and the persisting message of
the remaining egalitarian Methodists and Baptists, the slaveholding elite
knew what they were up against and set out to remedy it.

While revivals and interracial religious fellowship did not disappear
from the region, the threatening egalitarianism fostered by some of the
evangelicals did diminish. David Barrow was faced with a cold response
to his antislavery pronouncements of 1798. The Methodists' resolutions of
1800 had a similar fate in the South. From Savannah to Richmond, non-
conforming evangelicals encountered rough treatment—sometimes even
death—at the hands of local chastising mobs. By the early years of the
new century, the Methodists and Baptists had no doubt that if they were
to survive and expand in the South and gain any access to the slaves,
they would have to dissociate themselves from any taint of antislavery.[90]
No evangelical embodied this shift better than Francis Asbury, who in
1783 wrote "We all agree in the spirit of African liberty" yet by 1809 could
utter with equal certainty, "What is the personal liberty of the African
which he may abuse, to the salvation of his soul . . . ?"[91] While the transition from a tentative antislavery to a compromise with bondage was not
without its reversals or ever fully completed, the job was more or less
finished among the evangelicals by the early years of the 1810s.

Of equal importance was the steady if partial suppression by white authorities of independent black churches from the late eighteenth century

89. Jacob Read to Charles Pinckney, June 18, 1807, quoted in Strickland, "The Great Revival and Insurrectionary Fears," 93 n. 62.

90. For discussion of this Methodist compromise with the social realities of the South, see
Donald G. Mathews, *Slavery and Methodism: A Chapter in American Morality, 1780–1845*
(Princeton: Princeton University Press, 1965), 3–61. W. Harrison Daniel indicates that the
white Baptists made their peace with slavery more readily, eliminating almost all dissent by
the latter years of the 1790s (Daniel, "Virginia Baptists and the Negro," 68–69). Essig argues
that the leaders of Virginia Baptists sought a new struggle against worldliness that would
maintain the group cohesion and righteousness that existed before the legislature guaran-
teed their religious liberty in 1785; slaveholding became the badge of greed and sloth and
was attacked with increased vigor. But local churches failed to share the fervor, and by the
late 1790s the Baptist elders evaded further contention by designating it a solely legislative
matter. James Essig, "'A Very Wintry Season': Virginia Baptists and Slavery," *Virginia Magazine of History and Biography* 88 (April 1980), 170–85. At the turn of the century, Methodists
throughout the South were assaulted as proponents of "Nigger religion," but they were especially persecuted in areas with large slave populations, such as Wilmington, Georgetown,
and Charleston, where they succeeded in winning many black adherents. See Johnson, *Ante-
Bellum North Carolina*, 345; *Autobiography of the Rev. Joseph Travis*, 52–54; Abel McKee
Chreitzberg, *Early Methodism in the Carolinas* (Nashville, Tenn., 1897), 78, 96–97.

91. Clark, *Journal and Letters of Francis Asbury*, 1:441, 2:591.

onward. Independent black Methodist congregations were particularly feared, because they came out of a much stronger antislavery and egalitarian tradition than the Baptists did. At the turn of the century, black Methodist churches that had some form of autonomy existed in New Bern, Tarboro, Wilmington, and Fayetteville in North Carolina, and in Georgetown and Charleston in South Carolina, with the strong possibility that still unidentified churches existed in other towns as well.[92] By 1815 the growing respectability of Methodism, coupled with the highly centralized administration the denomination could use against local churches, had allowed white officials to bring all but the Charleston church fully under their sway.

The movement against independent black Baptist churches began earlier, in large part because they and New Light evangelizing appeared sooner than similar Methodist efforts. In the early 1790s in Southside Virginia, where Baptists were the overwhelming choice of the church-going inhabitants, blacks broke with whites to form churches of varying degrees of independence in at least three different locations: Williamsburg, Charles City, and Allen Creek in Mecklenburg County. The reason for this splintering was the same in every case: actions had been taken by white authorities to force blacks to cease preaching and baptizing new members.[93] While in each case blacks resisted submitting to the edicts, Williamsburg, which retained a black minister, had by 1791 allowed the Dover Association "to visit them and set things in order," and "the most orderly" in Allen Creek had allowed a new white minister to reorganize them. The church in Charles City "ended in confusion," apparently the fate of autonomous blacks. The experiences of these churches make it clear how volatile an issue black preaching and pastoring could become. Indeed, it could have been the issue on which blacks—slave and free— would prove themselves the most willing, regularly and tenaciously, to challenge white authority publicly.[94]

92. All but the New Bern and Tarboro churches have been previously identified. For references to these two churches, see ibid., 2:326, 382.

93. See Robert B. Semple, *A History of the Rise and Progress of the Baptists in Virginia* (Richmond, Va., 1810), 112, 114–15, 221–22.

94. The degree of autonomy achieved by these churches, however, must not be overstated. Many were the result of the departure of white members who felt constrained by the large black presence and, after splitting, were monitored by the new white church. The proximity of the few clearly independent black churches to white Baptist churches in the same town, and membership in regional associations, could have had moderating influences on the blacks, despite the Baptists' decentralized associational structure. While Luther Jackson identifies three churches that "seemed to be distinctly independent organizations" in Southside Virginia, all three of them would fit into this characterization. Black Baptist congregations simply seem not to have been as feared as their Methodist counterparts were. By

In 1818 the founders of the Charleston AME church were bucking a powerful tide. Advancing a combination of evangelicalism, democratic ideology, and black autonomy, which the white elite had deliberately worked to stamp out since the turn of the century, they continued to be a glaring challenge to the completion of white hegemony. What is most astounding is that the AME church existed for as long as it did in Charleston, given the strength of the forces it came up against. The Denmark Vesey affair of 1822 revolved around the uncovering of a dangerously extensive plot to rise against the whites, but that plot itself issued from the relentless effort of whites to close the African church, which embodied the egalitarian evangelicalism so many African Americans cherished.

David Walker carried this tradition of resistance to slavery and rebellious black religion to the North. His likely exposure to the Vesey affair introduced him to one of the most complex expressions of black resistance in the postrevolution South. Moreover, he probably was familiar with the ideological and organizational strategies for resistance that had been forged over the years in black communities extending from Charleston to the James River. His life so far had been spent in a territory filled with the persistent resistance of resourceful outlying slaves, isolated individual rebels, black evangelicals struggling to maintain some independence, and even scheming black merchants who despite interdictions kept a toehold on the marketplace. Having come of age in a town dominated by slaves, Walker knew well their lives, the extent of their will to resist, and their actual moments of defiance. His years in Charleston exposed him to many free blacks who cooperated and interacted with slaves and who were committed to the institution's overthrow. These years undoubtedly sparked his revolutionary evangelicalism and equipped him with the courage to extend his vision over a far broader terrain.

David Walker probably left this great center of black life with the hope of uniting the rebellious spirit manifest in so many loosely connected regions of the South into one ideologically united force that could overcome slavery once and for all and finally achieve the peace and equality that was Christ's promise. Carrying on in the tradition of Gabriel, of the rebels of 1801–2, and of Denmark Vesey and Peter Poyas, Walker recognized that egalitarian evangelicalism had the potential to spread among and embolden the mass of discontented slaves and free blacks. Fleeing the recent discouragements of Charleston and its ferocious vise of reaction, and grounded in the lessons of the tumultuous lowcountry, Walker headed for the unknown turf of the North.

1815 it was hoped that a softened evangelicalism and a reduced black religious autonomy would neutralize the threat religion posed to slavery.

3

"Even here in Boston, pride and prejudice have got to such a pitch"

Settling Down in Massachusetts

> *Do any of you say that you and your family are free and happy, and what have you to do with the wretched slaves and other people? So can I say, for I enjoy as much freedom as any of you, if I am not quite as well off as the best of you. Look into our freedom and happiness, and see of what kind they are composed!! They are of the very lowest kind—they are the very* dregs!*—they are the most servile and abject kind, that ever a people was in possession of!*
>
> —David Walker's *Appeal*

David Walker probably left Charleston, South Carolina, sometime soon after the trial of Denmark Vesey and his conspirators. A number of free blacks followed this course. Morris Brown, Henry Drayton, Charles Corr, Amos Cruckshanks—all leading figures in founding and sustaining Charleston's AME church—and most likely others made a hasty departure for Philadelphia as soon as the plot was uncovered.[1] A few free blacks, such as Prince Graham and Quash Harleston, were forcibly transported from

---

1. John B. Matthews, James Eden, London Turpin, Alexander Harleston, and Smart Simpson—all signatories of the original Charleston AME petition (see Appendix A)—were in Philadelphia in 1822 for conference meetings, probably after the Vesey affair. See Daniel A. Payne, *History of the African Methodist Episcopal Church,* ed. C. S. Smith (Nashville, Tenn., 1891), 38–39. Any African church member who had been to the North in 1822 was either highly discouraged or outright prevented by the Charleston authorities from remaining in town after the plot was uncovered.

the state as punishment for involvement with Vesey.[2] Many other unnoted and discouraged free blacks left South Carolina as well, in the wake of the reaction to the conspiracy and the razing of the African church.

Although the latter part of 1822 seems like a logical time for Walker to have left Charleston, determining the date precisely is difficult. His departure could have come as late as the middle of 1824 or so, which would have allowed him just enough time to travel to Boston, situate himself, and still be inscribed in the 1825 Boston City Directory, as he was. Yet he almost certainly left earlier. In a number of places in the *Appeal,* Walker refers either to having made lengthy journeys in the United States or to being familiar with characteristics of the South and West, which strongly suggests time spent there. Two passages in particular point to such travels. He opens the *Appeal* with the following statement:

> Having travelled over a considerable portion of these United States, and having, in the course of my travels, taken the most accurate observations of things as they exist— . . .

and concludes the work with this testimony:

> I do not speak from hear say—what I have written, is what I have seen and heard myself. No man may think that my book is made up of conjecture—I have travelled and observed nearly the whole of those things myself, and what little I did not get by my own observation, I received from those among the whites and blacks, in whom the greatest confidence may be placed.

The most likely time for Walker to have made these trips would have been after his departure from Charleston.[3] Although he may have moved about somewhat before arriving in Charleston, his preeminent concern at that time was probably getting to that town and seeking employment there. Extensive travels would have been much more likely during the uncertain interim between leaving Charleston and arriving in Boston.

Where exactly Walker journeyed in the South and West is open to conjecture. An excursion to Savannah is a likelihood, and voyages up the Savannah, the Cooper, the Cape Fear, or other rivers are also possible. But Walker leaves us no further clues. It is not even clear to what "West" he was referring. Did he mean the trans-Appalachian West of Tennessee and Kentucky and the Ohio River valley, or the Old Southwest of Missis-

2. Charles Spencer Smith, *A History of the African Methodist Episcopal Church* (Philadelphia, 1922), 14. See also Appendix B.

3. *Appeal,* 1, 76; see also 13, 21, 28, 62.

sippi and Alabama, or simply the western portions of the Carolinas or of some state like Pennsylvania? While the degree to which slavery existed in the "West" of which he spoke suggests the regions of the Old Southwest, where reliance on slave labor was great, the locus of his travels cannot be pinpointed with any kind of certainty. The possibility also remains that Walker did not penetrate far into the Southwest at all, and that he relied on his own readings and discussions with others to inform himself on that developing region.

In his passage northward, a sojourn in Philadelphia is not unlikely. Philadelphia had long served as a magnet for free blacks and fugitive slaves leaving the South. It was a major port, where ships transporting many of them regularly stopped; employment prospects were good; and the free black population was large (well over 10,000 by the mid-1820s) and offered support to many new arrivals in the form of kin, friends, and community institutions. Moreover, it was the seat of the African Methodist Episcopal Church and Bishop Richard Allen, as well as the new home for some recent leading exiles from that denomination in Charleston.

This connection with the AME Church could well have been what brought Walker to Philadelphia. While a search through the pertinent records of the Mother Bethel AME Church and through municipal tax records, censuses, and directories did not yield a David Walker, sections of the *Appeal* suggest that he spent time in that city.[4] Walker's discussion of Bishop Allen and his achievements is so direct and intimate that it implies some personal exposure to the man. Walker refers glowingly to Allen on a number of occasions, but one is particularly reverential:

> Having overcome the combined powers of devils and wicked men, [Reverend Allen] has under God planted a Church among us which will be as durable as the foundation of the earth on which it stands. Richard Allen! O my God!! The bare recollection of the labors of this man, and his ministers among his deplorable wretched brethren, (rendered so by the whites) to bring them to a knowledge of the God of Heaven, fills my soul with all those very high emotions which would take the pen of an Addison to portray. It is impossible my brethren for me to say much in this work respecting that man of God. When the Lord shall raise up coloured

4. Minute and Trial Book, Bethel AME Church, 1822–35 and 1838–51, Historical Society of Pennsylvania, Philadelphia. The City Tax (Real & Personal) Records for the city's largest black ward, Cedar, are incomplete; records for 1820–25 do not exist. The Poor Tax Register is equally incomplete; a search around these dates was unfruitful. On the long shot that he might appear in the 1820 census, the appropriate records were searched, but in vain. Walker does not appear in the Philadelphia Directory from 1819 to 1825.

historians in succeeding generations, to present the crimes of this nation, to the then gazing world, the Holy Ghost will make them do justice to the name of Bishop Allen, of Philadelphia. Suffice it for me to say, that the name of this very man . . . though now in obscurity and degradation, will notwithstanding, stand on the pages of history among the greatest divines who have lived since the apostolic age, and among the Africans, Bishop Allen's will be entirely pre-eminent.[5]

This is a description from a devout disciple, one who knows well whom he is following. The degree of his reverence betokens a strong possibility that Walker had contact with Allen's preaching and works in the Philadelphia black community. Although the evidence is finally only circumstantial, this possibility, joined with the flight of a number of black Charlestonians to Philadelphia and with other prospects the city offered, argues for Walker's presence there at some point after leaving the South. A similar search for him in New York City uncovered no traces.

Of the date of Walker's arrival in Boston we can be much more certain. He must have arrived there no later than the latter months of 1824, because his name appears in the 1825 Boston City Directory, a volume issued early each year. He was also assessed a tax in 1825 for his used-clothing store in Dock Square.[6] Walker is not listed in any tax records for 1824. The fact that in both the Boston City Directory and the tax book he is listed as a used-clothing dealer points also to a late-1824 arrival, as he would have needed time to locate a shop, gather inventory, and settle himself domestically.

In 1825 Walker must have been largely concerned with establishing himself economically in Boston. Tax records for this period regularly listed both place of residence and employment, but for Walker only his shop is listed, indicating that he probably lived there during this transitional year. The Directory also places him only at his shop. The source of the initial capital needed to start the shop is not clear. If he borrowed money, no records of the transaction remain. The requisite start-up money, however, probably was not that great, and he must have arrived in town with some money in hand. The possibility that someone he was referred to or came to know soon after arrival helped to establish him in the business cannot be dismissed because he settled into the trade so soon after reaching Boston.

This possibility is strengthened by the fact that blacks were coming to dominate the used-clothing business in Boston at this time. It was one of

5. *Appeal,* 58–59.
6. City of Boston, Valuation Book, Ward 4, 1825, Boston Public Library.

the few entrepreneurial activities open to them and a number of blacks went into it. While only three black used-clothing dealers were listed in the 1825 and 1826 city directories, others were probably missed, as was common for blacks in such directories.[7] By 1827 there were at least seven, and over the next three years the numbers mounted dramatically: ten in 1828, fourteen in 1829, and twenty in 1830.[8] Why their presence was burgeoning at this time is not clear, but it was evident that there was a demand for their wares and that respectability was attached to the trade. The *Boston Evening Transcript* noted in October 1831: "The increase of second hand clothes warehouses has been very rapid within a few years, and there is abundant proof that their occupants pursue a business worth following." Near the central wharves almost all these shops were concentrated on Brattle Street or streets immediately adjacent. The *Evening Transcript* declared, "Brattle Street is almost monopolized by them."[9]

David Walker found some of his most important relationships in this business. By 1830 no less than six of his close friends and political associates traded in old clothing and in shops essentially right next door to him: Frederick Brimsley, William Brown, John Eli (Ely), Coffin Pitts, John Scarlett, and Henry Tyler. Numerous small black businesses, especially barbers and bootblacks, were also located in this tiny district, and several of them became key colleagues of Walker's: James Barbadoes and John Pero were a door or two down on Brattle Street, while Victor Villeneuve, Louis Blancard, Cato Freeman, Oliver Nash, and William G. Nell were within a block of his establishment. Owning a small business facilitated Walker's entrance into established black Boston.[10]

But there were also risks to dealing in used clothing. In this time before the availability of easily produced, inexpensive, ready-made clothing, a considerable market for secondhand clothing existed. Thieves often looked to steal a variety of garments and accessories from people's wardrobes, and then to sell them at secondhand shops. While a few shop owners knowingly trafficked in such items, the majority monitored their vendors closely to be sure they were not marketing illicit wares. Frederick

7. For example, Frederick Brimsley, a close associate of Walker's, was missed in 1826. Although there is only one clothing dealer listed in 1826—David Walker—one man sold fruit and clothing and another was a clothes cleaner, a trade often dealing in used clothing (Boston City Directory, 1825, 1826).

8. The numbers were probably greater, for the figures come only from those listed in the Boston City Directory, 1827, 1828, 1829, 1830.

9. *Boston Evening Transcript,* October 24, 1831.

10. All information on addresses comes from the Boston City Directory, 1825–30.

Brimsley alerted the police to a young man who was trying to sell him stolen goods in 1830. He also led a movement to license used-clothing dealers as a way to sanction them and eliminate the "fences."[11]

Despite this commitment to honesty and vigilance, the dealers could still suffer at the hands of suspicious police. In February 1828 John Scarlett, John Eli, and David Walker were brought before the state court on charges of having received stolen goods. After arguments for the defendants were presented, all were "acquitted by the Jury without hesitation." Yet the precariousness of the trade was once again impressed on them.

That brief trial provides unique insight into Walker's character. The court was advised that these men "conduct their business in a fair and honorable manner" and that "they were accustomed to give early information of suspicious persons to the Police." Even more revealing was the statement that "a crowd of witnesses of the first standing in society" had "testified to their [i.e., Walker et al.] integrity and fairness in their dealings, and moral characters, to be envied by some of a fairer complexion."[12] It is unfortunate that these witnesses, who could well have been white, were not identified by name. Nevertheless, the extent to which Walker had by early 1828 come to be known and respected by people of merit in the community, and the testament to Walker's civic and personal uprightness, is unmistakable.

In 1826 David Walker strengthened his connection with Boston's black community. Early in that year he rented a room on Beacon Hill on Southack Street,[13] which was in the heart of the Sixth Ward and had the highest concentration of blacks anywhere in the city.[14] A number of black men, and possibly their families, lived in the same building with Walker, along

11. *Boston Daily Courier,* February 12 and August 26, 1830. See also the *Boston Evening Transcript,* October 24, 1831, for an expression of public concern over used-clothing dealers receiving stolen goods.

12. All quotations in this and the preceding paragraph are from the *Boston Daily Courier,* February 12, 1828.

13. City of Boston, Valuation Book, Ward 4 and Ward 6, 1826, Boston Public Library.

14. In 1830 Ward 6 had 605 black inhabitants, one-third of the total black population (1,875) of the city. The adjacent Ward 7, on the northeastern end of Beacon Hill, accounted for 450 blacks, and Ward 5, across Cambridge Street from the bottom of Beacon Hill, had 185 more. Thus, in 1830 some 56 percent of Boston's black population was concentrated on Beacon Hill (66 percent if the ward in the immediate outskirts of the Hill is included). The north slope of Beacon Hill was commonly called "Negro Hill" in the antebellum era. The other area with a significant black population in 1830 was the North End, which bounded the city's wharves. There, in the First and Second Wards, 300 blacks lived, a number of them mariners. (Data from James and Lois Horton, *Black Bostonians: Family Life and Community Struggle in the Antebellum North* [New York: Holmes & Meier, 1979], 4.)

with several white tenants.[15] The surrounding buildings were filled with men and women who would soon become his close associates.

On February 23, 1826, standing before the Reverend Isaac Bonney, David Walker married Eliza Butler.[16] No record of their meeting or courtship is available, but marriage and death certificates indicate that Eliza had been a resident of Boston from birth.[17] Her father, Jonas Butler, had also been born in Boston, but whether as a slave or a free man is not known. Walker had married into a well-established black Boston family. This liaison gave him an entrance into the black community, which he would have lacked as a single, unconnected male from the South. A child also must have arrived soon, for according to the 1830 federal census

15. Despite the high number of blacks relative to the overall black population, the Sixth Ward was by no means demographically dominated by blacks, nor did racial segregation along the rigorous pattern of twentieth-century urban America exist in any but an embryonic form. Alongside the 605 blacks in the Sixth Ward were 3,898 whites. Blacks and whites still lived close by in the Boston of 1830.

16. The Reverend Isaac Bonney (1782–1855) had another fateful encounter with an eminent antebellum African American. In 1838 or 1839, after having moved to New Bedford, Massachusetts, Frederick Douglass sought out a church where he could renew the relationship with organized religion that had been damaged for him by the hypocrisy of the church in the South. Douglass had a predilection for the Methodist church and ventured to join its most prominent representative in town, the Elm Street Methodist Church. This church was presided over by none other than Reverend Bonney, who itinerated for more than forty years among several congregations in Connecticut, Rhode Island, and Massachusetts and was one of New England's most popular preachers.

About his first encounter with the church, Douglass wrote: "Although I was not allowed a seat in the body of the house, and was proscribed on account of my color, regarding this proscription simply as an accommodation of the unconverted congregation who had not yet been won to Christ and his brotherhood, I was willing thus to be proscribed, lest sinners should be driven away from the saving power of the gospel." But he soon realized that this isolation had nothing to do with one's relationship to grace and everything to do with skin color. Remaining after church one Sunday for the serving of the sacrament, Douglass, who until then had been confined with the handful of black members to the gallery, descended with them to receive the Host, but they had to wait in the farthest corner from the altar until all the whites had been served. Bonney then beckoned: "Come forward, colored friends!—come forward! You, too, have an interest in the blood of Christ. God is no respecter of persons. Come forward, and take this holy sacrament to your comfort." Disgusted with Bonney's patronizing tone, the black members' acquiescence to it, and the lack of real fellowship in this church, Douglass refused the offer, walked out of the church, and never returned. Eventually he settled on a small, local gathering of black Methodists. See Frederick Douglass, *My Bondage and My Freedom,* ed. Philip S. Foner (1855; reprint, New York: Dover Publications, 1969), 351–53. See also William B. Sprague, ed., *Annals of the American Pulpit; or, Commemorative Notices of Distinguished American Clergymen of Various Denominations,* 9 vols. (New York, 1873), 7:452–54.

17. Register of Marriages in Boston, 1800–1849, and Registry of Deaths in Boston, both housed in City Hall, Government Center.

Walker by then had two boys and one girl under the age of ten in his household.[18]

In the middle of the same year, Walker took another significant step into the heart of Boston's black community. On the evening of July 28, 1826, he was duly initiated into the first degree of Prince Hall Masonry. A few weeks later, on August 14, he was elevated to the Master's degree and received fully into Boston's African Lodge. Entrance into the Prince Hall Masons gave Walker immediate access to some of the most prominent members of Boston's black community: the Reverend Thomas Paul, minister of the First African Baptist Church; John T. Hilton, hairdresser, Grand Master of the Lodge in 1827, and a leading community spokesman; Walker Lewis, hairdresser and militant abolitionist; and James Barbadoes, also a hairdresser and indefatigable political organizer. Walker would now have regular contact with these men and many other similarly minded and positioned members.[19]

With admission into the African Lodge, Walker entered the most long-lived institution of Boston's blacks. Black Freemasonry in America has a history stretching over 200 years, beginning in 1775 when Prince Hall and several other free blacks of Boston were initiated into a lodge of British soldiers then resident in the city.[20] After British troops left Boston in March 1776, Prince Hall and his fraters remained without an official lodge warrant and were therefore unable to initiate new members. Having sought a charter from the white Massachusetts Grand Lodge after the Revolution and been refused, they were chartered by the Grand Lodge of England in May 1787 as African Lodge #459. Freemasonry quickly spread among numerous free black males in Boston, and within the next several years into black centers along the northeastern seaboard. Unchartered and unrecognized by white American Masons, black Masons denominated

18. 1830 Federal Census, Massachusetts, Suffolk County, Boston, Ward 5, p. 197.

19. Prince Hall Records, Minutes of African Lodge, Boston, 1807–46, compiled by H. V. B. Voorhis, housed at Grand Masonic Lodge of Massachusetts, Boston. I extend my thanks to Roberta Hankammer, Head Librarian at the Grand Masonic Lodge, for alerting me to these invaluable records.

20. Little is known of Prince Hall's early history. Born in Barbados around 1748 the son of an Englishman and a free black woman who was part French, Hall arrived in Boston in March 1765 and by 1770 had acquired property and sufficient education to become a Methodist preacher. He eventually had a congregation in Cambridge, Massachusetts, and he was a prominent member of Boston's black community almost from his arrival in the city. The most thorough treatments of Hall's life are Lorenzo Greene, "Prince Hall: Massachusetts Leader in Crisis," *Freedomways* 1 (Fall 1961), 238–58; and Sidney Kaplan, *The Black Presence in the Era of the American Revolution, 1770–1800* (New York: New York Graphic Society, 1973), 181–92.

themselves "Prince Hall Masons" when their founder died in 1807, marking themselves off racially as well as honoring Hall.

Prince Hall used the Masons to struggle against slavery, the slave trade, and racial oppression. Their separation from the American Masons actually enhanced the independence and political strength of their lodge by freeing them of any resident authority while still granting them the right to charter other lodges. African Lodge #459 thereby gained the unintended and exclusive power to establish in numerous communities black lodges that could reinforce solidarity while promoting antislavery and the fight for black civil rights. By late 1787 Prince Hall and his associates were petitioning the legislature for some sort of program for black education. In 1788 they were instrumental in abolishing the slave trade in Massachusetts by advertising the infamous episode of a kidnapping and sale in the West Indies of three free black men from Boston, who were eventually returned. Speeches that Hall gave at the lodge provided evidence of his belief that Freemasonry could serve the ends of black freedom. In a 1797 address, he reminded his brothers:

> Our Grand Master Solomon did not divide the living child, whatever he might do with the dead one; neither did he pretend to make a law to forbid the parties from having free intercourse with one another, without the fear of censure, or be turned out of the synagogue.

In that same year new lodges had been chartered in Providence and Philadelphia. Earlier correspondence between Hall and the eventual first Grand Master of the Philadelphia lodge, Absalom Jones, revealed an inspired unity of interest. Prince Hall, responding to an earlier query, wrote on September 16, 1789:

> May God prosper you in . . . all your undertakings for the good of your African brethren. . . . We here are not idle, but are doing what we can to promote the interest and good of our dear brethren that stand in so much need at such a time as this.

Jones promptly replied: "It afforded us much satisfaction to find that you are united with us in laboring in the same vineyard." By 1814 a lodge was opened in New York City and three more were opened in Philadelphia, which established an unprecedented institutional interconnectedness among black communities in the Northeast, regardless of how irregular that correspondence may have been. No black organization even vaguely resembling that of the African lodges for institutional durability, long-term political objectives, and geographical extent existed during their first decades. Not until the appearance of the African Methodist Episcopal Church in 1816, many of whose leaders were also Masons, would its eventual superior in breadth be formed. By his death in December 1807, Prince Hall and his numerous followers had laid the foundation for a system of correspondence among black leaders that significantly aided their effort to unite nationally in the next decades and to realize a new and more powerful political organization.[21]

By 1826 the African lodges were continuing to grow. Claims over the years by white Masons that African Lodge #459 had become dormant when Prince Hall died, and thus lost whatever legitimacy it may have had, are easily refuted by extant minutes from meetings spanning the years 1807 through 1825.[22] More lodges were added in New York City, Baltimore, Washington, D.C., and Alexandria, Virginia—the latter two known especially for their opposition to the slave trade in the District of Columbia and for their willingness to assist runaway slaves.

A resurgence of interest in the Boston lodge apparently occurred around 1826. A number of new members were inducted in that and following years, efforts were made to strengthen ties with and jurisdiction over several other lodges (which in fact led to a rupture with the New York City lodges), and in 1827 the aggressive leadership of then Grand Master John T. Hilton led the lodge to declare its independence from any other lodge in the world and establish itself as the Grand Lodge for Prince

21. Much of my material for the discussion in this paragraph comes from Greene, "Prince Hall" and Kaplan, *Black Presence*. See also William H. Grimshaw, *Official History of Freemasonry Among the Colored People in North America* (1903; reprint, New York: Negro Universities Press, 1969), 67–95, 108–25; Benjamin Quarles, *The Negro in the American Revolution* (Chapel Hill: University of North Carolina Press, 1961), 4–18; Prince Hall, "[Extract from] A Charge Delivered to the African Lodge, June 24, 1797, at Menotomy, Massachusetts," in Benjamin Brawley, *Early American Negro Writers* (Chapel Hill: University of North Carolina Press, 1935), 96–99; Harry E. Davis, *A History of Freemasonry Among Negroes in America* (Cleveland: United Supreme Council, 1946), 9–97. See also the two interesting pieces of correspondence from 1797 between Boston and Philadelphia in which, among other things, the Reverend Peter Mantone states to Hall: "We would rather be under you, and associated with our Brethren in Boston, than to be under those of the [white] Pennsylvania Lodge; for, if we are under you, we shall always be ready to assist in the furtherance of Masonry among us" (Harry E. Davis, "Documents Relating to Negro Masonry in America," *Journal of Negro History* 21 [1936], 425–26).

22. Regarding this criticism and others pertaining to the legitimacy of African Lodge #459's charter, see the report in *Proceedings of the Grand Lodge of the Most Ancient and Honorable Fraternity of Free and Accepted Masons of the Commonwealth of Massachusetts . . . Quarterly Communication, March 8, 1876* (Boston, 1876), 64–91. For the minutes, see Prince Hall Records, Minutes of African Lodge, Boston, 1807–46.

Hall Masonry in North America, a move to which most of the other lodges assented.

This dramatic action reflected the mounting tendency among reform-minded Northern blacks in the late 1820s to create their own racially autonomous organizations. While continuing to affirm the same Masonic principles as their white brothers, the African lodges simply removed themselves from the debate over their legitimacy and officially entitled themselves. Yet this action also highlighted the fact that the African lodges were much more than mere imitations of the white institutions, that they were instead black creations created first and foremost to serve black-determined ends. Unlike white Masonry, African Masonry has its roots in the protest against slavery and racial discrimination. Throughout the antebellum era, it would continue to serve as a prominent vehicle in this struggle. By the late 1820s the high level of self-awareness and confidence embodied in African Lodge #459 reflected the degree of political commitment and racial consciousness attained by black Masons throughout the Northern seaboard.[23]

The relationships David Walker formed in the African Lodge were some of the most central ones of his life in Boston, and they would be reinforced by his participation with these associates in other significant events and institutions of the Boston black community. One principal annual event celebrated by the whole community was a parade marking the end of the Atlantic slave trade by England and the United States. While blacks in New York City and Philadelphia traditionally celebrated the abolition of the foreign slave trade on January 1 from as early as 1808, similar black celebrations in Boston date from the same year but were held on July 14. This event always drew most of the leading members of black

23. Grimshaw, *History of Freemasonry Among the Colored People,* 124–25, 131–37, 165; Minutes of African Lodge, Boston, 1807–46, in Prince Hall Records. For an example of the level of intensity of the Mason's antislavery rhetoric, see *An Address, Delivered Before the African Grand Lodge of Boston, No. 459, June 24th, 1828, By John T. Hilton: On the Annual Festival, of St. John the Baptist* (Boston, 1828).

Gary Nash tends to miss this central characteristic of antebellum black masonry in his discussion of it in Philadelphia. He understands it principally as an institution that attempted to reinforce the middle-class respectability of its black members and their relative distance from the uneducated and flamboyant mass of blacks. That it served to one extent or another to highlight the educated and economic elite of a given black community is undeniable, but—as I shall explore further in this chapter—it also did much more: it was entwined with the celebrations of the community at large, it reflected that community's strong sense of collective responsibility, and it gave important voice and organization to political aspirations with which few blacks would disagree. Nash separates the black Masons from the mass of blacks more than is justified. See Gary Nash, *Forging Freedom: The Formation of Philadelphia's Black Community, 1720–1840* (Cambridge: Harvard University Press, 1988), 218–19, 222.

Boston. In 1820 the marshals of the "African Celebration," as most newspapers called it, included Thomas Dalton and William Brown, eventual Masonic brothers of Walker.[24]

By at least 1824, large celebrations of Haitian independence began to appear in Boston, probably in conjunction with an upsurge of interest among blacks in emigration to the Caribbean republic.[25] In July 1824 the Reverend Thomas Paul, who had spent some months in Haiti as a missionary and had met President Jean Pierre Boyer, endorsed Haitian emigration and praised the country's prospects. In 1825, while addressing another such gathering, he compared the Haitians to "the Israelites of old."[26] In 1828, at the traditional time for this particular event—early September—there was a grand celebration both for Haiti's independence and for the arrival in Boston of Prince Abduhl Rahhaman, a recently emancipated slave who was actually a prince of the African kingdom Footah Jallo and was touring the North to raise funds to purchase his family and return there. The parade began at the African Meeting House on Belknap Street and moved down Beacon Hill until arriving at the new quarters of the African Lodge on Cambridge Street for dinner and toasts. The leaders of the day's events read like a roster of the African Lodge: C. A. De Randamie, William Brown, George Holmes, Porter Tidd, John T. Hilton, Thomas Dalton, James G. Barbadoes, John Brown, James H. Howe, and David Walker the Second Marshall. The speakers praised Haiti, castigated the slavers, and looked forward to the day of universal emancipation. Within just a few years, Walker had become a respected organizer and speaker.[27]

24. *Columbian Centinel,* July 14, 1820. On the 1808 celebration, see William Bentley, *The Diary of William Bentley, D.D.,* 4 vols. (Salem, Mass.: Essex Institute, 1905–14), 3:372–73: "On 14 July, the Africans celebrated in Boston the freedom of their Colour by the laws of some European nations." Apparently January 1 commemorations were not held in Boston, and the July 14 date was chosen "for convenience, merely." See William B. Gravely, "The Dialectic of Double-Consciousness in Black American Freedom Celebrations, 1808–1863," *Journal of Negro History* 62 (Winter 1982), 303. The possibility also exists that July 14 was the date Massachusetts blacks traditionally associated with their emancipation.

25. Interest in Haitian emigration had been strong among blacks in Boston and elsewhere, at least since 1818. In that year, the Reverend William Bentley of Salem, Massachusetts, gave a vivid description of an emigration meeting at which Prince Saunders and Reverend Paul spoke (*Diary of William Bentley,* 4:522–23). See also Philip Staudenraus, *The African Colonization Movement, 1816–1865* (New York: Columbia University Press, 1961), 82–87; and Arthur O. White, "Prince Saunders: An Instance of Social Mobility Among Antebellum New England Blacks," *Journal of Negro History* 60 (1975), 526–35.

26. *Columbian Centinel,* September 3, 1825.

27. *Freedom's Journal,* September 5, and October 24, 1828. Regarding the interesting history of Prince Abduhl Rahhaman, see Terry Alford, *Prince Among Slaves* (New York: Harcourt Brace Jovanovich, 1977).

Along with several other members of the African Lodge, David Walker also played a signal role in fostering *Freedom's Journal* in Boston. Generally deemed the first national black newspaper, *Freedom's Journal* had its roots in the rising anticolonizationist movement among free blacks in the North and became an important instrument for uniting black reformers throughout the region. On March 16, 1827, its inaugural issue was released in New York, but almost four weeks earlier a meeting had been held at Walker's house to consider "giving aid and support to the 'Freedom's Journal.'" Attended and addressed not only by Walker but also by George Holmes, John T. Hilton, William (or John) Brown, and Reverend Paul, the meeting endorsed the paper as one from which "great good will result to the People of Colour" and promised "our utmost exertions to increase its patronage."

A year later, in April 1828, they met again at the Reverend James Lee's Methodist meetinghouse "for the purpose of enquiring whether the Freedom's Journal had been conducted in a manner satisfactory to the subscribers and to the Coloured community at large." Such a democratic assessment of and participation in the paper showed how much it was the creation of the members of a number of black communities, not simply of the editors in New York City. The Boston contingent lauded the journal for its "defence and support of the African cause" and resolved that it was "well worthy of our unremitted exertions." Although *Freedom's Journal* ceased publishing by the middle of 1829 and during its latter months suffered from severe editorial conflict, its presence in Boston served as a rallying point for political activists there and strengthened their ties with one another.[28]

Walker also figured prominently in the Massachusetts General Colored Association (MGCA). This seminal organization intended not only to promote the interests of local blacks but also ultimately to speak for blacks nationally. Unfortunately none of its records are extant, but the span of its existence can be determined with fair accuracy as 1828 (or perhaps 1826) through 1833, in which year the Association's members agreed to subsume themselves as an auxiliary in the New England Anti-Slavery Society.[29] In September 1828 Thomas Dalton was listed as president of the

28. *Freedom's Journal,* March 16, 1827, and April 25, 1828. For a lengthy discussion of *Freedom's Journal* and another paper that followed it, *Rights of All,* see Bella Gross, *"Freedom's Journal* and the *Rights of All," Journal of Negro History* 17 (1932), 241–86. For another example of a community discussion of *Freedom's Journal* and its objectives, see the case of New Haven in the newspaper, August 10 and 17, 1827.

29. The earliest reference to the organization I have found so far is in *Freedom's Journal,* September 5, 1828. But James and Lois Horton give 1826 without giving a source for that date (*Black Bostonians,* 57). Regarding their affiliation with the New England Anti-Slavery

MGCA and appears to have continued in that role throughout its existence. Other members of the MGCA who belonged to the African Lodge
were James Barbadoes, John T. Hilton, and Walker Lewis. James Gould of
Freedom's Journal was its treasurer at least as late as mid-1831.[30] The
most famous statement of the society was made by Walker himself in
December 1828 in a vigorous speech calling for a nationally organized
movement led by blacks to defeat slavery.[31] Its broad vision was unprecedented for a black political association of its time and represented the
remarkable level of awareness attained by a number of blacks in Boston
by the late 1820s.[32]

Residential proximity further strengthened their connectedness. By
1827 Walker and his family had moved to Belknap Street, in the heart of
Beacon Hill's north slope. Tax assessment records for the Seventh Ward
make it possible to determine who his neighbors were. It is not surprising
that many were fellow Masons or members of the MGCA. Immediately
around him on his side of the block were Masons John Pero and George
B. Holmes. Frederick Brimsley, fellow clothier and member of the MGCA,
was right next door, as was also a leading African Baptist and MGCA
adherent, Coffin Pitts. Directly in front of him on the opposite side of the
street were Masons John Courreaux, William Vassal, and William Brown.
Also facing him was the residence of the black Methodist minister, Samuel Snowden, a man with whom Walker formed a close relationship, perhaps along the lines of a father-son model.[33]

By no later than early 1829 Walker became a homeowner on Bridge
Street, just across Cambridge Street from Beacon Hill in a section of the
West End then undergoing heavy development. Only two associates now

---

Society, see the notice quoted in William Cooper Nell, *The Colored Patriots of the American
Revolution* (Boston, 1855), 346.

30. *The Liberator,* August 13, 1831.

31. *Freedom's Journal,* December 19, 1828.

32. The African Abolition Society, a black political association even more elusive than the
MGCA, also existed at this time and Walker probably had some connection with it. It played
an important organizational role in the African Celebration in Boston on July 14, 1829, and
its members led that year's procession. The only reference that can be found to it so far is
that in *Genius of Universal Emancipation,* September 2, 1829.

33. Valuation Book, Ward 7, 1827, Boston Public Library. Regarding Walker's relationship
with Snowden, it is important to note that Snowden, like Walker, was born in the South. He
moved to Boston around 1810 and became a preacher in 1815. The intensity of Snowden's
commitment to Methodism suggests, as with Walker, an exposure to that faith before arriving in the North. This was probably the case, because Snowden came from Maryland, the
seat of the Methodist church in America. For Snowden's birthplace, see Death Certificates
(1850), Registry of Births, Marriages, and Deaths, at Boston City Hall. See also Caleb H.
Snow, *A History of Boston,* 2nd ed. (Boston, 1828), 417.

lived next door to him: Aaron Gaul and the co-founder of the MGCA, William G. Nell. Yet by 1829–30 a large number of Walker's associates had moved across Cambridge Street to the overwhelmingly white Fifth Ward.[34]

A study of census and tax records makes it clear why these blacks who were so committed to their neighborhoods would move into almost totally white areas: availability of affordable housing.[35] The Fifth Ward in 1830 was a solid working-class neighborhood, and inexpensive homes were available for purchase from such real-estate magnates as George Parkman—from whom Walker, for example, bought his home.[36] Black home ownership in the Fifth Ward was dramatically higher than in any other of the city's wards; of the twenty-four black-headed households in the ward, nine of them (or 37.5 percent) were homeowners.[37] This was an extraordinary number for a community that by mid-century listed only 1.5 percent of its members as owners of real property.[38]

These households, however, were not scattered randomly throughout the Fifth Ward, but bunched in clusters of homeowners and tenants in specific sections. Blacks continued to live in close proximity. Not only did Nell and Gaul live near Walker, but just around the corner on Cambridge Street was Thomas Cole. Intersecting Bridge Street just above Walker's house was Vine Street, which had at least two black homeowners on it, one of whom was Cyrus Foster, a Revolutionary War veteran and deacon at the African Baptist Church. Three blocks away on Chambers Street was another small cluster, which included Walker's longtime friend William Kerr. But the highest concentration of blacks lived several blocks away from Walker in the northwest corner of the ward running along the Charles River. At least five blacks owned houses on these few blocks,

34. According to the 1830 census, the Fifth Ward had a total population of 6,138, of whom 5,953 were white (1830 Federal Census, Massachusetts, Suffolk Co., Boston, Ward 5).

35. The following analysis relies on the City of Boston, Valuation Book, Ward 5, 1829, 1830, and 1831 and on the 1830 Federal Census for Ward 5.

36. Parkman was not one to cut an easy deal. He held title to the house jointly with Walker and would not release it until payment had been completed within the next six years at the rate of $266.00 a year—a huge sum for Walker. See Suffolk Deeds (Grantee), 330: 208–9, in Suffolk County Registry of Deeds, Boston. Walker's death fated his wife, Eliza, to lose the house. By 1831 Walker's name had disappeared from assessment records for the house and Parkman's had returned. Such harsh terms surely prompted Walker to write in the *Appeal*: "But I must, really, observe that in this very city, when a man of color dies, if he owned any real estate it most generally falls into the hands of some white person. The wife and children of the deceased may weep and lament if they please, but the estate will be kept snug enough by its white possessor" (10).

37. This figure does not include the eleven households for which ownership or lack of it was not determinable. Thus, the rate of ownership could be even higher.

38. Horton, *Black Bostonians,* 10–12.

including Walker's Masonic brothers James Howe and William Brown, the popular abolitionist barber Peter Howard, and Robert Roberts, a servant and early Negro Convention member. James G. Barbadoes, fellow Mason and secretary of the MGCA, was also a tenant in this neighborhood. While it is apparent that between 1825 and 1830 a number of prominent blacks left Beacon Hill's north slope for the Fifth Ward, it is also equally apparent that many did so because of the availability of inexpensive housing. As a result, black enclaves that replicated on a smaller scale the conditions on the other side of Cambridge Street developed. Moreover, their actual closeness to former neighbors on the north slope—in several cases just a block away—makes it clear that Walker was not fleeing the dense black settlement of Beacon Hill.

Most of these associates were also deeply committed to the church, but unlike David Walker most appear to have belonged to the African Baptist Church. Officially constituted in 1805, the First African Baptist Church was founded by blacks who were moved by current religious revivals but also sought to avoid discrimination in seating and in other matters encountered in the white Baptist churches. The church was literally at the very center of Boston's black community; its recently erected meetinghouse (1806) on Belknap Street became the heart of the newly developing community on the north slope. It embodied a growing racial awareness and pride that only increased with the size of Boston's black population. Spurred on by the oratory and relentless organizing of its famous minister, the Reverend Thomas Paul, the church quickly became a resource for black education and political activism. It is thus no surprise that some of its leading members, and its minister, were close associates of David Walker. John T. Hilton, William Brown, James G. Barbadoes, William G. Nell, Thomas Dalton, and probably others were both Masons and church members.[39]

Yet Walker's lack of affiliation with the African Baptist Church is also no surprise; it only reinforces the likely fact that he was early reared in and had a deep commitment to the black Methodist church. That David Walker, who was clearly interested in contacts with Boston's leading black figures, would opt to join the less powerful but semi-independent black Methodist May Street Church only confirms that devotion. Founded in 1818 by the Reverend Samuel Snowden while continuing under the nominal supervision of the white Bromfield Street Methodist Church, the May Street Church moved into a newly erected brick building on October 24, 1824. Church membership had grown from twenty-three in its first year to

39. George A. Levesque, "Inherent Reformers—Inherited Orthodoxy: Black Baptists in Boston, 1800–1873," *Journal of Negro History* 60 (1975), 491–500; Horton, *Black Bostonians,* 40–42; Daniels, *In Freedom's Birthplace* (Cambridge: Houghton Mifflin, 1914), 21–23.

eighty-four by June 1827 and services were "usually filled with hearers." Moreover, in March 1826 a second independent black Methodist church was established under the Reverend James Lee on Center Street.[40] The black Methodist churches in Boston remained separate from the African Methodist Episcopal organization in Philadelphia, which would not have a presence in Boston until 1838, when the Reverend Noah C. W. Cannon created the first AME congregation there, probably from the remnants of James Lee's church. The May Street Church, however, remained under the control of the Bromfield Street Church until 1903.[41]

The powerful personality and antislavery activism of the Reverend Samuel Snowden must have drawn Walker to this church. Unlike Thomas Paul and like Walker, Snowden was from the South and had been born a slave. Both were famous for holy vituperations of their homeland's attachment to slavery. Reverend Snowden's antislavery vehemence may well have outpaced the more moderate Paul, and this might also have drawn Walker. Like Walker, Snowden always opened his house to fugitives. On the day he died in October 1850, thirteen fugitives arrived at his door. He also had a special mission to black mariners, who favored his church overwhelmingly, and he had helped any number of them who feared kidnapping when they were in Southern ports. Many of these seamen also probably knew Walker, whose shop provided them with wares and hospitality. Perhaps he saw in Snowden, who was born about 1765 and who everyone, including white abolitionists, affectionately called "Father Snowden," some resemblance to his own father, who was purportedly a slave.[42]

Walker and most of his associates were members of the artisanal/shopkeeper stratum of Boston's black community. This layer was basically the upper level of that community. With the exception of a handful of individuals, a professional class of ministers, doctors, lawyers, and teachers was virtually nonexistent in the black Boston of this time. For a man to be a hairdresser, a clothes dealer, a carpenter, or a tailor was to be in the forefront of black society. For example, twenty-nine members (five of

40. Snow, *History of Boston,* 386, 417–18.
41. The most important work in helping me understand the history of antebellum Boston's black churches was Roy Finkenbine's "Boston's Black Churches: Institutional Centers of the Antislavery Movement," in Donald M. Jacobs, ed., *Courage and Conscience: Black and White Abolitionists in Boston* (Bloomington: Indiana University Press, 1993), 169–89. See also Payne, *History of the AME Church,* 143; Robert Hayden, *Faith, Culture, and Leadership: A History of the Black Church in Boston* (Boston: Boston NAACP, 1983), 18–19; Horton, *Black Bostonians,* 43; Snow, *History of Boston,* 417–18; and "Coloured People of Boston," *African Repository and Colonial Journal* 13 (1837), 90–91.
42. Oliver Johnson, *William Lloyd Garrison and His Times* (Boston, 1879), 71–72; *The Liberator,* January 3, 1851; *National Anti-Slavery Standard,* October 31, 1850.

them were probable members) of the African Lodge and ten other non-Masonic associates of Walker's worked at the following trades: fifteen hairdressers and barbers, five clothes dealers, three ministers, five bootblacks, three waiters, and one each as sawyer, tender, tailor, blacksmith, musician, clothes cleaner, laborer, and possibly cook[43] (see Appendix C). Applying Leonard Curry's system of occupational classifications, 31 percent of Walker's associates at the time were of the artisanal, entrepreneurial, and professional Group C, 51 percent were of Group B, which included people engaged in transportation, food service, and (my only adjustment to Curry's categories) personal service, such as waiters and hairdressers, and 18 percent (Group A) held positions such as laborers, mariners, and bootblacks.[44] Black society at large had a quite different distribution: 9 percent in Group C, 23 percent in Group B, and 68 percent in Group A. Those whose work was not identified were either semi-skilled, unskilled, or unemployed.[45] And while only 32 percent of the over-

43. This enumeration is compiled from membership lists and lists of officers contained in the Minutes of African Lodge, Boston, 1807–1846, in Prince Hall Records. The lists I used pertain only to the years 1826–30. For a partial list of the members of the MGCA, see John Daniels, *In Freedom's Birthplace,* 36n. See also *Freedom's Journal,* March 16, 1827, and April 25, 1828. Information on employment is from the Boston City Directory, 1825–30, and from Horton, *Black Bostonians.* Of the 35 identifiable members of the Lodge, 10 had indeterminable jobs. Of the 10 other associates, the employment of only one could not be determined. For a complete listing of the people and their work, see Appendix C.

44. See Curry, *The Free Black in Urban America,* app. B, 258–59, for his discussion of these job categorizations. Curry placed personal service workers in the Group A category, which I believe underrates the skill of hairdressers and waiters (who may also have been cooks and caterers) and the fact that they often managed their own establishments and had concerns typical of shopkeepers.

45. See Appendix D. This figure and others pertaining to employment are derived from the 1826 Boston City Directory. A total of 66 people worked in jobs considered artisanal/entrepreneurial in that year.

The reckonings obtained from the 1826 Directory are rough. I chose that Directory because it had more names listed than any other Directory for the years 1825–30, but it still listed only 356 adults—a smaller number than the actual number of black adults working in Boston for that year. Some individuals do not have their work attributed and others do not have it done with precision. Still others might change work from one year to the next. Women are underrepresented (only 74 women, 40 of whom are identified simply as widows and only 11 of whom have their jobs identified, are listed). Women were a sizable but hidden part of the labor force; if they lived and worked in a white household they were not listed. Another problem is that the number of mariners is probably grossly understated; many who were at sea were not recorded. In 1837 the Boston Auxiliary of the American Union for the Relief and Improvement of the Coloured Race identified 171 black mariners in the city, a figure that depicts the realities of a major port much more accurately than the 1826 figure of 30 (see "Coloured People of Boston," *African Repository,* 90). Nevertheless, directories can offer a useful, if approximate, overview of the character of employment in antebellum cities, and it is in this general manner that I use them here. For an excellent

all population were engaged in Group B and C employment, 82 percent of Walker's circle were so employed.

Among David Walker and his associates, therefore, a significantly high number, relative to the overall black population, were engaged in skilled and/or entrepreneurial trades, were homeowners, and were evidently educated to one extent or another and politically active. The shared interests of these people, their frequent association through secular and religious organizations, and their residential proximity helped them to forge a social bond that was vital and enduring. Moreover, they endorsed a program that was fiercely antislavery and antidiscriminatory, that was committed to black improvement especially through education, and that virtually obliged service to the black community at large by fostering a strong sense of collective responsibility and racial awareness. A distinct and highly visible cohort within Boston's black community, they were the ones who delineated the system by which whites excluded them and other blacks from numerous opportunities.

While relatively higher levels of home ownership, income, and education created a sense of distinctiveness among Walker's circle, they also voiced concerns and interests that were common to all free blacks in Boston in the late 1820s. Their awareness of their differentness did not preclude them from feeling connected with the mass of blacks. The degree of economic and social stratification among blacks in Boston at this time was actually quite small, especially when compared with that among the city's white population. Basically all blacks in Boston were poor, and all were subject to extreme discrimination. Differences in income were never enough to create glaring dissimilarities in condition among segments of the black population.

Moreover, following a skilled trade did not necessarily mean financial security, for skilled blacks found it difficult to obtain work and, once they did, to be paid a fair wage.

In 1827 a black commentator observed: "Very few black Bostonians are mechanics; and they who are, almost universally relinquish their trades for other employments. This, I suppose, is principally owing to the want of patronage on the part of the public." English traveler Edward Abdy reported in 1834 that a black Bostonian he knew "had experienced great difficulty in obtaining an employment in which he could get his bread decently and respectably: with the exception of one or two employed as printers, one blacksmith, and one shoemaker, there are no colored me-

---

discussion of the relative utility of city directories, and an example of their use in determining the occupations of free blacks and their range, see Curry, *The Free Black in Urban America,* app. B, 258–66.

chanics in the city."[46] An artisan might therefore find himself more impoverished than a seemingly less valuable general laborer who probably had
greater job security.[47] A lack of economic opportunity was generalized
throughout the whole black community at this time and kept almost everyone at a roughly similar level of poverty and insecurity.[48]

No black in 1820s Boston, regardless of station, escaped the almost
daily sting of discrimination and harassment. David Walker concluded an
April 1828 speech by speaking of "the very derision, violence and oppression, with which we as a part of the community are treated by a benevolent and Christian people." A local observer from 1827 put it more tersely:
"We are an oppressed and degraded race."[49] White derision and even violence had always dogged blacks wherever they went in the city.

The 1820s witnessed only a stepping up of such attacks, an increase
noted then throughout the North. Hosea Easton, an associate of Walker's,
vividly described how "universally common" in the streets of Boston were
taunts, especially from the young, about blacks' physical features, intellectual capacites, and poverty. He added: "Cuts and placards descriptive
of the negroe's deformity, are everywhere displayed. . . . Many of the
popular book stores, in commercial towns and cities, have their show-
windows lined with them. The barrooms of the most popular public
houses in the country, sometimes have their ceiling literally covered with
them. This display of American civility is under the daily observation of
every class of society, even in New England."[50]

46. *Freedom's Journal*, November 9, 1827. Edward S. Abdy, *Journal of a Residence and
Tour in the United States of North America from April 1833 to October 1834*, 3 vols. (London,
1835), 1:121.

47. Evidence from the Fifth Ward supports this predicament. While two laborers (Jonathan Cash and Peter Gray) owned houses in that ward, a barber (William Kerr) and a tailor
(John White) rented.

48. In black Boston in 1850 more than 77 percent of all employed free black males worked
in unskilled, semi-skilled, or personal service forms of labor. Conversely, in the same year,
less than 6 percent of free black males worked as artisans. According to these figures,
employment opportunities for free black males appear to have actually worsened in Boston
by the late antebellum era. See Curry, *The Free Black in Urban America*, 260. Such dismal
economic prospects for blacks were not the case throughout the North. By the 1820s, for
instance, Philadelphia had some enormously wealthy free blacks and growing economic
stratification within the black community. James Forten, Hagar Ballard, and Elizabeth
Wilson all had estates in excess of $40,000, and dozens more were valued above $3,000. The
rate of property ownership, although declining in the 1820s, still hovered around 10 percent.
Nothing comparable existed in black Boston, even by 1830—which further validates the
relative economic homogeneity of Boston. Nash, however, indicates that blacks in Philadelphia were also facing increased occupational restriction and by 1830 were being forced
out of such traditional black trades as coach-driving, carting, and dock work. See Nash,
Forging Freedom, 214–16, 246–53.

49. *Freedom's Journal*, November 9, 1827, and April 25, 1828.

50. See Hosea Easton, *A Treatise on the Intellectual Character, and Civil and Political*

Outside of facilities in their own neighborhood, a frequent gathering place for blacks both for leisure and for celebrations was the Common, only a few blocks from the north slope of Beacon Hill. And they were just as regularly harassed and sometimes forced off the Common by white toughs. As early as 1797 Prince Hall vividly discussed the situation in Boston and on the Common in particular:

> Patience, I say; for were we not possessed of a great measure of it, we could not bear up under the daily insults we meet with in the streets of Boston, much more on public days of recreation. How at such times are we shamefully abused, and that to such a degree, that we may truly be said to carry our lives in our hands, and the arrows of death are flying about our heads. Helpless women have their clothes torn from their backs. . . . And by whom are these disgraceful and abusive actions committed? Not by the men born and bred in Boston,—they are better bred; but by a mob or horde of shameless, low-lived, envious, spiteful persons—some of them, not long since, servants in gentlemen's kitchens, scouring knives, horse-tenders, chaise-drivers. I was told by a gentleman who saw the filthy behavior in the Common, that, in all places that he had been in, he never saw so cruel behavior in all his life; and that a slave in the West Indies, on Sundays or holidays, enjoys himself and friends without molestation. Not only this man, but many in town, who have seen their behavior to us, and that, without provocation, twenty or thirty cowards have fallen upon one man.[51]

The annual celebrations in Boston by blacks commemorating the end of America's participation in the Atlantic slave trade were always harassed by groups of whites. Lydia Maria Child recalled: "It became a frolic with the white boys to deride them [the black celebrants] on this day, and finally, they determined to drive them, on these occasions, from the Common." At one event, however, Child recounted that the blacks vowed to resist the plans of the white youths and that as hundreds of whites chased a much smaller number of blacks down the north slope, Colonel George

Condition of the Colored People of the United States (Boston, 1837), 40–42, reprinted in Dorothy Porter, ed., *Negro Protest Pamphlets: A Compendium* (New York: Arno Press, 1969). Cartoons grotesquely lampooning blacks were gaining in popularity throughout the United States in the 1820s, ridiculing especially the emerging black middle-class and creating a comic black character type that reinforced the idea that blacks were unfit for freedom. For several examples of such cartoons in Philadelphia and for an insightful discussion, see Nash, *Forging Freedom,* 253–59.

51. Prince Hall, "[Extract from] a Charge Delivered at Menotomy, Massachusetts," 98–99.

Middleton, a black Revolutionary War veteran, confronted them with a musket and commanded them to stop. Bloodshed was only narrowly avoided by the diplomatic intervention of Child's father.[52] White-inspired violence was not at all uncommon on Beacon Hill, and in fact it seems to have increased as the black population became more concentrated there. Raids following African celebrations were almost expected in the 1820s and were not unusual at other times.[53] The persons and neighborhoods of free blacks were always vulnerable to wanton attacks from whites.

Two other factors contributed to a developing sense of commonality among blacks in Boston. As the overall free black population grew steadily during the first three decades of the nineteenth century and strengthened their awareness of themselves through mere numbers, these people came to be concentrated in two or three neighborhoods. By 1830 two-thirds of Boston's blacks (1,240) lived either on Beacon Hill or in the tangential West End. Other neighborhoods existed, especially near the wharves in the North End, but the heart of the community was on the north slope, symbolized by the African Meeting House erected there. This residential convergence of people who shared conditions and status on a broad basis greatly reinforced a sense of community and could work against tendencies to stratify socially.[54]

The most prominent figures in black Boston were on remarkably close terms with the more ordinary members of their community. Close living quarters, an imposed lack of occupational opportunity, and poverty fostered this situation. Thomas Dalton, the eloquent senior warden of the Masons and co-founder of the MGCA, was a bootblack. David Walker's shop was popular for clothing purchases among black mariners and laborers, as well as a famous gathering spot for conversation.[55] Walker also had a black seaman, James Middleton, and a black laborer or hairdresser, William Henry, living in his house on Bridge Street in 1830, probably as boarders. Such an arrangement was common among black homeowners

52. As transcribed in Nell, *Colored Patriots,* 26–27.

53. See broadsides containing doggerel satirizing black speech, which nonetheless describe actual white-led riots that occurred on Beacon Hill in July 1827 and 1828: "Dreadful Riot on Negro Hill!" Rare Book, Broadside Collection, vol. 54-10, Library Company of Philadelphia; and "The Riot on Negro Hill" at Boston Public Library Rare Book Room. Regarding riots in the same place on July 14, 1826, see Curry, *The Free Black in Urban America,* 100. See also the description of a riot between blacks, sailors, and Irishmen on Ann Street, a black neighborhood in the First Ward, on July 15, 1829, in *Columbian Centinel,* July 18, 1829.

54. It is important to bear in mind just how small geographically was the community on Beacon Hill, where in 1830 more than 1,000 blacks lived. It really comprised only a handful of blocks, which occupied about one-quarter to one-half square mile.

55. This use of his shop parallels that of Denmark Vesey's, where political conversations and plotting occurred regularly.

trying to make ends meet. But Henry Highland Garnet adds another perspective on Walker's use of his house. Writing of him in his slim biography, Garnet noted: "His hands were always open to contribute to the wants of the fugitive. His house was the shelter and the home of the poor and needy."[56] This was not a romanticized recollection of Walker, but rather a faithful description of a standard method for dealing with temporary indigence in a community with a strong sense of collective and racial responsibility. It also furthered contact between those who had a little bit more with those who had almost nothing.

Yet the methods Walker and his circle adopted for combating the evils confronting them were not always those of the rest of the community. Walker and his associates believed that the key to the uplift of the race was a zealous commitment to the tenets of individual moral improvement: education, temperance, Protestant religious practice, regular work habits, and self-regulation. But by no means did the mass of blacks adhere so faithfully to these values. Many were neither church-going nor temperate, and they were not committed to study and displayed little interest in adopting the reformers' prescriptions for self-improvement. A number of them preferred the dance halls of the North End or the gambling, dog fights, drinking, and sexual carousing that also flourished there and on the north slope.[57] These were the people to whom Maria Stewart, a fond admirer of David Walker and a leader among Boston black reformers in the early 1830s, spoke when she asserted that dancing is not

> criminal in itself . . . [but] has been carried on among us to such an unbecoming extent that it has become absolutely disgusting. . . . Had those men among us who had an opportunity, turned their attention as assiduously to mental and moral improvement as they have to gambling and dancing, I might have remained quietly at home and they stood contending in my place.

She further admonished:

> Our money, instead of being thrown away as heretofore, [should] be appropriated for schools and seminaries of learning for our children and youth. We ought to follow the example of the whites in this respect. Nothing would raise our respectability, add to our peace and happiness, and reflect so much honor upon us, as to be

56. Garnet, *Walker's Appeal, With a Brief Sketch of His Life*, vi.

57. For a vivid description of what was called "Satan's seat" on the north slope in 1817, see the report of the Reverend James Davis quoted in George A. Levesque, *Black Boston: African American Life and Culture in Urban America, 1750–1860* (New York: Garland Publishing, 1994), 382–83.

ourselves the promoters of temperance, and the supporters, as far as we are able, of useful and scientific knowledge.[58]

While by no means denying the historical impact on African Americans of being subject to centuries of "deprivations, fraud, and opposition" (59), and that white advance was in part founded on theft from blacks, Stewart nevertheless asserted:

Our condition as a people has been low for hundreds of years, and it will continue to be so, unless by true piety and virtue, we strive to regain that which we have lost. White Americans, by their prudence, economy, and exertions, have sprung up and become one of the most flourishing nations in the world, distinguished for their knowledge of the arts and sciences, for their polite literature.[59]

Stewart, Walker, and others of their circle wanted to participate more fully and successfully in the mainstream American economy and middle-class culture. By no means was this desired because of their preference for things white or because of some wish to highlight their difference from and superiority to the mass of blacks. Rather, it was sought after because they were convinced that the needs, independence, and dignity of African Americans would be best served by adherence to these values and aspirations. Moreover, they believed deeply that few individuals would really be allowed greater involvement with the economy or educated culture until the level of cultivation and aspiration was elevated for all blacks and until they had abandoned forever any trace of connection to the culture of slavery.

Certain that they knew what was best for African Americans, they developed a strong sense of mission to their race to inspire them to a greater allegiance to the tenets of individual moral improvement. This led them to have a deep commitment to their community and to working within it. Hosea Easton is an excellent example of this sort of orientation. A highly skilled blacksmith, a friend of Walker's through the MGCA and their service to *Freedom's Journal,* representative to the first Negro Convention in Philadelphia in 1831, and author of a learned 1837 treatise on the character and condition of blacks in the United States, Easton's adult years were devoted to working for the improvement of the mass of black Americans. In Boston, Easton turned his talents not to securing a com-

58. Maria Stewart, "An Address Delivered at the African Masonic Hall," in Marilyn Richardson, ed., *Maria W. Stewart, America's First Black Political Writer: Essays and Speeches* (Bloomington: Indiana University Press, 1987), 60.

59. Ibid., 58, 59.

fortable living for him and his family but rather, at great risk to his own financial station, to educating black youths in iron work and basic literacy, because no white-run establishment would take on black apprentices. In 1837 he wrote the following about his enterprise, which ultimately failed from lack of white patrons:

> At an early period of my life, I was extensively engaged in mechanism, associated with a number of other colored men of master spirits and great minds. The enterprise was followed for about twenty years, perseveringly, in direct opposition to public sentiment, and the tide of popular prejudice. So intent were the parties in carrying out the principles of intelligent, active free men, that they sacrificed every thing of comfort and ease to the object. The most rigid economy was adhered to at home and abroad. A regular school was established for the instruction of the youth connected with the factory, and the strictest rules of morality were supported with surprising assiduity; and ardent spirits found no place in the establishment.[60]

Individual control and regularity are of prime importance here; every person involved in the enterprise was expected to strive for self-improvement. But such exertions were always made within the overriding framework of the group and serving it. Because of the degree to which blacks in Boston had to depend on themselves to provide education and apprenticeships for their people, an individual who did possess a skill often felt a great responsibility to extend knowledge of it to others as well. In this spirit, Benjamin Roberts, a successful black printer, also opened his shop to black youths. Others made similar efforts.[61]

These individuals promoted self-esteem and racial pride and made real sacrifices to do so. And though they encouraged the acquisition of skills that would improve individual competitiveness in the marketplace and facilitate individual mobility, those who acquired those skills were always admonished to use them somehow in service to the community, to help uplift the less advantaged and needy, of whom there were many in black Boston. While individual advancement and the values of Anglo-American middle-class culture were heralded by the reformers, they also never abandoned the black population to pursue individual ends or for some sort of self-serving accommodation with the white hierarchy that would leave the needs and aims of the mass neglected.

David Walker embodied this commitment almost perfectly. The *Appeal*

60. Easton, *Treatise,* 44–45.
61. Horton, *Black Bostonians,* 76–77.

was a clarion call to those who had the skills, education, and religious vision to extend them to the less endowed in the black community so that they also might enter the struggle with greater zeal and intelligence:

> Men of colour, who are also of sense, for you particularly is my APPEAL designed. Our more ignorant brethren are not able to penetrate its value. I call upon you therefore to cast your eyes upon the wretchedness of your brethren, and to do your utmost to enlighten them—*go to work and enlighten your brethren!* . . .
>
> For I believe it is the will of the Lord that our greatest happiness shall consist in working for the salvation of our whole body. . . .
>
> Remember, to let the aim of your labours among your brethren, and particularly the youths, be the dissemination of education and religion.[62]

Never is stress placed on using abilities and knowledge merely for individual advancement. Indeed, the *Appeal* is premised on the notion that each individual has a divine summons to use his or her skills to advance the cause of the oppressed race. No one in Boston addressed this particular responsibility more forcefully or regularly than David Walker.

Yet the commitment of Walker and the reformers to these values and aspirations, and their belief in the absolute efficacy of them, far surpassed the faith that the mass of blacks had in them. How successful they were in persuading them to change is suspect. The fact that they repeatedly and so stridently demanded adherence raises real questions about how many converts they won. Addressing a gathering at the African Masonic Hall, Maria Stewart said:

> Talk, without effort, is nothing; you are abundantly capable, gentlemen, of making yourselves men of distinction; and this gross neglect, on your part, causes my blood to boil within me. Here is the grand cause which hinders the rise and progress of people of color. It is their want of laudable ambition and requisite courage.

She further rebuked:

> There are temperate men among you; then why will you any longer neglect to strive, by your example, to suppress vice in all its abhorrent forms? You have been told repeatedly of the glorious results arising from temperance, and can you bear to see the whites

62. *Appeal*, 28–30.

arising in honor and respectability without endeavoring to grasp after that honor and respectability also?

After recounting how a bootblack had told him he was perfectly happy with his station, an exasperated Walker expostulated: "Oh! how can those who are actuated by avarice only, but think, that our Creator made us to be an inheritance to them for ever, when they see that our greatest glory is centered in such mean and low objects?"[63]

Indeed, as these passages forcefully reveal, the reformers—filled with a deep faith in their rightness—could adopt toward their intended audience chastising and condescending tones that might well alienate them more than persuade them. Hundreds of blacks could be rapidly rallied in Boston in the 1830s to protect a fugitive from extradition to the South,[64] but few answered the call to join a temperance society or attend a lecture on moral improvement.

Thus a somewhat fragmented community developed among blacks in Boston: a community in which all shared a common concern to protect the often tenuous freedom blacks held in the North and to remove the weight of discrimination weighing on all blacks while they could have widely differing interpretations of how a person should use that freedom. Those who usually led the attack against the problems faced by the community as a whole were determined to resolve them in part through specific ends that were often pursued largely by themselves. This is not to say that these leaders were neither important nor respected, but rather that all the values and goals they voiced so regularly and publicly by 1830 were by no means shared by the community as a whole. Despite the clearly discernible fabric of solidarity and collective responsibility woven throughout black Boston, there were also real divisions that separated various strata in the community and that could work against blacks acting in concert.

Boston had proven to be no refuge from the degraded status imposed on blacks in the rest of the United States. Indeed, Walker's experiences in the city only deepened his understanding of the relative unfreeness of blacks throughout America. Boston of the late 1820s fully reflected the North's unfolding movement toward a more aggressive racism founded on the increasingly fortified belief that blacks were inherently inferior to whites, as well as socially threatening, and were to be confined to the most menial work and least attractive living conditions. Through such

63. Stewart, "Address at the African Masonic Hall," 58, 60; *Appeal,* 29.
64. See, for example, Leonard Levy, "The Abolition Riot: Boston's First Slave Rescue," *New England Quarterly* 25 (March 1952), 85–92.

imposed conditions the abject status of African Americans was reinforced and thus seemingly confirmed.

But precisely the opposite occurred in black Boston among its leading members. The trend to cordon blacks off only further united them around their race and similarity of conditions. It also heightened their awareness of themselves as a distinct political entity that had objectives very specific to themselves. It is no surprise that in 1827 the Boston African Lodge declared its total independence of any white Masonic lodge. The steadily worsening conditions for blacks—which pushed them increasingly into a compact and largely economically homogeneous community—actually fostered a growing sense of independence among many of them and facilitated organizing.

By late 1828 Walker and his allies were riding a surge of faith that it was an unusually auspicious time to motivate blacks in Boston and beyond to take collective actions that served to do more than meet the basic needs of individual and community existence. They had to be moved to believe that they could change their status, that they were not destined to occupy an inferior place in society to which they had to accommodate themselves. They had to be brought to intuit their strength and their entitlement to use it, and to begin to see that blacks over a much broader geographical range than Boston could be linked with one another and take common action. To these ends, David Walker devoted the remaining year and a half of his life.

4

"To make them think and feel, and act, as one solid body"

The Appeal *and the Black Reform Movement*

By the late 1820s the free black communities of the North had come of age. Resting on a settled infrastructure of numerous benevolent organizations, black churches, residential proximity, and a deep-seated ethos of mutual assistance, black communities, especially in such major centers as Boston, New York City, and Philadelphia, had not only become fully aware of themselves as distinctive entities with their own specific needs, but were much more assertive in pronouncing that difference publicly and pursuing their own ends. Black political activity in the North had become more organized and confident. The American Colonization Society was near the zenith of its popularity, and black communities throughout the North were under increasing pressure to marshal an effective opposition to it. Despite some setbacks and divisions within their own ranks, free blacks met this highly concerted threat to their existence in the United States with a good deal of success. Indeed, black resistance to the colonization movement was the single most important factor in dissipating the Society's strength by the mid-1830s. *Freedom's Journal* was also part of this anticolonizationist effort and contributed to developing a network among black reformers and intelligentsia that ran throughout the northern and mid-Atlantic states and even into some towns in the South. These immensely important organizational labors reinforced the maturing free black communities' awareness of themselves and of their potential to work in concert with each other.

An irrepressible enthusiasm for combination was spreading rapidly among a number of notable free blacks in the North. Having achieved a sufficient degree of internal strength and articulateness in their own communities, these figures increasingly looked beyond their localities and sought out ways to unite with blacks in distant cities and towns. Samuel Cornish, Presbyterian minister and editor of *The Rights of All,* the short-lived replacement for the defunct *Freedom's Journal,* projected in a September 1829 editorial an excited vision that was typical of his time. Writing of the need to establish associated leagues of uplift throughout free black society, he exclaimed:

> One general agent whose duty it shall be to continue travelling from one extremity of our country to the other, forming associations communicating with our people and the public generally, on all subjects of interest, collecting monies, and delivering stated lectures on industry, frugality, enterprise &c., thereby [might link] together, by one solid chain, the whole free population, so as to make them think and feel, and act, as one solid body, devoted to education and improvement.[1]

Such a vision of a tight-knit union of interest among free black communities simply did not exist in any coherent form before the mid-1820s. If earlier examples of such thinking can be found, they can only be determined incidental when held up against the pervasiveness of such hopes by the late 1820s and early 1830s.

David Walker was in the forefront of this impassioned movement for racial union. Instrumental in forming the Massachusetts General Colored Association (MGCA) in 1828, Walker also articulated its organizational foundations:

> The primary object of this institution, is, to unite the colored population, so far, through the United States of America, as may be

1. *Rights of All,* September 18, 1829.

practicable and expedient; forming societies, opening, extending, and keeping up correspondences, and not withholding anything which may have the least tendency to meliorate *our* miserable condition.[2]

The MGCA was the most advanced embodiment of this new impulse to organize nationally. While the African Methodist Episcopal (AME) Church, the African Methodist Episcopal Zion (AMEZ) Church, and the Prince Hall Masons were extending themselves throughout the North at the same time, none of them was as frankly political as the MGCA or working so explicitly to unite blacks on a national scale. Although the life of the MGCA spanned only a brief five years, it heralded a dramatic change in African American political consciousness and organization and presaged the creation of the National Negro Convention movement only two years later. The *Appeal* was part and parcel of this rising new spirit, and it promoted racial solidarity and moral elevation with a fervor identical to that in Walker's speech to the MGCA.

These changes were a product of a particular moment in time. The excited and hopeful vision of union and black strength that blossomed in the late 1820s issued from the growing interconnectedness among the educated elite of free blacks in the North and the simultaneous maturation of settled, self-aware free black communities in several Northern cities and towns.

Black Boston, New York City, and Philadelphia had come into their own in the 1820s, but such important secondary centers of black life as New Haven, Connecticut, and Providence, Rhode Island, had also become well-rooted along the northeastern seaboard during the same decade. Historians of both black New Haven and Providence designate the early 1820s as the time when those communities became distinct and coherent entities within the two cities. In both cases the historians pointed to the creation of independent local black churches as heralds of the new neighborhoods—in New Haven in 1824 the African Ecclesiastical Society, which by 1829 became the Congregational United African Society, and in Providence in 1820 with the convening of the African Union Church.[3]

2. David Walker, "Address Delivered Before the General Colored Association at Boston," in John Bracey et al., eds., *Black Nationalism in America* (Indianapolis: Bobbs-Merrill, 1970), 30.

3. Robert G. Sherer, "Negro Churches in Rhode Island Before 1860," *Rhode Island History* 25 (January 1966), 9–25; Julian Rammelkamp, "The Providence Negro Community, 1820–1842," *Rhode Island History* 7 (January 1948), 20–33; Robert A. Warner, *New Haven Negroes: A Social History* (1940; reprint, New York: Arno Press, 1969), 80–90. While he places much more weight on the role of expanding independent black households in fostering autono-

While the black population of both towns numbered in the hundreds well before 1820, the creation of separate churches was specified as the "first outward manifestation of the rise of a Negro community." The 1820s also witnessed the formation of a new Masonic lodge in Providence, as well as the African Improvement Society in New Haven—which under the auspices of white philanthropists helped local blacks create their own Sabbath schools, secular evening schools, and a temperance society. These educational and benevolent efforts gained blacks some limited economic advancement and furthered the coalescing of their communities.[4]

New Haven and Providence were not alone in experiencing such growth. The black populace of other northeastern towns—such as Albany in New York; Hartford, Middletown, and New London in Connecticut; and Salem and New Bedford in Massachusetts—underwent similar changes institutionally and in group-consciousness. These changes were also often forecast with the creation of a separate or nearly separate black church and are discussed at greater length later in this chapter.

The growth of black enclaves in various cities and towns was inseparable from the development of an educated and socially involved local black leadership. Chapter 3 identifies this group and their activities in Boston. Similarly structured circles, often centered around religious leaders, arose in the other cities too. Philadelphia is a prime example. There the core group of clergymen Richard Allen, Absalom Jones, and John Gloucester and the merchant James Forten were essential to shaping almost every significant religious, benevolent, and educational organization in the city from the 1790s through the first three decades of the nineteenth century. Separate black Methodist, Episcopal, and Presbyterian congregations were founded by the three ministers respectively, and Allen, Jones, and Forten were the principal petitioners to Boston for an African Masonic lodge in 1797. Their influence was equally felt in a number of the mutual aid and educational societies that arose during these years in black Philadelphia.[5]

---

mous black institutions, Robert Cottrol designates 1820 as the year when significant intra-community organizing took off in black Providence. See Robert Cottrol, *The Afro-Yankees: Providence's Black Community in the Antebellum Era* (Westport, Conn.: Greenwood Press, 1982), 47–48, 57–59. For further general discussion of the Providence community, see *Creative Survival: The Providence Black Community in the 19th Century* (Providence: Rhode Island Black Heritage Society, 1984).

4. Rammelkamp, "The Providence Negro Community," 24. Robert Sherer, however, does emphasize the equal importance of the years 1835–48 in giving form to the Providence community ("Negro Churches in Rhode Island," 24–25). For the African Improvement Society, see *Genius of Universal Emancipation,* December 4, 1829, and January 1, 1830.

5. For more extensive discussion of the Philadelphia black community and its leaders, see Carol V. R. George, *Segregated Sabbaths: Richard Allen and the Rise of Independent Black Churches, 1760–1840* (New York: Oxford University Press, 1973); Nash, *Forging Free-*

New York City had a similar intertwining development of community and leadership. Peter Williams Jr.—son of the Methodist Peter Williams Sr., who helped lay the foundation for what would become by 1820 the AMEZ Church—early affiliated with the Episcopal faith and became the priest of the first black Episcopal parish, St. Philip's, in 1819. James Varick, a founding member in 1810 of one of black New York's most important benevolent associations—the New York African Society for Mutual Relief—was also ordained as the first bishop of the AMEZ Church in 1822. Samuel Cornish, the co-founder of *Freedom's Journal,* was largely responsible for also founding the city's First Colored Presbyterian Church in 1822. When Cornish's responsibilities at *Freedom's Journal* became too heavy by 1827 and he had to step down from his pastorate, Theodore Sedgwick Wright, former agent for *Freedom's Journal* and a Presbyterian educated at Princeton Seminary, became in 1829 the church's next minister, a position he held until his death in 1847. These men, along with a number of other men and women, were involved with creating and sustaining a number of mutual aid, moral improvement, and educational societies. In the 1830s many of them also participated in the Negro Convention Movement.[6]

Smaller cities and towns also witnessed a rise of prominent leaders. The Reverend Nathaniel Paul, brother of Boston's Thomas, helped found the Union Street Baptist Church in Albany as well as the First African Society of that town.[7] In 1826 and years after, the Reverend Jeremiah Asher participated in organizing the African Religious Society in Hartford, which in a few years became the black Talcott Street Congregational Church. By 1840 Asher had become a leading member of Providence's black community and the minister of its Baptist church.[8] In New Haven, Scipio C. Augustus, John Creed, and Bias Stanley joined with white antislavery Congregationalist Simeon Jocelyn and others to form the African Ecclesiastical Society in 1824. By 1830 this society had become the Congregational United African Society on Temple Street and the center of

---

dom; and Julie Winch, *Philadelphia's Black Elite: Activism, Accommodation, and the Struggle for Autonomy, 1787–1848* (Philadelphia: Temple University Press, 1988).

6. Daniel Perlman, "Organizations of the Free Negro in New York City, 1800–1860," *Journal of Negro History* 56 (July 1971), 181–97; David E. Swift, "Black Presbyterian Attacks on Racism: Samuel Cornish, Theodore Wright, and Their Contemporaries," in David W. Wills and Richard Newman, eds., *Black Apostles at Home and Abroad: Afro-Americans and the Christian Mission from the Revolution to Reconstruction* (Boston: G. K. Hall, 1982), 43–47; Rhoda G. Freeman, "The Free Negro in New York City in the Era Before the Civil War" (Ph.D. diss., Columbia University, 1966), 380–94.

7. J. Marcus Mitchell, "The Paul Family," *Old Time New England* 63 (Winter 1973), 75.

8. David O. White, "The Fugitive Blacksmith of Hartford: James W. C. Pennington," *Connecticut Historical Society Bulletin* 49 (Winter 1984), 10; Jeremiah Asher, *Incidents in the Life of the Rev. J. Asher* (London, 1850), 36–49.

black community development.[9] Jehlial Beman of Middletown, Connecticut, a town near New Haven where "many persons of colour reside," led the local African Americans in creating an African congregational church in 1827 and in promoting support for *Freedom's Journal.* Several years later his son Amos, an important figure himself in late-1820s Middletown, began preaching at Hartford's Talcott Street Church before becoming the Temple Street Congregational Church's first settled black preacher in 1838 and a leader of New England's antislavery movement.[10] In the early 1820s Deacon Charles Spicer began to shape an officially sanctioned AME congregation in New Bedford, one of the first churches of that denomination in New England.[11] By the late 1820s there were black leaders throughout the eastern seaboard who embodied the newfound cohesion of numerous communities.

The rise of these leaders and the communities they founded contributed significantly to the vision of black solidarity and uplift that was so characteristic of many black thinkers and activists in the late 1820s and 1830s. As prominent members established themselves and the institutions that reinforced their stature, they reached beyond their localities to associate with leading figures of other towns and cities.

Several factors helped forge these liaisons. As early as 1789 the Free African Society in Philadelphia the African Union Society in Newport, Rhode Island, and similar African organizations in Boston and Providence corresponded concerning the possibility of repatriating in Africa with the assistance of early white colonizationist William Thornton. Henry Stewart, a black Philadelphian, even traveled to Newport and Boston to discuss the plan. The plan was never enacted, but it brought such significant blacks as Prince Hall, Absalom Jones, and Richard Allen into contact, probably for the first time.[12] The Prince Hall Masonic movement had a similar function. By 1797 Boston had chartered Masonic lodges in Philadelphia and Providence, and in 1814 New York City was added. This reinforced the connection between Hall, Allen, Jones, James Forten, and other black leaders. By 1826 the addition of new lodges in more cities extended the network.

Denominational activism among blacks also fostered links. The Reverend Thomas Paul, founder of the African Baptist Church in Boston, helped

9. Warner, *New Haven Negroes,* 80–84.

10. Robert Warner, "Amos Gerry Beman—1812–1874: A Memoir on a Forgotten Leader," *Journal of Negro History* 22 (January 1937), 200–205; *Freedom's Journal,* August 17, 1827.

11. Payne, *History of the AME,* 36, 37.

12. William H. Robinson, ed., *The Proceedings of the Free African Union Society and the African Benevolent Society, Newport, Rhode Island, 1780–1824* (Providence: Urban League of Rhode Island, 1976), 16–34; Floyd Miller, *The Search for a Black Nationality: Black Colonization and Emigration, 1787–1863* (Urbana: University of Illinois Press, 1975), 3–20.

establish and briefly served the African (later Abyssinian) Baptist Society in New York City in 1809. He also made a number of speaking tours in the Northeast that familiarized him with blacks in many towns and cities. His brother Nathaniel, a Baptist minister in Albany in the 1820s, collected in several New England towns subscriptions that were critical in the initial support of Providence's United African Society and helped found that society in 1820. Another brother, Benjamin, served as minister at the Abyssinian Baptist Church and aided New York City's antislavery movement.[13] Samuel Cornish had roots in Philadelphia, where he was closely associated with the powerful Presbyterian minister John Gloucester and expected to replace him on his death in 1822. Theodore Wright was also connected with black Philadelphia, where his father was an early organizer against the colonization movement. Once in New York City, Wright further extended his involvement with black Presbyterianism. He was present at the August 1829 celebration of New Haven's Temple Street Church and addressed "several hundred of his colored brethren."[14]

Richard Allen's creation of the AME denomination in 1816 expanded these religious connections. Before 1816 Allen was minister of a black Methodist church that was separate from but officially subordinate to St. George's Methodist Episcopal Church. Nevertheless, the two churches had quarreled for years over issues of jurisdiction, and when the minister of St. George's forced the issue in 1816, Allen and his flock made a final and decisive break and became the African Methodist Episcopal Church. By 1820 the denomination had more than 7,000 members, most of them concentrated in the Philadelphia–Baltimore–southern New Jersey region and in the soon-to-be-defunct Charleston District. Yet by the late 1820s the AME Church had successfully spread west into Ohio and the Pittsburgh region, where activist Lewis Woodson was minister, and north into New York and New England. After the Vesey affair, this expansion was greatly aided by the infusion of experienced figures fleeing Charleston, many of whom, like Morris Brown, Charles Corr, Amos Cruckshanks, and Henry Drayton, quickly became leading elders of the church, or, like John B. Mathews, James Eden, London Turpin, Alexander Harleston, and Smart Simpson, became prominent circuit riders and resident preachers. Annual regional conferences in Philadelphia, Baltimore, and New York brought many of these figures together regularly and helped maintain communication among them and with Allen.[15]

While not as extensive as the AME Church, other totally autonomous

13. Mitchell, "The Paul Family," 73–75; Woodson, *History of the Negro Church,* 88–90; Sherer, "Negro Churches in Rhode Island," 13–14; *The Rights of All,* June 12, 1829.

14. Nash, *Forging Freedom,* 200, 262–63; Swift, "Black Presbyterian Attacks on Racism," 45–47; *The Rights of All,* September 18, 1829.

15. George, *Segregated Sabbaths,* 79–115; Payne, *History of the AME Church,* 19–63.

African churches were also formed in this period. The AMEZ Church arose in New York City in 1820 after continuing disputes with white leaders over ordination of black preachers led to a complete secession by the black parishioners. Initially affiliated with the AME Church, but unable to resolve differences between the two and chafing under Allen's insistence on his preeminent position in the hierarchy, the New York wing broke with Philadelphia in 1822, created the AMEZ denomination, and elected their own bishop, James Varick. Throughout the 1820s, however, the AMEZ Church was primarily a New York City church, having only loose connections with affiliated churches in New Haven and Philadelphia. Laboring under similar problems with white ministerial paternalism, Peter Spencer and his black Wilmington, Delaware, congregation broke with the local Methodist church in 1813 to found the African Union Church (AUC). Although Spencer attempted unsuccessfully to ally with the AME Church in 1816, and oversaw the limited expansion of his church beyond Delaware, the AUC remained throughout the 1820s an even more local church than the AMEZ, finding most of its adherents in Wilmington and outlying towns.[16] Yet these three denominations all shared a commitment to furthering separate African churches and had fairly regular—if not always amicable—contact with one another. Altogether, they constituted another loose grid of communication among blacks. Thus by the 1820s numerous steadily extending strands of Masonic, religious, and benevolent ties moved their way through Northern black society and drew a growing number of black leaders closer together.

The slow but steady reaction of numerous black communities against the rise of the American Colonization Society (ACS) began to weave these strands into an organized network. Constituted in Washington, D.C., in late December 1816, the ACS, brainchild of New Jersey Presbyterian minister Robert Finley, intended to help impoverished and persecuted free blacks help themselves by strongly encouraging them to emigrate to a colony on the West African coast that the ACS would help establish. The organization quickly attracted a number of leading political figures—especially from such border states as Maryland and Virginia, where large numbers of free blacks lived alongside a much larger number of slaves. John Randolph, Richard Lee, and Bushrod Washington, all of Virginia, and Francis Scott Key and Senator Robert Goldsborough of Maryland, gave instant respectability to the Society and its apparently benevolent objectives. But the national political leader who became the most closely asso-

16. Lewis V. Baldwin, *"Invisible" Strands in African Methodism: A History of the African Union Methodist Protestant and Union American Methodist Episcopal Churches, 1805–1980* (Metuchen, N.J.: Scarecrow Press, 1983), 37–80.

ciated with the ACS was Henry Clay of Kentucky. Fired by the rapid growth of the organization in the 1820s, Clay would in part stake his political ambitions throughout that decade on the unsuccessful effort to secure federal support for the ACS and its colony in Liberia.[17]

African Americans in Philadelphia wasted no time responding to the ACS and its plan. On January 15, 1817, a mass meeting of well over 1,000 blacks was held at Richard Allen's Bethel Church to oppose the colonization movement unequivocally. Just a few days after this mass gathering, a committee of eleven local leaders, which included Allen, Absalom Jones, James Forten, and John Gloucester, reiterated this opposition in a meeting with Robert Finley in Philadelphia. When a branch of the ACS was formed in that city during the summer of 1817, hundreds of black citizens once again convened to protest its presence and intentions and to signal their support for blacks who were still enslaved. As Gary Nash has observed, in Philadelphia the colonization movement actually had a powerfully coalescing effect on the black community and solidified its members' commitment not to desert the slaves but to stay in their homeland and fight slavery.[18]

No other community in the North acted with the swiftness or forcefulness of Philadelphia. A partial but important explanation for this delay is that black leaders in the North had never been without some interest in the idea of a mass return to Africa or some other place where African Americans might settle and govern themselves. For some years before the founding of the ACS, Paul Cuffe, a successful Afro-Indian maritime merchant who lived in Westport, Massachusetts, had worked to create a viable site on the west coast of Africa suitable for both African American colonization and mercantile exploitation. Widely connected with white philanthropists in the North and in England, Cuffe had by 1815 also gained the support of Robert Roberts, Thomas Paul, and Prince Saunders in Boston, Peter Williams in New York, and Allen, Jones, and Forten in Philadelphia, as well as numerous black leaders in such port towns as Newport and New Bedford. These figures became interconnected through the African Institutions Cuffe helped to create in Boston, New York, Phila-

17. The standard source on the creation and operation of the ACS is Philip Staudenraus, *The African Colonization Movement, 1816–1865* (New York: Columbia University Press, 1961). However, a provocative recent article challenges the Staudenraus thesis that religiously inspired benevolence fueled the ACS. Douglas Egerton argues that fears of social turmoil brought on by the widespread presence of a racially oppressed and ignorant lower class were far more central to the inception of the ACS than benevolent impulses. See Egerton, "'Its Origin Is Not a Little Curious': A New Look at the American Colonization Society," *Journal of the Early Republic* 5 (Winter 1985), 463–80.

18. Nash vividly re-creates the drama of these several meetings and their impact on the community's cohesion and consciousness (*Forging Freedom*, 235–40).

delphia, and Baltimore with the object of furthering interest in an African American colony in Africa. The coincident rise of the ACS with the swelling excitement around Cuffe's project initially inclined the black merchant and other black leaders, such as Allen, Forten, Jones, and Russell Parrott, to listen to the representatives of the ACS and even consider endorsing it, especially since a number of friendly white philanthropists were associated with it. Once it became clear, however, that no blacks would be included in the leadership of the ACS, that the organization depicted black racial characteristics in derogatory terms, and that the Philadelphia black community was overwhelmingly opposed to the plan, the leaders separated themselves from it. Although Paul Cuffe died shortly thereafter, in September 1817, Allen, Forten, and others continued to weigh quietly the possibility of black-led emigration.[19]

By 1818 a number of black leaders, first brought together by Cuffe around his project, were regrouping over the prospect of emigrating to Haiti. Prince Saunders first promoted this emigration. A Boston native, Saunders had been educated in England and traveled widely by 1818, having served as King Henri Christophe's envoy from Haiti to the Court of St. James and his agent to recruit schoolteachers there. While in London, Saunders was befriended by Thomas Clarkson and William Wilberforce, British abolitionists. Clarkson was then corresponding with Henri Christophe about the possibility of black Americans emigrating to Haiti. Clarkson won Saunders over to this cause and encouraged him to seek Henri's support as well. But Saunders had by then fallen into the suspicious king's disfavor and decided to go directly to the United States in the fall of 1818, where he toured Boston, New York City, and Philadelphia, praising Haiti and calling on African Americans to emigrate there and participate in its great mission to advance the black race. In Boston he received the support of Thomas Paul, and in Philadelphia the support of Russell Parrott and James Forten. While Saunders was generating some enthusiasm in these cities and regained the confidence of Henri, Clarkson had won the king over to the emigration plan, and he offered to put a ship and $25,000 at his envoy's disposal. But he was unable to secure it before the king, plagued by a recent stroke and civil war, committed suicide in October 1820.[20]

19. Lamont D. Thomas, *Rise to Be a People: A Biography of Paul Cuffe* (Urbana: University of Illinois Press, 1986). The entire book is useful, but pp. 65–119 address the matters I discuss. See also Miller, *Search for a Black Nationality,* 21–53; and Winch, *Philadelphia's Black Elite,* 29–39.

20. The most thorough study of early interest in Haitian emigration among African Americans is Julie Winch, "American Free Blacks and Emigration to Haiti, 1804–26," *Documentos de Trabajo,* Centro de Investigaciones del Caribe y America Latina, Universidad Inter-

Interest in Haitian emigration nevertheless continued. Spurred by overtures in 1824 from Haiti's new president, Jean Pierre Boyer, and his apparent interest in converting the Catholic nation to Protestantism, Thomas Paul gathered a few emigrants together in Boston. Meanwhile, late in the same year, Richard Allen, James Forten, Samuel Cornish, Peter Williams, and other leading blacks—working in conjunction with Haitian agent Jonathan Granville—were organizing the Haytien Emigration Society of Coloured People in their respective cities as well as in Baltimore. The movement was especially strong in New York, where Loring Dewey, a white agent who had broken with the ACS over his support of Haitian colonization, endorsed the new society and was joined by a number of other whites. By late 1824 several hundred prospective emigrants in each city readied themselves for departure, encouraged by Boyer's promise of a travel stipend and a land grant, and within a few months well over 1,000 colonists had left for the black republic. By April 1826 the Haitian government estimated that 6,000 African Americans had settled on the island. Yet by the same date more than one-third of them had returned to America, disgruntled over the harsh conditions and discouraged by the numerous cultural obstacles. If African Americans had found a more favorable environment in Haiti, more might have emigrated there and kept alive some hopes for removal from the United States. Sentiment among blacks for leaving the country may have been deeper in the 1820s than has been acknowledged, especially because horrible conditions and prospects for blacks continued and white racism was mounting. The widespread excitement about the Haitian project tends to support this conjecture. While the Haitian Emigration Societies had provided another opportunity for black leaders to orchestrate their energies and strengthen their bonds, the conclusion by mid-1826 was that emigration was a disappointing failure and had to be reassessed.[21]

Leading Northern blacks turned now to fight the ACS with a renewed vigor. This dramatic change was heralded by the beginning of *Freedom's Journal* in March 1827. *Freedom's Journal,* edited by Samuel Cornish and John Russwurm in New York City, was initially an anticolonizationist publication, and probably begun in part as a response to the publication two years earlier of the ACS organ *African Repository*. The newspaper imme-

americana de Puerto Rico, 33 (August 1988). My brief recounting of events relies heavily on her work. See also Arthur O. White, "Prince Saunders: An Instance of Social Mobility Among Antebellum New England Blacks," *Journal of Negro History* 60 (October 1975), 526–35; Miller, *Search for a Black Nationality,* 74–75.

21. White, "Prince Saunders," 534; Miller, *Search for a Black Nationality,* 76–82; Nash, *Forging Freedom,* 243–45.

diately gained the favor of most prominent Northern black leaders. Meetings among blacks occurred in several cities to assent to the objects of the newspaper and to vow material assistance. Agents for the paper arose in all the principal cities and in many of the secondary cities as well: David Walker and Thomas Paul in Boston, Scipio Augustus in New Haven, Nathaniel Paul in Albany, and Theodore S. Wright in Princeton—to name only a few. Articles written by James Forten and Richard Allen appeared in the *Journal,* as did the speeches and sermons of Russell Parrott, John T. Hilton, David Walker, Peter Williams, Nathaniel Paul, and others. And of course editorials by Cornish and Russwurm were regularly featured. Weekly reporting focused on numerous notable figures from black communities throughout the North and described their noteworthy—often political, educational, or religious—events. Underlying it all was the conviction that African Americans were here to stay, that their communities were coalescing and steadily improving, and that every point in the colonizationists' program would be challenged.

For the first time, the various strands of religious, Masonic, and benevolent networks concentrated into one forum that was known and distributed throughout the North and even in some towns in the South. In an 1837 oratorical recollection, Theodore Wright captured the hope and significance this newspaper embodied:

> The principle of expatriation, like a great sponge, went around in church and state [in 1817], among men of all classes, and sponged up all the benevolent feelings which were then prevalent, and which promised so much for the emancipation of the enslaved and down-trodden millions of our land. . . . But, sir, there were hundreds of thousands of men in the land who never could sympathize in this feeling; I mean those who were to be removed. . . . They resolved to cling to their oppressed brethren. They felt that every ennobling spirit forbade their leaving them. They resolved to remain here, come what would, persecution or death. . . . This was the spirit which prevailed among the people of color, and it extended to every considerable place in the North and as far South as Washington and Baltimore. . . . Although they were unanimous, and expressed their opinions, they could not gain access to the public mind: for the press would not communicate the facts in the case—it was silent. In the city of New York, after a large meeting, where protests were drawn up against the system of colonization, there was not a single public journal in the city, secular or religious, which would publish the views of the people of color on the subject. . . . Ah, Mr. President, that was a dark and gloomy period.

The united views and intentions of the people of color were made known, and the nation awoke as from slumber. The *Freedom's Journal,* edited by Rev. Sam'l E. Cornish, announced the facts in the case, our entire opposition. Sir, it came like a clap of thunder.[22]

Although Wright's recounting of the degree of black opposition to colonization does not fully reckon with the smattering of sympathy among some blacks for the colonization movement, particularly in the pre-1827 period, it is essentially correct while displaying with vivid accuracy the frustration African Americans experienced in attempting to get their opinions published and circulated. It also makes clear how the *Freedom's Journal* became the point of convergence for anticolonization activity in numerous places and forged a radically new mode of communication and organization among free blacks. Black leaders could now talk among themselves on a weekly basis, witness the methods for problem-solving and progress of numerous communities, and develop a much more united and sophisticated response to the ACS. The last several months of *Freedom's Journal*'s brief two-year existence were given over to the procolonizationist editorializing of John Russwurm, who had been recently converted to the ACS after many months of pressuring from that organization. Nevertheless, ensuing black journals and newspapers, from the short-lived *Rights of All* in 1829 onward, were uniformly opposed to ACS-directed colonizationism and would carry on the first paper's central function of providing a discursive and informational forum that brought and bound together the educated black leadership of the North.

The culmination of this steady drive toward ever more regular and broader organization among the black leadership of the North was the beginning of the Negro Convention Movement in September 1830. The national ties forged through *Freedom's Journal* became institutionalized through the conventions, which met annually through 1835 and engendered later national and state conventions. The Negro Convention Movement was as much the result of "an awakening spirit in our people to promote their elevation" as it was an organized response to the ACS and the immediate need to address the threat of Cincinnati and other cities to expel their free black residents.[23] It drew largely on the support of individ-

22. Theodore S. Wright, "The Progress of the Antislavery Cause," in Carter G. Woodson, ed., *Negro Orators and Their Orations* (1925; reprint, New York: Russell & Russell, 1969), 87–88.

23. "Minutes and Proceedings of the Second Annual Convention, for the Improvement of the Free People of Color in These United States" (1832), in Howard H. Bell, ed., *Minutes of the Proceedings of the National Negro Conventions, 1830–1864* (New York: Arno Press, 1969), 35.

uals who had helped build the North's black communities and ties between them in the 1810s and 1820s: Richard Allen, Scipio C. Augustus, James Forten, Peter Spencer, Hosea Easton, James Barbadoes, Robert Roberts, Samuel Snowden, Peter Williams, Bias Stanley, John Creed, Samuel Cornish, Theodore S. Wright, Lewis Woodson, Jehial Beman, James W. C. Pennington, John Scarlett, and even former Charleston residents Henry Drayton and Morris Brown and a host of lesser known figures, participated actively in fostering the conventions either as delegates or as local representatives who solicited funds, gathered information, and worked for the moral improvement of their communities.[24]

The members of the convention movement, however, did not want it to be simply an annual meeting where black leaders gathered, but rather the organizational nexus of a national instrument whose purpose was to uplift the whole of African American society. To this end the convention movement hoped to have agents in "each and every village, town, city, or county, in the different states of the union" with clear-cut functions:[25]

> We have selected four valuable subjects for rallying points, viz.: Education, Temperance, Economy, and Universal Liberty. We hope to make our people, in theory and practice, thoroughly acquainted with these subjects, as a method of future action. . . . We hope to unite the colored population in those principles of Moral Reform. . . . In order to this [sic], we will appoint agents to disseminate these truths among our people, and establish auxiliaries wherever practicable, that the same leaven of righteousness and justice may animate the body politic.[26]

These agents would be the educated, religious, temperate, and antislavery leaders of their local communities. Charged with the local task of sowing moral improvement, they were also linked with the overarching national network that strove to make ironclad the net that might organizationally and ideologically unite all African Americans. The members of the convention movement were fired with the same vision Samuel Cornish had of "one solid chain, the whole free population . . . [thinking, feeling, and acting] as one solid body, devoted to education and improvement."[27] Clearly there was a broad base of agreement among black leaders

24. Sources for these names and many others are in the Minutes and Proceedings of the Annual Conventions from 1830 to 1835, contained in Bell, *Minutes . . . National Negro Conventions.*

25. "Minutes of the Fourth Annual Convention" (1834), 32–33, in ibid.

26. "Minutes of the Fifth Annual Convention" (1835), 26–27, in ibid.

27. *Rights of All*, September 18, 1829.

in the North about what needed to be done. Although these visions of connectedness and consensus were far from being fully realized, and in fact never would be, the organizational distance free blacks had traveled in the first three decades of the nineteenth century was nevertheless remarkable. Peter Osborne, a leading New Haven African American, encapsulated this hope and sense of progress in an 1832 speech at that town's African church:

> What has been done within a few years, since the union of the colored people? Are not the times more favorable to us now, than they were ten years ago? Are we not gaining ground? Yes—and had we begun this work forty years ago, I do not hesitate to say that there would not have been, at this day, a slave in the United States.[28]

Walker's *Appeal* issued naturally out of this matrix of solidifying black communities, interconnected leaders, and high hopes for black improvement and freedom. First of all, Walker himself played an active part in the building of this matrix in the late 1820s and either knew personally or was familiar with a number of the other leading participants in it. He forged the black reform movement's zeal for unity as much as it shaped him. In December 1828 in a speech reprinted in *Freedom's Journal,* Walker asked rhetorically: "Ought we not to form ourselves into a general body, to protect, aid, and assist each other to the utmost of our power . . . ?" Later in the same speech, he proclaimed:

> Two millions and a half of colored people in these United States, more than five hundred thousand of whom are about two-thirds of the way free. Now, I ask, if no more than these last were united (which they must be, or always live as enemies) and resolved to aid and assist each other to the utmost of their power, what mighty deeds could be done by them for the good of our cause?[29]

As with the Negro Convention Movement, Walker placed the educated black leadership at the center of this mandate to attain black unity. In his *Appeal* he repeatedly called to the educated of the black communities to bring literacy, religion, and political awareness to the uneducated and discouraged:

28. *The Liberator,* December 1, 1832.
29. Walker, "Address Delivered Before the General Colored Association at Boston," 31, 32–33.

> Men of colour, who are also of sense, for you particularly is my
> APPEAL designed. Our more ignorant brethren are not able to pen-
> etrate its value. I call upon you therefore to cast your eyes upon
> the wretchedness of your brethren, and to do your utmost to en-
> lighten them—*go to work and enlighten your brethren!*—Let the
> Lord see you doing what you can to rescue them and yourselves
> from degradation. . . .
>
> There is a great work for you to do, as trifling as some of you
> may think of it. You have to prove to the Americans and the world,
> that we are MEN, and not *brutes,* as we have been represented, and
> by millions treated. Remember, to let the aim of your labours
> among your brethren, and particularly the youths, be the dissem-
> ination of education and religion.[30]

David Walker was speaking first of all to a literate black audience. It was
this handful of educated members of each black community who Walker
believed could reach out the most extensively and effectively to the illiterate, the less aware, and the demoralized. They would be the linchpin to
uplifting and mobilizing the mass of blacks.

For Walker, and for the entire black reform movement, educating was a
highly political task. While a few small African schools associated with
churches and benevolent organizations were nurtured in the leading
cities, and limited public education was available to blacks in some cities
by the 1820s, educational resources for blacks in the North were sharply
curtailed and consigned the overwhelming majority of African Americans
to illiteracy and the restricted awareness and vision that that condition
usually imposes. Walker and other black leaders were bitterly aware that the
educational privation of blacks was used to label them inherently ignorant
and unable to learn save for the most rote lessons. Walker fumed:

> The Christians, and enlightened of Europe, and some of Asia, see-
> ing the ignorance and consequent degradation of our fathers, in-
> stead of trying to enlighten them, by teaching them that religion
> and light with which God had blessed them, they have plunged
> them into wretchedness . . . and to add to their miseries, deep
> down into which they have plunged them tell them, that they are
> an *inferior* and *distinct race* of beings. . . .
>
> For coloured people to acquire learning in this country, makes
> tyrants quake and tremble on their sandy foundation. Why, what is
> the matter? Why, they know their infernal deeds will be made

30. *Appeal,* 28–30.

known to the world. . . . The bare name of educating the coloured people, scares our cruel oppressors almost to death.[31]

Knowing how to read and inquire was considered such a potent tool that such skills in African Americans were stamped subversive.[32]

As perhaps this group's first task, Walker expected them to read the *Appeal* to those unable to do so. Along with the mandates he issued to educate the ignorant, he also opened and closed the *Appeal* with the specific directive that the literate read that pamphlet to the unschooled. In the preamble immediately preceding page one in the third edition, Walker counsels all African Americans "to procure a copy of this Appeal and read it, or get some one to read it to them, for it is designed more particularly for them." The confusing antecedent to "them" in the final clause is the literate "some one," for Walker had made it clear throughout his work that "men of colour, who are also of sense, for you particularly is my APPEAL designed."[33] A few pages from the end, he chastises: "Some of my brethren, who are sensible, [for not taking] an interest in enlightening the minds of our more ignorant brethren respecting this BOOK, and in reading it to them, just as though they will not have either to stand or fall by what is written in this book."[34]

This strategy for uplifting and informing the mass of blacks is basically identical to that employed by the Negro Convention Movement. For example, a committee that included James Barbadoes was constituted at the Third Annual Convention in 1833 to investigate the African colonization movement and report on the findings. The inquiry damned the movement—in terms David Walker would have relished—as "that great BABEL of oppression and persecution" that "must shortly be numbered with the ruins of the past." Immediately on presenting their adopted report, the convention authorized the printing of 3,000 copies of the report "in handbills for distribution, by the members of the Convention." Alongside their more general efforts to create educational and moral improvement societies, the delegates personally circulated in their neighborhoods material

31. *Appeal,* 19, 31–32.
32. Walker makes instilling in individuals the ability to frame appropriate questions and answer them intelligently the central task of his *Appeal* and its distributors: "But against all accusations which may or can be preferred against me, I appeal to Heaven for my motive in writing—who knows that my object is, if possible, to awaken in the breasts of my afflicted, degraded and slumbering brethren, a spirit of inquiry and investigation respecting our miseries and wretchedness in this *Republican Land of Liberty!!!!!!*" (*Appeal,* 2).
33. *Appeal,* preamble, 28.
34. *Appeal,* 71n. See also p. 72n, where he asks, "Why do the Slave-holders or Tyrants of America and their advocates fight so hard to keep my brethren from receiving and reading my Book of Appeal to them?"

intended to heighten residents' awareness of activities dangerous to the race. Although the report did not contain material as potentially inflammatory as that of the *Appeal,* it did condemn the colonization movement in no uncertain terms and relied on a distribution system that was virtually the same, especially in the North, to that employed by Walker.

It is important to recognize that the *Appeal* pertained much more to spreading knowledge among blacks and uplifting their characters than it did to violent resistance and slave revolt. Armed rebellion, for Walker, was subordinate to inspiring deprived blacks with the word of God and with the truth about their capacities and their history. Slavery, of course, was the greatest crime against God, and Walker would never discount the option of violent attack on it, especially by those whose outraged faith and morality could no longer endure it. Knowledge of the truth entailed awful responsibilities and the Bible made clear that one of them might be the duty to resist unlawful authority.

But Walker was eager to forgo confrontation so long as the white power structure assented to the essential liberty of African Americans and to their entitlement to a spiritual and secular education:

> I say, let us reason; had you not better take our body, while you have it in your power, and while we are yet ignorant and wretched, not knowing but a little, give us education, and teach us the pure religion of our Lord and Master, which is calculated to make the lion lay down in peace with the lamb, and which millions of you have beaten us nearly to death for trying to obtain since we have been among you, and thus at once, gain our affection while we are ignorant? . . . Treat us then like men, and we will be your friends. And there is not a doubt in my mind, but that the whole of the past will be sunk into oblivion, and we yet, under God, will become a united and happy people. The whites may say it is impossible, but remember that nothing is impossible with God.[35]

Violence had to remain an option, because slavery was the most blasphemous and intolerable of sins and Christians could be brought to the point where it was demanded that they resist rather than continue to submit to its abominations. Nevertheless, Walker hoped to avoid this crisis and finally wanted only the opportunity for his people to participate fully without obstacle in the expanding free labor economy and the culture of Protestant moral improvement. His pamphlet could not make this position more clear.

Yet historians have largely tended to overlook this essential preoccupa-

35. *Appeal,* 69–70.

tion of Walker's in favor of identifying him and his *Appeal* exclusively with a call for violent resistance and some form of racial separatism. In their seminal 1974 study of black abolitionism and emigrationism, *They Who Would Be Free,* Jane and William Pease characterized David Walker and his *Appeal* this way: "The logical climax of discontent, the *Appeal* was atypical of its time in tone, goal, and focus."[36] This conventional assessment ignores the extent to which Walker and his booklet were in the mainstream of the blossoming black reform movement of the late 1820s and reflected positions held by many other African Americans. The error, however, is not an unusual one, for it issues from the common understanding that antebellum black social and political thinkers were strictly divided between those promoting the path of individual moral improvement and assimilation into the larger white American society and those calling for some direct action against slavery and racial discrimination through racial solidarity, possible acts of resistance, and separation from whites.[37] While the former is usually portrayed as the more constructive and realistic path, it is also overwhelmingly pointed to as the one adopted by the majority of antebellum blacks. Thus those calling for any form of resistance or strident racial solidarity are inherently seen to be at odds with the apparently more conservative and cautious values of moral improvement that might lead to successful assimilation. The Peases themselves evince this dichotomy when they make Walker stand not only for the proponent of slave revolt but also as the one who "more nearly reflected the temper of the decade" when he stated in 1828 during his address to the Massachusetts General Colored Association that blacks must unite themselves by forming societies and extending correspondences through which, the authors seem to be suggesting, they would cultivate the sobriety, thrift, industriousness, and plainness that would help them advance in a white American society.[38] This passage, however, actually reflected similar themes embodied in the *Appeal.*

This dichotomy has more often than not obscured the degree to which black proponents of political activism, racial solidarity, and even resistance understood the tenets of moral improvement to be central components of their strategies. Perhaps the main reason this connection has been neglected is that historians widely associate adherence to moral

36. Jane H. and William H. Pease, *They Who Would Be Free: Blacks' Search for Freedom, 1830–1861* (New York: Atheneum Press, 1974), 26.

37. See, for example, Frederick Cooper, "Elevating the Race: The Social Thought of Black Leaders, 1827–1850," *American Quarterly* 24 (December 1972), 604–25; and Monroe Fordham, *Major Themes in Northern Black Religious Thought, 1800–1860* (Hicksville, N.Y.: Exposition Press, 1975).

38. Pease, *They Who Would Be Free,* 27.

improvement with an imitation of the white middle class, which is seen as the source and chief beneficiary of these values. Thus anyone in the black community espousing them must desire wholehearted assimilation into white middle-class America, or, conversely, anyone calling for some sort of racial separatism and resistance must be inherently suspicious of these values, for they are supposed to be the benchmark of the desire to assimilate peacefully. If they are not clearly one or the other of these, the figure must then be interpreted as somehow caught in the grips of a confusing paradox.

Nowhere are these positions more clearly revealed than in Frederick Cooper's discussion of antebellum black activist and sometime emigrationist Martin Delany. Cooper opens with an essential statement on moral reform, "The crusade for moral reform apparently demonstrates a wholehearted acceptance of the moral values of white middle-class America," and then introduces Delany:

> Race pride and racial solidarity coexisted with conventional moral values. The paradox is most evident with Martin Delany. He boasted that "there lives none blacker than himself." He laid much emphasis on racial solidarity and self-help, denounced white oppression and suggested schemes for emigration. Yet no one believed more strongly than Delany in the morality of white America: industry, frugality, abstemiousness, the need for a practical education, careers that would be "useful" to society as a whole.[39]

Because of this confusing dichotomy, an activist's desire to see his people's lives well regulated must be understood as strangely contrary to aspirations for political autonomy and racial solidarity.

While it had been undeniably prominent in advancing the culture of individual moral improvement, the white Anglo-American middle class nevertheless had no special claim on the utility of these tenets. While many reform-minded blacks believed that whites might respond more favorably to black freedom and equality if the race clearly assented to Protestantism, temperance, education, and industriousness, blacks adopted moral improvement not simply as a way to gain the favorable notice of whites but for their own politically and racially motivated reasons as well. The reformers deemed the pursuit of these tenets essential to achieving the "one solid body" they so zealously sought. Speaking in Hartford in 1839, the black Garrisonian and Congregational minister Amos Beman declared that all African Americans must strive for "middle class" moral improvement and regularity as a way to achieve "race pride and unity in

39. Cooper, "Elevating the Race," 616.

the task of destroying slavery."[40] Those values could contribute to the solidarity of the group politically and to individual self-respect by replacing destructive habits that some African Americans might readily acquiesce to in a society that posed as many psychologically damaging barriers to and judgments against them as white America did in the 1820s.[41] Walker had little to say about the impact that blacks' becoming better educated, more religious, and more attuned to developing inner skills that regularized one's life and built individual integrity would have on whites.

But he had everything to say about the impact on blacks themselves. For Walker, assenting to these values and habits was an act of empowerment and even resistance, for he knew full well that an integral part of white America's oppression of blacks was to deprive them of the opportunity to acquire knowledge and to discourage habits that did not generate individual and collective respect.

David Walker clearly represented the values, beliefs, and aspirations articulated by the cadre of Northern black reformers in the late 1820s. While an open appeal for slave revolt was surely rare, he reflected the increased willingness of blacks by the late 1820s to avow publicly their outrage at the persistence of slavery and to consider new methods for fighting and ending it. Violent resistance was by no means excluded, and more blacks in Boston and elsewhere in the North may have been involved with Walker in circulating the *Appeal* than can be readily identi-

40. Amos G. Beman Papers, Scrapbook II, 26–28, Beinecke Library, Yale University.

41. Paul Faler, while emphasizing class rather than race, reached similar conclusions about the commitment of some shoemakers in antebellum Lynn, Massachusetts, to what he calls the new code of industrial morality, which included temperance, education, regular work habits, Protestant worship, and firm regulation of one's inner impulses. While he designates one group of shoemakers who assented to these values as doing so in order to enhance their mobility by identifying themselves more fully with their control-minded employers, another stratum adhered to them because they believed this morality fostered self-respect and independence and made them more able to combat the mounting efforts of their employers to exploit and dupe them. Although very loyal to their class, they had concluded that activities such as drinking, gaming, and bawdy partying, which had characterized the culture of workingmen in the eighteenth century, had become counterproductive in this new era of radical transformations in the economy and the workplace. But these values were always intended to advance working-class interests, not those of the manufacturers. This stratum of shoemakers was the catalyst behind organizing worker newspapers, cooperatives, and lecture societies. As Faler summarized: "Self-imposition of a rigorous code of moral conduct was not a way to respectability but rather a means of preserving personal pride and obtaining a sense of power and self-confidence at a time when the worker always seemed subject to outside control. He was proclaiming his independence from those external forces that governed him—whether employer or liquor" (393). See Paul Faler, "Cultural Aspects of the Industrial Revolution: Lynn, Massachusetts, Shoemakers and Industrial Morality, 1826–1860," *Labor History* 15 (Summer 1974), 367–94.

fied—a matter that will be examined in the next chapter. David Walker and his *Appeal* embodied the increasing political awareness and assertiveness of the Northern black leadership by the late 1820s, and their conviction that slavery was the cause of all the ills confronting blacks in America and that they had to work urgently to extirpate it.

In July 1829 Boston blacks vehemently displayed their impatience with the doctrine of colonizationism and social expedience. During a speech given by a white minister at the African Meeting House on July 14—the traditional day for the African Celebration in Boston—many blacks left abruptly "with visible dissatisfaction" because they believed the minister was not sufficiently sympathetic to the slaves or direct enough in his description of their plight. They created such agitation that it required the efforts of one of their own ministers to quell them. But soon they were up again. When the guest minister went on to counsel them to show whites that they deserved freedom by evincing self-government, and to understand that the slaves could not be emancipated "before they could be qualified" for it, "a very audible murmur ran round the house" voicing unmistakable disapproval. An effort by an agent of the ACS to endorse these arguments only precipitated a "more earnest and decisive" growling. The sympathetic white reporter understood their frustration; they were only speaking "the language of nature" and pursued "the simple question of right, not of expediency."[42]

That reporter was William Lloyd Garrison, whose own edging toward immediatism after hearing such rumblings and footsteps could only have been accelerated by the far more precise articulations of Walker. Garrison paid his own respects to Walker's convictions and his insights into the destructiveness of slavery and racism, if not to Walker's angrier strain.

Garrison clearly recognized the depth of allegiance blacks in Boston and in the North felt for Walker, that he was "regarded among his people as a man inspired"—as one of the *Liberator*'s early white commentators described him.[43] Garrison's awareness was not simply one of respectful observation. The black community—especially Boston's—would supply *the* critical moral and financial support for his paper in its early years. Garrison wanted to avoid the financial instability of his mentor, Benjamin Lundy, who by April 1830 had to shift his weekly *Genius of Universal Emancipation* to a monthly schedule because too few will "patronise a weekly publication, devoted to the important subject of African Emanci-

42. *Genius of Universal Emancipation,* September 2, 1829.
43. *Liberator,* April 30, 1831.

pation."[44] When Garrison arrived in Boston in spring 1830 filled with plans for this new abolitionist newspaper, he immediately began building a deep relationship with the city's black community, a public who had already given him much evidence of their willingness to patronize an aggressively antislavery newspaper. Lundy had never committed so much energy to forging ties with Baltimore's black community, and he also remained sympathetic to the ACS and Haitian colonization until at least as late as 1831. Of course, Garrison would win the hearts and minds of many African Americans by excoriating these very positions.

But Garrison also gave Walker no short shrift in the *Liberator*. Despite his own problems with the *Appeal,* Garrison prominently and largely favorably covered Walker and his work in the *Liberator*'s first half-year. No less than nine articles—some of them lengthy—appeared in the newspaper between January and June 1831.[45] Garrison unquestionably used this forum partly as a way to establish his understanding of and sympathy for the sensibilities of the black community. No doubt it earned him much credibility, just as Lundy's bitter condemnation of the *Appeal* in April 1830 must have further sunk his journal's hopes.[46]

Throughout the nineteenth century and beyond, the leaders of black America all made clear that they not only endorsed David Walker and his work but also considered him one of the great inspirational leaders for African Americans. Henry Highland Garnet, Maria Stewart, Amos G. Beman, and Frederick Douglass—figures whom the Peases would consider much more in the mainstream of antebellum black activism—as well as W. E. B. Du Bois—gave Walker credit for being a central influence on their lives. Garnet issued a famous edition of the *Appeal* containing his interview of Walker's widow and his own call for slave resistance. In orations in 1831 and 1833, Boston's famous black abolitionist and missionary, Maria Stewart, reflected the near reverence with which many in the local community regarded Walker:

> Many will suffer for pleading the cause of oppressed Africa, and I shall glory in being one of her martyrs; for I am firmly persuaded, that the God in whom I trust is able to protect me from the rage

44. *Genius of Universal Emancipation,* July 1830.

45. *Liberator,* January 1, 8, 22, and 29; February 5, 19; April 30; and May 14 and 28, all in 1831.

46. See also Donald M. Jacobs, "David Walker and William Lloyd Garrison: Racial Cooperation and the Shaping of Boston Abolition," in Donald M. Jacobs, ed., *Courage and Conscience: Black and White Abolitionists in Boston* (Bloomington: Indiana University Press, 1993), 9–17.

and malice of mine enemies, and from them that will rise up against me; and if there is no other way for me to escape, he is able to take me to himself, as he did the most noble, fearless, and undaunted David Walker. . . .

But where is the man that has distinguished himself in these modern days by acting wholly in defence of African rights and liberty? There was one, although he [i.e., David Walker] sleeps, his memory lives.[47]

In 1863 Amos Beman still used Walker and his work to uplift his people. In discussing central texts that must be distributed among the Union soldiers, he proposed:

There are some books and publications of special importance in the present crisis of our affairs, which should be in the hands of all, especially of all our soldiers: First that book of *facts,* by W. C. Nell of Boston, also that volume of fire, "Walker's Appeal," and "Garnet's address to the slaves" should be scattered over the land, as thick as autumnal leaves.[48]

In 1883 no less a towering figure than Frederick Douglass was remembering David Walker as an inspirational pioneer in the defense of black freedom and rights whose labors preceded even those of Garrison and Lundy:

The question is sometimes asked, when, where and by whom the Negro was first suspected of having any rights at all? In answer to this inquiry it has been asserted that William Lloyd Garrison originated the Anti-slavery movement, that until his voice was raised against the American slave system, the whole world was silent. With all respect to those who make this claim I am compelled to dissent from it. I love and venerate the memory of William Lloyd Garrison. . . . [Yet i]t is no disparagement to him to affirm that he was preceded by many other good men whom it would be a pleasure to remember on occasions like this. Benjamin Lundy, an humble Quaker, though not the originator of the Anti-slavery movement, was in advance of Mr. Garrison. Walker, a colored man,

47. Maria Stewart, "Religion and the Pure Principles of Morality, the Sure Foundation on Which We Must Build" (1831) and "An Address Delivered at the African Masonic Hall" (1833), in Richardson, *Maria W. Stewart,* 30, 57.

48. Amos Beman's scrapbooks, 2:4. William Cooper Nell was the black author of *Colored Patriots of the American Revolution* (1855).

whose appeal against slavery startled the land like a trump of coming judgment, was before either Mr. Garrison or Mr. Lundy.[49]

While Douglass went on to mention earlier proponents of emancipation, such as Samuel Hopkins and John Wesley, it is clear both that he associated Walker with the origins of the organized antislavery movement and that the *Appeal* was seen as a righteous opening salvo defending African American integrity and power.[50]

Even as late as 1940, W. E. B. Du Bois lauded the *Appeal* as "that tremendous indictment of slavery" that represented the first "program of organized opposition to the action and attitude of the dominant white group [and included] ceaseless agitation and insistent demand for equality." For Du Bois, the Niagara Movement and the National Association for the Advancement of Colored People were only descendants of a program first articulated and implemented by Walker.[51]

The fact that these supposedly more conventional proponents of black liberty could find such a pivotal place for Walker in their lives indicts any assignment of Walker and his booklet to the dangerous fringes of antebellum black activism. They and others like them were evidently moved by his call for African Americans to make a commitment to liberty, solidarity, and improvement that was so fierce that they would finally resist any force unresponsive to less aggressive persuasion.

49. Frederick Douglass, "Our Destiny Is Largely in Our Own Hands: An Address Delivered in Washington, D.C., on 16 April 1883," in John W. Blassingame and John R. McKivigan, eds., *The Frederick Douglass Papers,* 5 vols. (New Haven: Yale University Press, 1992), 5:68–69.

50. In a work that combined visionary descriptions of God's retribution against slaveholders with attacks on slavery as irrational, brutal, and unrepublican, the Reverend W. Paul Quinn of Pittsburgh even appropriated intact a four-page section from the *Appeal* (without giving credit to Walker) in order to urge whites to immediate repentance. Walker's language was far more compelling than Quinn's. This is one further example of the quiet but significant ways in which the *Appeal* circulated and wielded influence. Compare *Appeal,* 40–43, with Paul Quinn, "The Origin, Horrors, and Results of Slavery, Faithfully and Minutely Described, In a Series of Facts, and Its Advocates Pathetically Addressed" (1834), in Dorothy Porter, ed., *Early Negro Writing, 1760–1837* (Boston: Beacon Press, 1971), 628–30.

51. W. E. B. Du Bois, *Dusk of Dawn: An Essay Toward an Autobiography of a Race Concept* (New York: Harcourt, Brace & Co., 1940), 192–93.

5

Getting the Good Word Out

Circulating Walker's Appeal

> *It is evident they have read this pamphlet, nay, we know that*
> *the larger portion of them have read it, or* heard *it read, and*
> *that they glory in its principles, as if it were a star in the east,*
> *guiding them to freedom and emancipation.*
> —*Boston Evening Transcript,* 28 September 1830

> *That he believes that all the negroes, though not in the first*
> *place knowing to the design of revolt, when it was*
> *accomplished, approved it.*
> —From the trial transcript of Babo in Herman Melville,
> *Benito Cereno*

The first edition of David Walker's *Appeal* was published in the fall of
1829. Printed on the title page was the statement "Written in Boston, in
the State of Massachusetts, Sept. 28th, 1829." The pamphlet was more
than likely printed in the North End shop of two white printers, David
Hooton and Matthew Teprell. Hooton had been used previously by the
African Lodge to print an address given by John T. Hilton, and both
printers were cited on the list of Walker's debts in his probate records.[1]

---

1. See *An Address, Delivered Before the African Grand Lodge of Boston, No. 459, June
24th, 1828, By John T. Hilton: On the Annual Festival, of St. John the Baptist* (Boston, 1828);
Probate Records of David Walker, No. 29332, Suffolk Co. Registry of Probate. Beyond these
two connections, little is known about the potentially significant relationship of these two
printers to Walker and to the Boston black community. Walker, however, had developed
some sort of liaison with them, for he, along with Thomas Dalton, was charged with seeing
that Hilton's address was printed.

A small controversy also arose around the authorship of the *Appeal*. An anonymous piece printed in March 1830 in the *Boston Daily Courier* insisted that Walker could not have been the author of the *Appeal*: "[He] who believes it to have been written by David Walker, the dealer in old clothes in Brattle Street, must have more abundant faith than falls to our humble share. It is not, cannot have been, the work of that man."[2] In a letter to *The Liberator* filled with unintended praise of Walker and printed in January 1831, another reader wrote that he was opposed to Walker and his *Appeal* "not because he is a man of color, but because I do not believe that he wrote it." He continued:

> For the matter brought forward in said pamphlet is the result of more reading than could have fallen to the lot of that man, and, at the same time, have left him so vulgar as he has been represented to me. (2)—Besides, sir, he could never have read all the authors quoted in his book, and seen of what true greatness consisted, and then bestowed such unbounded praise upon one [i.e., Richard Allen] whose name the political, the moral, and the religious world will be found equally indifferent about handing to those who may come after us (3)—To say nothing of the excellent criticisms upon the speeches of the most talented men of the age—all of which discover to us a greater degree of education than we have any reason to believe that he possessed.[3]

Their certainty was evidently founded on the assumption that no black person could possibly have had the level of learning and reading that Walker manifested in his work. William Lloyd Garrison did not question Walker's authorship of the pamphlet or his scholastic and moral ability. He addressed the issue in notes appended to the January letter:

> We are assured, by those who intimately knew him, that his Appeal was an exact transcript of his daily conversations; that, within the last four years, he was hurtfully indefatigable in his studies; that he was not "vulgar," either in manners or language; and that he was a blameless professor of religion.

The *Appeal* bears a highly personal, emotional tone that marks it as the work of someone who had experienced the humiliations, revelations, disappointments, and rage of which he wrote. As I have established in earlier chapters, a number of events and experiences mentioned in the *Appeal*

2. *Boston Daily Courier*, March 22, 1830.
3. *The Liberator*, January 29, 1831.

can either be directly linked to Walker or ascribed to him with a high level of probability. The mayor of Boston at the time, Harrison Gray Otis, conducted his own investigation of the *Appeal* and its author by sending a young associate to Walker's shop to question him. According to this investigator, Walker affirmed that "he openly avows the sentiments of the book and authorship."[4]

However, Walker may have shown his work to associates before having it printed and circulated. Given his closeness to a number of potentially interested figures in Boston, and the degree to which his *Appeal* expressed strategies and opinions that they could have voiced or endorsed as well, Walker may well have received suggestions and/or encouragement from others in his endeavors. This is not to imply that the *Appeal* was somehow written by a team. The style of the document is simply too personal and distinctive to have been written by anyone other than a single impassioned author. Yet this would not preclude the possibility that he showed his work to others who would be most interested in its content. Walker shared his work with others after it was completed; why not also consult like-minded associates before publishing this highly social work? While Walker unquestionably wrote the *Appeal,* he may very well have received comments on it from others, and clear indications of their willingness to assist in realizing its objectives, before the pamphlet ever went to press. One piece of evidence that supports this position is that the white mariner from Boston who brought the *Appeal* into Savannah in early December 1829 testified that he received the copies "from a Negro man named Ely a clothier in Brattle Street."[5] This "Negro man" was David Walker's close friend and political associate, John Eli, whose clothing shop was next door to Walker's at 38 Brattle Street.

The *Appeal* appears to have first surfaced publicly in Savannah. On December 11, 1829, the Savannah police department seized sixty copies of the *Appeal.* Earlier a white steward of a Boston brig that had recently landed in Savannah delivered this parcel of pamphlets to a prominent local black Baptist preacher, the Reverend Henry Cunningham, who "immediately returned it on ascertaining the character of its contents." Cunningham probably alerted the police to its presence, for soon afterward the steward was arrested and questioned thoroughly by the police. The steward, however, claimed to be "totally ignorant of the nature of the

4. Letter from Boston Mayor Harrison Gray Otis to the Mayor of Savannah, William T. Williams, February 10, 1830; reprinted in *Richmond Enquirer,* February 18, 1830.

5. Williams to Otis, December 12, 1829, Records of Chatham County, Georgia, Mayor's Letter Book, 1821–44, Georgia Historical Society, Savannah. I express my appreciation to Barbara Bennett, assistant director of the Society, for her help in identifying this and other letters.

contents" of the parcel and was discharged after having his baggage inspected. Nevertheless, the police apprised Mayor William T. Williams of the seizure, and Williams then promptly notified Charleston's Intendant, Henry L. Pinckney, as well as Boston's Mayor, Harrison Gray Otis, of the dangerous development. Soon, Governor George Gilmer of Georgia was alerted, and on December 21 he circulated a communication among the state legislators, urging them "to meet [the problem] promptly and effectually." By the end of the year, the state had marshaled its machinery to attempt to cut off further circulation of the *Appeal* and hurriedly wrote new laws for the quarantining of all black sailors entering Georgia ports, punishing with serious penalties the introduction of seditious literature into the state and tightening laws against slave education.[6]

The pamphlet had started its fire, and the perception officials had of its significance was made even more acute by recent insurrectionary developments in the South. Governor Gilmer laid out fears of the authorities concisely:

> The plots devised some years ago in Charleston, and very lately in Georgetown, South Carolina, the late fires in Augusta and Savannah, have shewn us the danger to be apprehended in the cities from the negroes. The information communicated [regarding the *Appeal*], presents this danger in a new shape.[7]

These were no small matters. A sizable portion of Augusta had been burned in April 1829, and further fires flared in October and November. The April fires had also destroyed most of the town's arms. Officials, including Governor John Forsyth and militia commander William W. Montgomery, were certain that slaves had started the fires.[8] A tradition of slave

6. Williams to Henry L. Pinckney, Intendant of Charleston, December 12, 1829; Williams to Otis, December 12, 1829; Williams to Governor George M. Gilmer, December 26, 1829, Records of Chatham County, Georgia, Mayor's Letter Book, 1821–44, Georgia Historical Society, Savannah. Williams to Gilmer, December 28, 1829, File II—Names, Georgia Department of Archives and History, Atlanta; Governor's Communication, December 21, 1829, in *Journal of the House of Representatives of the State of Georgia, 1829–1830* (Milledgeville, Ga., 1830), 353–54; Clement Eaton, "A Dangerous Pamphlet in the Old South," *Journal of Southern History* 2 (August 1936), 326–29. Eaton's article is essential reading in tracing the trail of the *Appeal.* Eaton makes one slip in his thoroughly researched study; on page 326 he states that Mayor Williams wrote Governor Gilmer that the pamphlet had been found in the possession of a slave. While that could certainly have occurred, the evidence he cites is a letter in which the white steward, not a slave, is discussed as the possessor. In tracing the movement of the *Appeal* and who was exposed to it, such a distinction is very important to make. See above, Williams to Gilmer, December 28, 1829.

7. *Journal of the House of Representatives of the State of Georgia, 1829–1830,* 353.

8. William W. Montgomery to Governor John Forsyth, Augusta, April 30, 1829, Record

arson only reinforced their suspicions about Augusta and the contemporaneous firing of Savannah. An apparently wide-reaching conspiracy in Georgetown had also been exposed sometime in the spring of 1829 and had alarmed authorities throughout that region of the South. In characteristic fashion, state officials treated the affair with great secrecy, but a letter from State Attorney General James Louis Petigru warning the presiding magistrate revealed the scope of the plot:

> I am afraid you will hang half the country. . . . You must take care and save negroes enough for the rice crop. It is to be confessed that your proceedings have not been bloody as yet, but the length of the investigation alarms us with apprehension that you will be obliged to punish a great many.[9]

These events set a fearsome background to the *Appeal*'s arrival in Georgia.

The role of the Reverend Henry Cunningham in the pamphlet's progress in the state remains unclear, as does the reason for his being specifically pinpointed to receive the parcel of books. Cunningham merits further examination. He was apparently born a slave in Savannah in the late eighteenth century and early on joined Andrew Bryan's First African Baptist Church, organized in 1788 and considered the first such church in America. Failing to receive a ministerial appointment from Bryan to new black churches being formed in 1802, Cunningham and a number of other prominent members of that church dissociated themselves from it and affiliated with the Reverend Henry Holcombe's white Baptist church. On January 1, 1803, Holcombe ordained Cunningham into the ministry and helped him organize the Second African Baptist Church on Savannah's prosperous east side. One historian of this church noted:

> Most of the members composing [it] were those residing in the city,—intelligent domestic servants and some mechanics,—who were ever under the eye of their owners, which gave them great protection and peaceable worship; and so that church became the pride of the young colored people of Savannah.

Group 4, File II, Box 174; Forsyth to Secretary of War John Eaton, Milledgeville, May 6, 1829, Governor's Letter Books, November 1809–October 1829, Drawer 62, Box 64, Georgia Department of Archives and History. See also Aptheker, *American Negro Slave Revolts*, 281–82.

9. James Petigru Carson, ed., *Life, Letters, and Speeches of James Louis Petigru: The Union Man of South Carolina* (Washington, D.C.: W. H. Lowdermilk & Co., 1920), 66.

While this church did not have the total autonomy of Bryan's, it appears to have been the most attractive church to Savannah's black artisans and slaves who hired their time.[10]

Like several other central black religious figures in the early ante-bellum South, Cunningham traveled to the North to continue his denominational work. Indeed, he helped form the African Baptist Church in 1809 in Philadelphia, where he remained as its first preacher until 1811, when he returned to Savannah apparently with enough money to purchase his freedom. The Southern imprint lasted long on the church, but Cunningham must also have established a number of Northern contacts and been exposed extensively to the vibrant black religious culture of early-nineteenth-century Philadelphia. These experiences probably left their stamp on him for many years after his return to the South, and he more than likely maintained some of the contacts he made there.[11]

By the early 1820s at the time David Walker was probably in Charleston, Cunningham had established himself, along with his associate, the Reverend Andrew Marshall of the First African Baptist Church, as one of the two leading black preachers in Savannah. He had also accrued the sanction of some local white philanthropists. In the 1823 Register of Free Blacks for Chatham County, Josiah Penfield was listed as guardian of both Cunningham and his wife. Penfield was a prominent white supporter of the African Baptist churches, assisting them from the late eighteenth century until his death in 1829. By 1828 Cunningham secured another guardian by the name of S. C. Dunning, also an active supporter of the African churches. These and other white benefactors lent a critical endorsement to the often delicate maneuvering the African ministers had to employ to maintain the portion of autonomy their church had achieved.[12]

This is the man to whom Walker chose to send sixty copies of his *Appeal*. Whether Cunningham actually requested the pamphlet is probably impossible to determine, but some reasonable speculations regarding him and his relationship with the work can still be made. During his time in Charleston, Walker may very well have become aware of Cunningham,

10. James M. Simms, *The First Colored Baptist Church in North America, Constituted at Savannah, Georgia, January 20, A.D. 1788* (Philadelphia, 1888), 56–59; E. K. Love, *History of the First African Baptist Church, from Its Organization, January 20th, 1788, to July 1st, 1888* (Savannah, Ga., 1888), 1–3; William B. Gravely, "The Rise of African Churches in America (1786–1822): Re-examining the Contexts," *Journal of Religious Thought* 41 (1984), 72.

11. Gravely, "The Rise of African Churches," 72; Nash, *Forging Freedom*, 201–2; Woodson, *History of the Negro Church*, 87.

12. Chatham County Registers of Free Persons of Color, 1817–64, Georgia Historical Society; Woodson, *History of the Negro Church*, 113; Love, *History of the First African Baptist Church*, 6, 20–22.

Marshall, and other figures in the African Baptist movement in Savannah. He might have selected Cunningham to receive copies because of his literacy, his religious stature, and the high regard in which he was held in the community. Such a person could give great authority to the *Appeal* in reading and distributing it to a local audience.

The possibility that Cunningham had an antislavery orientation should by no means be excluded. His apparent peace with the slave system and deferential tone toward important whites were no different from those exhibited by Morris Brown, a man whose possible connections with the Vesey affair have never been fully discredited. These postures were the sine qua non of prominent black leadership in any Southern town and should not be automatically identified with the actual feelings and opinions of the leader.[13] They were often skillfully contrived masks crafted with an acute awareness of the demands of racial protocol and hierarchy. Andrew Marshall, Cunningham's close religious associate and with whom he shared the same white benefactors, struggled for years to keep his church and its deeply loyal members from coming under the jurisdiction of a white Baptist church that aggressively pursued him. Yet the manner in which he presented this actually combative position was revealingly characterized by one of his white opponents in a letter to Mayor Williams in 1833: "Our advice has been uniformly disregarded, and, though frequently asked, has on no occasion been followed." Clearly, Marshall had regularly enacted a ritual of deference by seeking the advice of the Baptist elders, and had just as regularly rejected it and followed his own course of religious autonomy.[14] Cunningham, whose historical relationship with his church and with the white church was different from Marshall, could nonetheless have easily been a supporter of Marshall, to whose church Cunningham had once belonged.

My point here is that Cunningham's interest in the *Appeal* cannot be automatically discarded. He had passed at least two years in the North and had unquestionably been exposed to black antislavery and reformist sentiment there. He himself had been born into slavery, knew full well its sufferings, and may have remained sympathetic to the thousands remain-

13. For an excellent example of the deferential language Cunningham could employ in his exchanges with white benefactors, see his letter to his supervising white church in Love, *History of the First African Baptist Church,* 14.

14. Ibid., 23. This dispute was relentlessly pursued by the white Sunsbury Baptist Association, which like so many other white religious authorities in the South "feared that such independence as the gospel taught was 'extremely dangerous' for the negroes to take in, being slaves" (ibid., 27). Indeed, the Association, despite Marshall's powerful white supporters, did bring the African church back under their supervision. For a fuller discussion of this conflict, see ibid., 10–28.

ing in it. And he was deeply committed to fostering some form of independent black religious worship, an activity that we have seen in several instances was inherently challenging to Southern social structure and either implied or made explicit some degree of resistance in its supporters. Even if Cunningham had not specifically requested the pamphlets, Walker probably reasoned that if he received copies he might either distribute them, read the work to groups, or simply read the *Appeal* himself and be aware of the efforts of its author. In selecting him, Walker—if he alone was responsible—made a decision consistent with his strategy to place his work in the hands of the educated, and with his experience that black religious figures wherever were often opposed to slavery and eager to help blacks elevate themselves. The preacher's decision to alert the authorities to the pamphlets' presence may well have been made because of his acute sensitivity at that time to the various dangers of accepting the parcel, not necessarily because he rejected its content outright.

Soon after the uncovering of the *Appeal* in Savannah, it appeared in the possession of a white editor, Elijah Burritt, in the state's capital. Burritt, a New Englander by birth, had spent the last twelve years in the South. He published a newspaper in Milledgeville, the *Statesman & Patriot,* which often took unpopular stands, especially regarding the tariff issue, states' rights, and the legitimacy of Cherokee land titles in Georgia. In early January 1830 Burritt received twenty copies of the *Appeal* at the local post office, and by early February the town's authorities learned that they were in his possession. Burritt, who had been in Augusta when the discoveries were made, was quickly arrested when he returned, and then released when no prosecutor appeared against him. A few days later he was rearrested and confronted with an incriminating letter he had received from Walker, which seemed to suggest a conspiratorial agreement. Burritt hoped to erase this suggestion by showing an earlier letter Walker had sent him, but succeeded in only deepening his guilt in the eyes of his accusers. Released again on a technicality, Burritt, knowing that the penalty for circulating insurrectionary material in Georgia was capital, fled the state that night and returned North. Efforts by Governor George Gilmer to extradite Burritt to Georgia were to no avail.[15]

15. Much of the material for this discussion of the Burritt affair was drawn from John E. Talmadge, "The Burritt Mystery: Partisan Journalism in Antebellum Georgia," *Georgia Review* 8 (Fall 1954), 332–41; and Cary Howard, "The Georgia Reaction to David Walker's *Appeal*" (M.A. thesis, University of Georgia, 1967), 62–89. See also Peter Tolis, *Elihu Burritt: Crusader for Brotherhood* (Hamden, Conn.: Archon Books, 1968), 84–85; Phillips, *Plantation and Frontier,* 2:150; Eaton, "A Dangerous Pamphlet," 328–29; Governor Gilmer to B. P. Stubbs, February 11, 1830, and Gilmer to Harrison Gray Otis, February 12, 1830, both in Governor's Letter Books, 1829–33, Drawer 62, Box 64, Georgia Department of Archives and

Elijah Burritt had in fact requested "one or more copies" of the *Appeal* in a letter to Walker sent on December 21, 1829.[16] The letter had a very respectful tone and conveyed useful information to Walker about the fate of the sixty copies delivered to Savannah, information certainly not necessary for him to supply in order to receive his books. It even closed with the cordial phrase "Very Respectfully." Although Burritt had read several pages of the pamphlet already and was familiar with its inflammatory character, he offered no condemnation of the text or of Walker's efforts to disseminate it. Indeed, Burritt indicated that laws will be passed imminently "in relation to the matters involved in its circulation." Despite awareness of the grave jeopardy in which this request might place him, he continued apace.

In his only statement on the *Appeal* in the *Statesman & Patriot,* Burritt never repeated the standard opprobrium heaped on it by both Southern and Northern officials. Nowhere were there such common lurid condemnations as "the extravagance of his sanguinary fanaticism, tending to disgust all persons of common humanity" or "the most wicked and inflammatory productions that ever issued from the press."[17] Only the comparatively benign observation that there is "little ground for misinterpretation" of the text was advanced.[18] While he affirmed Governor Gilmer's maxim that "more should be *done* than said" about this work whose "object . . . was to circulate the poison of general principles," he reprinted a long column from the *Boston Centinel* that included lengthy passages from some of the angriest and most vengeful sections of the *Appeal,* and then discussed them with a largely morally neutral voice. Proclaiming a desire to educate the public about the pamphlet and its lack of "any digested or concurrent plan of rebellion," he was in fact violating the governor's maxim and the long-standing Southern tradition of greatly restricting public discussion of slave conspiracies or unrest. Such excerpting of the *Appeal* was extremely rare in the South primarily because it could contribute to the circulation of the ideas among African Americans.

Why such mild censure at a time of public anxiety while exhibiting a far greater interest in excerpting and explaining a text which supposedly left

---

History; *The Georgian,* March 13, 1830. Tolis (*Elihu Burritt,* 85) incorrectly identifies the governor of Georgia at this time as George M. Troup. Troup, an ardent states'-rights man who relentlessly pursued Cherokee lands, was at this time a U.S. Senator from Georgia, but he had served as governor of Georgia from 1823 to 1827. See Robert Sobel and John Raimo, eds., *Biographical Directory of the Governors of the United States, 1789–1978,* 4 vols. (Westport, Conn.: Meckler Books, 1978), 1:288.

16. See the complete letter in *Milledgeville Southern Recorder,* July 31, 1830.
17. *Nile's Register,* March 27, 1830; *Richmond Enquirer,* January 28, 1830.
18. *Milledgeville Statesman & Patriot,* January 2, 1830.

"little ground for misinterpretation"? Although he was a Democrat, Burritt probably believed, like some Southern Whig editors, that the *Appeal*'s threat was overstated and perhaps used to generate opposition to the tariff and perceived Northern meddling in Southern affairs. In fact, he made it clear that he did not believe the work raised the threat of any "immediate mischief."[19]

It is likely that Burritt also opposed slavery. He was born in Connecticut into a family that included famous peace activist and abolitionist Elihu Burritt. After his flight to the North, he befriended New Haven abolitionist Simeon Jocelyn, who in an 1832 letter to William Lloyd Garrison described Burritt as having "facts on the subject of slavery most horrible and [he] would make one of the most commanding and interesting agents for our society that can be found—he is pious and warmly devoted to the cause of the oppressed."[20] Burritt, who died in Texas in 1837 in an ill-starred colony there, never worked for Garrison, but the likelihood that he had antislavery sympathies is high. They may have inclined him to have been very curious about Walker's denunciation of slavery and to have accorded the stalwart author a certain respect.

Burritt may well have believed that room still existed in Georgia and the South for some limited and careful inquiries, if not debates, over slavery. As with his more vigorous opposition to Georgia's Native American policy, airing the *Appeal* and his reflections on it was simply one more way for him to evince his commitment to public debate and human rights. But the very arrival of the *Appeal* was in fact helping to close any remaining openings both in Georgia and throughout the South. *Le Liberal,* a New Orleans weekly sympathetic to free people of color and mildly antislavery, thrived until it was terminated in March 1830 as the furor around the *Appeal* mounted there.[21]

Regardless of his motivations, Burritt almost certainly did not intend a subversive circulation of the *Appeal.* He made no secret of having written the letter to Walker, and once the copies were received he privately lent or sold single copies to several local eminent citizens, including slaveholders.[22] And in the January 2, 1830, issue of his *Statesman & Patriot,* Burritt fueled public vigilance and efforts to suppress the pamphlet by referring to its effort "to circulate the poison of general principles."

19. See, for example, the *Richmond Daily Whig,* January 8, 1830, for a lampoon of the panic and "the ridiculous farce" of legislative secrecy adopted to address this issue. In 1828 Burritt had been an enthusiastic supporter of Andrew Jackson. See Tolis, *Elihu Burritt,* 92 n. 18.

20. Tolis, *Elihu Burritt,* 86.

21. This matter is discussed more fully later in the chapter.

22. *Milledgeville Southern Recorder,* July 31 and August 14, 1830.

Burritt became the victim of his numerous political enemies and the ambitions of his associate editor, John G. Polhill. Burritt was an outspoken opponent of Georgia's mounting effort to expropriate Cherokee lands while he endorsed the tariff of 1828 and the federal government's right to regulate commerce. For this he earned the enduring enmity of Governor George Gilmer and other influential political figures. The fact that he was a Northerner only deepened their suspicions. By late 1829 his wife was sure that he "had become extremely unpopular even with his own party" and that they "had conspired to ruin him."[23]

When Polhill appeared at the governor's office in early February 1830, while Burritt was in Augusta, with sixteen copies of the *Appeal* and a supposedly incriminating letter from Walker, all addressed to Burritt, the officials were quite ready to rush to judgment. Despite counsel from some to await Burritt's return, Polhill, who had known from the editor that he possessed a few copies of the *Appeal* and had even lent some to slaveholding friends, nevertheless claimed to have feared Burritt's intentions when he discovered the unknown additional pamphlets and the letter from Walker requesting he "comply according to engagement."[24] In fact Burritt later made clear that this request was simply for payment to some banking house in Boston for the twenty copies, a standard procedure he proposed in his December letter to Walker.[25] By his return a few days later, the probably desired effect had already been realized: a groundswell against Burritt that would lead to his hasty flight was amassing. As of July 1830 Polhill had gained full title to the *Statesman & Patriot* and all the tools of its production and changed its name to the *Federal Union.* His self-interest in fostering the controversy was evident. Although precisely what Burritt's intentions were will probably never be known, it is nearly certain that they were founded on some blend of curiosity, arrogance, and humanity.[26]

Burritt was by no means the only white Northerner in Georgia in 1830 who opposed the state's policy toward the Cherokees. Emboldened by the election of Andrew Jackson to the Presidency in 1828, state officials, led by Governor George Gilmer and U.S. Senator George M. Troup, appropriated certain Cherokee lands for new counties and then extended the laws

23. *Milledgeville Southern Recorder,* August 14, 1830.

24. *Milledgeville Federal Union,* August 7, 1830.

25. *Milledgeville Southern Recorder,* August 28, 1830.

26. The vitriolic and public debate over Polhill's and Burritt's intentions can be followed in the *Milledgeville Federal Union,* July 17, 1830; July 31, 1830; August 7, 1830; August 14, 1830; August 21, 1830; September 25, 1830; October 2, 1830; and in the *Milledgeville Southern Recorder,* July 24, 1830; July 31, 1830; August 14, 1830; August 28, 1830; September 11, 1830; September 18, 1830; October 9, 1830.

of the state to these lands. The tribe was then strongly encouraged to cede its lands to Georgia and to emigrate to new territory west of the Mississippi. Jackson made it clear that the loud Cherokee protests would find no favor with the federal government. The tribe did, however, receive much sympathy from the numerous Protestant missionaries who had lived among them for decades, many of whom were Northerners affiliated with the Congregationalist-dominated American Board of Commissioners for Foreign Missions (ABCFM). Among a number of courageous white supporters, two were particularly outspoken: Samuel Worcester and Elizur Butler, both of the ABCFM. When the Georgia legislature decreed, in a move to eliminate these and other missionaries, that all whites working among the Cherokees must be licensed by the state and take a loyalty oath to it, Worcester, Butler, and a few other men opted for a harsh imprisonment rather than submit to the state. Amid much publicity, Worcester had his case brought before the U.S. Supreme Court. In one of his most famous decisions—*Worcester v. Georgia,* Chief Justice John Marshall ruled in March 1832 that Georgia had no jurisdiction over the Cherokee lands or government and thus found Worcester illegally imprisoned. Although President Jackson refused to enforce the Court's ruling against a defiant Georgia, Governor Giles finally decided to pardon Samuel Worcester after deciding that the missionary's imprisonment served no further end and would actually add tension to the rising Nullification crisis.[27]

Worcester and Butler, however, were apparently involved in another controversy in Georgia. While writing his reminiscences of antislavery days, Samuel May, the Garrisonian abolitionist, inquired of a friend from Louisiana, a Dr. W. H. Irwin, what he remembered of Walker's *Appeal* in the South. Irwin, according to May,

> replied that he was living in Georgia in 1834, was acquainted with the Rev. Messrs. Worcester and Butler, missionaries to the Cherokees, and knew that they were maltreated and imprisoned in 1829 or 1830 for having one of Walker's pamphlets, as well as for admitting some colored children into their Indian school.[28]

27. The Cherokees, despite their own efforts, those of the missionaries, and the Marshall decision, began a forced relocation to the Oklahoma Territory in 1834. The political background to this tragedy, the Cherokees' involvement with the missionaries, and the specific activities of Worcester and Butler are thoroughly explored in William G. McLoughlin, *Cherokees and Missionaries, 1789–1839* (New Haven: Yale University Press, 1984), 239–99. See also Francis Paul Prucha, *American Indian Policy in the Formative Years: The Indian Trade and Intercourse Acts, 1790–1834* (Cambridge: Harvard University Press, 1962), 224–49.

28. Samuel J. May, *Some Recollections of Our Antislavery Conflict* (Boston, 1869), 134. A mounting controversy also surrounded the admission of slaves to Cherokee schools. As Georgia authorities attempted to impose their laws over the Cherokees' expropriated lands,

There is, however, no further evidence that they did have copies of the *Appeal,* and the friend's memories of thirty or so years ago may certainly have lacked some precision. Georgia authorities may also have conveniently linked the two prominent missionaries with the *Appeal,* repeating an often-used racial ploy to inflame a Southern populace against resident Northerners.

But the two Congregationalists may also have shared Burritt's interest to familiarize themselves with this novel and infamous work. Both these men, as well as their associates from the ABCFM, had antislavery leanings, most likely of the sort common to Northern colonizationists who truly found slavery economically and morally repugnant but who also considered racial integration impossible and/or impractical.[29] Yet they considered their position on slavery a delicate one: while they in no way wanted to endorse or foster the institution, they did acknowledge its existence among a number of Cherokees and were concerned to not alienate them or their nonslaveholding brethren by forcing the issue.[30] To do otherwise, they believed, would jeopardize their decades of work among this tribe.

Slaveholding, however, was not widespread among the Cherokees. According to an 1835 census of the Eastern Cherokee Nation, of 16,542 members only 207 were slaveholders, and they held 1,592 black slaves. Of those masters, only 3 held more than 50 slaves, and 83 percent had fewer than 10.[31] The vast majority of Cherokees were simply too cash-poor to buy or own slaves. Some observers also noted that the slavery of blacks among them was milder than that imposed by white Americans. British traveler T. Hamilton commented in 1833 that the slaves among the Creeks—a tribe closely related to the Cherokees as a fellow member of the Five Civilized Tribes—were "unhabituated to severe labour [and] described their bondage as light, and spoke of their master and his family with affection." He added:

> To the lash they are altogether unaccustomed, and when married, live in houses of their own, round which they cultivate a patch of

they arrested Sophia Sawyer, an ABCFM missionary, in 1832 for instructing slaves in a school for Cherokees. Some slaveholders among the tribe allowed a few of their black slaves to attend these schools. Both Butler and Worcester, teachers themselves, were strong supporters of these schools. See R. Halliburton Jr., *Red over Black: Black Slavery Among the Cherokee Indians* (Westport, Conn.: Greenwood Press, 1977), 81; Theda Perdue, *Slavery and the Evolution of Cherokee Society, 1540–1866* (Knoxville: University of Tennessee Press, 1979), 88–89.

29. In fact, Samuel Worcester's cousin, Professor Samuel M. Worcester, was an ardent supporter of the ACS at Amherst College in the late 1820s. Staudenraus, *African Colonization Movement,* 132–33.

30. Halliburton, *Red over Black,* 93–96.

31. Ibid., 57; Perdue, *Slavery and the Evolution of Cherokee Society,* 58–59.

ground. The negro and Indian children are brought up together on a footing of perfect equality, and the government of the family seemed entirely patriarchal.[32]

Despite the presence of slaveholding, their nationwide dispossession and eventual forced removal bore a disturbing resemblance to the forced migration of the nation's black inhabitants. These significant similarities were not lost on the missionaries. In a widely publicized series of letters written under the nom de plume "William Penn," Jeremiah Evarts, another ABCFM missionary who worked closely with Worcester, asserted that "the world has pronounced its irrevocable sentence" on the slave trade and thus asked, "Is it more clearly wrong to take Africans from their native land, than it is to make slaves of the Cherokees upon *their* native land? or, on penalty of their being thus enslaved, driving them into exile?"[33]

Burritt, Worcester, and Butler were all sensitive to this link. While most likely none of them—including Burritt—had anything to do with broad distribution of the *Appeal,* Worcester and Butler could well have known of the work and been interested in it. They may have received a copy— possibly through a network of white missionaries and reformers involved with the Cherokees, who sympathized with at least some of the frustrations voiced by Walker. Moreover, there were other missionaries working among the Cherokees, especially Methodists, who were associated with Worcester and Butler and who were much more vehement in their opposition to Georgia authorities. Indeed, they could sometimes sound like Walker himself. An ABCFM missionary, Daniel Butrick, recounted the sermon of one Methodist circuit rider to some Cherokees.

> Near the close of the discourse the speaker imagined a council in hell—which extended to some of the state legislatures—and also included the President of the United States—all for the purpose of rob[b]ing the Cherokees of their country and breaking them up as a Nation. . . . [The preacher] also imagined a council held by Christians, by holy angels, and finally by the Father, Son, and Holy Ghost for the purpose of saving the Cherokees; and he predicted the Salvation of the Nation. This much affected the minds of some, even produced groaning and tears.[34]

32. T. Hamilton, *Men and Manners in America,* 2 vols., 2nd American ed. (Philadelphia, 1833), 2:132–33.

33. "'William Penn' Essays," no. 22, in Jeremiah Evarts, *Cherokee Removal: The "William Penn" Essays and Other Writings,* ed. Francis Paul Prucha (Knoxville: University of Tennessee Press, 1981), 172–73.

34. Daniel Butrick to Jeremiah Evarts, September 22, 1830, as cited in McLoughlin, *Cherokees and Missionaries,* 290.

While the Congregationalist Butrick was repelled by the emotionalism of the sermon and response, there were missionaries in Georgia—again, usually Methodist—who were quite willing, as William McLoughlin observes, to place "the powerful God of Christianity . . . on the side of social and political justice for the Indians" and to use that God, as does Walker, to support a nationalistic impulse.[35] Although the ABCFM rejected this tone and interpretation, Worcester, Butrick, Butler, and others prepared a manifesto in late December 1830 that called on "all benevolent people" to pray for assistance to the injured Cherokee nation. This document was modeled on a Methodist manifesto written three months earlier.[36] In admittedly widely varying degrees, all the missionaries manifested the capacity to attach religious significance to the Cherokees' search for justice. The real possibility remains that they might also have seen a connection between the plight of the Cherokees and that of African Americans and that the casting of both those struggles in religious terms may have helped them make the link.

Walker may have also pinpointed figures such as Burritt, Worcester, and Butler to receive the *Appeal* for several reasons: their commitment to Christian benevolence; their application of it to an oppressed people, the Cherokees; and their likely antislavery position, which could be powerfully linked with their awareness of the Cherokees' plight. By no means did Walker exclude the possibility of blacks allying with whites in pursuit of racial justice. Walker stated this quite explicitly in his speech before the MGCA:

> But some may even think that our white brethren and friends are making such mighty efforts, for the amelioration of our condition, that we may stand as neutral spectators of the work. That we have many good friends yea, very good, among that body, perhaps none but a few of those who have ever read at all will deny; and that many of them have gone, and will go, all lengths for our good, is evident, from the very works of the great, the good, and the godlike Granville Sharp, Wilberforce, Lundy, and the truly patriotic and lamented Mr. Ashmun, late Colonial Agent of Liberia, who, with a zeal which was only equalled by the goodness of his heart, has lost his life in our cause, and a host of others too numerous to mention. . . . Now all of those great, and indeed, good friends whom God has given us I do humbly, and very gratefully acknowledge. But, that we should co-operate with them, as far as we are

35. Ibid.
36. Ibid., 255–56, 291–92.

able by uniting and cultivating a spirit of friendship and of love among us, is obvious.[37]

Walker was clearly impressed by the degree of commitment to racial justice—or at least to the abolition of slavery—exhibited by certain white philanthropists, and he must have considered that his pamphlet might gain some favor among them, especially because of its Christian premises.

The fact that these three missionaries worked among the exploited Cherokees also could have served to draw Walker's attention to them. Walker believed the Native Americans would probably be likable allies in the struggle against slavery and racial oppression. He was certain of their unwillingness to submit to slavery:

> Why do they [i.e., white slaveholders] not get the Aborigines of this country to be slaves to them and their children, to work their farms and dig their mines? They know well that the Aborigines of this country, or (Indians) would tear them from the earth. The Indians would not rest day or night, they would be up all times of night, cutting their cruel throats.[38]

Even though a small number of Cherokees themselves held black slaves, Walker may have calculated that their love of freedom, combined with the degree of their current oppression at the hands of whites, might be enough to push them into solidarity with the slaves.

Other black rebels concluded similarly. In a letter forwarded to Virginia's Governor John Floyd from Southampton County after the 1831 Nat Turner insurrection, the mysterious "Nero" proclaimed the existence of a vast network of black and white conspiratorial agents throughout the

37. *Freedom's Journal,* December 19, 1828. See also John Bracey et al., eds., *Black Nationalism in America* (Indianapolis: Bobbs-Merrill, 1970), 32. In the *Appeal,* 71, Walker also states: "Those philanthropists and lovers of the human family, who have volunteered their services for our redemption from wretchedness, have a high claim on our gratitude, and we should always view them as our greatest earthly benefactors." Walker's favorable focus on white philanthropists is highlighted by his commentary on Jehudi Ashmun, a man who had recently died in Africa while helping to carve out the original Liberian settlement. Evidently a colonizationist, Ashmun nevertheless probably gained Walker's sanction by not being a slaveholding colonizationist in the Henry Clay mold, and for actually having gone to Africa with African Americans to help them build a community where they might elevate themselves. In so interpreting Walker's perspective on Ashmun, one must bear in mind that Walker also cites among his list of benevolent whites Granville Sharp, the English philanthropist who led the movement to create Sierra Leone, England's African colony for blacks resident in the island nation.

38. *Appeal,* 63.

South who would continue the tumult only begun by Turner. One of his highest hopes was that "we could enlist the Indians of Georgia in our common cause—and we are not without hopes that we shall."[39] Later developments, in fact, revealed that their hopes were not misplaced; the Seminoles of Florida and the hundreds of runaway slaves who lived among them or nearby as maroons proved fearsome allies in their wars with the United States Army in the mid-1830s.

Nero suggests more tantalizing possibilities regarding the involvement of Burritt and other whites in antislavery activities in the Deep South:

> We have never been foiled in but one instance, and that was when we confided in the abilities of Burrit of Georgia. Our holy cause most surely was then in jeopardy, and had it not been for a most masterly maneuver of our Chief, who was then in Georgia, Burritt would have lost his worthless life, and our fond hopes would have been blasted, lucky for us, that Burritt did not know the person of our chief, for had he, most probably he would have betrayed him. That circumstance however has been of service to us—it has mad[e] us more circumspect—made us more cautious in making confidants. We have now many a white agent in Florida, S. Carolina and Georgia, but they are not Burritts. Such are some of the fond prospects on which I dwell, and for which I live.[40]

While Nero's statement on "many a white agent" may be more bluff than actuality, his information on Burritt is nevertheless intriguing because there was little public coverage of his encounter with Georgia authorities in the North.[41] "Nero" thus may well have had some form of contact with a person or organization familiar with Burritt.

Nero was probably connected with the early Negro Convention Movement and related early abolitionist circles. He refers to efforts to build a Negro college and to working with people in Ohio and upper Canada, issues of central concern to the early convention movement. He also lauds "the generous sympathies of White people" and how "they contribute largely to our enterprize." The Tappan brothers and other wealthy,

39. The Nero letter is held in the Slave and Free Negro Letterbook, Executive Papers of Governor John Floyd, Virginia State Library, Richmond. The letter is reprinted in full in Ira Berlin, ed., "After Nat Turner: A Letter from the North," *Journal of Negro History* 55 (April 1970), 144–51; the sentence quoted is on page 147.

40. Berlin, "After Nat Turner," 149.

41. Brief references were made to Burritt in the *Boston Daily Courier,* March 22, 1830, and in *Genius of Universal Emancipation,* March 5, 1830.

white philanthropists were prominent financial supporters of the first Negro Conventions. And despite his fiery rhetoric, Nero repeatedly proclaimed that "knowledge and information must move our machinery" and that only through "the business of education and improvement" can oppression and revenge finally be eliminated.[42] Stress on education and moral improvement were two of the most commonly voiced themes of the Conventions' members. Among the few white participants in the first Convention during the summer of 1831 was New Haven's Reverend Simeon Jocelyn, who definitely knew Elijah Burritt and his story by early 1832 and was likely familiar with him by the summer of 1831.[43] Other participants in the Conventions and early abolitionism were probably similarly familiar. Indeed, information about Burritt could have traveled relatively freely within the confines of these circles. Nero's awareness of Burritt and his activities is difficult to explain otherwise unless we make the problematic assumption that the editor was indeed his agent.

The possibility that the letter was a hoax cannot be ignored. Some of the claims of the author are far-fetched and dramatically diabolical: traveling as "a mendicant Negro," their leader "has visited almost every Negro hut and quarters" in the South over the last three years; 300,000 men North and South will be ready to rise "when our plans are matured"; extensive financial, moral, and armed support from whites in the North existed, and $167,000 had already been raised for them in Haiti; the cadre of leaders "pledged ourselves in a goblet made of the skull of a slaveholder, and . . . signed our name to articles of confederation with our own life blood." Many of his proclaimed methods fit neatly with Governor Floyd's outlining of the Northern abolitionist conspiracy: the Post Office and printing presses will supply a "machinery of vast power" to deliver subversive literature and letters in cipher to the agents; their leaders will manipulate the ignorant slaves with preaching and arouse in them a conviction of righteousness for their cause. Stock stereotypes were also deployed. All Nero's agents were well paid and "a Yankee, you know, will hazard his life for money"; only the blacks, not the white agents, have a sufficient "savage state" and "ferocity" for a "promiscuous slaughter of women and children." All these claims compounded lent much credibility to the designs Floyd described.

Yet, if Floyd or someone else had it planted, its most obvious function—to arouse the white populace and validate Floyd's representations—was never served. Floyd never published the letter, although he

---

42. This mixing of calls for revolt with calls for study and peaceful improvement is basically identical to that of Walker. For all the above references to Nero, see Berlin, "After Nat Turner," 145–47.

43. Tolis, *Elihu Burritt,* 86.

may have included it in a packet of documents pertaining to slave insurrection that he circulated among legislators during an address to them on December 6, 1831. We can never be certain, however, because the packet is not extant.[44] Floyd also held the letter, along with a copy of the *Appeal* and the *Liberator*, in a special file for abolitionist material. All of this suggests that Floyd believed the letter genuine and took its information very seriously.

The other possibility is that the letter *was* sent by an ardent opponent of slavery in Boston, and it did describe, however aggrandized, antislavery structures and potentials that did exist in the South. We simply will never know for certain. But Nero's mention of "many a white agent" may in fact have been referring to a knowledge of a loose-knit collection of white missionaries, editors, businessmen, peddlers, sailors, or whatever from the North who lived or moved about in the South and who may have sympathized to one degree or another with blacks and their plight. While the impression he gives of a tightly knit organization is surely inflated, his pointing to the existence of white sympathizers in the South with whom some of his circle were familiar is probably not off the mark. Nero undoubtedly wanted to intimidate Governor Floyd of Virginia and projected a specter of ubiquitous subversion. Yet his descriptions, rather than being mere unfounded imaginings, were hyperboles or exaggerations of reality. Lesser degrees of what he described did in fact exist in the North and South. And—much as with Walker—the energetic optimism in his tone is as much a reflection of the intense hopefulness for change that blacks in reform circles experienced in the early 1830s as it was a swaggering bravado. Walker himself may have been aware of such a coterie of white connections. The receipt of the *Appeal* by Burritt, Worcester, and Butler may be evidence of that possibility. This was not the last time whites figured into the circulation of the booklet.

Only a week or two after first appearing in Georgia, the *Appeal* arrived in Virginia. On January 7, 1830 Governor William Giles alerted the Virginia General Assembly that a free black carrying several copies of the *Appeal*

---

44. Floyd stated the following in the address: "From the documents, which I herewith lay before you, there is too much reason to believe those plans of treason, insurrection and murder, have been designed, planned and matured by unrestrained fanatics in some of the neighboring States, who find facilities in distributing their views and plans amongst our population, either through the post office, or by agents sent for that purpose throughout our territory." Message of Governor Floyd to the Virginia Legislature, December 6, 1831. Reprinted in Henry Irving Tragle, *The Southampton Slave Revolt of 1831: A Compilation of Source Material* (Amherst: University of Massachusetts Press, 1971), 432.

had been apprehended.[45] This man had apparently been circulating the pamphlet among Richmond's blacks before being captured. Initially, one particular free black, Thomas Lewis, had been sought by the unidentified figure who carried the *Appeal* into the city. This mysterious person appears to have been Walker's emissary, since he carried not only thirty copies of the pamphlet but also a letter from the author to Thomas Lewis, who was singled out for receipt of the copies.[46] Upon his arrival in Richmond, he discovered that Lewis had just recently died. Claiming to have then inquired of "a gentleman of the City [presumably white with such a title] for advice" on what to do with his package, he was counseled to circulate its contents, although the local resident never read the booklets, assuming "them to be of the class of fanatical tracts upon the subject of religion, now profusely scattered through the country." He promptly distributed all copies. However, Mayor Joseph Tate was notified of these events early enough to retrieve twenty of the pamphlets and to have Walker's agent apprehended. Tate then notified Governor Giles on or about January 5, and he in turn apprised the General Assembly. On January 7, with much haste, the General Assembly convened an extraordinary closed-door session to discuss the matter and lay plans for reckoning with it.[47]

As with the arrival of the *Appeal* in Georgia, evidence of its appearance in Richmond and Virginia is very sketchy. We know only that Walker's agent was a free black. He could have been a mariner who came up the James River, but he could also have traveled by land. That he knew Walker, however, seems likely, because he carried a letter from him, a letter that is itself suggestive. Its most important implication is that Walker probably did not know the Thomas Lewis to whom he sent the parcel—in fact, Lewis probably never solicited the pamphlets. Walker opened and closed the very brief letter with the two following sentences:

Esteemed Sir,—

Having written an Appeal to the Coloured Citizens of the World it is now ready to be submitted for inspection, of which, I here

45. For information cited here pertaining to the circulation of the *Appeal* in Richmond, see Governor William Giles to Linn Banks, January 7, 1830, Executive Letter Book, Reel 14, Virginia State Library, Richmond.

46. This important letter, the only extant copy of Walker's handwriting, is in the Slave and Free Negro Letterbook.

47. *Richmond Daily Whig,* January 8, 1830. See also James Stuart, *Three Years in North America,* 3rd ed., 2 vols. (Edinburgh, 1833), 2:75–76.

with send you *30 c* which Sir, your Hon., will be please to sell, among the Coloured people. . . . If your Hon should want any more of these *Books* please to direct any communication to me at c/o 42 Brattle St. where all Letters or advices eminating from your Hon. will mee[t] with a hearty and greatful reception.

The tone of the first sentence indicates that Walker was introducing Lewis to the existence of the pamphlet, but it also seems to assume that the man will be interested in selling them. In the last sentence, Lewis's unfamiliarity with Walker seems further confirmed by the fact that Walker gave him his address and encouraged him to write. Walker's offer of this information also indicates that Lewis probably did not request the pamphlets.

Why then did Walker send thirty pamphlets and a letter to this particular man? Again, we cannot know with certainty, but an important connection does exist. While my search for Thomas Lewis through Hustings Court Minutes, city and county censuses, personal property and land tax lists, and other municipal records did not definitely yield this man, it did establish that a large number of free blacks with the last name of Lewis lived in the Richmond/Henrico County region of Virginia in the late 1820s and early 1830s. Boston of the same era was not without several black Lewises itself: there was Joseph Lewis, a clothes dealer at 8 Brattle Street; A. J. Lewis, a hairdresser; and Walker Lewis, also a hairdresser.[48] Walker Lewis was in fact a friend of David Walker and a fellow Prince Hall Mason. Some of these Boston Lewises may have been from this large Richmond pool, having migrated to a northeastern urban port, which was not uncommon among upper South free blacks of that time.

Black Lewises from Richmond and Virginia were living in Boston at later dates and could have been in Boston during Walker's time there. Esther Lewis was born in Richmond and died in Boston at the age of sixty-eight on October 24, 1870. Her husband, George, also came from Richmond. Another George Lewis hailed from Virginia and was seventy-six when he died on July 20, 1867. Winnie Lewis died on March 11, 1875, at the age of forty-five and was born in Richmond.[49]

It was possible that Walker was alerted to Thomas Lewis as a likely recipient of the *Appeal* by someone familiar with him in Boston. Such personal communication links certainly functioned widely among free blacks in the North and upper South—especially since so much migration occurred between these two areas—and may have contributed to the tar-

48. All these names are from the 1830 Boston City Directory. However, there probably were a number of other black Lewises living in Boston.

49. *Index of Boston Deaths,* City Hall, Government Center.

geting of other people to receive the *Appeal*. As antislavery black reformers did in the North, Walker sought out individuals in the South who were literate and who he had decided would be receptive to the religious and antislavery orientation of his pamphlet. Such persons would be the most ardent and effective distributors of the work.[50]

Walker appears to have followed an identical strategy in North Carolina. The *Appeal* most likely entered that state through the port of Wilmington. Sometime early in August 1830 "a well disposed free person of Color" notified local authorities that Walker's pamphlet was circulating in the town and showed them a copy.[51] An immediate further investigation determined that Walker "had an Agent in this place (a slave) who had received this book with instructions to distribute them throughout the State particularly in Newbern, Fayette[ville], & Elizabeth [City]."[52] This agent was Jacob Cowan, probably the slave of a local large slaveholder, Thomas Cowan.[53] Cowan had received 200 copies of the work and was evidently

50. Walker could have been aided in this search by his important connection with *Freedom's Journal*. By 1829, Joseph Shepherd of Richmond was regularly listed as the newspaper's agent in that city. He could not have been unaware of Walker, whose name was listed in the same column of agents as his and whose activities in Boston were discussed in the paper on a number of occasions. Walker could have used this liaison to help him gain a useful knowledge of the black community in Richmond and/or to introduce materials there. See, e.g., *Freedom's Journal*, January 2 and March 28, 1829.

Freedom's Journal and its initially strong anticolonization and pro-emancipation stands were well received by many literate, reform-minded free blacks in the upper South. One man, who identified himself only as "A Free Coloured Virginian," wrote in July 1827:

> The appearance of a paper from the North, edited by persons of our own colour, and devoted to the interests of our long oppressed and stigmatized race; cannot fail to awaken the liveliest joy and gratitude in every bosom, that is not callous to humanity and virtue. We, at the south, are peculiarly interested in its welfare, for we are those on whom its effects may operate most beneficially. (*Freedom's Journal*, July 6, 1827)

Such an enthusiastic response to the new newspaper may have led Walker to believe that an equally ardent support would greet the arrival of the *Appeal*.

51. James F. McRae, Magistrate of Police, to Governor John Owen, Wilmington, August 7, 1830, in Governor John Owen, Letterbook, 1828–30, vol. 28, North Carolina State Archives.

52. McRae to Owen, August 7, 1830.

53. Marshall Rachleff, "Document: David Walker's Southern Agent," *Journal of Negro History* 62 (January 1977), 100–103. Regarding Jacob Cowan's probable ownership by Thomas, see *Cape Fear Recorder*, April 5, 1817, in which an advertisement placed by Thomas Cowan offered a reward for the retrieval of his slave Primus, who had been absent for some time. A further search for evidence linking Jacob to Thomas was unfruitful. Immediately above this announcement was another from New Hanover County authorities officially outlawing Primus, a condition that made it legal to kill him on sight if necessary. Primus had been "lurking about in said county, committing depredations on the property of the good citizens thereof" for some time. Apparently, Thomas's slaves had a tradition of rebellious activity.

literate, for he acknowledged understanding the above instructions, although he—like so many other figures caught with the *Appeal*—denied that he followed the directives. The letter does appear to have come from Walker, or from another agent in New York City.[54] Nevertheless, the method of enclosing written instructions with the pamphlets was repeated in North Carolina.[55]

Cowan kept Wilmington authorities "ignorant of the extent to which the books may have circulated," but he was well situated to distribute them broadly.[56] According to one news story, Jacob (or James) Cowan "had a very indulgent master, who allowed him to keep a tavern," where he held the pamphlets "for their more efficient distribution." By the time of his arrest several accomplices were imprisoned with him.[57]

Numerous police magistrates were notified of the recent events and warned to guard against the pamphlet's circulation.[58] As of September 3, 1830, white authorities in Fayetteville had not detected the pamphlet's presence in their town, despite sending undercover agents into the black community.[59] Officials elsewhere in the state were not so fortunate. Cowan and others handling the *Appeal* in Wilmington must have had connections with local runaways, for evidence exists that runaways from settled encampments near the town were in part responsible for carrying the pamphlet to other areas of North Carolina and forwarding Walker's directives. In early November 1830 a man named Moses, who had escaped

54. A letter written by the Wilmington Magistrate of Police, James F. McRae, fifteen months later noted that Cowan had "received a letter of instructions from Walker or the agent who had shipped the pamphlets to him from New York." The parcel must have had some indication that it came from New York. See James F. McRae to Police of Mobile, Wilmington, November 3, 1831; reprinted in Rachleff, "Document," 101.

55. Jacob Cowan's rebelliousness was not contained with his apprehension in Wilmington. Soon after he was arrested, he was transported to Charleston "with instructions to have him sold into the interior of other Southern States, where he would be deprived of the opportunity afforded by a Sea port town to receive and distribute such books." He was shortly purchased by a Mobile, Alabama slaveowner. By about October 1831, however, Cowan had been implicated in a local conspiracy in which his literacy again may have played an important part. One of the conspirators declared "that a letter had been received from Mobile Stating that there would be a war soon between the Whites and the Blacks. Tis possible that this fellow Jacob Cowan communicated this intelligence and that he had Secretly excited and encouraged the Conspiracy of which they were found guilty" (McRae to Police of Mobile, November 3, 1831, and David Crawford to Governor John Gale Jr., Mobile, November 18, 1831; both in Rachleff, "Document," 101, 102).

56. McRae to Owen, August 7, 1830.

57. *Boston Daily Courier,* August 12 and 26, 1830.

58. Governor Owen to the Police Officers of the Principal Towns in the State, Raleigh, August 19, 1830, Letterbook, 1828–30, vol. 28, North Carolina State Archives.

59. L. D. Henry, Magistrate of Police of Fayetteville, to Governor Owen, Fayetteville, September 3, 1830, Letterbook, 1828–30, vol. 28, North Carolina State Archives.

enslavement in the New Bern region two years earlier, was recaptured and held in a jail in the same area with a number of other long-standing runaways. One evening the wife of the jailer eavesdropped on the men and learned of an extensive network of slaves and runaways conspiring throughout eastern North Carolina. One branch of this system connected with Wilmington through "a fellow named Derry . . . [who had] brought some ofthose pamphlets" to New Bern and possibly as far north as Elizabeth City.[60] The men stated that a number of captains had been selected and "that they had runners or messengers to go between Wilmington, Newbern & Elizabeth City, to 'carry word'—& to report to them."

This was no mere braggadocio. Runaways in this region were profuse and had plagued authorities and slaveholders for decades.[61] Dense swamps and pine barrens offered a multitude of safe "haunts" in which runaways gathered, sometimes creating settled encampments and arming themselves. Draining of these extensive swamps had only begun in the early nineteenth century. Most runaways knew of a number of these havens and linked themselves together: the conspirators above often collected near New Bern at Brice's or Price's Creek, familiar to all runaways in the district. As in 1795 and 1821, the runaways periodically organized themselves into such a threat that only the military could suppress them. Advertisements for their apprehension attest to the runaways' striking mobility.[62] They moved regularly and effortlessly between such towns as Wilmington, Fayetteville, New Bern, and their hinterlands, and usually with the assistance of their fellow slaves, especially those working the region's innumerable rivers and tributaries. Traveling to points north of New Bern along the coast was equally common. A trip to Elizabeth City near the Virginia line was no problem, nor was one to Raleigh. Advertisements for runaways also made it clear that they were often aided by non-runaways who usually knew where their lairs were. Communication and commonality of interest between the two groups was impressive and would be key in extending the *Appeal*'s circulation.[63]

Many of these runaways were repeaters. Notable among them was Tom

60. J. Burgwyn to Governor Owen, New Bern, November 15, 1830, Letterbook, 1828–30, vol. 28, North Carolina State Archives.

61. Anyone doubting their numbers should read the painstaking documentation of slave runaways in Freddie L. Parker, ed., *Stealing a Little Freedom: Advertisements for Slave Runaways in North Carolina, 1791–1840* (New York: Garland Publishing, 1994). For example, see ibid., 563–669, for runaways in the state's southeastern region. Of course, this book cannot account for the many unadvertised runaways.

62. Throughout Parker, *Stealing a Little Freedom.*

63. See, for example, David S. Cecelski, "The Shores of Freedom: The Maritime Underground Railroad in North Carolina, 1800–1861," *North Carolina Historical Review* 71 (April 1994), 179, 181, 197–99.

Whitfield, held in the same jail with Moses and one of the key figures in the conspiracy. Tom, an accomplished house painter, was described as a "most notorious bad character," had run away no less than three times since 1821, and had recently been recaptured. Abner, another captured runaway, had been out for eight or nine years and was also a captain.[64] Tom, among many others, was known to "lurk" about "Gastons Island, on Price's Creek," where he had gathered a number of rebellious runaways, and was coordinated with others who had collected on the Newport River and near Wilmington. Individuals such as Tom and Abner were deeply disaffected with slavery and found it extremely difficult to manufacture even a veneer of submission to it. They were familiar with the underground world of runaways and with the network binding them together throughout coastal North Carolina. Tom, a skilled artisan, may also have been literate and able to read "those pamphlets" from Wilmington whose movement he oversaw. Indeed, his exposure to the *Appeal* may well have transformed him from being a mere irritant to local slaveholders to becoming a committed ideologue who sought to organize a cadre of similarly motivated runaways to threaten the institution of slavery regionally. While not seeking Tom specifically, he was the sort of person, like Cowan, whom Walker wanted to reach because of his likely receptivity to the pamphlet's message and his capacity to circulate it broadly.

By late 1830, white authorities throughout eastern North Carolina were increasingly worried about a possible slave insurrection; their anxieties focused especially on Walker's pamphlet and the threat posed by runaways. The rebel leaders conspired to begin the uprising before or during Christmas festivities and fully believed that once they initiated action "the other negroes would then rise and help them." The white reprisals in Wilmington after the *Appeal*'s arrival during the summer of 1830, however, led them to postpone moving until after the new year. The plan outlined above was given added credence when officials went to some of the hidden sites identified by Moses and found houses, food, and weapons. At one spot, "a place of rendezvous for numbers," eleven houses were burned. In another, screws for loading guns were found buried, and a nearby white woman had regularly prepared and hidden beef for runaways. Officers in the New Bern region were certain that "a conspiracy among the black people of this and the neighbouring counties exists, for the purpose of exciting an insurrection."[65]

64. Burgwyn to Governor Owen, November 15, 1830; Parker, *Stealing a Little Freedom*, 632, 647, 659. By April 1831 Whitfield was gone again (Parker, 773).

65. J. Burgwyn and Jno. J. Pasteur to Governor Owen, New Bern, November 15, 1830, Letter Book, 1828–30, vol. 28. Slaves involved in this plot also probably planned to take advantage of the social disruption created in coastal North Carolina by the celebration at Christmastime of Jonkonnu, an Afro-Caribbean ritual introduced into the region sometime in

People from nearby counties also complained about outliers. Representatives of Lenoir and Wayne Counties worried in late 1830 about large numbers of blacks who congregated in unpatrolled regions of the counties.[66] At the same time, petitioners from southeastern North Carolina were even more frank and anxious:

> The petition of sundry Inhabitants of the Counties of Sampson Bladen New Hanover and Duplin humbly sheweth that our slaves are become almost uncontroulable they go and come when and where they please and if an Attempt is made to correct them they fly to the Woods and there Continue for Months and Years committing grievous depredations on Our Cattle hogs and sheep and many other things. And as patrols are of no use on Account of the danger they subject themselves to and their property. Not long since three patrols two of which for Executing their duty had their dwelling and Out houses burnt down, the other his fodder stacks all burnt.[67]

Runaways in 1830 found boldness in their numbers and security and mobility in the numerous and interconnected refuges that ran throughout southeastern and coastal North Carolina. Whites worried about their property and social stability were not overreacting when they proposed the raising of large militias in 1830 to pursue the outliers into their fastnesses and shoot the ones who did not submit immediately. They were responding realistically to the particularly pronounced threat runaways posed in this region in 1830 and with the knowledge of their menace over the past decades.[68] Walker seems to have known of their presence and capacities as well.

---

the late eighteenth or early nineteenth century. Jonkonnu gave its slave practitioners the opportunity over several days to dress in exorbitantly colored and arrayed clothes, to gather together in large groups while conducting their own dance through the streets of towns, and to solicit small favors, such as liquor, food, and money from local whites. Whites who were unwilling to make an offering or too poor to do so were often subjected to taunts and insults by the celebrants. The social inversion and temporary freedom allowed the slaves could create explosive social situations, as Elizabeth Fenn makes evident in her article "'A Perfect Equality Seemed to Reign': Slave Society and Jonkonnu," *North Carolina Historical Review* 65 (April 1988), 127–53.

66. General Assembly Session Records, November 1830–January 1831, Box 6, "Petitions," North Carolina State Archives.

67. Ibid.

68. Historians tend to overlook the degree to which runaways and their communities have risen at particular times in America to become socially very threatening, opting instead to understand them as irritating to slaveholders but otherwise isolated and posing no threat to slavery or local society. The major exception to this interpretation is Herbert Aptheker's seminal essay "Maroons Within the Present Limits" (1939).

In the New Bern and Washington area, authorities watched the black population apprehensively. A strong possibility exists that the *Appeal* in fact reached New Bern as early as September 1830.[69] But by December, alerted to the circulation of the *Appeal* in counties below and on edge about the approaching holidays and the relaxation of regulations, officials banned all unsupervised meetings of blacks. Nevertheless, on about December 10 "a Quaker . . . preached in the Methodist Meeting House to a Congregation composed amongst others of many Slaves."[70] John Gray Blount, a prominent local citizen and state legislator, recounted:

> His observations respecting our Slaves were highly improper and most of them say he used the following strong language "that the Slaves of the South were a degraded & oppressed People that the just judgment or vengeance of God was now hanging over the heads of their masters on account of it and that the time would soon come when they would all be free."[71]

The similarity of the sermon's language to that in the *Appeal* was not lost on Blount and his associates.

To add to the anxiety New Bern citizens had, "a negro well clothed & with plenty of money who says he belongs to a man in Columbia S.C." arrived in town from New York at the same time that the Quaker passed through. His claim of seeking his wife in the North and then having made arrangements with his owner to return, which secured him his current pass, was treated with great suspicion by local officials, especially after this young and healthy man suddenly became so lame he could walk no more. But Blount was even more suspicious about

> his coming to this place to get to Columbia when there is scarcely a week when Vessells are not passing from new york to Charleston & also the additional one of his pass fixing the 1st of January for him to be at Columbia which would make it seem necessary for him to be in motion about Christmas, the time when slaves have the greatest lattitude and he could best communicate to them his business.[72]

69. Charles Edward Morris, "Panic and Reprisal: Reaction in North Carolina to the Nat Turner Insurrection, 1831," *North Carolina Historical Review* 62 (January 1985), 45.

70. John Gray Blount to Joseph B. Hinton, Washington, December 13, 1830, in David T. Morgan, ed., *The John Gray Blount Papers,* 4 vols. (Raleigh: North Carolina Department of Cultural Resources, 1982), 4:542–43.

71. Blount to Hinton, December 14, 1830, in ibid., 4:544.

72. Ibid., 544–45.

The prospect of an unknown black male from New York—the probable source of some of the copies of the *Appeal* in the state—moving about the low country at a time when regulations among slaves were relaxed was simply too disquieting for Blount.

Blount may also have been concerned about the fact that in New Bern resided one of North Carolina's two agents for *The Rights of All,* John C. Stanley. While a few months earlier he may not have known of the journal, by early September, one of the state's leading newspapers—the *Cape Fear Recorder*—carried two prominent articles about *The Rights of All* and its two North Carolina agents. The *Recorder* was quick to observe that there "is now no doubt in our minds that a conspiracy for exciting insurrection in the South is carrying on, by the free coloured people of the North . . . and that emissaries have been dispersed, *for some time,* throughout the Southern States, for the purpose of disseminating false principles and infusing the poison of discontent." The leading tools in this covert circulation were *The Rights of All* and that "execrable pamphlet," the *Appeal.* The *Recorder* was certain that a handful of free blacks in North Carolina such as Stanley were "giving countenance to pernicious publications." Adding to that fear was the fact that the other agent, Louis Sheridan of Elizabethtown, promptly wrote a letter to the *Recorder* and disavowed any current connection with the "mischievous publication" or with its "principles subversive of law and order." His earlier involvement with *Freedom's Journal* he explained was intended only to promote the moral improvement of free blacks. However, his assertion that he "was not aware that David Walker . . . was one of the authorised agents of the paper" could only have been false: Walker's name was always listed with his in the box for agents.[73]

Other events further heightened tensions. A friend of Blount's in Raleigh wrote to him that a black woman in Hillsborough had told some white children "that the negroes were to rise & kill all the white men— some of the handsomest of the white women would be spared for wives for the leaders."[74] In nearby Chapel Hill a white preacher who was probably an itinerant secretly assembled some local blacks one evening, but "students found it out, & went & found him inflaming the worst passions of human nature—& from his baggage he was suspected, & charged with having Walkers pamphlets."[75] Fortunately for him, he somehow managed to escape. Blount's correspondent, in the same letter, then recounted how a black man replied to a letter in which a prominent Presbyterian

73. *Cape Fear Recorder,* September 3 and 10, 1830. For list of agents in *The Rights of All,* see, for example, June 12, 1829.

74. Hinton to Blount, December 20, 1830, in Morgan, *John Gray Blount Papers,* 4:546.

75. Hinton to Blount, December 23, 1830, in ibid., 547.

minister of Raleigh put forth a plan for colonizing 400 blacks in Liberia. Governor Owen had recently described him as "an intelligent free man of Bladen County," a county adjacent to New Hanover.

> He wrote for an answer that he would not go & the people of Colour were fools to go—that if the United States would free the negroes & give them a territory for them to colonize within their limits—or in Canada—they would go there—if they would give them no freed territory—they must free the negroes & admit them to all the rights of Citizens & amalgamate with the whites without distinction—or the whites must take their certain doom—for come sooner or later it would be said. Very nearly the identical views & language of Walkers pamphlet. We are on a mine, it would appear—the match, I hope will be snatched from the destructive hand.

Apparently something did explode near New Bern on or about December 25, 1830. According to newspaper reports, "sixty armed slaves" had assembled in a swamp near New Bern and selected Christmas morning as the time to commence their rebellion. The local militia, however, was alerted, surrounded the swamp, and "killed the whole party." Disturbances ensued in the Wilmington region, where it was reported—despite efforts to conceal it—that "there has been much shooting of negroes in this neighborhood recently, in consequence of symptoms of liberty having been discovered among them." James Barbadoes, a friend of Walker's in Boston, repeated in *The Liberator* in February 1831 that sixty slaves had been killed in New Bern the past Christmas and that it was "owing to Walker's inflammatory pamphlet."[76]

By December 1830, social relations in North Carolina seemed upside down, and some pointed to David Walker's pamphlet as the subversive lever. In the same month, a committee appointed by the governor to investigate the recent disturbances reported:

> An extensive combination now exists to excite in the minds of the slaves and coloured persons of this, and the other slave holding States, feelings and opinions subversive of good order, and utterly incompatible with the relation in which we stand towards that class of our population. . . .
>
> Designs have been certainly contemplated, and perhaps plans actually formed, to subvert the relation of master and slave. . . .

76. *Boston Evening Transcript*, January 10, 1831; *The Liberator*, February 12, 1831; Aptheker, *American Negro Slave Revolts*, 289–90.

The actual detection of the circulation of the incendiary publication, . . . and the accidental but partial discovery of designs, perhaps not fully developed or digested, which have been entertained by some slaves at points of the State remote from each other, . . . leave no doubt on the minds of your Committee, that the time has arrived . . . to act with firmness and decision.[77]

Such fears prompted North Carolina, along with a number of other states, to reinforce its laws against slave literacy and independent religious activity and against the mobility of free blacks and their ability to interact with slaves. Nevertheless, acts of resistance would remain at a high level throughout 1831 among African Americans in North Carolina.

The *Appeal*'s appearance in other places in the South was noted as well. On March 27, 1830, police in Charleston, South Carolina, arrested Edward Smith, a white mariner from Boston, for distributing several copies of the *Appeal* among local black longshoremen.[78] Seized soon after a black informant set him up to be overheard by the captain of the guard, Smith stated in sworn testimony before the Guard Committee that he had been visited aboard his brig in Boston "by a decent looking black man whom he believed to be a Bookseller & that he required of him that he Should give them [i.e., the pamphlets] secretly to the Black people." Smith "consented & promised the man that he would do as directed," even though he knew nothing about the pamphlets' contents and only later read a few lines and discovered "that it was something in regard to the imposition upon negroes." But, loyal to his pledge despite his vague knowledge of the questionable contents, he distributed three to six pamphlets among the blacks who unloaded the ship's cargo.[79] Thus at least a few copies reached the local black community.

Smith's claim to have had little knowledge of the contents of the pamphlets and to be distributing it primarily because he had promised to do so was similar to that advanced by the white mariner in Savannah.[80] The argument is not convincing. Almost all the figures caught with copies of

77. General Assembly Session Records, November 1830–January 1831, Box 6, "Joint Committee Reports," North Carolina State Archives; also reproduced in Charles L. Coon, *The Beginnings of Public Education in North Carolina: A Documentary History, 1790–1840*, 2 vols. (Raleigh, N.C., 1908), 1:477–78.

78. William H. and Jane H. Pease, "Walker's *Appeal* Comes to Charleston: A Note and Documents," *Journal of Negro History* 59 (July 1974), 287–92. Unless otherwise noted, all of the following discussion on the *Appeal* in Charleston comes from this source.

79. While Smith claimed to the authorities that he brought only three copies to Charleston (290), he was overheard saying to the black informant that he had carried six (289).

80. The apprehended mariner in Savannah actually disavowed all knowledge of the pamphlet's contents.

the *Appeal* indicated that they were doing something suggested to them by another, more understanding party. The free black caught circulating copies in Richmond claimed to have asked a white gentleman what to do with them, thus casting himself as a submissive character who obeyed instructions from whites. Jacob Cowan in Wilmington acknowledged receipt of the pamphlets and the letter but maintained he did not obey the instructions. Smith's defense, which portrayed him as less intelligent than he was, was largely in line with these other descriptions of personal passivity. The repetition of this form in places remote from each other suggests that it may have been contrived in advance.

It is very possible that Smith was approached in Boston by the same person who approached the white steward of the boat bound for Savannah. John Eli, a friend and political associate of Walker's, had contacted the white steward; he, Walker, or an associate could easily have done it for the Charleston boat too. Their interest in white sailors for these two ports can in part be explained by the extreme suspicion in which black mariners in the North were held by local authorities in these two towns. Indeed, in 1822, after the Vesey plot, Charleston had passed a law that required all black sailors entering the harbor to be quarantined in the local workhouse at the ship captain's expense for the duration of their ship's visit there. Smith even commented on this inconvenience when he noted to another black man that the removal of the ship's black cook "was a great Shame as it turned Every thing into Confusion on board the vessel."[81] A black sailor in Charleston after 1822 had almost no chance of having enough time to distribute material. Savannah, which enacted its own quarantine law soon after the discovery of the *Appeal* there, was only slightly better in that it did not yet have formal machinery for removing black seamen. Walker was fully aware of this problem at certain Southern ports. In a new footnote added to his third edition—published in the first part of 1830 and thus after the events in Savannah and probably Charleston—Walker asked:

> Why do the Slave-holders or Tyrants of America and their advocates fight so hard to keep my brethren from receiving and reading my Book of Appeal to them? . . . Why do they search vessels, &c. when entering the harbours of tyrannical States, to see if any of my Books can be found, for fear that my brethren will get them to read?[82]

81. Pease, "Walker's *Appeal* Comes to Charleston," 290.
82. *Appeal,* 72n.

He knew that a white sailor with materials simply would not attract the concern a black sailor would. Thus Smith and the other mariner were probably targeted to carry the booklets, because they were white.

Of course, the two white men might have had some ideological reasons for assisting Walker, but that would be difficult to determine. Sailors, however, had long been known for their tendency to become involved with unconventional ideas and subversive political activities. In part, their very mobility could expose them to cultures and different ways of thinking, which more geographically rooted people would find threatening. The rise of the Seamen's Bethel Movement in the early 1820s was, among other things, an effort among philanthropists and ministers to regularize the lives and thinking of these mobile laborers. Bethels would be opened in all ports to provide sailors with facilities to shield them from the pervasive temptations of alcohol and prostitution. Once in the Bethels, the sailors would receive regular exposure to Christian doctrine and be encouraged to fulfill their religious duties daily, both in port and at sea. To reinforce this pattern established in the Bethels, sailors were given Bibles and numerous religious tracts to take with them on voyages. These items were also distributed to ships' captains to be placed on board.

Early proponents of the Bethel Movement were quite aware that sailors often filled their free time on ship with reading, and they sought to regulate what the mariners read. A report of the Boston Seamen's Friend Society in 1831 observed: "Sailors, though often careless in port, where there is much to occupy their attention, are very easily induced to read when at sea, and hence it is important that every vessel should be furnished with some suitable books."[83]

Otherwise, they feared irreverent or subversive readings would be chosen. A minister in Portland, Maine, recounted in 1821 how a young sailor, scared by his use of oaths, asked another sailor for a book to help him overcome the problem. Hoping for "a Testament or Bible," he was instead offered "a French novel by Rousseau."[84] Edward Smith himself stated that he did not have any idea of the *Appeal*'s contents until he skimmed a few pages during free time on board ship. Members of the Bethel Movement wanted to keep sailors' minds and conversations from going in unconventional directions, by attempting to remove from ships all literature that

83. *Third Annual Report of the Board of Directors of the Boston Seamen's Friend Society* (Boston, 1831), 11. Copy available at the Rare Book Room, Boston Public Library.

84. Edward Payson, D.D., *An Address to Seamen, Delivered at Portland, October 28, 1821; At the request of the Portland Auxiliary Marine Bible Society* (copy available at the Boston Public Library Rare Book Room).

deviated from their conservative understanding of Christian doctrine and responsibility. They were far from fully successful.

Racial mixing on board ships and in ports was very common and could foster sympathetic bonds between blacks and whites. Sailors were often involved in assisting runaway slaves in port towns, and it was not at all unusual for whites as well as blacks to participate. Former slave William Grimes made his escape from Savannah in the early 1820s through just such a racially mixed network of Boston sailors.[85] One British officer, Basil Hall, observed:

> Perhaps the only place in the world where a black has, to all intents and purposes, an equal chance with the rest of mankind, is on board a ship-of-war. He is there subjected to the same discipline, has the same favour shown if he behaves well, and suffers a like punishment for the like faults. I think it's generally allowed in the English navy, that under like circumstances, black seamen are as useful and as trust-worthy as the rest of the crew.[86]

J. S. Buckingham, a British journalist who visited the United States in the 1840s, made similar observations about a frigate docked in Norfolk. He found that "no distinction was made between black and white" and that "the white seamen [did not] evince the slightest reluctance to be associated with them [i.e., the blacks] on terms of the most perfect equality in the discharge of their duties."[87] Most in the American merchant marine at the time would have agreed with this outlook on the relative racial equality reigning on shipboard.

The rise of the Bethel Movement at this time was intended to counter among sailors thinking and socializing considered threatening by some prominent upholders of the prevailing social order. The Bethels encour-

85. Grimes, *Life,* 50–53. For numerous examples in North Carolina, see Cecelski, "Shores of Freedom," 176–78, 188–204.

86. Basil Hall, *Travels in North America in the Years 1827 & 1828,* 2 vols. (Philadelphia, 1829), 2:213.

87. J. S. Buckingham, *The Slave States of America,* 2 vols. [London, 1842], 2:471–72). For a stimulating and detailed discussion of how black sailors "partially and temporarily circumvented the racist norms of American society" through work in the maritime trades, see W. Jeffrey Bolster, "'To Feel Like a Man': Black Seamen in the Northern States, 1800–1860," *Journal of American History* 76 (March 1990), 1173–99. For a broader examination of the rough equality prevailing among black and white sailors in the eighteenth-century Atlantic world, see Marcus Rediker's pathbreaking book, *Between the Devil and the Deep Blue Sea: Merchant Seamen, Pirates, and the Anglo-American Maritime World, 1700–1750* (Cambridge: Cambridge University Press, 1987), and Peter Linebaugh and Marcus Rediker, "The Many-Headed Hydra: Sailors, Slaves, and the Atlantic Working Class in the Eighteenth Century," *Journal of Historical Sociology* 3 (September 1990), 225–52.

aged racial separation by initially serving only white sailors and only later creating segregated homes for blacks.[88] They wanted to keep sailors from the "dangerous" ideas circulating in ports and on ships and from promiscuous mixing of various sorts—sexual, racial, and political—which characterized marine life. An extensive effort to bring conservative Christian doctrine to mariners was in part intended to reduce the possibility that they would accept these threatening ideas and engage in subversive or insubordinate activities.[89] Edward Smith and the unidentified white sailor in Savannah were likely exposed to such a subculture and were perhaps even deliberate participants in some of its subversive actions. Walker and his associates sought mariners who had been shaped by this subversive shipboard experience as allies in the critical seaborne wing of the *Appeal*'s distribution.

On March 8, 1830, four blacks were arrested in New Orleans on charges of circulating the *Appeal*. A local free black shop owner, Robert Smith, was accused "of circulating or loaning out" the pamphlet. Neither the number of copies involved nor the mode of delivery was clear; Smith's account of how he came to possess them was "confused and unsatisfactory." Another free black, Samuel Dundass, was connected with two slaves, one named Ned and the other unidentified, who had a copy of the *Appeal*. All "gave different and contradictory answers" to queries about their receipt of it and relationship to it. As was the case with so many of the *Appeal*'s other agents, all four men were literate.[90]

The pamphlet arrived in New Orleans at an anxious time. The public had learned in December 1829 that a schooner from Norfolk headed for New Orleans with 197 slaves was almost commandeered by a number of them when they revolted. A similar plot around the same time on another

88. The first home for black seamen appears to have been established in New York City in 1837 under the financial auspices of the American Seamen's Friend Society. It was managed by William P. Powell, a black sailor who was sympathetic to the plight of black sailors and abolitionism. See Philip S. Foner, "William P. Powell: Militant Champion of Black Seamen," in *Essays in Afro-American History* (Philadelphia: Temple University Press, 1978), 88–90.

89. A Charleston newspaper argued in 1821 for the utility of religion in regulating sailors in very frank terms. Concerned with serious problems over piracy along the southeastern seaboard, the paper advanced that "if there be no other restraints imposed upon their dishonesty, than such as arise from a slavish fear, there is but a very imperfect security indeed against mutiny, piracy, murder, and all the dreadful and enormous crimes committed on the high seas" (*Charleston Courier*, January 18, 1821). A number of these pirates were American sailors who had jumped ship rather than continue with the brutal rule and economic exploitation common among many captains. Pirate ships also regularly had racially mixed crews. For example, a boat captured in the Caribbean in May 1821 had twenty-eight white crewmembers and ten black (*Charleston Courier*, May 19, 1821).

90. *Baton Rouge Gazette*, March 20, 1830; *Boston Daily Courier*, April 1, 1830.

New Orleans brig was discovered by white authorities at the last moment. By early 1830, fears about the hundreds of nonresident slaves and free blacks who arrived weekly in the busy port were mounting.[91] Suspicious fires flared up simultaneously in the city. In about February 1830 one British traveler counted "three incendiary fires" while he was there for a month and noted that people were "in a constant state of alarm." He blamed the problem on the brutal treatment of the slaves by whites, and he believed that soon the South would be overwhelmed "with some dreadful calamity." On March 12 a slave named Jean Baptiste was cornered as he was about to ignite a fire in a shop. Authorities hoped he "would make some discovery concerning the cause of the many fires, which have for some time past desolated our city." Helpful or not, he was executed soon afterward.[92]

The *Appeal* heightened the public anxiety and may have furthered the unrest as well. Conspiring and resistance flourished in March and April soon after its discovery. Just before March 30 a number of African Americans and a handful of white allies rose north of New Orleans in the vicinity of Opelousas. Nineteen blacks and several whites fell in the conflict, and fifteen of the ringleaders were executed after the rebels' defeat. A plan for a general uprising against the whites was also uncovered, and one slave was executed for murdering his master. The latter conspirators may have been connected with the arsonists in New Orleans.[93]

The arrival of the *Appeal* fueled aggression against freedom of the press and speech and against free blacks. The Louisiana State Legislature passed two very restrictive acts in March 1830. The first threatened anyone who might "write, print, publish, or distribute any thing *having a tendency* to create discontent among the free coloured population of this state, or insubordination among the slaves therein" with life imprisonment or death. Equally condemned and punished was "any public discourse" intended to create any of these ends. Legislators also reinforced laws against slave literacy. While these laws were meant to make capital the dissemination of any publications like the *Appeal,* its principal local victim was *Le Liberal,* "the only liberal paper at New Orleans [and] which occasionally inserted articles favourable to the black population." It along

91. *Boston Courier,* December 31, 1829. One British observer, S. A. O'Ferrall, estimated that "within the last two months [of late 1829/early 1830], 5000 negros have been sold here," giving a vivid picture of the number of nonresident blacks brought constantly into the port. S. A. O'Ferrall, *A Ramble of Six Thousand Miles Through the United States of America* (London, 1832), 197.

92. O'Ferrall, *A Ramble,* 196; *Baton Rouge Gazette,* March 20, 1830; *Niles' Register,* April 24, 1830.

93. *Boston Daily Courier,* April 26, 1830; *Niles' Register,* April 24, 1830.

with any speech or writings raising even the slightest question about slavery and white superiority were suppressed.[94]

The *Appeal* and its free black champions equally contributed to the passage of ferocious anti–free black legislation, for which Louisiana quickly gained notoriety. Following the example of Cincinnati, which attempted to legislate the removal of its free black population in late 1829, and fearing a mounting and uncontrolled black population, Louisiana lawmakers passed acts expelling from the state all free blacks who had moved there after 1825. Those refusing to depart and those attempting to migrate there risked imprisonment and hard labor for life. The legislature also levied harsh penalties against any free blacks who entered the port as seamen and did not depart with their vessel. While these acts were of dubious constitutionality and—like Ohio's—proved largely impossible to enforce, they made vivid the fears Walker's work generated. By the end of 1830 his remarkable capacity to circulate the pamphlet in some of the farthest reaches of the South was well established and dreaded.[95]

David Walker was especially interested in disseminating the *Appeal* in the South, where he believed its message of resistance and divine concern was most needed. Yet the work also moved in the North, and with relatively greater ease. The Boston community, white and black, had been aware of the pamphlet ever since controversy around it developed, for it was noted in local newspapers. But one Boston newspaper emphasized its impact:

> Since the publication of that flagitious pamphlet, Walker's Appeal, for the consequences of which, if we mistake not, some fanatical white man will have to answer, we have noticed a marked difference in the deportment of our colored population. It is evident they have read this pamphlet, nay, *we know* that the larger portion of them have read it, or *heard* it read, and that they glory in its principles, as if it were a star in the east, guiding them to freedom and emancipation.[96]

The Reverend Amos Beman, minister of the African Congregational Church in New Haven by the late 1830s, remembered that the circulation of the *Appeal, The Liberator,* and William Lloyd Garrison's *Thoughts on African Colonization* among blacks in the region of New Haven and Mid-

94. Stuart, *Three Years in North America,* 2:208–9, 211; O'Ferrall, *A Ramble,* 197–200.

95. Stuart, *Three Years in North America,* 2:209–10; *Richmond Enquirer,* March 30, 1830; *Boston Daily Courier,* May 21, 1830.

96. *Boston Daily Evening Transcript,* September 28, 1830.

dletown in Connecticut in the early 1830s gave them the courage to take a public stand against the colonization movement.[97] The booklet also appeared in Providence, where a copy was owned by a member probably of a local white family, Jane Congdon.[98] It also must have circulated in Philadelphia. In early issues of *The Liberator,* "Leo" of Philadelphia engaged in a heated exchange with "J.I.W." over the impact and value of the pamphlet, indicating its circulation at least among that city's black intelligentsia.[99] It is certain that it circulated in New York City and other important Northern towns, even though there is no hard evidence of that now.

This paucity of material on the *Appeal* in the North probably points to the relatively greater emphasis Walker placed on circulation in the South and to the fact that local Northern authorities were much less threatened by its presence when it did arise and consequently took little if any note of it. Moreover, because of its volatile reputation—even among abolitionists—blacks in the North who were familiar with it were hesitant to discuss it openly.

Thus Walker's *Appeal* made appearances in the United States from New Orleans to Boston. The scale of its identifiable circulation is impressive, but it still leaves open questions about how much further it penetrated into Southern slave society and just what the impact of that penetration was. Gauging the breadth of circulation beyond the incidents that were clearly substantiated, and determining just what happened to copies of the pamphlet that were not retrieved by authorities in the South or were simply never discovered, is extremely difficult.

Yet some possibilities encourage judicious speculation. One was noted above, where runaways and itinerant preachers distributed the pamphlet

---

97. Warner, *New Haven Negroes,* 100; Scrapbook II, p. 87, Amos Beman Papers, James Weldon Johnson Collection, Beinecke Rare Book Library, Yale University, New Haven.

98. See rare copy of the first edition of the *Appeal* at the Library Company of Philadelphia. In it is inscribed

> Jane Congdon
> my Book
> in Providence
> 1830

A search of available Providence directories from 1824 to 1836 did not yield a Jane Congdon. No black Congdons at all were found. However, a number of white Congdons were listed, several of them appearing to have been moderately prosperous; one owned a hardware store, two others owned a metal manufactory. One Hodge Congdon, a black man, was on the founding committee of the African Union Meeting House, and this Baptist church eventually moved, curiously enough, to Congdon Street. The white family of that name must have been sufficiently prominent to merit having a street named after them. See Cottrol, *Afro-Yankees,* 58; and *Creative Survival: The Providence Black Community in the 19th Century* (Providence: Rhode Island Black Heritage Society, 1984), 55.

99. *The Liberator,* January 29, and February 5 and 19, 1831.

along the eastern seaboard in North Carolina. Preachers in particular were feared because of the sanction their stature in the community could lend to the *Appeal* and because their frequent mobility gave them the opportunity to circulate it. In Virginia in December 1831, Governor John Floyd, referring specifically to the recent Nat Turner uprising, but also in general to the numerous rebellious acts and plots that had occurred in his state and in North Carolina from 1829 to 1831, exclaimed:

> The most active among ourselves, in stirring up the spirit of revolt, have been the negro preachers. They had acquired great ascendancy over the minds of their fellows, and infused all their opinions, which had prepared them for the development of the final design: . . . ; [they] have been the channels through which the inflammatory papers and pamphlets, brought here by the agents and emissaries from other States, have been circulated amongst our slaves.[100]

Floyd had been especially concerned about the circulation of the *Appeal* and *The Liberator,* which he considered instrumental in knitting together the spirit of resistance pervading Virginia and North Carolina at that time. Concern over the possible role of black preachers in distributing the *Appeal* was also very strong in these two states because they had many more of these figures than did states farther south. Along with the preachers and outliers, other likely members of such a network were the numerous mobile black laborers who existed not only throughout eastern North Carolina but also in various areas of Virginia, South Carolina, and Georgia. All these figures had a tradition of participating in underground communication networks in the South and could have provided vital support in broadening the pamphlet's distribution (see Chapter 2).

An even more difficult route to follow, but perhaps a more fruitful one, is to consider how much members of black communities were exposed to the *Appeal* and its ideas by having literate individuals read it to them. This could have increased geometrically the number of individuals exposed to it. Walker placed great hope on motivating literate people to share the *Appeal* with those unable to read it, and in several instances apparently targeted such people to receive the pamphlet. He may have known much more about social reading patterns in the black community than could be evident to us by simply reading the *Appeal* or even considering where he distributed the pamphlet. Large groups of people in various

---

100. Communication of Governor John Floyd to the Virginia Senate and House of Delegates, December 6, 1831, in *Journal of the House of Delegates of the Commonwealth of Virginia* (Richmond, Va., 1831), 10.

black communities gathering together to have materials read to them was not at all uncommon, especially when the overwhelming majority of these people were illiterate. For example, the Boston newspaper cited above stated quite confidently: "The larger portion of them have read it, or *heard* it read." The Reverend Amos Beman participated in large groups that assembled in Middletown, Connecticut, to hear the pamphlet read in one sitting. The following passage makes clear how that work and *The Liberator* fortified them for new political organizing.

> It was in Middletown that we saw the first number of the *Liberator,* and its clarion voice sank deep into our mind. That paper, and "Walker's Appeal," and the Address of Mr. Garrison, and his "Thoughts on Colonization," were read and re-read until their words were stamped in letters of fire upon our soul.—The first time we ever spoke in a public meeting was in that city, in behalf of the *Liberator,* and against the Colonization Society.[101]

A remarkable passage from one of a series of lengthy letters on the *Appeal* written by the anonymous author "V" in 1831 lends even further weight to the belief that such reading in a public forum was a widespread pattern in black communities. After stating that lawmakers in the South were wise in their wickedness by making it penal to teach slaves to read, he explained:

> [A] few years since, being in a slave state, I chanced one morning, very early, to look through the curtains of my chamber window, which opened upon a back yard. I saw a mulatto with a newspaper in his hand, surrounded by a score of colored men, who were listening, open mouthed, to a very inflammatory article the yellow man was reading. Sometimes the reader dwelt emphatically on particular passages, and I could see his auditors stamp and clench their hands. I afterwards learned that the paper was published in New-York, and addressed to the blacks. It is but reasonable to suppose that such scenes are of common occurrence in the slave

101. Beman Papers, Scrapbook II, p. 87, Beinecke Rare Book Library, Yale University. See also Warner, *New Haven Negroes,* 100. In the same article, Beman emphasized the great importance attached to public readings of inspiring works intended to fire blacks for antislavery organizing: "One of the last things which we did before we left to attend the Convention [of Colored Men in the State of Connecticut in September, 1854], was to read the Address of Wm. L. Garrison to the colored people of this country."

states, and it does not require the wisdom of Solomon to discern their tendency.[102]

The author's comment that it is "reasonable to suppose that such scenes are of common occurrence in the slave states" is amply supported by evidence from slave narratives. Like any other artisanal skill, literacy was a highly valued skill that not only benefitted the individual but also was often shared socially in communities that were largely illiterate. In the late eighteenth century, the slave divine Jupiter Hammon admonished African Americans who could read the Bible to read it to groups of the uneducated and tutor them in literacy. In the early 1830s before fleeing slavery, Frederick Douglass organized a clandestine Sabbath school in Maryland's Eastern Shore town of St. Michaels, where he and two other literate slaves taught and read to as many as forty illiterate slaves. A white man recollected from his childhood days on his father's South Carolina plantation how the crippled slave Dick taught himself how to read and passed many winter evenings reading the Bible and other religious literature to "sometimes a score or more" of his fellows from the quarters. A free black in New Orleans recalled how in 1859 word of John Brown's execution spread swiftly and far among blacks because unwitting whites gave newspapers to literate slaves, who would then secretly read them to the whole community. James Henry Hammond wrote in 1861 of the blacks on his large lowcountry plantation in Silver Bluff, South Carolina, that he had a dozen slaves who read as well as he did and that "they teach each other and I never interfere with it, though it is against the law." Clarence Mohr has noted about African American society in Civil War Georgia that "every city had numerous literate slaves and free blacks who were willing teachers and conveyors of news and information."[103] The

102. *The Liberator*, May 14, 1831. Also reprinted in full in Truman Nelson, *Documents of Upheaval: Selections from William Lloyd Garrison's the Liberator, 1831–1865* (New York: Hill & Wang, 1966), 14.

103. Jupiter Hammon, "An Address to the Negroes in the State of New York," in Porter, *Early Negro Writing*, 319–20; Frederick Douglass, *Narrative of the Life of Frederick Douglass, An American Slave*, ed. Benjamin Quarles (Cambridge, Mass.: Belknap Press, 1960), 112–14; J. G. Clinkscales, *On the Old Plantation: Reminiscences of His Childhood* (1916; reprint, New York: Negro Universities Press, 1969), 43–47; Janet Duitsman Cornelius, *"When I Can Read My Title Clear": Literacy, Slavery, and Religion in the Antebellum South* (Columbia: University of South Carolina Press, 1991), 84; Clarence Mohr, *On the Threshold of Freedom: Masters and Slaves in Civil War Georgia* (Athens: University of Georgia Press, 1986), 209; Drew Gilpin Faust, "Culture, Conflict, and Community: The Meaning of Power on an Ante-Bellum Plantation," *Journal of Social History* 14 (Fall 1980), 96 n. 26. Eugene Genovese (*Roll, Jordan, Roll*, 563) finds a similar availability of literate slaves to assist the illiterate and spread

role of these structures in the circulation of the *Appeal,* while extremely difficult to document, cannot be dismissed. Walker was surely at least aware of them.

Opportunities for slaves to learn how to read and write were always available. One route was the secretive one: the person used hidden readers and devious tactics to gain instruction from unwitting whites. The most famous person who took this route was Frederick Douglass. Blacks trained as artisans often had to learn how to cipher and how to do some basic reading. Favorite slaves were sometimes selected by owners to learn how to read, and literate slaves and free blacks often shared their knowledge with others of their race.

But perhaps the most common avenue to literacy for blacks was instruction by a white person who considered it their religious duty to teach their slaves how to read Scripture. Janet Cornelius, in a recent study of literacy among slaves, established the depth of this conviction among evangelical slaveholders throughout the South, many of whom felt the duty so deeply that they actively opposed efforts by state legislatures to proscribe slave literacy and education, even at times of panic such as that wrought by the arrival of the *Appeal.* Despite their deep-seated conservatism and unflagging commitment to slavery, the Scotch-Irish and Huguenot Protestants of the South Carolina upcountry fought a losing battle in the early 1830s against Whitemarsh Seabrook and the state's nullificationists to prevent passage of a law prohibiting slave literacy. Nevertheless, they regularly violated these laws privately, as did other white evangelicals throughout the South—such as Charles Colcock Jones of Georgia—who found that the laws were affronts to individual conscience and biblical mandates.[104]

In the upper South through the eighteenth century and later, Quakers, Methodists, and Baptists were particularly known for teaching their slaves how to read. In about 1820 an evangelical slave owner in Maryland so enraged his neighbors by teaching his many slaves to read the Bible that he was forced to go armed to his Sunday schools.[105] Soon after the *Appeal* reached North Carolina, debate in the state legislature over restricting slave literacy raised the issue of teaching slaves to read Scripture. A Mr. Dick of Guilford County, a region heavily settled by Quakers, argued against "that clause of the bill which prohibits Slaves from being taught to read."

---

political information, even in the most unfavorable and isolated environments, as in the Deep South's Black Belt.

104. See Cornelius, *"When I Can Read My Title Clear,"* esp. 37–58, 105–24.

105. Adam Hodgson, *Remarks During a Journey Through North America in the Years 1819, 1820, and 1821, in a Series of Letters* (New York, 1823), 217–18.

Many of his constituents . . . considered it to be their duty to teach their Servants to read, that they might obtain a knowledge of the Scriptures, and he thought if Slaves were not taught to write, so that they could hold no correspondence with each other, the purpose of the friends of the bill would be answered.[106]

But his position was lost to those who were convinced that the reading skills of slaves would be applied more regularly to works like Walker's pamphlet than to the Bible. Likewise, Governor John Floyd fretted after the Nat Turner uprising about the misdirected benevolence of "our females . . . [who] were persuaded that it was piety to teach negroes to read and write, to the end that they might read the Scriptures—many of them became tutoresses in Sunday Schools and, pious distributors of tracts, from the New York Tract Society."[107]

Governor Floyd had reason to voice fear. In the same letter, following the above passage, he wrote:

Then commenced the efforts of the black preachers, often from the pulpits these pamphlets and papers [i.e., from the New York Tract Society] were read—followed by the incendiary publications of Walker, Garrison and Knapp of Boston, these too with songs and hymns of a similar character were circulated read and commented upon—we resting in apathetic security until the Southampton affair.[108]

This passage embodied the three central fears of Southern authorities regarding slave literacy: reading was an inherently dangerous skill to teach blacks; black preachers through their combination of religious stature and not uncommon literacy could be a principal threat in fomenting revolt; literate blacks read to large groups of illiterates and thus facilitated the flow of information through underground channels. These fears were not unfounded; indeed, one literate slave, especially one with mobility, could potentially proselytize for revolt hundreds who then themselves could go out and recruit.[109] This sort of structure was actually rein-

106. *Raleigh Register,* December 9, 1830.

107. Governor John Floyd to Governor James Hamilton of South Carolina, Richmond, November 19, 1831 in Miscellaneous Mss. Collection, Box 88, John Floyd File, Library of Congress, Manuscript Division, Washington, D.C. This letter is also reprinted in Henry Irving Tragle, *The Southampton Slave Revolt of 1831: A Compilation of Source Material* (Amherst: University of Massachusetts Press, 1971), 275–76.

108. Floyd to Hamilton, November 19, 1831.

109. Thousands of miles away and nearly a century later, African revolutionaries demon-

forced in the late colonial era by Anglican missionaries of the Society for the Propagation of the Gospel who were established in towns along the eastern seaboard. They often trained one or two slaves to read the Bible and make simple interpretations of it, and then returned the students to their communities armed with Bibles and readers to instruct and read to their fellow slaves.[110] The church depended on literate slaves employing their skills for the benefit of the whole slave community.

Walker must have been aware of such social reading patterns within black communities in both the North and South. A report to the North Carolina legislature in December 1830 summarized in effect why states throughout the South at that time were cracking down swiftly against opportunities for blacks to gain literacy.

> One source of great evil . . . from which the most serious danger may be apprehended, is, the teaching slaves to read and write; thereby affording them facilities of intelligence and communication, inconsistent with their condition, destructive of their contentment and happiness, and dangerous to the community.[111]

Literacy among slaves, although possessed only by a very small minority, was probably nevertheless more widespread than current historians are inclined to acknowledge. Janet Duitsman Cornelius estimates that as many as 10 percent of antebellum slaves may have been literate.[112]

Of course, just as teaching slaves to read was no guarantee that they would confine their reading to specific texts such as the Bible, it also gave no certain assurance that their understanding and interpretation of Scripture would not vary from conventional conceptions of it held by the predominant white Protestant culture. Not only was the mere ability to read and spread information among their compatriots a threat, but their literacy also opened the possibility of an exploited people fundamentally reinterpreting central texts of their oppressors, especially a work as com-

---

strated exactly how this mechanism could work among a largely illiterate people. Jomo Kenyatta, leader of anticolonial actions against the British and future president of Kenya, recalled: "In 1921 Kenya nationalists, unable to read, would gather round a reader of [Marcus] Garvey's newspaper, the *Negro World,* and listen to an article two or three times. Then they would run various ways through the forest, carefully to repeat the whole, which they had memorised, to Africans hungry for some doctrine which lifted them from the servile consciousness in which Africans lived" (as quoted in Lawrence Levine, "Marcus Garvey and the Politics of Revitalization," in John Hope Franklin and August Meier, eds., *Black Leaders of the Twentieth Century* [Urbana: University of Illinois Press, 1982], 120).

110. This process is discussed at much greater length for Wilmington, North Carolina, in Chapter 1.

111. Coon, *Beginnings of Public Education in North Carolina,* 2:479.

112. Cornelius, *"When I Can Read My Title Clear,"* 8–9, 62–63.

plex as the Bible. Such reinterpretation could shape the extent as well as the character of the circulation among blacks of the *Appeal* and other contemporary ideologies of revolt. The ability to ground calls for resistance in a text as widely legitimated as the Bible could be critical in justifying those calls. Earlier discussions of the plots of Gabriel Prosser and Denmark Vesey have shown just how much emphasis was placed on this strategy.

In Charleston in 1710, Dr. Francis Le Jau, the resident representative of the Church of England, chose a number of slaves to receive a Christian education, which included learning to read and write. No sooner had he commenced, however, than "the best Scholar of all the Negroes in my Parish . . . was like to Create some Confusion among all the Negroes in this Country." The scenes of apocalyptic judgment in the Book of John "made an Impression upon his Spirit," and he spoke to his master and others about "a dismal time [when] the Moon wou'd be turned into Blood, and there would be dearth of darkness." This created much excitement among the local slaves, but Le Jau refused to acknowledge any other problem than that he had not "judgment enough to make good use of [his] Learning." He missed that this man was using his literacy to interpret the Bible in a way that would make sense out of his people's current oppression.[113]

James Habersham, one of Savannah's largest slaveholders, had a similar experience with one of his favored slaves, David. Habersham sent David to England to get a religious education and then serve as a missionary among Habersham's slaves. Yet once he returned and began his mission in 1775, he preached that "God would send Deliverance to the Negroes, from the power of their Masters, as He freed the Children of Israel from Egyptian Bondage."[114] David may also have been influenced by whites in Charleston using such imagery as the momentum toward revolution accelerated in the colonies. Concerned that David preach only a spiritual deliverance, Habersham returned him quickly to England. Despite his highly controlled religious education, David still pursued an interpretation of Scripture that rendered his education useless to his master and made David a potentially dangerous agitator.

The Bible always held the possibility of being converted into a subversive text legitimating resistance to corrupt authority or, at the very least,

---

113. Francis Le Jau to the Secretary, February 1, 1710, St. James Parish [Charleston District], in Frank J. Klingberg, ed., *The Carolina Chronicle of Dr. Francis Le Jau, 1706–1717* (Berkeley and Los Angeles: University of California Press, 1956), 70.

114. James Habersham to Robert Keen, May 11, 1775, Savannah, "The Letters of Hon. James Habersham, 1756–1775," in *Collections of the Georgia Historical Society*, vol. 6 (Savannah: Georgia Historical Society, 1904), 6:244.

clearly sympathizing with the plight of the oppressed and offering them hope of eventual deliverance. It was with an acute awareness of this possibility after Nat Turner that such people as Bishop William Capers of South Carolina and the Reverend Charles Colcock Jones of Georgia organized a closely regulated mission to the slaves as a way of preventing them from veering in this interpretive direction.[115] Walker's use of Scripture in precisely this way was thus following a path already well worn by rebellious black Christians.

With the assistance of underground networks and patterns of communal reading, the circulation of the *Appeal* was undoubtedly much broader than we can document, and the impact the pamphlet had on African Americans and on events during the turbulent years of 1829–31 is equally difficult to ascertain. But the *Appeal* did help animate slave resistance in North Carolina in late 1830 and clearly prompted legislation restricting black mobility, education, and fraternizing there and in South Carolina, Georgia, and Louisiana.

While no direct connection between the pamphlet and resistance in Virginia can be established, the tradition of rebellious liaisons between blacks in that state and in northeast and coastal North Carolina suggests that there was a relationship. Religion was a thread that continued to bind many blacks in this region together. Stationary and itinerant black Baptist preachers were located throughout these counties, and some blacks maintained an adherence to Methodism fueled in part by a persisting antislavery position among a few white Methodists, and the fact that the denomination continued to reach out actively to blacks. The uprisings of 1830 in North Carolina were distinguished by their close attachment to religious figures and tenets: a black Baptist preacher circulated the *Appeal* in Wilmington; a Quaker preached against slavery to blacks in New Bern; an itinerant minister who had copies of the pamphlet was found meeting secretly with slaves in Chapel Hill. This region, running from north of Richmond south to Wilmington, had a tradition of fusing religion with resistance that extended at least as far back as the era of Gabriel's conspiracy. It would be no surprise if this tradition was still active in 1830 and 1831.

In the early hours of the morning of August 22, 1831, Nat Turner and his party of conspirators began in Southampton County, Virginia, an insurrection that within a matter of hours would leave at least fifty-five white

115. For further discussion of this mission to the slaves, see, for example, Albert Raboteau, *Slave Religion: The "Invisible Institution" in the Antebellum South* (New York: Oxford University Press, 1978), 152–80; Donald G. Mathews, *Religion in the Old South* (Chicago: University of Chicago Press, 1977), 136–50.

women, men, and children dead, many of them gruesomely murdered. The details surrounding this cataclysm have often been described and need not be repeated here,[116] but the religious underpinnings of the uprising, and its connection with blacks in nearby counties of North Carolina, are striking.

Religious revivals had been sweeping Virginia and North Carolina in 1831 and reflected the current evangelical fervor evident in many parts of the nation during this Second Great Awakening. Such activity was particularly intense in southeastern Virginia, where "in August [1831], extensive revivals of religion were prevailing."[117] Racial mixing was common at these revivals until Turner's revolt. One such meeting occurred in mid-August at Barnes's Methodist Church, located in the southeast corner of Southampton County near Hertford County in North Carolina. What made this camp meeting of more than passing interest was that one of the principal preachers was Nat Turner. Although a Baptist, Turner was a respected preacher who, according to some accounts, had preached to diverse audiences as far north as Richmond and as far south as southern Northampton County in North Carolina.[118] Blacks from as far away as Winton, North Carolina, and from more easterly counties of Virginia attended this meeting, in large part to hear Turner.[119]

Apparently, significant plotting for the imminent uprising occurred at Barnes's.[120] Some whites later detected a rebellious spirit among the blacks there, a few even claiming that some blacks had attempted to ride over them. At the camp meeting, Nat gained many sympathizers, who revealed their loyalty by wearing red bandannas around their necks. Beyond covert machinations that probably occurred, the action that most clearly revealed Nat's plans was the biblical passage on which he chose to preach: the unleashing of the first of the four apocalyptic horsemen in

116. See the following for detailed accounts of the insurrection, its antecedents, and its impact: William Sidney Drewry, *The Southampton Insurrection* (1900; reprint, Murfreesboro, N.C.: Johnson Publishing Co., 1968); Aptheker, *American Negro Slave Revolts,* 293–324; F. Roy Johnson, *The Nat Turner Slave Insurrection* (Murfreesboro, N.C.: Johnson Publishing Co., 1966); F. Roy Johnson, *The Nat Turner Story* (Murfreesboro, N.C.: Johnson Publishing Co., 1970); Stephen B. Oates, *The Fires of Jubilee: Nat Turner's Fierce Rebellion* (New York: Harper & Row, 1975); Tragle, *Southampton Slave Revolt;* Peter Wood, "Nat Turner: The Unknown Slave as Visionary Leader," in Leon Litwack and August Meier, *Black Leaders of the Nineteenth Century* (Urbana: University of Illinois Press, 1988), 21–40.

117. *The Liberator,* October 1, 1831; reprinted in Tragle, *Southampton Slave Revolt,* 115.

118. Johnson, *Nat Turner Story,* 69; see also the useful map of his suspected travels on p. 70.

119. Drewry, *Southampton Insurrection,* 157.

120. Along with Drewry, see also *Richmond Constitutional Whig,* August 29, 1831, reprinted in Tragle, *Southampton Slave Revolt,* 51–52.

Revelation 6:2:[121] "And I saw, and behold, a white horse: and he that sat on him had a bow; and a crown was given unto him, and he went forth conquering and to conquer." Like numerous rebels before him, Turner legitimized the will to resist through the Bible.

The likelihood that communication about the revolt was spread from Barnes's is high. A few days after the uprising began, a free black Baptist preacher, London Gee, who lived near the meetinghouse but just over the North Carolina line, was arrested in Murfreesboro along with another black Baptist preacher from nearby Northampton County, Sam Brantley.[122] A black preacher in Nansemond County, which had sent participants to Barnes's, was taken up and condemned for involvement in the conspiracy.[123] In the Southside county of Prince George, a slave named Christopher, "a blacksmith by trade and a preacher by profession," was tried and condemned on September 1, 1831, for being connected with Nat Turner and being responsible for sending communications to blacks in New Kent County, north of the James River.[124] White authorities were so certain of the religious and clerical origins of the rebellion that the commentary of a letter-writer in Winton, North Carolina, reflected the belief of many:

> The whole affair was arranged by the negro preachers who have been suffered to hold their meetings at pleasure, by day and by night; and so the scoundrels have been permitted to poison the minds of the negroes.[125]

Moreover, many whites believed that Turner rose a week too early and thus fouled plans for a much broader and concerted rising to be commenced on the last Sunday of August. Thomas Borland wrote to Governor Stokes that several blacks had testified that "the blacks in Southampton

121. Drewry, *Southampton Insurrection*, 114.
122. Solon Borland to Roscius C. Borland, Murfreesboro, August 31, 1831, in Governors' Papers, Montfort Stokes, State Series 62, Division of Archives and History, Raleigh; Johnson, *Nat Turner Slave Insurrection*, 131.
123. Drewry, *Southampton Insurrection*, 115n. See also Tragle, *Southampton Slave Revolt*, 94.
124. Drewry, *Southampton Insurrection*, 156; *Richmond Enquirer*, September 2, 1831, reprinted in Tragle, *Southampton Slave Revolt*, 58–59.
125. Johnson, *Nat Turner Slave Insurrection*, 133. Solon Borland of Murfreesboro wrote: "Religion has been brought to their aid. Their leaders, who you know are preachers, have convinced many of them that to die in the cause in which they are engaged affords them a passport to heaven—many have said so when about to be put to death" (Solon Borland to Roscius C. Borland, Murfreesboro, August 31, 1831). Governor Floyd's position on the role of preachers is discussed above. Further examples can be found throughout Johnson, *Nat Turner Slave Insurrection*, 117–35.

. . . thought the Sunday on which they began the work of death, to be the last Sunday in the month."[126] Borland further apprised Stokes:

> The insurrection was well known among the Negroes to be about to take place, & such intention communicated to a considerable distance; . . . the last Sunday (evening) in August was the day fixed on & named to black congregation [in or near Suffolk, Virginia in Nansemond County] by a black Preacher named Grimes, who told them, where they were to meet him, armed in the best manner possible, and after a funeral sermon he would preach, pass thro' the country as soldiers and destroy the whites.

The rebellious movements radiating out of Southampton County clearly spread into North Carolina. Immediately upon being alerted to the Southampton revolt, a slave rapidly left his owner's residence some fifteen miles southwest of Murfreesboro with "a forged pass & made a bold attempt to reach [Southampton] . . . having told a Negro before he left home, there would be a war between the black and white people." His haste was considered very suggestive of foreknowledge. A man was also discovered traveling through the Edenton area dressed as a woman and suspected of circulating information.[127] Unfounded rumors also flourished and moved quickly in North Carolina in the wake of the spreading panic over the massacre, and several attacks anticipated imminently by hundreds of marching African Americans never had any basis in reality.[128] Yet the willingness of whites to believe these exaggerations was aided significantly by the fact that most of these counties had experienced incidents of slave resistance or conspiring in the recent past—especially in late 1830—and were probably not unaware of the persisting tradition of interconnections between slave activity in southeastern Virginia and that in northeastern and coastal North Carolina. It is no surprise that the first reports of the Southampton uprising immediately prompted speculation

126. Borland to Governor Stokes, September 18, 1831. Numerous instances of this belief were cited. See, for example, the letter of S. B. Emmons to *The Liberator*, October 1, 1831, in which he wrote that a fellow traveler in Virginia "mentioned that the slaves commenced an attack one week too soon, owing to some miscalculation. This circumstance I have seen corroborated by other accounts" (reprinted in Tragle, *Southampton Slave Revolt*, 115). See also Moses Ashley Curtis, Personal Diary, 1830–36, vol. 6, entry dated September 9, 1831, in Curtis Papers 199, Southern Historical Collection, University of North Carolina, Chapel Hill.

127. Both examples are in Borland to Governor Stokes, September 18, 1831.

128. A number of eastern counties came under the grip of such panics in the days and weeks immediately after Turner's uprising. For a thorough discussion of these fears, see Morris, "Panic and Reprisal," 29–52.

about whether the rebels "were . . . connected with the desperadoes who harassed N. Carolina last year."[129]

The cause for alarm in southeastern North Carolina was not unfounded. Plans and movements of slaves in that region appear to be directly related to the arrival of news there about Nat Turner. On about September 5 a slave named Dave was charged with conspiring to rebel with other blacks from Sampson and Duplin Counties. Their plan was to march in two columns toward Wilmington, murdering whites, burning plantations, and rallying blacks as they marched. In Wilmington they expected to be met by 2,000 black rebels who would assist them in taking that city and then march with them back toward Fayetteville.[130]

They almost certainly had some contact with similarly minded rebels in Wilmington, for on September 10 authorities in that town learned that a number of local blacks were planning an extensive uprising. In concert with rebels in other counties, those in Wilmington had settled on a day in early October to commence the work. Three months after the uncovering of the plot and the undertaking of a thorough investigation, a Wilmington diarist, Moses Ashley Curtis, was able to write confidently:

> The insurrection seems to have embraced two or three counties, & intercourse was kept up by occasional despatches through those who were occasionally sent on business to Wilmington. Officers were appointed in part [sic] in the different counties, military stores collected in small quantities I believe, & on the 4th of Oct were to have taken W[ilmington]. —A troop of some hundred were to come down from the upper counties under their Generalissimo, & to be joined by the insurgents here. —But they were detected & we saved.[131]

---

129. *Richmond Compiler,* August 27, 1831; reprinted in Tragle, *Southampton Slave Revolt,* 49.

130. Morris, "Panic and Reprisal," 38–41.

131. Curtis Diary, entry dated December 8, 1831. Another Wilmington resident, Charlotte De Berniere Hooper, also commented on the degree of coordination among the conspiring parties: "Their confessions were corroborated by others who have been taken up since & who had never seen them so could not have concerted a story. . . . They all agree in stating that the 4 of Oct was the day or night fixed on for the taking and burning Wilmington" (Charlotte Hooper to John De Berniere Hooper, Wilmington, September 20, 1831, in John De Berniere Hooper Papers, file 5, Southern Historical Collection, University of North Carolina; *Cape Fear Recorder,* September 21, 1831, and November 9 and 16, 1831). For further details on the conspiracy and the panic in Wilmington, see *Cape Fear Recorder,* September 14, 1831.

The extensiveness of the plot is confirmed by the fact that at least four-teen slaves were executed in three different counties: New Hanover, Sampson, and Duplin.[132]

Just like Turner's comrades, these rebels not only participated in but took advantage of the religious revivals occurring in their region. Plans had been made for "the blacks from several counties . . . to assemble and commence their work" during a Baptist camp meeting in early October.[133] Indeed, many of the conspirators were affiliated with the Methodist church and most likely used their separate assemblies, such as those afforded by class meetings and love feasts, to assist in planning and rally-ing for the uprising. Curtis observed:

> There was a peculiar feature displayed in the late insurrection. Most of the culprits were members of the methodist church, some of them in high repute for honesty. On some plantations, in fact it is almost a general rule, they set down a negro who joins the church for a rogue and one who becomes a preacher for an arch villain.[134]

The belief in the rebels' close relationship to the Methodist church was so widely held that the Front Street Methodist Episcopal Church (since 1886, Grace) of Wilmington felt compelled to respond to it. In their quar-terly report at the end of 1831, the officials stated:

> Whereas, it has been reported, that all the persons executed in this place for conspiracy were members of the Methodist Episcopal Church some of them sustaining the relations of Leaders and preachers to said Church, which report we fear has been indus-triously circulated with design to prejudice the public mind against us as a people.
>
> Therefore Resolved, that we the members of the quarterly con-ference feel it our duty to contradict said report and to give a short

132. Curtis Diary, entry dated December 8, 1831.
133. Curtis Diary, entry dated September 10, 1831.
134. Curtis Diary, December 8, 1831. According with Curtis's observation on the rebels' "high repute for honesty" was Charlotte De Berniere's comment that "all the ringleaders are men who *live at their ease,* pay moderate wages, & are in every respect better situated than poor white people" (Charlotte Hooper to John De Berniere Hooper, September 20, 1831, John De Berniere Hooper Papers). It is evident from this statement that these slaves hired their own time and thus were probably artisans, perhaps in the building trades. The combi-nation of religious and economic leadership in these men is impressive and remarkably similar to that invested in the leadership of the Denmark Vesey conspiracy.

statement of facts. Of the Ten persons executed, *three* were connected with our communion of whom one alone sustained a good standing. None of them were leaders or Preachers. We further state that no coloured preachers are connected with this station. And there are only *Two* in the bounds of the South Carolina Conference, both of whom are men of respectable character and talents.

This statement only confirms the popular conception of the rebels' relationship with the Methodist church. At least three of the leaders were on the rolls of the church—a significant number—and the passage does not even count those who might have considered themselves Methodists but were not officially enrolled in a church. Perhaps even more important, it does not contend at all with the highly possible Methodist affiliation, official or unofficial, of the numerous rebels who were not considered leaders but shaped the popular white assessment more than the leaders did. The statement that there were no black preachers in the conference suffers from a similar problem in that it does not calculate the possibility that a preacher who declared himself a Methodist might not have had a certified relationship with the conference. It was not at all uncommon for black preachers to circulate in this broad region and to claim a denominational affiliation that had not been sanctioned officially.[135]

The structural similarities to Turner in planning for and implementing resistance are no mere coincidence; they bespeak the common fusion of religion and rebellion in this region of particularly committed evangelicals. While the conspirators in the Wilmington area were probably not in direct contact with those in Southampton, it is not implausible that the Wilmington rebels knew of events in Virginia through channels other than newspapers and white heralds. The underground lines of communication among blacks in eastern North Carolina probably equaled more aboveboard sources in utility and were much more likely to be enthusiastic about the turn of events. During Thomas Gray's famous examination of Nat Turner, he asked the condemned man if he knew of more-extensive and concerted plans of rebellion. Turner replied:

> I do not. When I questioned him as to the insurrection in North Carolina happening about the same time, he denied any knowledge of it; and when I looked him in the face as though I would search his inmost thoughts, he replied, "I see sir, you doubt my word; but

135. "Minutes of the 4th Quarterly Conference, 31 December 1831," Grace Methodist Episcopal Church, Quarterly Reports, 1807–52, New Hanover Room, New Hanover County Public Library, Wilmington.

can you not think the same ideas, and strange appearances about this time in the heaven's might prompt others, as well as myself, to this undertaking."[136]

This seemingly cryptic response is actually highly suggestive of a common mental outlook and connections, religious and otherwise, existing among blacks over this wide geographical area. While Turner denied personal involvement in any broader plans, his reply by no means excluded the possibility that further planning may have occurred among others and on bases similar to his own.

The impulse to create a direct connection between Nat Turner and David Walker has been so strong that commentators, even at the time of the Southampton revolt, could not resist it. Benjamin Lundy, editor of the antislavery newspaper *Genius of Universal Emancipation* and journalistic mentor of William Lloyd Garrison, believed that Turner was probably exposed to the *Appeal:* "The pamphlet of David Walker, which [Turner] had probably seen, had professed much religious zeal, and urged insurrection on the alleged authority of the New Testament."[137] Lundy, a Quaker, reviled the *Appeal,* claiming in early 1831 that a "more bold, daring, inflammatory publication, perhaps, never issued from the press, in any country."[138] However, he was not without self-interest in this assessment; his newspaper and *The Liberator* were widely indicted in the South for stirring up the black rebels. He thus blamed all the 1831 uprisings on Walker,—"if in fact they owed their origin to any publication whatever."[139]

Later historians have continued to weigh the possibility that Walker may have influenced Turner. Albert Bushnell Hart believed that the *Appeal* "may possibly have influenced" Turner, but Herbert Aptheker finds Hart's position dependent on the unsubstantiated assertions of Lundy. Aptheker himself concludes that no "causal relation between any antislavery literature and Turner's action" has yet been proven and that none can be assumed until such evidence is forthcoming.[140] Vincent Harding also finds no certainty of contact between the two, but nevertheless crafts

136. Thomas R. Gray, *The Confessions of Nat Turner, the Leader of the Late Insurrection in Southampton, Va.* (Baltimore, 1831), reprinted in Tragle, *Southampton Slave Revolt,* 316.

137. [Thomas Earle], *The Life, Travels, and Opinions of Benjamin Lundy* (Philadelphia, 1847), 249.

138. *Genius of Universal Emancipation,* April 1830.

139. Earle, *Life, Travels, and Opinions of Benjamin Lundy,* 247. Governor Floyd of Virginia, of course, was another prominent proponent of the belief that the *Appeal* contributed to the 1831 disturbances.

140. Albert B. Hart, *Slavery and Abolition, 1831–1841* (New York, 1906), 217–18; Aptheker, *American Negro Slave Revolts,* 107–8.

an insightful and moving chapter around the fact of their striking similarities.[141]

It is important to bear in mind that David Walker intended an extensive
penetration of the *Appeal* into the hinterlands around port towns and that
he hoped these areas surrounding one port would overlap with areas similarly seeded with the *Appeal* by people from other nearby ports. The
booklet could have progressed toward Southampton from Richmond and
Norfolk and/or up from the North Carolina lowcountry, perhaps by way of
two of the county's major rivers—the Chowan and the Meherrin—which
emptied into the Albemarle Sound by Edenton and were regularly navi-
gated by black boatmen.

Walker, possibly following the organizational strategy of Denmark
Vesey in the Charleston region, planned to extend networks of distribution and communication out from the ports that would rely on mobile
laborers and especially on a select group of educated, evangelical, and
politically motivated blacks whom he believed existed in all Southern
ports. These individuals he directed to take charge exclusively of organizing strategic details in their region and to begin to uplift and empower the
mass of local blacks, in large part by introducing them to the essential
ideas and aspirations of the *Appeal*. The remarkable breadth with which
the *Appeal* spread in some states like Virginia, North Carolina, and Georgia attest to the fact that Walker aptly relied on some local distributional
systems.

Indeed, the *Appeal* probably played just such a critical role in the extensive conspiracy in Wilmington in September 1831. In 1860 the Garrisonian abolitionist Lydia Maria Child recalled meeting in the late 1830s an
elderly black woman named Charity Bower, who had earlier fled from
slavery in Edenton, North Carolina, and who had recounted that there
was "a great deal of shooting in Wilmington, (N.C.) just before the
Prophet Nat's [Turner] time. The reason of it was this. A colored Baptist
preacher named Spaulding had one of Walker's books. He lent it to another and his master saw him reading it. The white folks got together and
read the book, and they had the colored folks up in no time."[142] John
Spaulding, a successful cooper, was almost immediately placed in chains
on a boat bound for New York and barred from ever returning to his
home. But Spaulding probably had enough time to apprise others of the

141. Harding, *There Is a River*. For Harding's discussion of Turner and Walker, see ibid.,
75–100.

142. Lydia Maria Child to Thomas Wentworth Higginson, Wayland, Massachusetts, March
17, 1860, in Patricia G. Holland and Milton Meltzer, eds., *The Collected Correspondence of
Lydia Maria Child, 1817–1880* (Millwood, N.Y.: Kraus-Thomson Organization Limited, 1979),
microfiche card 45, letter 1209. For futher information on Charity Bowery, see Lydia Maria
Child, "Charity Bowery," *Liberty Bell*, 1839, 26–43.

work and communicate its conviction to them. In a related incident, Lydia Child remembered that Billy McNiel, a slave and "the best carpenter in Wilmington," was shot and killed.

These events with the *Appeal* and its abettors had to have occurred in or about August and/or September 1831, for Wilmington's newspaper, the *Cape Fear Recorder,* noted the commencement in early November 1831 of the trial of Billy McNeil [*sic*] and other slave conspirators for their role in the September plot.[143] Billy and the other convicted conspirators were executed several days later on November 12. While Charity seems to conflate Billy's capture and murder, her memory of events was largely accurate.

Spaulding was precisely the sort of individual Walker wanted to receive the *Appeal:* he was a literate preacher, was clearly excited by the pamphlet, and contributed to its circulation in the region. It is very likely that the pamphlet influenced the associated rebels in neighboring Sampson and Duplin Counties where it could easily have traveled and thereby fulfilled Walker's organizational objectives for at least one region.

Walker likely sought by mobilizing each one of these discrete regions to create a grid of overlapping networks ideally capable of uniting blacks throughout the South. These sorts of networks were exactly what black reformers were hoping to foster among blacks in the North. Why not—through an albeit more secretive route—in the South as well? If there was a confluence of agents, then, in Southampton from the North, South, and East, this may well have been in accord with Walker's grand organizational vision.

At this point we can only speculate whether Turner actually saw or was aware of David Walker's *Appeal.* Yet it is clear that the world Nat Turner inhabited—that of Southside and northeastern North Carolina—was one where the *Appeal* might receive a favorable reception. The continuing influence of Walker in southeastern North Carolina can also be reasonably discerned in the rebellious actions taken there in September 1831. Only eight months earlier his pamphlet had been circulating among black residents of Wilmington and nearby outliers, some of whom may have carried it as far north as New Bern and Elizabeth City. An impact on insurrectionary events in 1831 cannot be dismissed. Vincent Harding summarizes best how we must reckon with this indeterminate impact:

> And what of Nat Turner? Did Walker's *Appeal* ever reach him as he waited for the proper sign in Southampton County? No record exists of that contact, if it ever occurred. But the contact was not necessary, for Nat Turner had long been convinced that the God of Walker's *Appeal* had always been in Southampton.[144]

143. *Cape Fear Recorder,* November 9, 1831.
144. Harding, *There Is a River,* 94.

Other events, however, must also be recognized for the contributions they made to this rebellious momentum from the late 1820s through the early 1830s. In some Upper South states by 1829, there was growing talk among whites of problems with slavery, if not of outright endorsement of abolition. The Virginia Constitutional Convention of 1829–30 revolved principally around the issue of political representation and the advantages reaped by Tidewater and lower Piedmont counties by having their thousands of slaves counted toward that representation. Before and during this assembly, many a delegate from the slave-poor counties of western Virginia had uncomplimentary public comments to make about the institution of slavery and those who profited from it.[145] Just to the west, a bill had been unsuccessfully introduced in the Kentucky House of Representatives "to provide for the constitutional emancipation of all slaves in the state."[146] These political events in Virginia directly contributed to renewed and large-scale slave resistance in the counties of Mathews, Gloucester, Isle of Wight, and adjoining counties. One correspondent of Governor Giles informed him:

> The common belief among the negroes of his county [i.e., Mathews] was, that the State Convention had been elected to decide on the question of their emancipation. That emancipation would be proclaimed at the next August Court. In case of failure, there were some who advocated insurrection.[147]

Slave unrest was also reported at the same time in the nearby lower part of Maryland's Eastern Shore. While initial reports of slave insurrection were soon disproven, it was established that two black preachers from the Baltimore African Methodist Episcopal Church were traveling among the slaves in the region hoping to form an AME congregation among them. However, they had apparently also been exciting "some of the Slaves with dangerous and nefarious notions about their freedom."[148] Similar rumors circulated among blacks in and around Wilmington during

---

145. See Alison Goodyear Freehling, *Drift Toward Dissolution: The Virginia Slavery Debate of 1831–1832* (Baton Rouge: Louisiana State University Press, 1982), 36–81.

146. As quoted in Earle, *Life, Travels, and Opinions of Benjamin Lundy,* 237. In *Niles' Register,* February 6, 1830, note was taken of a recent "animated debate on a bill to prevent the importation of slaves into Kentucky." The author commented further: "[The fact that] slavery has been highly injurious to Kentucky, is undoubted; and that measures will be taken to rid the state of its slave population, so far as may be consistent with what are esteemed the rights of property, is entirely manifest to us."

147. Palmer, *Calendar of Virginia State Papers,* 10:567–69.

148. *Niles' Register,* July 17, 1830; *Genius of Universal Emancipation,* July 1830; *Boston Daily Courier,* August 28, 1830.

the summer of 1830, for at the same time the *Appeal* was discovered there the local police magistrate also alerted Governor Owen to the

> fact recently brought to light, viz. that a very general and extensive impression has been made on the minds of the negroes in this vicinity that measures have been taken towards their emancipation on a certain and not distant day [and that that] has excited no little uneasiness in our community.[149]

Chances are good as well that many blacks, especially those in and around port cities, were aware of the debate over abolition in England and the social turmoil helping to fuel it in the West Indies. Antislavery agitation had been stepped up in England in 1830, and new techniques—such as wide-scale petitioning and mass demonstrations—were employed to secure broad popular support for the cause. In the British West Indies, rumors similar to those circulating in Virginia and North Carolina regarding impending emancipation spread even more extensively and greatly increased the willingness of slaves to rebel.[150] Outbreaks occurred in Tortola, Antigua, and the Bahamas alone in 1830 through early 1831, followed by the much larger Christmas Rebellion of 1831 in Jamaica. Rebelliousness was sweeping the Caribbean basin at this time, and reports on resistance there, as well as rumors of abolition, could easily enter the South by way of the black sailors who were the foundation of the two regions' intimate maritime interconnections.[151] Once emancipation was under way after 1832, slaves as far in the interior as Kentucky heard of it "in a very short time [and] expected they would be free next."[152]

A number of African Americans were also aware of liberation struggles occurring contemporaneously in Europe and linked their own movement

149. James F. McRae to Governor Owen, Wilmington, August 7, 1830.

150. Michael Craton, "Slave Culture, Resistance, and the Achievement of Emancipation in the British West Indies, 1783–1838," in James Walvin, ed., *Slavery and British Society, 1776–1846* (Baton Rouge: Louisiana State University Press, 1982), 100–122; Michael Craton, *Testing the Chains: Resistance to Slavery in the British West Indies* (Ithaca, N.Y.: Cornell University Press, 1982), esp. 291–300.

151. Julius S. Scott's dissertation, "The Common Wind: Currents of Afro-American Communication in the Era of the Haitian Revolution" (Ph.D. diss., Duke University, 1986), makes clear the degree to which such accounts and rumors moved during this revolutionary era among African Americans on the various islands of the West Indies and between them and their fellow enslaved in the United States South. Their principal vehicle of communication, maritime activity, had only expanded between the two regions during the early decades of the nineteenth century, and one can therefore safely assume that a lively communication continued between them.

152. *Narratives of the Sufferings of Lewis and Milton Clarke, Sons of a Soldier of the Revolution, During a Captivity of More than Twenty Years Among the Slaveholders of Kentucky* (Boston, 1846), 118.

with those on the other side of the Atlantic. One writer, identified only as "A Colored Philadelphian," wrote to *The Liberator* just before the Nat Turner uprising:

> When we take a retrospective view of things, and hear of almost every nation fighting for its liberty, is it to be expected that the African race will continue always in the degraded state they now are? No. The time is fast approaching when the words "Fight for liberty, or die in the attempt," will be sounded in every African ear throughout the world.[153]

African American activists often voiced nationalist sentiments similar to those underlying revolutions in France, Germany, Greece, and elsewhere. Walker himself referred regularly to ongoing struggles in Greece and Ireland and held them up as a prod to rebellious activity on the part of his own people.[154] Moreover, information on current revolutionary movements in Europe was readily accessible, for newspapers throughout the United States covered them closely. Walker even ridiculed South Carolina newspapers for their common exclamation over Turkish barbarities against the insurgent Greeks while they advertised slaves for sale on the next page.[155]

David Walker's *Appeal* did not generate slave resistance in the South. The slaves did not need Walker to tell them what they had been doing all along; they would have continued their rebelliousness had the *Appeal* never appeared among them. Indeed, Walker was a product of their tradition of resistance rather than the other way around. Yet the pamphlet was nevertheless a rallying point in several locations for conspiring and resistance and could have sustained other efforts. It lent aid and comfort to the rebellious in the manner of earlier great rebels by speaking directly to the individual and historical integrity of African Americans and to their special relationship with God. And it made it poignantly clear that many blacks in the North knew the slaves' suffering well and were committed to struggling with them to end slavery forever. Nothing like this had ever come out of the North before, especially not by the brave hand of a man who publicly avowed authorship. While the *Appeal* did not make the turbulence of 1829–31, it did act in concert with the insurrectionary spirit, broadened its meaning and hope, and sought to direct it in a way that would unite blacks throughout the South.

153. *The Liberator,* August 20, 1831.
154. See, for example, *Appeal,* 7, 12–13.
155. Ibid., 12–13.

6

History and Oratory

The Intellectual Background of the Appeal

The *Appeal* issued from a well-established tradition of black antislavery and religious oratory. Many of the themes and issues touched on by Walker in his work had already been addressed by an array of prominent black orators. Walker followed in the footsteps of a number of powerful black ministers and community leaders who spoke out often on matters of concern to African Americans. The uplifting of individuals and of the entire race through education and general moral improvement had long preoccupied black spokesmen, despite the fact that a new urgency attached to this concern. In 1787 Jupiter Hammon exhorted his fellow blacks, "Let all the time you can get be spent in trying to learn to read."[1] Prince Saunders signaled the creation of the Pennsylvania Augustine Edu-

---

1. Jupiter Hammon, "An Address to the Negroes in the State of New York" (1787), in Porter, *Early Negro Writing*, 319–20.

cation Society with the hope that its members "will never be weary in labouring for the promotion of the cause and interests of science and literature among the rising generation of the people of colour."[2] In 1809, at the conclusion of his oration commemorating the end of the foreign slave trade, a New York City minister, Joseph Sidney, issued an admonition common to these speeches, that his people endeavor

> to convince the world that we are not only capable of self-government, but also of becoming honourable citizens and useful members of society. Let it be our business to demonstrate to the conviction, even of the enemies of our freedom, that sobriety, honesty, and industry, are among the distinguishing traits in our characters.[3]

In 1828, a leading black abolitionist of Philadelphia, William Whipper, summarized the view of many that "the means of ameliorating our condition . . . [are] by a strict attention to education."[4]

David Walker was not the first to speak of a vengeful God who would not tolerate competition from any earthly masters or wait long the release of his people. By the eighteenth century, blacks were already looking to God as a liberator and one who would mete out stiff justice to the enslavers. The slave preacher David and the preacher observed by the Reverend Francis Le Jau in early Charleston are just two examples of the development of this perspective.[5] This outlook deepened during the era of the American Revolution as calls for liberty were joined with evangelical appeals by black and white orators alike.

Blacks in the postrevolutionary North continued to advance this promise of divine concern. Attempting to explain God's awareness of the suffering of African Americans and to warn that they must not weaken and abandon their faith, Prince Hall counseled in 1797:

> Let us by the blessing of God, in whatsoever state we are, or may be in, to be content; for clouds and darkness are about him; but justice and truth are his habitation; who hath said, Vengeance is

2. Prince Saunders, "An Address Delivered at Bethel Church, Philadelphia; on the 30th of September, 1818. Before the Pennsylvania Augustine Society, for the Education of People of Colour," in ibid., 91–92.

3. Joseph Sidney, "An Oration Commemorative of the Abolition of the Slave Trade in the United States" (1809), in ibid., 362.

4. William Whipper, "An Address Delivered in Wesley Church on the Evening of June 12, Before the Colored Reading Society of Philadelphia, for Mental Improvement" (1828), in ibid., 115.

5. Both these figures are discussed in Chapter 5.

mine and I will repay it, therefore let us kiss the rod and be still, and see the works of the Lord.[6]

"Othello," an anonymous black essayist writing in *The American Museum* in 1788, warned repeatedly that American slavery was "an outrage to Providence and an affront offered to divine Majesty, who Has given to man His own peculiar image." He chided, "Ye sons of America, forbear!— Consider the dire consequences that will attend the prosecution, against which the all-powerful God of nature holds up his hands and loudly proclaims, desist!"[7]

While many Northern black orators in the early nineteenth century chose to emphasize the relatively more pacific doctrine that God created all humankind of one blood and that to enslave any person was thus a sin against God, others continued to stress God's wrathful avenging character more directly, especially after 1820. Nathaniel Paul, of the African Baptist Church in Albany, rhetorically asked the slaveholders: "Are there no forebodings of a future day of punishment, and of meeting the merited avenger? Can he retire after the business of the day and repose in safety?"[8] While the angry and impatient deity is more pervasive in the *Appeal,* his characteristics are essentially the same as those described by numerous African American speakers who preceded Walker.

Walker also refers variously to Africa, and specifically to Egypt, as the source of learning and civilization that was only later transferred to Greece and Rome. Moreover, he asserted, Egyptians were yellow and/or dark-skinned, and thus black Africans became the source of European civilization.[9] Yet Walker was by no means the first African American to advance these theories. Prince Hall argued that Moses was tutored in geometry and the law by an Ethiopian, Jethro, and empowered to accomplish what he did by this teaching.[10] Thus Hall described one of the roots of Judaism, and in a sense of Christianity, as stemming from a black man. An almost requisite component of orations given on January 1, in celebration of the end of America's participation in the foreign slave trade, was a paean to Africa's original innocence, fruitfulness, and peace, unspoiled until the arrival of the European slave traders in the late fifteenth century.[11]

6. Prince Hall, "A Charge Delivered to the African Lodge, June 24, 1797, at Menotomy," in Porter, *Early Negro Writing,* 75.

7. Othello, "Negro Slavery" (1788), in Woodson, *Negro Orators,* 15, 21.

8. Nathaniel Paul, "An Address Delivered on the Celebration of the Abolition of Slavery in the State of New York, July 5, 1827," in ibid., 66–67.

9. See, for example, *Appeal,* 8, 19–20.

10. Porter, *Early Negro Writing,* 72. Of Jethro's teaching, Hall said: "This is the first and grandest lecture that Moses ever received from the mouth of man."

11. See, for example, Peter Williams, "An Oration on the Abolition of the Slave Trade;

Yet some of these encomiums went beyond lauding Africa simply on its own terms and turned to celebrate it rather as one of the world's great exemplars and even sources for learning and virtue. In 1813 George Lawrence exclaimed: "Africa! thou was once free, and enjoyed all the blessings a land and people could. Once held up as the ornament of the world, on thy golden shores strayed Liberty, Peace and Equality."[12] But in 1814 William Hamilton of New York City went much further and proposed that we consider Africa the divinely created "original . . . for the growth of man in his first state of existence." Observing that Africa "can boast of her antiquity, of her philosophers, her artists, her statesmen, her generals; of her curiosities, her magnificent cities, her stupendous buildings, and of her once widespread commerce," Hamilton focused on Egypt as the actual center of these African triumphs and claimed that Egypt probably spread them as far as China. He was certain, however, that the original inhabitants of sub-Saharan Africa were Egyptians and that they introduced civilization into this vast region centuries ago. Moreover, this connection implicitly equated Egyptians' complexion with that of black Africa. Thus, for Hamilton, the whole of Africa was the place "where fair science first descended and the arts first began to bud and grow," and this was an achievement of black-skinned, not white-skinned, people.[13]

Walker's fame was in many ways staked on the scathing indictments he directed against the contradiction of American republicanism existing alongside slavery. This was not a problem that had escaped the attention of white thinkers and orators since the days of the Revolution, but for an African American to come forward and ridicule and accuse American pretensions was a bold and, possibly dangerous action, even in the late 1820s. Nevertheless, at least several black impeachments of the nation's principles had preceded Walker's. In 1788 the forthright "Othello" stated: "Slavery unquestionably should be abolished, particularly in this country; because it is inconsistent with the declared principles of the American Revolution." He expressed grave concern about how Europe would judge this "strange inconsistency," but of much greater worry was divine judgment:

Delivered in the African Church in the City of New York, January 1, 1808"; Henry Sipkins, "An Oration on the Abolition of the Slave Trade; Delivered in the African Church, in the City of New York, 2 January 1809"; and George Lawrence, "Oration on the Abolition of the Slave Trade, Delivered on 1 January 1813." All are in Porter, *Early Negro Writing,* 346–48, 367–68, 376–77.

12. Porter, *Early Negro Writing,* 377.

13. Ibid., 392–94

That the Americans . . . —after making the most manly of all possible exertions in defense of liberty—after publishing to the world the principle upon which they contended, viz., "that all men are by nature and of right ought to be free," should still retain in subjection a numerous tribe of the human race merely for their own private use and emolument, is, of all things, the strongest inconsistency, the deepest reflection on our conduct, and the most abandoned apostacy that ever took place since the Almighty fiat spoke into existence this habitable world. So flagitious a violation can never escape the notice of a just Creator, whose vengeance may be now on the wing, to disseminate and hurl the arrows of destruction.[14]

This indictment is almost at the pitch of Walker's and focuses, like Walker, not only on the secular implications of hypocrisy but, even more important, on the religious.[15] Another challenge, while less direct and extensive, followed after this one. An essay published in 1808 by the African Society in Boston argued:

If there are so many that are now slaves, then, surely, those that remain ought to be free, as it is the right and privilege of every man.

Did not America think it was a privilege truly desirable to be enjoyed, when her mother nation was about to invade her land, and bring her under their dominion . . . ? Well, if so, what must be said of America, or especially that part which treats the African in ways similar to those which we have mentioned?[16]

By the late 1820s, at or about the same time Walker was writing, other black leaders were coming also to emphasize this paradox. William Whipper of Philadelphia, after highlighting the commitment of the leaders of '76 to liberty and independence, wondered then why

these wise men, who hate the very idea, form, and name of slavery as respects themselves, are holding and dooming an innocent posterity . . . to slavery in their own country. . . .

May the letter and spirit of the constitution of the United States

14. Woodson, *Negro Orators,* 15, 19.

15. It is also interesting to note here how once again God is linked with the preservation and advance of democratic virtues and will chastise those who stand in their way.

16. A Member of the African Society in Boston, "The Sons of Africans: An Essay on Freedom. With Observations on the Origin of Slavery" (1808), in Porter, *Early Negro Writing,* 18–19.

stare them in their faces—May the unalienable rights of man stand
as a mirror for them to view their words, until they are ashamed of
their deeds.[17]

John Hilton, a member of Boston's African Lodge with Walker, addressed
the organization in June 1828:

> But brethren, it is a source of pain to me to state that while we are
> here, partially enjoying the fruits of liberty, within these peaceful
> walls, there are in this boasted land of liberty, christianity and
> civilization, over twenty hundred thousand of our race kept in per-
> petual slavery, without one ray of hope, of their ever being re-
> leased from their state of bondage, but by death.[18]

Walker was not only familiar with the speech; he helped to secure publication of it.

Walker reserved some of his most galling venom and outrage for the
detractors of black character, especially Thomas Jefferson, who so decisively advanced the hypothesis of innate black inferiority in his *Notes on
the State of Virginia*. In many ways, Jefferson speculated about how much
capacity blacks had for intellectual and moral advance, precisely because
he wanted to explain why they were enslaved within the world's leading
republic. We will consider Jefferson and Walker more fully in the next
chapter; it is enough to note here that no African American prior to
Walker had attacked the Virginian's hypotheses with anywhere near as
much vehemence or scope. While several challenged the idea of black
inferiority—usually by claiming equality with whites through Christ—
none went to the source of this calumny like Walker. Indeed, few who
followed Walker challenged Jefferson as greatly, with the exception of the
eminent New York physician James McCune Smith.

Nevertheless, a precedent for this aspect of the *Appeal* can be found. In
a commemorative speech on January 2, 1809, New York orator William
Hamilton summarized and took on Jefferson's charges without specifically
identifying the president:

> The proposition has been advanced by men who claim a pre-emi-
> nence in the learned world, that Africans are inferior to white men
> in the structure both of body and mind; the first member of this
> proposition is below our notice; the reasons assigned for the sec-

17. Ibid., 114.
18. John T. Hilton, *An Address Delivered Before the African Grand Lodge of Boston, No.
459, June 24th, 1828* (Boston, 1828).

ond are that we have not produced any poets, mathematicians, or any to excel in any science whatever; our being oppressed and held in slavery forms no excuse, because, say they, among the Romans, their most excellent artists and greatest scientific characters were frequently their slaves, and that these, on account of their ascendant abilities, arose to superior stations in the state; and they exultingly tell us that these slaves were white men.

My Brethren, it does not require a complete master to solve this problem.[19]

Hamilton then briefly went on to sketch a refutation of these charges in a lengthy paragraph—the only known attack on Jefferson before the *Appeal*. While far from establishing a clear precedent for discussion of this matter—and Walker could have been unaware of the address—it still makes clear that the problems posed by Jefferson were being considered at least among the literate leadership in the black community well before Walker took them head-on in 1829.

The essential interrelatedness of exploited blacks throughout the world was one of Walker's most distinctive pronouncements. No one had asserted it previously with such vehemence. Walker recognized that the security of African Americans was in jeopardy so long as blacks anywhere in the world were enslaved and treated like subhuman brutes. He injected into the liberation struggles of American blacks an international urgency that had been lacking. Yet Nathaniel Paul voiced a similar sentiment in 1827 when he wrote:

We do well to remember, that every act of ours is more or less connected with the general cause of the people of color, and with the general cause of emancipation. Our conduct has an important bearing, not only on those who are yet in bondage in this country, but its influence is extended to the isles of India, and to every part of the world where the abomination of slavery is known.[20]

Paul too reflected the swelling hopes of many African Americans by the late 1820s that broad improvement in the conditions and character of black people in the United States could lead ultimately to the elevation of blacks throughout the world. Indeed Walker probably read this particular passage well before he began the *Appeal,* as it appeared in *Freedom's Journal* on August 10, 1827.

19. William Hamilton, "An Address to the New York African Society, for Mutual Relief, Delivered in the Universalist Church, January 2, 1809," in Porter, *Early Negro Writing,* 36–37.
20. In ibid., 74–75.

One of the most striking documents from this era was Robert Alexander Young's cryptic *Ethiopian Manifesto,* published in New York City in early 1829 just a few months before the *Appeal.*[21] In merely seven pages Young proclaimed that God had implanted equal natural rights in black and white alike and that blacks must "be responsible but to God" and begin drawing themselves together "in a body politic." Much more emphatically than Paul, Young declared that Africans all over the world were united through race, common exploitation, and a special bond to God. Yet he counseled the aggrieved "to submit with fortitude to your present state of suffering," deepening their faith in God while waiting for him to send a champion—probably from Grenada—to free them from slavery and their degradation. Despite his wrath over slaveholders and their barbarity, Young believed a sort of quietism was the best course for Ethiopians to follow until God acted.

Was Walker familiar with this significant manifesto? We cannot be sure. No reference to Robert Alexander Young or his work exists in *Freedom's Journal, The Rights of All,* or any other black writings or oratory from that time, including the *Appeal.* But Walker never referred to Vesey either, even though he was surely aware of that influential individual. How extensively his work circulated—if at all—and what his involvement was with the New York black community remains a mystery. Moreover, even if Walker had read the *Ethiopian Manifesto* he would have vehemently disagreed with its caution against resistance and any form of black political activism before the arrival of God's leader, who would initiate all. Yet Walker would have embraced Young's public excoriation of slavery and insistence on black unity.

Most of the principal themes Walker undertook in his work did not originate with him and had been mined by previous authors, although they were rarely expressed with the high-pitched intensity so common in his rhetoric. Walker could have been influenced by some of these writers and orators, and if such a determination could be made it would be an important one. But whether he was influenced or not, he was not certainly the first to address these topics.

In terms of printed sources on which Walker relied, the *Appeal* shows that he used the studies of Josephus, Plutarch, Oliver Goldsmith on the Greeks, Jesse Torrey on the domestic slave trade, and Frederick Butler on America for a significant portion of his knowledge of history. And of course the Bible profoundly colored his understanding of ancient history and his interpretation of history's direction.

21. Robert Alexander Young, *The Ethiopian Manifesto, Issued in Defence of the Black Man's Rights in the Scale of Universal Freedom* (New York, 1829).

But Walker's most important sources of printed information, historical and otherwise, were probably newspapers, particularly the *African Repository and Colonial Journal* and *Freedom's Journal*. The *African Repository*, house organ for the American Colonization Society (ACS), contained numerous articles extolling the level of civilization achieved by the sub-Saharan peoples of Africa. Part of the white colonizationists' plan for attracting black emigrants to their organization and to Liberia was to make clear that they were aware of black Africa's rich history and that they were not just more chroniclers of African darkness, ignorance, and degradation. At the same time they called for the conversion of heathen Africa, they represented themselves as respecters of its worthwhile secular achievements and applauded the connection of African Americans with that legacy. Many articles from the *African Repository* were reprinted in *Freedom's Journal*, especially by the latter months of 1828 when John Russwurm was being courted by the ACS.

Throughout the *Appeal*, Walker exhibited a concern about history—about Egypt's history and the sources of Western civilization, about the character of ancient slavery, and about the place of providence in history. From its beginning in March 1827, *Freedom's Journal* had regular lengthy and intelligent articles on all these issues. The likelihood that they influenced Walker is high. For example, a central assertion of Walker's *Appeal* was that Egyptians not only participated in the development of Western civilization, but were its very progenitors.[22]

22. The body of archaeological and historical data on Egypt available to Europeans was relatively limited through the eighteenth century. As British and French penetration into Egypt and the Nile basin expanded in the latter decades of the eighteenth century, artifacts and writings from ancient Egypt began to be collected and studied closely, both extending the amount of information available about that civilization and spurring new energetic debates over its relationship to Western civilization. For example, in the late 1760s Scottish explorer James Bruce sought the source of the Nile and in the process became a great admirer of ancient Egypt. He placed its roots in Upper Egypt in the heart of black Ethiopia. Yet by the early nineteenth century, data on ancient Egypt remained scanty, especially compared with what would be available by the end of that century, and ideological motivations figured significantly in how that data was interpreted. Martin Bernal explores the critical operation of ideological assumptions in shaping perspectives on Egypt in his important and controversial book *Black Athena: The Afroasiatic Roots of Classical Civilization,* vol. 1: *The Fabrication of Ancient Greece, 1785–1985* (New Brunswick, N.J.: Rutgers University Press, 1987). He argues that the understanding among European thinkers that Egypt was the source of Greek and Western civilization was virtually axiomatic from the time of Herodotus to the late eighteenth century.

By the latter decades of the eighteenth century, debate over the character of Egypt and its relationship to Europe heated up again and continued lively well into the nineteenth century. The debate revolved principally around the question of whether Egypt through its far-flung colonies played a preponderant role in shaping Hellenic civilization—and thus that of the West as a whole. While scholars like English historian William Mitford continued to

> When we take a retrospective view of the arts and sciences—the
> wise legislators—the Pyramids, and other magnificent buildings—
> the turning of the channel of the river Nile, by the sons of Africa or
> of Ham, among whom learning originated, and was carried thence
> into Greece, where it was improved upon and refined. . . . I say,
> when I view retrospectively, the renown of that once mighty peo-
> ple, the children of our great progenitor I am indeed cheered.[23]

This was significant for Walker not only because it removed the source of
European intellectual development from the Romans and Greeks, but
even more because he argued that Egyptians were black and related to all
the other black inhabitants of Africa.

> Some of my brethren do not know who Pharaoh and the Egyptians
> were. . . . For the information of such, I would only mention that
> the Egyptians, were Africans or coloured people, such as we are—
> some of them yellow and others dark—a mixture of Ethiopians
> and the natives of Egypt—about the same as you see the coloured
> people of the United States at the present day.[24]

Thus black Africans and, by descent, modern African Americans were the
source of civilization, not white Europeans.

These themes were equally asserted in *Freedom's Journal,* especially in
the early issues. One anonymous author declared:

> Mankind generally allow that all nations are indebted to the Egyp-
> tians for the introduction of the arts and sciences; but they are not
> willing to acknowledge that the Egyptians bore any resemblance to

---

support the notion of Egypt's central part in Greek culture, other younger scholars, such as
the German Karl Otfried Muller, who were deeply influenced by the entwining doctrines of
nationalism and romanticism, disparaged the significance of the Egyptian connection and
emphasized both the autochthonous roots of Grecian civilization and the impact of inva-
sions from the north. Bernal stresses that the movement to sever the Egyptian liaison occurred at the same time Europe was expanding its imperial control of the world and articulating for the first time elaborate ideologies of cultural and racial superiority over those
regions. Their defenses of expansion were premised on the essential difference of the peoples of such vast areas as Africa and Asia from those of Europe and of their supposed
inability to effectively rule and improve themselves. Yet Walker and his associates at *Freedom's Journal* and elsewhere, all of whom were very much a part of this renewed debate,
were eager to maintain the essential link between Egypt and Greece/Europe as a way to
establish the fundamental cultural solidarity of black Africans and thus African Americans
with Europe. As the nineteenth century unfolded, their position would lose more and more
ground.

23. *Appeal,* 19–20.
24. *Appeal,* 8.

the present race of Africans; though Herodotus, "the father of history," expressly declares that the "Egyptians had black skins and frizzled hair." All we know of Ethiopia, strengthens us in the belief, that it was early inhabited by a people, whose manners and customs nearly resembled those of the Egyptians.[25]

Another author referred to the settlement of the Grecian towns of Argos, Athens, Delphi, and others by the Egyptians, and noted that Pythagoras, Solon, Homer, Herodotus, and Plato all "made their noble journies of intellectual and moral discovery" to Egypt.[26] Still others argued that "China should be considered as a colony of Egypt" and that the Carthaginians—who "were originally Egyptians"—"dispersed themselves over all the islands and seaports of Europe, Asia, and Africa."[27] Thus Egypt became the foundation of virtually all the world's great civilizations.

But most important, several argued, was the original Egyptian civilization, which settled and colonized sub-Saharan Africa and allowed that region to share in the glory of Egypt's intellectual, political, and scientific achievements. With links not only by pigmentation but now also by set-

25. *Freedom's Journal,* April 6, 1827. Another author went even further and pointed out how Herodotus had denoted the Ethiopians as surpassing "all other men in longevity, stature, and personal beauty." At the height of Egyptian civilization, even white men found black Africans to be the most beautiful of humans. *Freedom's Journal,* July 20, 1827.

26. *Freedom's Journal,* July 13, 1827.

27. *Freedom's Journal,* August 24 and 31, 1827. Alexander Hill Everett, white opponent of the ACS and gradual abolitionist, argued an identical position in his 1827 work, *America; or, A General Survey . . .* (London, 1828), 204–17. In a section replete with confident evidence for the blackness of Egyptians, the complexity and dominance of their civilization, the vastness of its geographical scope and influence, and its positive relationship to the creation of Judaism, Christianity, and European civilization, Everett summarized his findings: "It appears, in short, that this race, from the period immediately following the deluge down to the conquest of Assyria and Egypt by the Persians, and the fall of Carthage, enjoyed a decided preponderance throughout the whole ancient western world." Walker could well have been familiar with this important scholarly work, or at least influenced by its manifestations in pertinent articles in *Freedom's Journal.*

Bruce Dain, "Haiti and Egypt in Early Black Racial Discourse in the United States," *Slavery and Abolition* 14 (December 1993), 139–61, explores the mounting interest that African American reformers after 1825 had in establishing the classical Egyptians as black and as the source of all civilization in the Mediterranean basin, using *Freedom's Journal* as one of his key sources and arguing that before 1825 African Americans concentrated on upholding Haiti as a symbol for Africans' capacity to improve and govern themselves. With the collapse in 1825 of the emigration project to Haiti, black reformers turned away from the example of Haiti—and its vivid connection with slave violence—and began to embrace the representation of Egypt and Africa as the seat of Western civilization. Dain notes a very important intellectual trend but neglects the degree to which these visions of Africa and Egypt were present in much earlier works of African Americans. See the discussions of Prince Hall, George Lawrence, and William Hamilton in this chapter above.

tlement, many authors felt justified in speaking of the region of Africa south and west of Egypt as an inherent, integral part of that culture rather than as a derivative satellite. Thus Africa, not just simply Egypt, came to stand in some instances for the source of world cultivation. One journalist observed:

> It would seem from even a slight examination, that the blacks . . . have not only a fair right to be considered as naturally equal to men of any other colour, but are even not without some plausible pretensions to a claim of superiority. . . . At more than one preceding period, they have been for a length of time at the head of civilization and political power, and must be regarded as the real authors of most of the arts and sciences which give us at present the advantage over them.[28]

Here blacks are Africans in general, not only Egyptians. Another, pointing to the ungratefulness of the Europeans and the vagaries of time, charged:

> How flagrant, has been the ingratitude of the Europeans, that to the descendants of their kindest benefactors, they have been most unjust and cruel. Their learning and their intelligence, and the basis of those very Sciences, by the improving of which, they have held a rank superior to the inhabitants of the other continents, came originally from the forefathers of the Africans, towards whom they have ever dealt with injustice and with disgrace to themselves.[29]

A commentator for the *African Repository* asserted that the area south of Ethiopia was settled by the Cushites or Ethiopians, who themselves participated in Egyptian civilization. The Cushites "gave to Africa, and through her to Europe and America, all the wisdom of the Egyptians." Thus Africa as a whole became a repository for a civilization that was then extended to the rest of the world. In many instances where this issue of civilization is discussed, Egypt and Africa are conflated. It is significant that this author also stressed that it was this "vast region from which our slaves are brought."[30] African American slaves found themselves in the

28. *Freedom's Journal,* July 13, 1827.

29. *Freedom's Journal,* August 31, 1827.

30. *African Repository and Colonial Journal,* March 1825, as excerpted in *Freedom's Journal,* December 5, 1828. This favorable orientation of the ACS suggests one more reason why Walker had some ambivalence about the impulses behind colonizationism. While obviously he excoriated people, such as Henry Clay, whom he believed used the organization simply

humiliating paradox of having descended from the people who were the source for the scientific and political tools with which the Europeans and Americans currently oppressed them.

But the conviction that they were the source of these talents was useful, because it allowed them to argue confidently against the increasingly common assertion that black Africans were of a species other than and inferior to the human species.[31] Commentators in *Freedom's Journal* boldly addressed the problem. One enumerated the slights in a manner that was a direct response to Jefferson's hypothesis of innate black inferiority while also referring to early craniological studies. Its tone is like that of Walker:

> The people of colour are ignorant and degraded—nothing can ever be made of them—God formed them to serve their fairer brethren—endowed them with faculties little superior to the tribe of Ourang Outangs. They want all the finer feelings of men—are an insensible and ungrateful race—and to render these prejudices still stronger, the craniologist exclaims, their retreating foreheads

to make their slave property more secure, he was not unfavorably affected by what he considered to be evidence of a spirit of true benevolence toward Africa and African Americans on the part of such famous colonizationists as Jehudi Ashmun. (For further discussion of Walker's attitude toward Ashmun and other white philanthropists, see Chapter 5, note 37.) Walker may have found further proof of this qualified benevolence of the ACS in this excerpted article. He indicates in the *Appeal* (69) that he was probably familiar with every issue "from its commencement" and its numerous positive articles on African civilization doubtless affected his thinking on these matters.

31. The mature expression of scientific racism in the United States did not arise until the early 1840s—well after the demise of *Freedom's Journal*—with the publication of Samuel Morton's *Crania Americana* (1839) and Josiah Nott's *Two Lectures on the Natural History of the Caucasian and Negro Races* (1844). Employing the findings of Swiss biologist Louis Agassiz on variation in plant and animal life according to climate and geographical locale, and Morton's own studies on a variety of human skull sizes from various regions, Nott hypothesized a number of divinely induced creations that uniquely fitted the offspring both mentally and physically for the environment in which they were placed. From two of these specific moments of creation arose black Africans and white Europeans. While they were from the same genus, Nott argued, they were not of the same species. This controversial notion of polygenesis directly challenged biblical authority on the singularity of creation from which all humans descended and the environmentalist argument popular among abolitionists which asserted that all humans had essentially the same internal tools, their expression varying only as a result of experience and environment. For a thorough discussion of the rise of scientific racism, see George Fredrickson, *The Black Image in the White Mind: The Debate on Afro-American Character and Destiny, 1817–1914* (New York: Harper & Row, 1971), esp. 71–96. For Josiah Nott's work, see his "Two Lectures on the Natural History of the Caucasian and Negro Races," in Drew Gilpin Faust, ed., *The Ideology of Slavery: Proslavery Thought in the Antebellum South, 1830–1860* (Baton Rouge: Louisiana State University Press, 1981), 206–38.

evidently denote them another race, something between man and the brute creation.[32]

Yet these detractions appeared ludicrous in light of the apparent fact of earlier African superiority:

> While Greece and Rome were yet barbarous, we find the light of learning and improvement emanating from this, by supposition, degraded and accursed continent of Africa, out of the midst of this very wooly haired, flat nosed, thick lipped, coal black race, which some persons are tempted to station at a pretty low intermediate point between men and monkies. It is to Egypt, if to any nation, that we must look as the real *antiqua mater* of the ancient and modern refinement of Europe.[33]

Given this assumption, the humanity of black Africans could not possibly be disputed. However, what black commentators did believe needed to be explained was why Africans currently found themselves in such a weakened and ignorant position, why—if they were the originators of civilization—were they now so degraded? To accomplish this task, they relied on arguments founded on the idea of, as one essayist put it, "the mutability of human affairs" and the very different circumstances and regulations under which modern slavery existed. The humanness of Africans and their ability to attain civilization and improvement on their own was not questioned; instead, certain historical circumstances were charged with hindering their inherent abilities. One author blamed the burning of the ancient library at Alexandria as the decisive event in rupturing sub-Saharan Africa's connection with the fountain of classical learning.[34] Another bemoaned how Egypt "began to fall before the rising greatness of their own accomplished and vigorous pupils" such as the Europeans and the Arabs.[35] But most speculators on the current status of black Africans

32. *Freedom's Journal,* April 13, 1827.

33. *Freedom's Journal,* July 13, 1827. Pompée Valentin, Baron de Vastey, a member of the Haitian nobility that was created in 1811 by that nation's beleaguered emperor, Henri-Christophe, and that collapsed with his suicide in 1820, argued a similar line in responding to the charges of Mazeres, a former French colonist of Haiti, that sub-Saharan Africa had always been degraded and savage. Vastey asserted, "Every body *knows* that the Greeks . . . were in a state of the grossest ignorance and barbarity . . . till civilized by colonies from Egypt." Moreover, the Egyptians unlike the Europeans and Americans, did not demoralize the people they colonized by enslaving and labeling them inferior, but rather "taught them to imitate themselves in the arts of society, and, in no great time, even to surpass their instructors." See *Freedom's Journal,* February 7, 1829.

34. *Freedom's Journal,* February 7, 1829.

35. *Freedom's Journal,* July 20, 1827.

probably would have agreed with the following seasoned appraisal of the vagaries of time:

> Each great division of the species has had in its turn the advantage in civilization, that is in industry, wealth, and knowledge, and the power they confer; and during this period of conscious triumph, each had doubtless been inclined to regard itself as a favoured race, endowed by nature and Providence with an essential superiority over all the others.—But on reviewing the course of history, we find this accidental difference uniformly disappearing after a while, and the sceptre of civilization passing from the hands of the supposed superior race into those of some other, before inferior, which claims in its turn, for a while, a similar distinction.[36]

Egypt had its moment, only to fall and be replaced by another. Some saw the successful Haitian revolution as a sign of the possible resurgence of African and African American culture, but it was by no means clear. The rise and fall of civilizations was simply an unavoidable product of our transitory life on earth.[37] Egypt and Africa had been only part of a cycle of which Europe and America were equal participants.

The proponents of this conservative understanding of history as one of irresistible ebb and flow did not mean that they believed each one of the predominating civilizations was equally tyrannical and culturally chauvinistic during its moment in the sun. While one writer in *Freedom's Journal* did discuss how Herodotus found the Egyptians "extremely proud of themselves, despising in their hearts all other nations, and regarding them as no better than brutes in human shape,"[38] the point was actually made much more often in the journal that the slavery imposed by the Egyptians on the Israelites was a fairly mild one, especially when compared with subsequent, more modern forms. One journalist remarked:

> I object to the practice of representing the slavery of Israel as the hardest ever endured; and of Pharaoh as the most unjustifiable of all slave-holders. It is not correct. . . . If I am not mistaken, the two facts can be fully made out, from the Hebrew account of their bondage:—
> 1. That it was not as hard as several kinds of modern slavery.

36. *Freedom's Journal,* July 13, 1827.

37. As the author of an article in the *African Repository* reflected, civilization "has often been exhausted in one country as it was awakened in another" (excerpted in *Freedom's Journal,* December 12, 1828). Alexander Hill Everett argues similarly in *America; or, A General Survey,* 204–6.

38. *Freedom's Journal,* August 27, 1827.

2. That Pharaoh not only had more plausible, but better reasons
for his course, than many modern slave-holders have.

Later he added: "Egyptian slavery was much milder than has been often
practised since, and is now practised by a good many who profess Christianity."[39] At least in terms of slavery, Egypt was not nearly as savage as
later, dominant civilizations. Indeed, the message was not only that Egyptian slavery was less brutal than modern forms, but also that the slavery
endured by Africans in America and in the West Indies ranked as among
the worst forms of slavery in all history. The fact that commentators elab-
orated on the specific and numerous privileges and opportunities enjoyed
by the enslaved Israelites, but not by African Americans, makes this undercurrent all the more apparent. The particular slavery instituted in the
New World, they argued, worked to hinder blacks from improving themselves much more than did the enslavement of the Israelites by the Egyptians. Thus African Americans might appear less capable and even less
human than previously enslaved races. These interpretations would have
an enormous impact on Walker's structuring of the *Appeal.*

The arguments used to defend this characterization of Egyptian slavery
were arranged largely in two categories—the cultural and psychological—and the source for the defense was the Bible. The main thrust of the
cultural argument was that the Israelites were largely unsupervised by the
Egyptians and could conduct their lives according to their own regulations and traditions so long as they met the relatively easy tribute and
levy of laborers required by Pharaoh. Several authors emphasized that
the "Hebrews were allowed to live separate to themselves, and retain
their own manners, customs and religion." They were not denied the opportunity to learn trades in textiles, woodworking, metallurgy, and jew-
elry. The great mass of the people appear to have enjoyed an education
and literacy. The Egyptians did not deny the Israelites the "right of private
property." In fact, they appear to have enjoyed the "undisturbed possession of the most fruitful part of the land, and the numerous flocks and
herds which they held . . . [and] a large part of their labour must have
been of the agricultural and pastoral kind, and probably applied to their
own exclusive benefit." One author even went so far as to claim:

Hebrews were received into Egypt at a time of unexampled scarcity when like to perish; and were, with their flocks and herds,
supported free of cost, (Gen. xlv.10, 11) while the Egyptians who
raised the grain laid up in store, (Gen. xli.34, 35) had to sell their

39. *Freedom's Journal,* June 29, 1827.

flocks, herds, and even themselves, for food for their families. Gen. xlvii.15–24.

Thus the Israelites enjoyed an economic and cultural freedom that seemed almost total when compared with the restrictions weighing on African American slaves and freedmen. Their mild enslavement could be construed as more of a generous rescue than a disaster—a justification that could not be applied to the cultural and physical disruption wrought by American slavery.[40]

These apologists for Egyptian slavery equally emphasized that pharonic slavery had a limited duration and lacked what they called a personal character. In discussing slavery as they believed it existed among the Jews but also inferentially among others in the ancient Middle East, one commentator argued that the Mosaic slave code lacked any concept of "perpetual and hereditary servitude." While non-Jewish people or "strangers" could be purchased or taken in war and held for the remainder of their lives, they had to be freed in the "year of jubilee," and their enslavement did not inhere to any of their offspring, who also had to be purchased before being made slaves. Fellow Jews could serve only as temporary servants or sojourners, not as salable slaves. Moreover, strangers who embraced Judaism after instruction were entitled to the same rights as other native Jews. Thus, the author concluded,

> It may be fairly inferred, not only from the unqualified injunction to proclaim a general emancipation in the year of jubilee, but from the text in relation to the heathen bondmen, that perpetual and hereditary bondage was not designed to be tolerated.[41]

40. *Freedom's Journal*, June 29, and July 13, 1827. It is important to add here that such discussions make clear that the identification of African Americans with the enslaved Jews of Genesis and Exodus was far from a perfect one. Many thoughtful African Americans, especially by the 1820s, were increasingly invested in associating themselves with the Egyptians and all that meant for their stature as civilized humans. Egyptians could also defensibly be described as black and African. Moreover, the growing tendency to depict American and West Indian slavery as the worst enslavements ever—a trend expressed most fully first by David Walker—demanded that any proponent reveal how the famous enslavement of the Jews was milder and allowed them many more opportunities to improve themselves than African Americans had. It also allowed the proponent to argue that when the Egyptians were slaveholders they were much more humane than the brutal Americans and thus make further feasible a black identification with the Egyptians. While the Exodus imagery of chosen people, enslavement, and deliverance remained arguably the principal metaphor for struggling African Americans, other significant contemporary forces could at times push blacks to mute that connection.

41. *Freedom's Journal*, July 27, 1827.

It was equally the case, they argued, that slavery was understood as adhering to nations of people rather than individuals. One could be enslaved by being from a group of people denoted outside the enslavers, but an individual was not described as inherently degraded or less than human by being from that group. In other words, labor could be demanded of these people, but a humiliating and dehumanizing control over the mind and body of the individual was not tolerated. The slavery existing among the Israelites and Egyptians was therefore characterized as "a national, rather than a personal bondage." Essayists in *Freedom's Journal* emphasized the limitations placed on the authority the master could exercise over the slave and the opportunities available to slaves to enhance their status and/or gain their freedom. Mutilation of any part of the slave's body, they claimed, was grounds for immediate manumission. Jewish girls sold into slavery were protected by various laws and could marry their owner and thereby automatically gain freedom. No law restricted slaves from attaining "eminence and power" or forced servile behavior from them. A slave could become an integral part of the owner's household and even reach "a highly confidential station." Slaves were not perceived as personal property totally subject to the will of the owner, and it was possible to gain freedom and participate more fully in the dominant society even though one came from a group designated as outsiders.[42]

Slavishness and degradation of character were not seen as inherently attached to the people of this group; their sole slavish attribute was that they could be purchased and forced to work for the benefit of another. Ancient slavery lacked the degrading psychological dimension so closely associated with modern slavery, especially the American version. One author neatly summarized what he and many others thought distinguished the slavery of the ancient Middle East:

> The odious and degrading distance between masters and slaves, which perpetual and hereditary slavery seldom fails to produce, could then have no existence. Freedom and servitude might pass among families and individuals, like the vibrations of wealth and poverty, without producing any degrading or permanent distinctions. . . . Personal bondage was, as far as the manners of the times would admit, divested of every degrading appendage . . . [and] the slavery extensively prevalent in subsequent ages, may read, in that venerable code, its own severe and unqualified reprobation.[43]

42. *Freedom's Journal,* July 13, and August 3, 1827.
43. Ibid.

The ancient Middle East lacked the concept that a particular people were permanently fitted by character for enslavement; there was no sense that the gap between master and slave was absolute and unbridgeable. Thus slaves in biblical times did not suffer the psychological damage created by the enslavers' constant reference to their inferiority and debased condition. Neither were they commanded to behave in ways that conformed to that description. Forced labor was expected; slavishness of character was not. The people enslaved by both the Israelites and the Egyptians were allowed in many ways to maintain their culture intact, and they also were enabled to preserve the integrity of their personality and their sense of self-worth. All this was denied to the African American slave and would contribute integrally to the psychological debasement that Walker believed was such a unique component of American slavery.

Numerous articles in *Freedom's Journal* addressed other areas of concern to Walker. In the first issues, laudatory columns on the history of Haiti, its revolution, and its most famous hero, Toussaint L'Ouverture, appeared regularly.[44] The journal also contained extensive discussions of slavery in the West Indies and of the swelling labors of the British abolitionists and public to outlaw the institution in the islands once and for all.[45] Exchanges on the American Colonization Society and colonizationism also appeared regularly in the journal, but Walker probably gained even more information about these activities from the *African Repository;* he claimed to have read every issue of the ACS's organ.[46] Various articles in *Freedom's Journal* also addressed the ongoing debate whether free or slave labor was more efficient and profitable.[47] As already noted in earlier chapters, the themes of African American improvement, education, and character were regularly treated in the newspaper, as were more general discussions of race and the history of racial attitudes. These articles provided Walker with some of his most important sources of information. David Walker's role as one of the principal supporters of the paper before it began publication, and as one of its leading agents once it commenced, virtually assured that he would be familiar with the contents of every issue.[48]

---

44. See, for example, *Freedom's Journal,* April 27; May 4, 11, and 18; June 15 and 29, 1827.

45. For example, *Freedom's Journal,* March 23 and 30; April 6; May 11; and September 14, 1827.

46. *Appeal,* 69.

47. *Freedom's Journal,* June 1, 1827.

48. See *Freedom's Journal,* March 16, 1827, for Walker's role in endorsing the plan to publish the journal.

It is important to acknowledge here, however, that the various assertions contained in the journal about the character and history of Egyptian
civilization, about the origins of European civilization, and about the nature of the slavery imposed by the Israelites and Egyptians were as indebted to the authors' ideological assumptions about black character and
slavery as they were to the still very limited body of archaeological, an-
thropological, and historical knowledge about early Egypt and Africa. For
example, the essayists actually had little data available to them beyond
the descriptions of the Bible about the conditions of Hebraic slavery, and
probably understated for their own purposes the degree to which Jews
individually were debased by their enslavement and had their status
passed on to their offspring. While the *African Repository* and *Freedom's
Journal* spoke in glowing terms of African civilization, equally strong
statements were issued by Europeans and Americans intent on reinforc-
ing the idea of persistent African barbarity.[49] The notions that the Egyptians were black or of mixed race and that they migrated extensively into
and civilized sub-Saharan Africa had long been debated and were currently widely challenged,[50] but as is often the case with ideologically
charged statements, the veracity of the thing asserted is not as important
as the fact that it is being asserted in the first place. That Walker and
other African Americans spoke increasingly of Egyptian significance by
the late 1820s pointed to the rise in black confidence and hopefulness

49. As noted in note 33, Haitian Baron de Vastey excoriated Africa's many detractors for
describing the continent as one "always sunk in barbarism, and that ignorance is essential
to the nature of her inhabitants" (*Freedom's Journal,* February 7, 1829). Vastey especially
focused on Mazeres, who claimed that Africans were hopelessly brutal and comprised a
species separate from Caucasians. In another work, Vastey successfully attacked Mazeres's
use of authorities to undermine his hypothesis. See Pompée Valentin, Baron de Vastey,
*Réflexions sur une lettre de Mazeres, ex-colon français, adressé à M.J.C.L. Sismonde de
Sismondi, sur les Noirs et les Blancs, la Civilisation de l'Afrique, le Royaume d'Hayti, etc.*
(Cap-Henri, 1816), 11–12.

50. Both Josiah Nott and Samuel George Morton argued in the early 1840s against this
claim—Morton by using skulls to show that Egyptians were not Negroes but Caucasoids,
and Nott by way of skull sizes and a superficial analogous treatment of Egyptian and Greco-
Roman art to demonstrate their essential affinity. They argued that originally Egyptians were
unmistakably white, related to black Africans only as masters to slaves, and that Egyptians
had never migrated into sub-Saharan Africa and influenced its culture, peoples in that region having been placed there by God through a separate act of creation and endowed with
capacities far beneath those of the first Egyptians. Once these two races mixed—as they
both theorize that they did—it spelled biological and intellectual catastrophe for the Egyptians. Others, like Karl Otfried Muller, were much less concerned with establishing the color
of ancient Egyptians than with discounting its relationship to the development of European
culture and the existence altogether of any civilization there. See Fredrickson, *Black Image
in the White Mind,* 74–75; Nott, "The Natural History of the Caucasian and Negro Races," in
Faust, *The Ideology of Slavery,* 212–19, 233; and Bernal, *Black Athena,* 240–46.

that had been occurring throughout the decade. These claims were being used to legitimize the membership of African Americans in European and American culture by depicting them as participants in the creation of Western civilization rather than as merely recipients of it. By establishing this relationship, they intended not only to bolster their own pride but also to gain greater opportunity and fuller citizenship for their people in American society.

Thus, regardless of the degree of historical accuracy in these various claims, the meaning of the discussions—with which David Walker was certainly familiar—held immense significance for him and his thinking about the peculiar condition of blacks in America and wielded great influence in his shaping of the *Appeal*. Most of Walker's statements about ancient civilizations and slavery can probably be traced to *Freedom's Journal* and the *African Repository*.

Walker also reflects another tradition that is of tremendous significance in the structuring of the *Appeal:* black oral culture and especially the centerpiece of its expressive life, extemporaneous black preaching. Walker's *Appeal* has its roots in an oral, not a print, culture. First of all, material written and printed by blacks—speeches, literary efforts, newspapers, or whatever—was scarce in the first three decades of the nineteenth century.[51] This fact among others made the publication of *Freedom's Journal* in 1827 so profoundly important for the literate members of the North's free black communities. Yet the *Journal* was only one of the earliest products of black-generated printed material, and the community remained overwhelmingly illiterate and indebted to oral forms of communication. The *Appeal* highlights and works within that prevailing pattern.

Walker intended the *Appeal* to be read aloud to groups, not quietly to oneself, as he made clear at numerous points in the work.[52] Its principal function was a public, not private, one. It was structured like an enthusiastically preached extemporaneous sermon intended to excite and inspire the audience to support some general ideas and plans—not like a formal discursive work whose goal was to demonstrate the validity of some

---

51. Dorothy Porter's outstanding and painstaking collection of early African American writings (*Early Negro Writing, 1760–1837*) is a testament to the great number of speeches, essays, petitions, letters, memoirs, poetry, and other forms of literary output by blacks printed in the early nineteenth century. Yet the majority of these productions were of speeches given on special occasions, such as the anniversary of the end of the slave trade, and were probably printed in limited quantities as a respectful commemoration of that year's orator. While they must have circulated to some extent among blacks and possibly influenced Walker, they were dwarfed by much more extensive and long-standing traditions of oral communication, the original form of most of these publications.

52. See discussions of this point especially in Chapters 4 and 5.

proposition or interpretation of the Bible. Walker's structuring of the *Appeal* reflected the strategy of many black religious leaders, including Richard Allen:

> We are beholden to the Methodists, under God, for the light of the Gospel we enjoy; for all other denominations preached so high-flown that we were not able to comprehend their doctrine. Sure am I that reading sermons will never prove so beneficial to the colored people as spiritual or extempore preaching.[53]

Walker favored the homiletic because it was the very heart of the oral culture he himself came out of. The greatest structural influence on the *Appeal* was unquestionably the hundreds of extemporaneous sermons that Walker had heard in black churches and that we will never be able to see or discuss because they were never written down. The words and images used to convey his ideas and plans, which he returns to again and again like refrains, give the impression of oral delivery, of an impassioned sermon. The *Appeal* lacks most of the standard rhetorical devices found in more conventional white or even black Protestant sermons. Although as a written document the work has at times a rough and haphazard edge marked by numerous brief digressions and heated expostulations, these qualities would be tolerated or even expected in an animated conversation or original speech.

Walker also used this form because he knew it would be immediately recognizable to the mass of African Americans and that this would allow him to reach and be intelligible to his intended audience. Like a folk preacher, Walker showed at many points in the text that he believed his writings had almost the force of the word of God. For example, late in the pamphlet he exclaimed, "Do they believe that I would be so foolish as to put out a book of this kind without strict—ah! very strict commandments of the Lord?"[54] Wanting to charge his words with authority before audiences who did not know him personally, he not only grounded what he had to say in reasonable arguments, but also put the entire work in a form used by religious leaders in these communities. This form and its authority Walker knew well from his own experiences in the South.

Finally, the entire *Appeal*—both its arguments and form—were deeply influenced by the Southern tradition of linking calls for slave resistance with Christian doctrine and biblical imagery. This was a practice that reached well into the eighteenth century but became particularly pro-

53. Richard Allen, *The Life Experience and Gospel Labors of the Rt. Rev. Richard Allen,* with an introduction by George A. Singleton (Nashville, Tenn.: Abingdon Press, 1960), 30.
54. *Appeal,* 71n.

nounced by the 1790s as revolutionary doctrine merged with the evangel-icalism swirling about the South. It was best expressed in such conspir-acies as Gabriel's, that of 1801–2, Denmark Vesey's, and Nat Turner's. I discuss this further in Chapter 7.

Taken separately, nothing in the various component parts of the *Appeal*, thematically or structurally, was really new with Walker. All the most important ideas and concerns he addressed had already been treated by other African Americans. Even Walker's extensive condemna-tions of American slavery as the most brutal in the history of the world, and of the charge of inherent black inferiority, had received a much briefer but nonetheless perceptive and barbed treatment in 1788 by "A Free Negro" in "Slavery," in 1809 by William Hamilton, and was poten-tially implied in the numerous articles in *Freedom's Journal* on ancient slavery discussed above.[55] The form he used to communicate all this was one of long-standing significance in black communities both North and South. As argued especially in Chapter 3, these patterns of commonality in the *Appeal* give further evidence of Walker's participation in main-stream antebellum black culture. They show that the pamphlet was not a product of a deranged mind or a hopelessly fringe political activism, and in view of the number of charges questioning Walker's sanity and political viability, by both his contemporaries and later historical observers, that is hardly an insignificant determination. Yet this very point also raises the critical question of what, if anything, was new or significant about David Walker's *Appeal*.

55. For a reprint of "Slavery," see Woodson, *Negro Orators and Their Orations*, 25–30.

7

"I am one of the oppressed, degraded and wretched sons of Africa"

An Exegesis of the Appeal

Elijah Muhammad spoke of how the black man was Original Man, who had been kidnapped from his homeland and stripped of his language, his culture, his family structure, his family name, until the black man in America did not even realize who he was.

—Malcolm X
from *The Autobiography of Malcolm X*

Servility long continued debases the mind and abstracts it from that energy of character, which is fitted to great exploits. It cannot be supposed, therefore, without a violation of the immutable laws of nature, that a transition from slavery and degradation to authority and power, could instantly occur.

—Governor Thomas Bennett
on the Denmark Vesey Affair

But it is time for me to close my remarks on the suburbs, just to enter more fully into the interior of this system of cruelty and oppression.

—David Walker's *Appeal*

David Walker's *Appeal* was one of the most important social and political documents to issue from America's antebellum era. It hearkened dramatic change in African American culture by synthesizing traditional elements of that culture into novel and compelling alloys, by proclaiming realms of the African American experience that had previously been left shuttered, and by offering a new, if demanding, way out of the painful political and existential conundrums confronting his black contemporaries. This chapter explores these changes and why they came when they did.

The impact and significance of the *Appeal* cannot be assessed simply in terms of the extent to which it generated slave resistance and provoked outrage and hysteria among Southern whites, and solidarity among Northern blacks. It must also be evaluated in terms of the black culture from which it issued and what it indicated about changes in that culture. While the *Appeal* was a hallmark of the coming of age and growing interconnectedness of the free black communities in the North, it was also a reflection of the degree to which Southern African American culture had come to shape the political and religious thinking of Northern blacks. This culture had even more deep-seated traditions of active resistance, more far-flung communication systems, and a more rebellious religion than had the North. Beyond the New York slave conspiracies of 1712 and 1741, the North did not have the level of insurrectionary rumblings common to the South.[1] This was no surprise. The density of the slave population in the North—except for New York City and a few areas in the Hudson River valley and northern New Jersey—never even approached the levels reached in the South's coastal plain running from Tidewater Virginia to south of Savannah. Moreover, most African Americans in the North were emancipated by the early years of the nineteenth century and thus had their major justification for revolt destroyed.

Because of the much lower slave population, far-reaching communication systems among blacks did not develop in the North anywhere near the extent to which they developed in the South. While the large number of African Americans involved in maritime activity in the North, especially in New England, undoubtedly led to the creation of networks among them in port towns, the absence of thousands of mobile black laborers and transporters in the North otherwise militated against the development of systems like those constructed in the South. From Southern ports networks spread inland, enhanced by the region's numerous intertwining waterways, and perhaps fostered a stronger sense of connectedness among blacks in the South than in the North, especially in and around such centers as Charleston and the Norfolk/Richmond area.

No discernible tradition of uniting the Bible and certain evangelical tenets with resistance and revolt existed among blacks in the North, as it clearly did in the South. Northern black culture simply did not produce a

1. For a useful introduction to the Conspiracy of 1741 and the lengthy trial transcripts issuing from it, see Daniel Horsmanden, *The New York Conspiracy,* ed. with an introduction by Thomas J. Davis (Boston: Beacon Press, 1971).

Martin and Gabriel Prosser, a Denmark Vesey, or a Nat Turner. Obviously the lack of slavery in the North by the early nineteenth century served to stifle such developments. Yet once African Americans in the North began to draw their increasingly settled communities closer together and to think in terms of assisting the slaves in some united way, evidence of a joining of evangelicalism with calls for resistance began to appear by the late 1820s. It is no surprise that those in the forefront of forging this union often were, like David Walker, Southerners who had contributed significantly to shaping free black communities in the North.

David Walker brought to the North the clear notion that armed black resistance founded on the word of God and on the underground organizational structures already existing among many blacks in the South was possible. Walker had a strong sense for the possibilities of wide-scale organizing among blacks in the South that came from having lived among them and their communication networks. This knowledge, coupled with his involvement in uniting Northern black communities, made Walker the perfect proponent not only for a national—even international—union of African Americans, but also for one intended to smash slavery finally and decisively. Walker would encourage this destruction by making use of and speaking to what he knew about black communities both North and South and about the attitudes and religious culture of their inhabitants.

More than any other black-generated document of its time, the *Appeal* announced the public commitment of a growing number of Northern blacks to end the sinful institution of slavery and to renovate the people that had been ravaged psychologically and materially by it. The pamphlet was thereby its era's paradigm of the extent to which the Southern African American culture of resistance and rebellious religion had come to merge with the flowering Northern culture of moral improvement to which ever more free blacks adhered. Premising all his actions finally on the need to advance the word of God to his people and to educate them for a productive and meaningful living, Walker never lost sight of the fact that his people's oppressors would invariably counter these actions and challenge his people to resist. For the new generation of black political activists who arose in the late 1820s, their broad-based commitment to individual uplift and improvement could never be separated from the need to resist and destroy the institution whose very existence and ideological assumptions denied their entitlement to participate in that culture.

But the pamphlet's meaning reached deeper still. David Walker's *Appeal to the Colored Citizens of the World* represented an entirely new effort to mobilize a vast number of blacks to challenge a system of racism in America that by the late 1820s Walker believed was coalescing into something historically unique in its viciousness. In pursuing this end, he selected an unusually personal form of exhortation which sought to make as vivid and concrete as possible how this system of oppression operated and how it ravaged the individual psyche. While Walker channeled into his work most of the major themes of African American protest and celebration—a unique compression in and of itself—this was not what made it the compelling document it would soon become. In a way that was unprecedented in scope and forthrightness, the *Appeal* grappled with the deleterious psychological impact the system of American slavery and racism had had on black individuals. Walker undertook the task of creating in the scarred a sense of personal power and worthiness that could lead them ultimately to forging a committed and intelligent solidarity truly capable of taking effective measures against the huge edifice of imposed degradation weighing on them. No one else more directly confronted the problem of how to motivate a people to pursue freedom and power who had become accustomed to not having it. The essence of the *Appeal*'s innovation and significance was contained in these insights and endeavors.

The key to understanding how all of this worked must begin with an appraisal of Walker's critical decision to orient his pamphlet around demonstrating the unique brutality of American slavery. Although a few earlier writers had addressed this issue, none had done it with the breadth or fervor that Walker applied to it, probably because the ideological matters contained in this idea of unique brutality had not reached the crisis point they were rapidly moving toward by the late 1820s. In a note immediately preceding the beginning of the preamble on page one of the *Appeal*, Walker wrote:

> It will be recollected, that I, in the first edition of my "Appeal," promised to demonstrate . . . to the satisfaction of the most incredulous mind, that we Coloured People of these United States, are, the most wretched, degraded and abject set of beings that ever lived since the world began, down to the present day, and, that, the white Christians of America, who hold us in slavery (or, more properly speaking, pretenders to Christianity), treat us more cruel and barbarous than any Heathen nation did any people whom it had subjected, or reduced to the same condition, that the Americans (who are, notwithstanding, looking for the Millenial day) have us.[2]

2. *Appeal,* i.

To solidify further his assertion of the historically unique situation of African Americans and to reveal implicitly the great influence the material in *Freedom's Journal* on ancient slavery had on him, Walker used the following passage in the opening paragraph of his Preamble:

> They tell us of the Israelites in Egypt, the Helots in Sparta, and of the Roman Slaves, which last were made up from almost every nation under heaven, whose sufferings under those ancient and heathen nations, were, in comparison with ours, under this enlightened and Christian nation, no more than a cypher—or, in other words, those heathen nations of antiquity, had but little more among them than the name and form of slavery; while wretchedness and endless miseries were reserved, apparently in a phial, to be poured out upon our fathers, ourselves and our children, by *Christian* Americans![3]

Walker's assertion of the unique brutality of American slavery actually had a good deal of basis in fact. Not in terms of the physical conditions of and the coercion applied to blacks, but rather in terms of the ideological machinery used to explain to both blacks and whites why blacks were enslaved in republican America.[4] After a further discussion of his work's intention to investigate in full the character of American slavery, his identification of that institution as "the source from which most of our miseries proceed," and an initial noting of differences between ancient and American slavery, Walker settled down to describe what he believed really constituted the basic difference between the two forms of slavery and what made the American without precedent:

> I call upon the professing Christians, I call upon the philanthropist, I call upon the very tyrant himself, to show me a page of history, either sacred or profane, on which a verse can be found, which maintains, that the Egyptians heaped the *insupportable insult* upon the children of Israel, by telling them that they were not of the *human family*. Can the whites deny this charge? Have they not, after having reduced us to the deplorable condition of slaves under their feet, held us up as descending originally from the tribes of *Monkeys* or *Orang-Outangs?* O! my God! I appeal to every man of feeling—is not this insupportable? Is it not heaping the most gross

---

3. *Appeal*, 1. For a lengthier discussion of this historical matter, see ibid., 7–10.

4. This is not to say that Walker neglected to cite the horrible physical cruelties imposed on blacks by white owners. For example, see a gruesome recounting of some of them in *Appeal*, 65–66.

insult upon our miseries, because they have got us under their feet and we cannot help ourselves? Oh! pity us we pray thee, Lord Jesus, Master.—Has Mr. Jefferson declared to the world, that we are inferior to the whites, both in the endowments of our bodies and our minds? . . . So far, my brethren, were the Egyptians from heaping these insults upon their slaves, that Pharaoh's daughter took Moses, a son of Israel for her own.[5]

His concern here with the idea that blacks were not human, and his desire to challenge it at its source in Thomas Jefferson's *Notes on the State of Virginia,* was a fundamentally ideological one, and it was principally with this matter that he would preoccupy himself in the balance of the work.[6]

Although others did address this idea in earlier works, none did so with the comprehensiveness or depth with which Walker pursued it. The ideological climate surrounding race was beginning to shift significantly by the late 1820s. Certainly Jefferson's speculations on the possibility of innate black inferiority were themselves dramatic new steps in racist thought and reflected new pressures being brought to bear on the ideology of slavery as a result of the American Revolution and its foundation in the universality of human freedom, equality, and dignity. Yet this thinking also existed within a rich mélange of postrevolutionary reflections and actions on race and slavery, which included sanctioning the end of slavery in the North, arguing on religious and political grounds for racial equality and abolition in the Upper South, and designing the first plans for removing the stain of slavery from American soil by freeing Southern blacks and helping them withdraw to lands far in the American interior or to another land altogether—speculation in which Jefferson himself participated.

This more flexible racial atmosphere of the late eighteenth century had rapidly dissipated by the turn of the century. By the late 1820s a remarkable hardening of proslavery and vicious antiblack attitudes was well under way among whites nationally—but especially in the urban North, where whites viewed anxiously the growing numbers of free blacks be-

5. *Appeal,* 10.
6. Jefferson was not the first to speculate on the possible connection between black Africans and apes and orangutans, or the most vehement in asserting that possibility. Among others, Edward Long of Jamaica wrote vividly in his *History of Jamaica* (1774) of the supposed sexual commerce between black Africans and the orangutan and their possession of similar levels of mechanical skills. In language strikingly like Jefferson's, Long argued that blacks could reasonably be considered "a different species of the same GENUS." See Winthrop D. Jordan, *White Over Black: American Attitudes Toward the Negro, 1550–1812* (Baltimore: Penguin Books, 1969), 482–97.

coming concentrated in visible and active communities of their own. These racial attitudes would find aid and comfort in referring back to the speculative thinking of so heroic an American as Jefferson.

Two strong undercurrents in American society of the time evinced the rise of this new racial antipathy: the mounting popularity of the American Colonization Society (ACS) and the growth of a body of laws and customs that enforced racial subordination. By 1820 the colonization movement— led by the ACS—was gathering a head of steam that would propel it to its greatest height of popularity in the late 1820s. The ACS had members who hated slavery, who were genuinely concerned for the welfare of free blacks, who believed free blacks were fully capable of improvement (although probably not at the level of whites) once removed from the stultifying repressions and prejudices of white society, and who saw in Africa a land of promise that had once contained noble civilizations and could again soon.[7]

This optimistic appraisal of African American and African character, however, was much more characteristic of colonizationists in the North— and specifically the educated elite of conservative reformers like Calvin Colton of Philadelphia and Ebenezer Baldwin and Leonard Bacon of Connecticut. The overwhelming majority of colonization supporters believed unquestioningly in black inferiority and in their unfitness to participate in American political and social institutions, and the ACS actually served to manipulate and encourage these prejudices by labeling them ineradicable if unfortunate, and thus the principal reason that blacks must emigrate. Most colonizationists would have readily agreed that African Americans were

> introduced among us by violence, notoriously ignorant, degraded and miserable, mentally diseased, brokenspirited, acted upon by no motive to honourable exertions, scarcely reached in their debasement by the heavenly light [and that they] wander unsettled and unbefriended through our land, or sit indolent, abject and sorrowful, by the streams which witness their captivity.[8]

By the late 1820s the ACS was arguably the principal source for defamatory representations of black character, and its institutionalization and endorsement by leading political and ministerial figures only lent greater legitimacy to the statements. While some of these descriptions were

7. George Fredrickson has a thoughtful discussion of this important aspect of the colonization movement in the 1820s in *Black Image*, 12–21.

8. Quoted in Leon Litwack, *North of Slavery: The Negro in the Free States, 1790–1860* (Chicago: University of Chicago Press, 1961), 21.

made with the understanding that it was the environment in which blacks developed that was ultimately responsible for fostering them, rather than some inherent character or biological flaw, many others perceived them as accurate depictions of African Americans. The cumulative effect was to solidify and extend racial prejudices, especially those identifying blacks as inferior and hopelessly incapable of contributing to American society, in a way both unconsidered and unnecessary in the more flexible early years of the republic.[9]

The rise of the colonization movement also signaled the much greater ease with which the slavery issue was being overlooked by the white American populace and how a black's place in America was increasingly being seen as confined solely to that of a slave. Although there were members of the movement who were antislavery and truly hoped colonizationism would lead eventually to full abolition, the ACS deliberately played down any such objectives—in order to secure national support for the program both from slaveholders who feared any suggestion of tampering with their property and more generally, from a populace north and south who were overwhelmingly either proslavery or at the least little troubled by the institution's existence. Thus the ACS made almost no comment or criticism about the material or moral conditions of the slaves, or about any threat they might pose to republicanism or national security. Instead, free blacks were made to shoulder the entire responsibility for the supposed threat that blacks as a race presented, because their freedom apparently left their almost irresistible tendency toward squalid poverty and degradation of character unchecked. Such was not the case with slaves, whose errant impulses and potential dangerousness were to be restrained by a caring but strict rigorous master. Slaves and slavery were not the social problematic; free blacks alone were in the sociology of the ACS. Thus, because colonizationism largely sanctioned the idea that the mass of free blacks—for whatever reasons—moved steadily toward degradation and inferiority to whites, slavery was more and more readily recognized as a necessary and acceptable institution for regulating an unruly population so long as they remained in the country. The ACS decision to downplay slavery as an issue was important not only

9. Henry Clay, the ACS's most prominent adherent, could hardly have hoped to dull the vicious effects of the statement "The free people of colour are . . . the most corrupt, depraved, and abandoned element in the population" by the trailing and equivocating qualification "It is not so much their fault as a consequence of their anomalous condition." For the mass of blacks remaining in the country, the significance of such assertions were the same as if they had been uttered by the most unregenerate white supremacist: blacks within the United States are irremediably inferior and threatening and are thus fit subjects for suppression. See *African Repository* 6 (March 1830).

as a tactical matter but in that it was a reflection of the nation's mounting comfort with the idea that black deficiencies and brutishness naturally fitted them for the role of slaves exclusively while they were within the boundaries of the United States.

From concluding that free blacks were an inherent threat to social security, it was just a short step to justifying the imposition of proscriptive and discriminatory measures against them. In the 1820s and after, an expanding body of laws and customs reinforced blacks' subordinate place in America by restricting their sphere of civic and political activity. While most adult black males in Massachusetts benefited from the expansion of the suffrage in the 1820s, blacks in the other Northern states, beginning with New York in 1821, actually witnessed either their disfranchisement or greatly restricted access to the ballot as the white male electorate was dramatically expanded. States throughout the North and the South continued to maintain anti-immigration laws that either denied free blacks the right to migrate into the state altogether or demanded that a bond be posted for the migrant's good behavior. Free blacks were also always subject to having their freedom questioned and always required to produce papers establishing it. In no state but Massachusetts could a black serve as a juror, and in all states restrictions were placed on the use of black testimony in court (especially if the other party in the case were white) and on blacks holding office.[10]

Blacks throughout the country were either denied access to or forced into inferior forms of public facilities, transportation, and inns. They were either banned from white churches or restricted to special galleries or pews within them. When public schools were opened to blacks, they were separate from and inferior to those for white youths. Laws prohibiting interracial marriage existed in all states at least through 1843, when Massachusetts repealed its sanction. The net effect of these and other far-ranging and various laws was to reinforce the idea that blacks existing outside of slavery required special regulation because they could not be relied on to regulate themselves and because they might overstep the boundaries society had placed around them. The natural condition for blacks in America was as slaves with a master to administer them; if they were allowed to step out of that state, special laws were necessary to replace the master.[11]

It was against this backdrop of pervasive racial hatred, proscriptive legislation, assertions of inherent black inferiority, and speculations on the humanness of blacks that Walker issued his indictment of American

10. See Walker's reference to these problems in *Appeal,* 8.
11. The two best sources for discussion of these restrictive laws are Litwack, *North of Slavery,* and Curry, *The Free Black in Urban America.*

slavery and racial attitudes as the most brutal ever. As if to summarize all the foregoing developments, Walker poignantly wrote:

> To crown the whole of this catalogue of cruelties, they tell us that we the (blacks) are an inferior race of beings! incapable of self-government!!—We would be injurious to society and ourselves, if tyrants should loose their unjust hold on us!!! That if we were free we would not work, but would live on plunder or theft!!!! that we are the meanest and laziest set of beings in the world!!!!!!—That they are obliged to keep us in bondage to do us good!!!!!!—That we are satisfied to rest in slavery to them and their children!!!!!!— That we ought not to be set free in America, but ought to be sent away to Africa!!!!!!!!—That if we were set free in America, we would involve the country in a civil war. . . .[12]

During the 1830s these elements would only become more pronounced as the rise of antiabolitionist fervor, especially in the North, fired the articulation of more elaborate antiblack and proslavery positions. While historians still debate whether American slavery and racism were unique—and, if so, how—most scholars would agree that Walker had rightly identified American slave society as unprecedented in the scope and system that it applied to describing its slaves as a race inherently inferior to the dominant class and in the degree to which it erected virtually impermeable racial barriers.[13]

This tendency of white America to describe African Americans as a special subordinate, more bestial caste within the human species, if not

12. *Appeal,* 66.
13. Over the last several decades, a debate has rumbled about whether the United States and the British sugar colonies were unique in the extent to which they erected nearly impenetrable racial barriers and developed an ideology of white racial supremacy, especially when compared with Spanish and Portuguese colonies in the Caribbean or South America, which were supposed to have had much more relaxed racial boundaries. Frank Tannenbaum, in his pioneering *Slave and Citizen: The Negro in the Americas* (New York: Alfred A. Knopf, 1946), has been the chief proponent of the position that the Spanish and Portuguese colonies had a milder form of slavery than the others and that the United States and the British colonies were unprecedented in their sweeping proscriptions of a wide variety of interracial liaisons and black political activity. While not denying that institutionalized racism acquired a rigor and pervasiveness in the United States that surpassed any similar efforts in Latin America, David Brion Davis, Eugene Genovese, Carl Degler, and others have challenged the Tannenbaum thesis, especially with regard to his assertion that slavery in Latin America was "softer" and less economically exploitative than it was to the north. For fuller discussions, see Davis, *The Problem of Slavery in Western Culture* (Ithaca: Cornell University Press, 1966); Degler, *Neither Black nor White: Slavery and Race Relations in Brazil and the United States* (New York: Macmillan Co., 1971); Genovese, *Roll, Jordan, Roll.*

to push them out of the human species altogether, and to deny them the capacity to possess the dignity that follows from the pursuit of elevated ideals and self-improvement—in effect to stop them at every approach from being able to participate in American society—Walker labeled unusually cruel in the history of slave societies. By the late 1820s Walker accurately perceived that solidification of this racist ideology was moving ahead with such momentum that blacks had to take urgent action if it were to be stemmed at all. The persistent popular call for an expansion of democratic egalitarianism during and after the Jackson administration made ever more pressing the simultaneous need to erect newer and more elaborately exclusive barriers to black participation in that expansion.

As a device for discussing this crisis in a condensed and dramatic form, Walker used Jefferson—a figure known to most—to symbolize the source and essence of this ideology and highlighted for his audience certain key passages from the famous Query 14 of his *Notes on the State of Virginia,* which informed the racial thought of the late 1820s. Walker wanted to make African Americans confront directly the painful fact that even with one of the most eloquent and generous proponents of liberty and equality in the United States they did not have a defender. He brought the full force of Jefferson's words to bear in one lengthy passage:

> "I [Thomas Jefferson] advance it therefore as a suspicion only, that the blacks, whether originally a distinct race, or made distinct by time and circumstances, are *inferior* to the whites in the endowments both of body and mind?"—"It," says [Jefferson], "is not against experience to suppose, that different species of the same genius [genus], or varieties of the same species, may possess different qualifications." (Here, my brethren, listen to him.) "Will not a lover of natural history, then, one who views the gradations in all the races of *animals* with the eye of philosophy, excuse an effort to keep those in the department of MAN as *distinct* as nature has formed them?"—I hope you will try to find out the meaning of this verse—its widest sense and all its bearings: whether you do or not, remember the whites do. This very verse, brethren, having emanated from Mr. Jefferson, a much greater philosopher the world never afforded, has in truth injured us more, and has been as great a barrier to our emancipation as anything that has ever been advanced against us. I hope you will not let it pass unnoticed. . . . For my own part, I am glad Mr. Jefferson has advanced his positions for your sake; for you will either have to contradict or confirm him by your own actions, and not by what your friends have said or done for us; . . . for I pledge you my sacred word of

honour, that Mr. Jefferson's remarks respecting us, have sunk deep into the hearts of millions of the whites, and never will be removed this side of eternity.—For how can they, when we are confirming him every day, by our *groveling submissions* and *treachery?*[14]

The statesman's lucid prose made it easy for Walker to lay out to his audience exactly what arguments needed to be attacked. And no figure better epitomized the uniqueness of American slavery than Jefferson, for while justifiably being heralded as one of the architects of a society in which people could participate in their own governance in unprecedented ways, his authority as a republican was also, paradoxically, lent to suggesting that a group within that society who were evidently human and thus fit to participate in it might in fact lack the moral and intellectual capacities for doing so. Their enslavement was thus a way to quarantine them and prevent them from corrupting the republic. No such ideological event had ever occurred in human history.[15] Jefferson's authority and the lack of challenge to his thinking on race allowed his speculations to sink deep into the consciousness of white America and be used almost reflexively to legitimize the most barbarous policies toward blacks. After noting another passage in which Jefferson suggested that blacks were inferior by nature, Walker exclaimed:

Do you believe that this assertion is swallowed by millions of the whites? Do you know that Mr. Jefferson was one of as great characters as ever lived among the whites? See his writings for the world, and public labours for the United States of America. Do you believe that the assertions of such a man, will pass away into oblivion unobserved by this people and the world? If you do you are much mistaken.[16]

14. *Appeal*, 26–28.
15. Jefferson himself was aware of this uniqueness. While certain that the novel political situation in America mandated the containment of blacks while they were within the country, he was equally assured that any prospect of their emancipation would also require unprecedented measures. After noting that the racial similarity of masters and slaves in ancient Rome allowed for their mixing after emancipation, he stressed that the supposed racial and moral dissonance existing between master and slave in America made such a policy impossible here. "But with us a second is necessary, unknown to history. When freed, he is to be removed beyond the reach of mixture." Again the extraordinary ideological environment demanded an understanding of and policies for slaves previously unheard of. Thomas Jefferson, *Notes on the State of Virginia,* ed. William Peden (New York: W. W. Norton & Co., 1972), 141–43.
16. *Appeal*, 15.

African Americans were entirely on their own in challenging this deep-seated thinking, but they had to accept the difficult duty to do so, for further delay meant only greater confirmation of the tenets underlying the racism. As Walker stressed, "I say, that unless we try to refute Mr. Jefferson's arguments respecting us, we will only establish them."[17] This was the great ideological assignment that Walker hoped to stir the mass of blacks to accept.

But for Walker it was essential that this authority not be challenged by logical argument alone. A fundamental part of what made American slavery uniquely brutal to Walker was the emotional and psychological toll it took on blacks. Jefferson wanted to address the issue of possible innate black inferiority as if it were just one more scientific hypothesis seeking a logical demonstration of either its validity or falsehood. He wrote:

> The opinion, that they are inferior in the faculties of reason and imagination, must be hazarded with great diffidence. To justify a general conclusion, requires many observations, even where the subject may be submitted to the Anatomical knife, to Optical glasses, to analysis by fire, or by solvents. How much more than where it is a faculty, not a substance, we are examining; where it eludes the research of all the senses; where the conditions of its existence are various and variously combined; where the effects of those which are present or absent bid defiance to calculation; let me add too, as a circumstance of great tenderness, where our conclusion would degrade a whole race of men from the rank in the scale of beings which their Creator may perhaps have given them. To our reproach it must be said, that though for a century and a half we have had under our eyes the races of black and of red men, they have never yet been viewed by us as subjects of natural history.[18]

Without denying the difficulty of the inquest or the subtlety with which scientific tools and methods had to be applied to study this elusive entity, Jefferson nonetheless emphasized that this long-delayed project now had to be started. Jefferson deemed it axiomatic that the hypothesis regarding black character could be tested solely through the use of scientific method and that it was a project undertaken alone in service to truth.

17. *Appeal,* 15. On the same page, Walker further emphasized this mission: "We and the world wish to see the charges of Mr. Jefferson refuted by the blacks *themselves,* according to their chance; for we must remember that what the whites have written respecting this subject, is other men's labours, and did not emanate from the blacks."

18. Jefferson, *Notes on the State of Virginia,* 143.

Moreover, his commitment to rational inquiry made clear his belief that the matter could be fully addressed at a significant remove from any emotionalism.

Prominent colonizationists of Walker's day—while not involved in Jefferson's proposed inquiry—nonetheless adopted a similar attitude of scientific distance from their own investigations and proposals. They represented themselves as reasonable and concerned individuals who had carefully observed society and arrived at certain logical conclusions about it regarding its racial affairs. In particular, they wanted to determine how any given environment might foster or stunt the development of healthy character. Walker quoted Henry Clay as saying:

> From their [the free blacks'] condition, and the unconquerable prejudices resulting from their colour, they never could amalgamate with the free whites of this country. It was desirable, therefore, as it respected them, and the residue of the population of the country, to drain them off.[19]

The abstract tone of the diagnosis makes it appear that Clay was only submitting to observable reality, that no moral question entered into the choice to decide not to challenge that reality. As with Jefferson, Clay's descriptions and conclusions were presented as based solely on a right understanding of the order of the world and as an effort to sustain that order. If profound implications for the object of the studies issued from the works, they were either largely ignored, as in the case of Jefferson, or heralded, as with the ACS solution but principally because of the degree to which they fostered order. The cause both believed they served first of all was a scientific inquiry into the proper place to be occupied by the various beings in creation, and they adopted tones that were intended to reinforce the idea that their inquiries lacked personal investment or any loathing for blacks.

Walker refused to accept this perspective as the terms on which the debate on race in America would occur, but at the same time he recognized the gathering strength of the trend. While believing that African Americans were quite capable of taking on the hypothesis of black inferiority in a logical, discursive way and had a duty to do so, he rejected Jefferson's presentation of the matter as one existing exclusively in the realm of science, as a pursuit of a broader understanding of natural history that could be met by continuing scientific study and debate alone.

For Walker, the hypothesis of black inferiority was first and foremost a moral abomination founded on a vicious racial hatred of blacks by whites

19. *Appeal*, 46.

and on a desire to make the exploitation of the labor of an already subject people more perfect. It had nothing to do with scientific inquiry and the pursuit of truth, and to treat it as though it did was only to legitimize white racist terms for discussing it and to suggest, however slightly, that perhaps blacks were not human. That they were human and capable of improvement was self-evident. Walker did not deny the fact of blacks' current inferiority to whites in terms of intellect and degree of civilized accomplishments, but he did not identify the source of that inferiority as an innate deficiency in character. Instead, he blamed it on the refusal of whites to uplift morally and intellectually the blacks who were under their supervision, or to allow independently motivated free blacks to improve themselves.

> See the inconsistency of the assertions of those wretches—they beat us inhumanely, sometimes almost to death, for attempting to inform ourselves, by reading the *Word* of our Maker, and at the same time tell us, that we are beings *void of intellect!!!!* How admirably their practices agree with their professions in this case. . . . If it were possible for the whites always to keep us ignorant and miserable, and make us work to enrich them and their children, and insult our feelings by representing us as *talking Apes,* what would they do? . . .
>
> Americans! notwithstanding you have and do continue to treat us more cruel than any heathen nation ever did a people it had subjected to the same condition that you have us. . . . I say, let us reason; had you not better take our body, while you have it in your power, and while we are yet ignorant and wretched, not knowing but a little, give us education, and teach us the pure religion of our Lord and Master. . . .[20]

Whites have been unbelievably cruel to blacks, and one of the fundamental ways in which they have distanced themselves from their horrible sinfulness is to claim that what they themselves have done to blacks is not at all their responsibility but is in fact the result of both a divine and a natural ordering of things. Repeatedly Walker returned to the theme that whites were simply incapable of facing honestly and fully the horror of their actions against blacks. Their avarice, hatred, and lust for power had rendered *them* so out of control that they could not see the crimes these forces had driven them to commit or how they wantonly provoked God.

20. *Appeal,* 62n, 69.

The whites . . . know that they have done us so much injury, they are afraid that we, being men, and not brutes, will retaliate, and woe will be to them; therefore, that dreadful fear, together with an avaricious spirit, and the natural love in them, to be called masters, (which term will yet honour them with to [*sic*] their sorrow) bring them to the resolve that they will keep us in ignorance and wretchedness, as long as they possibly can, and make the best of their time, while it lasts.[21]

Vehement and highly personalized emotional response to Jefferson's proposal was integral to Walker's strategy for subverting and finally counteracting the vicious effects of this thinking on blacks' understanding of themselves. In part, Walker was one more early-nineteenth-century representative of the attack on the sort of rationalism Jefferson so neatly embodied. To introduce the emotional element was to refute the validity of discussing the issue as a solely intellectual one while asserting the integralness of emotional expression to the life of humans. Part of Walker's strategy for establishing the humanness of blacks was to have them emote vigorously as a way to make clear that they were not dulled, beaten beings and that they did not acquiesce to the charge of inferiority like beasts would in fully accepting their owner's authority. Varied and powerful emotional expression was essential to what was human, proponents of romanticism asserted. Thus the very act of blacks emoting argued for their humanness. As he wrote with frightening economy, "You are not astonished at my saying we hate you, for if we are men, we cannot but hate you, while you are treating us like dogs."[22] The whole of the *Appeal* is riddled with similar emotional expostulations by Walker against the cruel system of white America. Sanctioning and stirring popular emotional response was a critical part of the logic of Walker's refutation of this system, striving to reveal that blacks responded just as whites would if such an evidently false charge were leveled against them.

The other and more important side of Walker's strategy of emotionalism, while clearly serving to challenge Jefferson's arguments, was, however, not intended so directly for the consumption of a white audience but was more oriented toward affirming the black individual's experience of this oppressive system and moving him or her from the psychic havoc it wrought on them to some new posture of internal coherency and self-respect. Walker believed that what was uniquely brutal about the American system of slavery and racism could not be fully elucidated without

21. *Appeal*, 61–62.
22. *Appeal*, 70n.

exploring the profound emotional turbulence that the system generated for blacks living under it. The rage, sadness, groveling, fear, guilt, confusion, and self-hatred that regular assertions of racial inferiority created in the individual were all vital parts to the successful operation of the system. Fully reckoning with this psychological toll was the key to ultimately healing that damage.

The weight of the pervasive charge of inferiority had severely damaged the ability of blacks to discern their best interests and to plot out courses for effectively acting in the world. One way in which this indictment incapacitated blacks was for it to generate such an intense defensive reaction on the part of individuals, to sweep them up in such a maelstrom of emotions that they were unable to act with any clarity. Walker in effect offered himself up as an example of how that dynamic worked. His numerous spontaneous outbursts in the *Appeal* were intended to be evidence of how emotionally painful and disruptive it was to directly confront the brutality of American racism. At one point, while excoriating ignorant blacks for aiding white slaveholders, he was temporarily so overwhelmed by the treachery that he cried out: "Oh Heaven! I am full!!! I can hardly move my pen!!!!" Here Walker himself came close to being unable to carry on his work due to the intensity of the experience. At another interval, after revealing the colonizationists' wish to keep blacks ignorant and degraded and thus docile, he exclaimed, "Here I pause to get breath," in order to regain his composure after facing the horror of their object. Elsewhere his outrage seemed to bring him dangerously close to losing control, as when he exclaimed: "Oh! my Lord how refined in iniquity the whites have got to be in consequence of our blood—what kind!! Oh! what kind!!! of Christianity can be found this day in all the earth!!!!!!"[23] The struggle to contain his emotions is evident here. Indeed, the entire *Appeal* embodied a constant wrestling with powerful emotions that were always threatening to overwhelm Walker, especially in the latter two-thirds of the fourth and final article. This was the great trial Walker or any African American would have to undergo in this confrontation. It was of great importance that Walker's remarkably vulnerable display of himself in his work—his very self-conscious immersion "fully into the interior of this system of cruelty and oppression"—was intended not to represent him as some uniquely sensitive individual but to stand for an experience any black American who was honest to himself or herself might have about the ideological environment of America. His pitched outbursts were usually placed in the context of an immediate recognition of something that had been done to "us" and that "we" could not be expected to re-

23. *Appeal,* 22, 52, 54.

spond to otherwise so long as that was done. His experiences were potentially accessible to anyone.

Yet most did not have those experiences, for it was a painful process that subjected one to great risk of emotional destabilization. One way in which the mere proposition of racial inferiority could seem to confirm its validity was by generating an emotional volatility in the object, which along with a consequent obscuring of rational faculties lent credence to the corollary of inferiority that blacks were incapable of regulating their internal life effectively. Thus it was very revealing that the *Appeal,* which sought so bravely to represent and give form to this volatility, was widely condemned by contemporary white readers like Benjamin Lundy, who wrote that Walker "indulges himself in the wildest strain of reckless fanaticism. . . . [The *Appeal*] is a labored attempt to rouse the worst passions of human nature, and inflame the minds of those to whom it is addressed." Harrison Gray Otis, mayor of Boston in 1830, dismissed its significance because of "the extravagance of [its] sanguinary fanaticism tending to disgust all persons of common humanity."[24] The effort was characterized as a paradigm of the individual out of control. They completely missed the fact that Walker was attempting to depict and, by so doing, affirm this experience of rage and temporary madness that confronting the racial brutality of America inevitably created in blacks. Not, however, so as to keep them locked into it, but rather as the most constructive—if not also painful and lengthy—process for finally releasing them from its long-term destructive effects and delivering them to a higher, more regulated, and compassionate inner life. Along these lines, it is of tremendous importance that Walker, regardless of how close to the edge of emotional chaos he would bring himself, always regained inner stability and resumed his work. He was a witness to the fact that one could overcome these passions and need not be consumed and driven by them.

Walker was caught in a dilemma on this issue of emotional expression: on the one hand, he wanted blacks to establish their humanity through their emotiveness, but at the same time the rage he sanctioned could be used to indicate their distance from responsible human regulation. He resolved this seeming conflict by asserting that the uniqueness of the pressures under which blacks were placed entitled them to uniquely intense emotional expression, that the frightening rage and spite were only the product of "your treating us like dogs." Thus he attempted to address potential objections from the white audience while licensing blacks to

24. *The Genius of Universal Emancipation,* April 1830; Harrison Gray Otis to Governor William Giles of Virginia, February 10, 1830 (reprinted in the *Richmond Enquirer,* February 18, 1830).

give vent to the crazy panoply of emotions roiling within them. Emotional release, of whatever sort, was an essential component of beginning the process of knowing oneself, of rejecting enslavement as fit for oneself, and of moving toward self-definition.

But Walker was not unaware of the problematic nature of these dignified objectives, of how profoundly difficult it could be to bring a long-oppressed people to enter into the process of individual self-discovery. On the one hand, he knew all too well how black individuals might resist the existential responsibility of self-determination. After lamenting the apparent unwillingness of Afro-Caribbeans to rise up against their white overlords whom they greatly outnumbered, he vociferated:

> Why do they not take possession of those places? Who hinders them? It is not the avaricious whites—for they are too busily engaged in laying up money—derived from the blood and tears of the blacks. The fact is, they are too servile, they love to have Masters too well!![25]

Walker was tormented by the fact that in certain situations of seeming great advantage, blacks refused to seize freedom and power for themselves, as though they simply did not want freedom and its obligations. At a critical point in his text, he recounted with pained disbelief how a female slave being led south for sale with some sixty other slaves had recently helped the slave trader recapture them after they had escaped and left him for dead. While this incident will be discussed more later, it is sufficient here to note that her sense of duty to the dealer, and her unwillingness to assume freedom, deeply distressed Walker and once again raised his fears that blacks had fully accepted slavishness.

And that particular fear was actually much more to the point for Walker. The problem for blacks was more fundamental than their deliberate unwillingness to take freedom for themselves. The problem was rather so deep an identification with the servile role assigned them by their white masters, and with the consequent belief that they owed all whites certain respectful duties, that they were prevented from perceiving themselves as entitled to freedom and personal empowerment, and thereby to seizing it when it was before them:

> I said above, because we cannot help ourselves, (viz. we cannot help the whites murdering our mothers and our wives) but this statement is incorrect—for we can help ourselves; for, if we lay aside abject servility, and be determined to act like men, and not

25. *Appeal,* 64.

brutes—the murderers among the whites would be afraid to show their cruel heads. But O, my God!—in sorrow I must say it, that my colour, all over the world, have a mean, servile spirit. They yield in a moment to the whites, let them be right or wrong—the reason they are able to keep their feet on our throats. Oh! my coloured brethren, all over the world, when shall we arise from this death-like apathy?—And be men!! . . . It shows at once, what the blacks are, we are ignorant, abject, servile and mean—and the whites know it—they know that we are too servile to assert our rights as men—or they would not fool with us as they do.[26]

Walker's use of a spare declarative clause yoked to the verb "to be" in the final sentence above—"we are . . . and mean"—is very significant. It indicates his deeply held belief that individual personality tended to move toward some unified conception of self premised on personal empowerment and self-esteem or on dependence and self-denigration. This is not to contend that Walker was unaware that contradictory impulses and ambivalent understandings of self coexisted in the individual mind, or that a person might suggest servility through his or her behavior while quietly maintaining within a patient strength and willingness to resist. These are all pointed to in his assertion, "They know, I say, if we *are* men, and see them treating us in the manner they do, that there can be nothing in our hearts but death alone, for them, notwithstanding we may appear cheerful."[27] Nor does it disavow his essential faith in the existence of an undying divine spark within each individual upholding personal dignity, righteousness, and power:

Man, in all ages and all nations of the earth, is the same. Man is a peculiar creature—he is the image of his God, though he may be subjected to the most wretched condition upon earth, yet the spirit and feeling which constitute the creature, man, can never be entirely erased from his breast, because the God who made him after his own image, planted it in his heart; he cannot get rid of it.[28]

Indeed, an integral part of his plan for resurrecting scarred African Americans and moving them to orient themselves around their higher sense of self was to kindle this spark into a flame.

Nevertheless, the pervasiveness of popular notions of black inferiority and African barbarity, the ignorance imposed on blacks by lack of educa-

26. *Appeal,* 62–63.
27. *Appeal,* 61.
28. Ibid.

tional opportunities and "right preaching," the disruption of familial and cultural bonds, and powerful, well-organized civil authorities throughout the nation ready to enforce white dominance left blacks dangerously short of ballast on which to stake constructive and empowering individual and group identity. Their sense of either not having continuity with the past or having issued solely from a bestial history, coupled with a lack of opportunity to determine their personal lives, left them with little genuine self-knowledge and thus more vulnerable to accepting definition given them by some other. Walker's great fear was that in the absence of clearly upheld alternative definitions of self and of the African American past, the individual's tendency to organize personality around a single dominant understanding of self would be unavoidably shaped by representations of black character and worth made by slaveholders.

Walker was acutely aware that the history of blacks in America was one largely of slavishness and degradation, all imposed. Any sense of connectedness with Africa and its triumphs was almost totally obscured. Save for scattered articles in newspapers and fledgling efforts by *Freedom's Journal* and *The Rights of All,* there were hardly any texts that represented African American history or culture in any favorable light, or even threw a sop to them for having persevered against adversity. By the late 1820s the understanding—for both blacks and whites—of black history and character was shaped almost exclusively by the fact of black enslavement from the moment of their arrival on the continent to the present day, save for a tiny minority of free blacks. Against this historical weight, Walker knew that it could be extremely difficult for blacks to perceive themselves as anything other than slaves, inferior, and rightfully subject to whites.[29] More than forty years earlier, an anonymous black

29. Walker himself clearly suffered at times from the pressure of this weight. At one point he exclaimed, "I aver, that when I look over these United States of America, and the world, and see the ignorant deceptions and consequent wretchedness of my brethren, I am brought ofttimes solemnly to a stand, and in the midst of my reflections I exclaim to my God, 'Lord didst thou make us to be slaves to our brethren, the whites?'" (*Appeal,* 28). However, he immediately claims to have dispelled his doubts by remembering that God's justice would not tolerate such a condition and that blacks would finally rise to smash it. Yet, while this apostrophe was in part intended to draw a tighter bond between Walker and his audience by showing that he was subject to the same doubts he had just represented them as having, it also revealed the depth of his anxieties about whether blacks would make the substantial changes he sought and whether God in fact endorsed them. About this important matter of religious belief and Walker, I shall have more to say later. Although he always appears to have resolved his doubts, their reoccurrence later in the text belies this sense of easy settlement. The existence of these doubts inside the individual who had done so much to excavate and challenge the system that sustained them testified to the boring of Jefferson's baleful speculations into the psyche of black America.

author eloquently described precisely this condition that Walker had explored in such painful detail:

> Would it be surprising if a slave, laboring under all these disadvantages—oppressed, insulted, scorned, trampled on—should come at last to despise himself—to believe the calumnies of his oppressors—and to persuade himself that it would be against his nature to cherish any honorable sentiment or to attempt any virtuous action?[30]

No other postulation but profound psychological disruption and ignorance could explain for Walker the perversion of natural instinct among blacks to the degree that "fathers [beat] their sons, mothers their daughters, and children their parents, all to satisfy the passions of unrelenting tyrants."[31] Part of the horrible brutality of American slavery was the manner in which it could transform blacks—despite their showing clear signs of individual and group strengths and resourcefulness—into the believers and even the agents of their own degradation.[32] His following reflection resonated with that anxiety and paradox:

> Oh! coloured people of these United States, I ask you, in the name of that God who made us, have we, in consequence of oppression, nearly lost the spirit of man, and, in no very trifling degree, adopted that of brutes?[33]

Thus Walker believed that blacks in the early nineteenth century were particularly vulnerable to accepting the definition proffered them by whites.[34] In so submitting, they acknowledged to one extent or another

30. "Slavery" by "A Free Negro" in Woodson, *Negro Orators,* 28.

31. *Appeal,* 22.

32. A particularly poignant representation of this process is contained in the slave narrative of Lewis Clarke, who as soon as he stepped on free Canadian land exulted in the full ownership of his own body for the first time. But he also remembered what the attitude of most of those who remained slaves was toward their bodies: "The slaves often say, when cut in the hand or foot, 'Plague on the old foot' or 'the old hand; it is master's—let him take care of it. Nigger don't care, if he never get well.'" (*Narratives of the Suffering of Lewis and Milton Clarke, Sons of a Soldier of the Revolution, During a Captivity of More than Twenty Years Among the Slaveholders of Kentucky* [Boston, 1846], 40).

33. *Appeal,* 26.

34. David Walker would rush to agree with Stanley Elkins's basic assessment that the experience of enslavement in America deeply affected and often damaged most blacks' sense of self and hindered their ability to create a core identity based on autonomy and

the appropriateness of whites' ultimate authority over them and their reliance on them not only for sustenance and moral regulation, but for
existential meaning as well. This act left blacks with a sense of debt and
obligation to whites mandating respect and civility toward them—both as
a result of the terms of the definition and because they had allowed
others to create meaning for them. So long as blacks conceded to whites
the right to define them, they would act as though they were obligated to
them and in ways that would confirm Jefferson's characterizations of
them. Until they accepted the responsibility of shaping their own identity
and rejected the authority of Jefferson and others to do so, they would
feel guilty about any challenge they raised to that authority, and that guilt
would impede their ability to act in their own best interests.

This is the message contained in Walker's critical recounting of a slave
woman's foiling of a daring mass escape of sixty blacks from their coffle.
This incident involved a black woman who, although being moved south
for sale, failed to participate in a well-orchestrated breakout of the men
from their chains, and instead helped one of the slave traders to escape
and raise neighboring whites to recapture the fleeing blacks.[35] For Walker,
the scenario stood as a paradigm of "the force of degraded ignorance and
deceit among us." How could one be so disoriented and degraded as to
protect these people? This question tormented him here and throughout
his work and was key to his understanding not only why blacks were
failing to determine themselves and resist more regularly and in larger

---

entitlement. See Stanley M. Elkins, *Slavery: A Problem in American Institutional and Intellectual Life,* 3rd ed. (Chicago: University of Chicago Press, 1976), 1–139.

One of the most integral thrusts of Walker's argument about the brutality of American
slavery was the degree to which it savaged the black personality, leaving it little to stand on
by way of its own making and thus more receptive to development by white masters.
Walker's zeal for motivating the individual led him to observe and evaluate black personality
minutely, and he often found it wanting if not downright politically counterproductive. But
Walker saw the process of degradation as an evolving one that touched every black in
America over time, not one that was essentially complete with the arrival in America of
captured, deracinated, and shocked Africans. And it is significant that Walker did not see
blacks as empty vessels waiting to be filled with meaning by their owners. While the pressures on blacks could understandably weary them into submission, evidence of their powers
as workers, as agents of change, and as a people special to God abounded. Blacks were not
the perfectly passive instruments of their master's will described by Elkins, but rather a
people capable of active agency, especially if they could be moved to identify with the
sources entitling that activity. Alternatives to passivity did exist, despite the relentless efforts of whites to eliminate all traces of those alternatives and blacks' own doubts and
anxieties about seizing them.

35. This event—as well as the reprinted newspaper account of it and Walker's reaction to
it—is contained in *Appeal,* 23–27. Unless otherwise noted, any quoted or paraphrased material in the following discussion comes from these pages.

numbers, but also what had to be overcome before he could effectively rouse them.

His response lay in his concept of "servile deceit." What he was referring to by this admittedly imprecise term was not an act of public lying— the woman to whom he attached it had not done any lying—but rather to an internal process that led individual blacks not only to deceive themselves about who they were and what the reality of their environment was, but also to deny their responsibility for gaining self-knowledge and crafting identity. This deceit led them almost ineluctably to being servile, given the specific world in which they existed, and to their belief that they owed certain duties to whites.

This woman perfectly embodied the black individual operating under servile deceit. Immediately after quoting the newspaper article and summarizing the horrible crimes of the slavers, Walker assaulted the assumptions he believed underlay the woman's actions:

> Brethren, what do you think of this? Was it the natural *fine feelings* of this woman, to save such a wretch alive? I know that the blacks, take them half enlightened and ignorant, are more humane and merciful than the most enlightened and refined European that can be found in all the earth.

Here he simultaneously attacks the notion that there might be anything elevated or natural in the feelings that led this woman to preserve the slave trader, while asserting that blacks had all the attributes of moral humanity—mercy, generosity, faith, civility. It is just that their expression in this particular setting could only be seen as elevated and obligatory by those who had deceived themselves on the scale of this woman.

> But I declare, the actions of this black woman are really insupportable. For my own part, I cannot think it was anything but servile deceit, combined with the most gross ignorance: for we must remember that *humanity, kindness* and the *fear of the Lord,* does not consist in protecting *devils.*

The fact that blacks had so fully assimilated the whites' designation of them as servile into their conception of self made them unable to acknowledge the reality of their barbarous treatment and their natural impulse to respectfulness and kindness had become perverted. They now believed these honorific gifts were rightfully offered to those who abused and dominated them. This was the ultimate expression of servile deceit. Blacks had come to believe that a necessary affinity existed between them and their white overlords.

Walker sought to undermine the foundation of this self-deception by challenging the notion that any bond at all existed here between master and slave, that it was sustained by anything natural (there "is no more harm for you to kill a man, who is trying to kill you, than it is for you to take a drink of water when thirsty") or by anything moral and Christian ("What has the Lord to do with a gang of desperate wretches . . . ? Any person who will save such wretches from destruction, is fighting against the Lord"). There was no obligation to these people, for no relationship founded on a mutually derived contract had ever been established. This was a relationship of coercion in which blacks and whites were in a state of war so long as whites exclusively continued to profit from and abuse blacks and assumed no responsibility for elevating them. The preponderance of whites had become nothing other than, as Walker repeated throughout the text, the "natural enemies" of blacks because they had robbed blacks of their inheritance of liberty.

With regard to this notion of bond, it is significant that Walker stressed that freedom was not a quality inhering to whites alone, which they could at their discretion give either partially or completely as a gift to deserving blacks:

> Should tyrants take it into their heads to emancipate any of you, remember that your freedom is your natural right. You are men, as well as they, and instead of returning thanks to them for your freedom, return it to the Holy Ghost, who is our rightful owner.[36]

Their supposed unique possession of liberty and the ability to discern the handful of blacks who were entitled to receive a modicum of freedom was an illusion created by whites to dupe blacks into believing they were justifiably enslaved and rightfully honored those who assumed the burdens of managing independence. Freedom was a gift from God alone, and no group of humans had ultimate control over either its production or distribution, save for the secular power to withhold the exercise of it upon due process from those who abused it. Whites did not have the power to create the internal experience of freedom for blacks, to determine it for them. That power existed fully and at all times within blacks themselves as a gift from God. Whites gave nothing to blacks upon manumission except the right to exercise the liberty they had immorally prevented them from so doing in the past. They were not giving blacks a gift, but rather returning what they had stolen from them and God. To pay respect to whites as the source of freedom was thus to blaspheme God by

36. *Appeal*, 71.

denying that he was the source of all virtues and the only one with whom one was justified in having a relationship of obligation and debt. Moreover, designating whites as the sole proprietors of freedom, and as the ones to whom blacks must appeal in order to receive it, only further solidified the ideology of black inferiority and deficiency.

Walker relentlessly attacked all notions that any familial ties or structures of mutual obligation which bound the master and slave together existed. One of the principal burdens of the *Appeal* was to communicate to African Americans that they were not dependent on or obligated to whites, that they were wholly free agents, and that they could come to assume responsibility for the moral application of that freedom. While collapsing one system of meaning, he hoped to resurrect the shattered slaves around independence and personal responsibility. Of course this challenged traditional patterns of work relations in the antebellum South based on paternalism, and upheld instead the possibility that black laborers could operate as independent economic agents ready to compete effectively in a market economy. Walker would have heartily endorsed this, yet he seems to have been convinced that blacks would not be capable of any of those economic transformations until each individual had struggled to reconstitute his or her identity.[37]

According to Walker, identity made perception. If so many blacks believed in their slavishness, they would then readily assume a bond and obligation between them and their masters that only assured their continuing dependency and degradation:

> How could Mr. Jefferson but have given the world these remarks respecting us, when we are so submissive to them, and so much servile deceit prevail among ourselves—when we so *meanly* submit to their murderous lashes . . . ?[38]

37. As economies in the plantation South became less and less reliant on interdependent black-white enterprise during the eighteenth century, and white planters were able to control the production process and the enslaved labor force more perfectly, a paternalistic ideology that characterized blacks as unable to sustain and direct themselves without planter assistance began to germinate and move toward the more articulate form it would acquire by the early decades of the nineteenth century. This process has been illuminated by Peter Wood, *Black Majority: Negroes in Colonial South Carolina from 1670 Through the Stono Rebellion* (New York: Alfred A. Knopf, 1974). This far-reaching paternalism, which has been exhaustively detailed and analyzed for the antebellum era by Eugene Genovese in *Roll, Jordan, Roll,* had by the late 1820s endowed slaves with some sense of obligation to their owners. While Walker was certainly aware of the structure of dependency and its impact on blacks' understanding of themselves, in the *Appeal* he is much more concerned with the existential consequences for blacks of their allowing whites to define them.

38. *Appeal,* 27.

Walker was well aware of the difficulties of challenging authority effectively when such a system of identification was operative. Not only was it difficult to get individuals to recognize slaveholders as their enemy, but once to that point any proposed plans of resistance could still be hampered by persisting doubts about their entitlement to take power and by guilt over a continuing sense of obligation to the authority.

Such examples of guilt and doubt abound even in the more self-actuated of slaves, such as those who have organized for running away. I shall cite just a few examples to illuminate this important psychological dynamic further. The famous fugitive William Grimes was plagued by doubts and guilt about having run away even though he had left a savagely cruel master and successfully settled in Connecticut:

> My conscience used sometimes to upbraid me with having done wrong, after I had run away from my master and arrived in Connecticut; and while I was living in Southington, Conn. . . . I went up on a high mountain and prayed to the Lord to teach me my duty, that I might know whether or not I ought to go back to my master.

He resolved his doubts only through extensive prayer. Sally Williams of North Carolina recounted how, after a severe beating, she contemplated running away but feared it was a sin. "She wondered if she were about to commit a sin, for she had been trained to such implicit obedience to her master, that she hardly dared think of resisting his will." She eventually fled to Fayetteville. Bethany Veney of Virginia had experienced conflicts throughout about lying in situations in which she was perfectly justified to do so. In one of the most intense of these conflicts, her husband had been trusted to spend one last night with her before he was sold South. They decided to run away and for Jerry to go first the following morning. Despite their imminent rupture being one of the most infamous cruelties of American slavery, they experienced tremendous guilt about their plan. "Then came the wish to secrete ourselves together in the mountains or elsewhere, till White [the slave trader] should be gone. . . . Then we remembered that White had trusted us, in letting him come to see me, and we felt ashamed for a moment, as if we had tried to cheat; but what *right* had White to carry him away, or even to own him at all? Our poor, ignorant reasoning found it hard to understand his rights or our own." This is a splendid example of what Walker called "the force of degraded ignorance and deceit among us," even upon two very reflective individuals.[39]

39. See Grimes, *Life,* 28–29; Sally Williams, *Aunt Sally; or, The Cross the Way to Freedom*

One of the greatest slave chroniclers of the antebellum era was Charles Ball, who eventually succeeded in running away to Maryland after several attempts. The deliberative and introspective Ball managed on a number of occasions to secure extra privileges and goods for himself through brilliant cunning. At one point he determined that he needed his master's sword for a forthcoming attempt at flight and underwent a revealing process:

> My master was an officer of militia, and had a sword which he wore on parade days, and at other times he hung it up in the room where he slept. I conceived an idea that this sword would be of service to me in the long journey that I intended to undertake. One evening, when I had gone in to see my master, and had remained standing at his bed-side some time, he closed his eyes as if going to sleep, and it being twilight, I slipped the sword from the place where it hung, and dropped it out of the window. I knew my master could never need this weapon again, but yet I felt some compunction of conscience at the thought of robbing so good a man.

This "so good a man" had only a few weeks earlier beaten Ball so severely that his shirt had fused with his skin from profusion of blood and he lay near death. Yet the doubt he experienced was based not on fear of further violence from this man, as one might expect, but on a profound trepidation about seizing something—the sword—which was uniquely identified with the master's power. Ball was careful to note that this sword was linked with one of the most important annual rituals repeated in communities throughout the nation—Parade Day—in which local hierarchies were displayed publicly and reinforced and, especially in the South, white solidarity and dominance was reasserted. Moreover, his master clearly had a preeminent position in this display as an officer of the militia. By stealing this sword, Ball in effect subverted the whole meaning of the ritual and ironically replaced his master with himself at the fore of the local force. By successfully taking the sword—which he did do—Ball symbolically seized a vast amount of power for himself but also lucidly revealed the great fear the rebel had to confront in denying the authority that was so extensively and forcefully upheld throughout society. Nowhere were Walker's preoccupations with the inner forces holding blacks back from seizing a power that lay directly before them more neatly encapsulated than in Ball's wrestling with the sword. If such anxieties grasped Ball—one who clearly had some conscious sense of entitlement,

(Cincinnati, 1858), 66–71; *The Narrative of Bethany Veney, a Slave Woman* (Worcester, Mass., 1889), 21.

however imperfectly formed, to power and self-determination, one can only imagine how much greater they may have been for those lacking his privileges, resourcefulness, and confidence.[40]

Real change could not begin to occur for African Americans until they could acknowledge and describe the conditions and system under which they existed. In the *Appeal,* Walker was in large part immersing himself in the heart of this uniquely brutal slavery in America and then naming and experiencing its numerous component horrors. What he performed was actually a detailed social and psychological excavation "of this system of cruelty and oppression."[41] His intent was to make more difficult any further hiding, by society or by individuals, from the realities of this system—how it operated and what its effects were. Walker believed that white America had literally gotten away with murder, because the people of the world identified it with the mask of humane republicanism it projected and had not seen the unspoken horrors hiding behind it.

> Our dear Redeemer said, "Therefore, whatsoever ye have spoken in darkness, shall be heard in the light; and that which ye have spoken in the ear in closets, shall be proclaimed upon the house tops."
>
> How obviously this declaration of our Lord has been shown among the Americans of the United States. They have hitherto passed among some nations, who do not know any thing about their internal concerns, for the most enlightened, humane, charitable, and merciful people upon earth, when at the same time they treat us, the (coloured people) secretly more cruel and unmerciful than any other nation upon earth. . . . God has however, taken off the fig-leaf covering, and made them expose themselves on the house top.[42]

Evidently Walker, like any good evangelical involved in spreading the truth and entitlement, is a part of this divine plan of exposure. Yet Walker was as concerned that individual African Americans not evade this reality as he was that America's crimes be posted before the eyes of the world. It was precisely blacks' unwitting will to believe in slaveholders as "enlightened, humane, charitable, and merciful people" that prevented them from really knowing them and responding appropriately to them.

Walker offered himself as an example of the fact that a black person

40. Charles Ball, *Fifty Years in Chains; or, The Life of an American Slave* (New York, 1858), 306.
41. *Appeal,* 6.
42. *Appeal,* 52–53, 54.

could plunge into the heart of the beast and experience its terrors and name them, emerge, and not only survive but somehow be strengthened and wiser. Despite the admittedly horrible burdens weighing on blacks in America, they did not have to be overpowered by them. Walker displayed himself as living proof of the fact that the possibility of an immediate and honest apprehension of the world that dismissed degrading deceit and hypocrisy, and the possibility of genuine change and growth, truly existed for African Americans. Through his painful and vulnerable display of himself in the process of naming and emoting, he made clear not only that it could be done but also how it could be done. One truly understood how a system of social oppression operated only by understanding how it operated on oneself. By knowing that, one could reject it more fully and deliberately and discern its subtle influences on one's life and weed them out. For Walker, all righteous social change had to begin with uncoerced, individual transformation.

As with any manifesto intended to move a large number of people to action, the *Appeal* was structured, both in images and in tones, to speak directly to the experiences of his black audience. As Walker emphasized, the work was written "in language so very simple, that the most ignorant, who can read at all, may easily understand."[43] It was filled with a great compassion for the sufferings of the slaves, and it labored to describe accurately what might comprise the lived experience of any number of them. Walker affirmed the pain, anger, confusion, and even deceit and self-loathing that were critical parts of a direct confrontation with American slavery by actually living them in front of his auditors. And he showed real sympathy for those who might mock and reject him, attributing their actions to an ignorance for which they were finally not responsible, and stressing their essential relatedness to each other.[44] Walker sought to gain the confidence of slaves through a sharing with them that revealed respect and love of them.

This integral effort to connect orator and audience was always oriented toward making inescapable the divine and ideological mandate challenging blacks to change these conditions, which they shared with Walker. Despite all the great psychological and social burdens weighing on blacks, and the great obstacles they posed to change, Walker believed that African Americans were doomed as individuals, as a race and as the children of God if they failed fully to challenge this ideology and the state structure that embodied and enforced it. As the discussion above on individual psychology attests, Walker was convinced that no social change of

43. *Appeal,* 71.
44. See, for example, *Appeal,* 30n, 31.

any substance could occur unless each individual underwent an internal, conscious struggle with American oppression and rose regenerated from it. Each African American had to undergo an internal revolution that wrought a fundamental shift in conception of self and led to an inner assent to one's entitlement to self-determination and to one's willingness to accept that responsibility. Only by such forceful inner assertion could the damage done by America's odious racial ideology begin to be cast off. Said Walker:

> There is an unconquerable disposition in the breasts of the blacks, which, when it is fully awakened and put in motion, will be subdued, only with the destruction of the animal existence. Get the blacks started, and if you do not have a gang of tigers and lions to deal with, I am a deceiver of the blacks and of the whites.[45]

Unleashing anger was essential to getting "the blacks started." Only through a full experience of this powerful emotion in which they rejected the structures and definition imposed on them by other people could they begin to move toward a clearer sense of what their true identity, this "unconquerable disposition," was. For African Americans, securing self-knowledge and identity in antebellum America had to have a base—to a degree unique to them—in rage, rejection, and defiance given the amount of pressure on them alone to comply with identities designed for them by others. Volatile emotional release had to play a crucial role for blacks—both for purging and for self-clarification.

But it was precisely this pressure to comply that made attempting and asserting self-definition extremely problematic for blacks. Undertaking this great effort was dangerous and required tremendous exertion. On what basis were blacks to believe that all this effort to build meaning, freedom, and community would in any way enhance their lives as members of the American nation? There was a much greater chance that it would lead to a precipitous decline in quality.[46]

45. *Appeal,* 25.
46. Walker actually had little to say to whites about changes he expected of them, as critical as such a designation would have been. Whites were to repent of their sins, to apologize to blacks for having abused them, to treat them like beings worthy of respect, and to help uplift them while they were still in their custody. Most of this was pronounced in quick order in the *Appeal,* 69–70. In no way did Walker grapple with the dynamics of the psychology of dominance or with the difficulties in changing it in whites on the scale of his hard-nosed and extensive assessment of the blacks, even though he despaired at one point that the notion of black inferiority had "sunk deep into the hearts of millions of the whites, and never will be removed this side of eternity" (*Appeal,* 28). Such a reality demanded much more serious attention from Walker, for it would make it impossible for blacks to be ac-

Faith in God's special love for African Americans and in his promises for them was to be the bedrock on which blacks would find the rationale and the courage to carry on this difficult work against what often seemed to be overwhelming odds. God would form the core of their newfound self. God was not introduced because of some mere tactical utility initiated by nonbelievers to manipulate the masses. Rather, Walker animated his work so richly with God's presence because an ever-growing number of blacks found in God and Christianity a source of abiding love and solace and because the religion's central images had to do with the deliverance of peoples from bondage and persecution. God affirmed the worth of every individual black person, and their equality with whites in the scheme of creation.

> Are we MEN!!—I ask you, my brethren! are we MEN? Did our creator make us to be slaves to dust and ashes like ourselves? Are they not dying worms as well as we? Have they not to make their appearance before the tribunal of Heaven, to answer for the deeds done in the body, as well as we? Have we any other Master but Jesus Christ alone? Is he not their Master as well as ours?—What right then, have we to obey and call any other Master, but Himself?[47]

Walker relentlessly repeated that God will deliver the blacks and rain wrath down on the whites who are too proud to atone for their sin against God's creatures:

> Will the Lord suffer this people [i.e., white slaveholders and hypocritical preachers] to go on much longer, taking his holy name in vain? Will he not stop them, PREACHERS and all? Americans! Americans!! I call God—I call angels—I call men, to witness, that your DESTRUCTION *is at hand,* and will be speedily consummated unless you REPENT.[48]

---

cepted and to participate effectively in American society. Yet he relied on motivating whites with the club of God's potential wrath, even though he believed that most had hardened their hearts against the deity and were committed to slavery. He counseled blacks that their faithfulness to God would lead them to triumph—with or without the whites. This is why Walker believed blacks could confidently undertake the demanding struggles, as we shall see in the following pages. While this lapse in analysis and strategizing once again pointed to Walker's overwhelming preoccupation with fomenting change in blacks, his failure to deal more substantively with how to make whites more genuinely receptive to black equality was a serious flaw in his plans for achieving realistic change in American society. It also seems implicitly to indicate his deep doubts about the degree to which whites could change their racial prejudices.

47. *Appeal,* 16.
48. *Appeal,* 43.

All this, he assured his audience, will come to pass and soon. Blacks need only have complete faith in God's love and promises.

Indeed, to enhance the authority of his own utterances in the *Appeal,* Walker associated them on several occasions with divine inspiration. At one point he proclaimed, "I write without the fear of man, I am writing for my God," and at another place he stated that his demonstration of the unusual barbarity of American slavery was supported "by the help of the Lord."[49] But his central statement on this matter linked him so closely with God that he seemed to be claiming direct revelation for his words:

> Some of my brethren, who are sensible, do not take an interest in enlightening the minds of our more ignorant brethren respecting this Book, and in reading it to them, just as though they will not have either to stand or fall by what is written in this book. Do they believe that I would be so foolish as to put out a book of this kind without strict—ah! very strict commandments of the Lord?— Surely the blacks and whites must think that I am ignorant enough.—Do they think that I would have the audacious wickedness to take the name of my God in vain? . . . He will show you and the world, in due time, whether this book is for his glory, or written by me through envy of the whites, as some have represented.[50]

In prophetic tones, Walker virtually equated his pronouncements with the word of God. His own articulate courage and confident finger-pointing were all intended to reinforce the idea that he was filled with God and spoke for him.

Yet even the zealot Walker revealed that he had painful moments of doubt concerning the very promises he celebrated. At a few points in the text, he ranged nervously for clearly demonstrative proof on which to base his belief.[51] The most personally revealing was:

> I aver, that when I look over these United States of America, and the world, and see the ignorant deceptions and consequent wretchedness of my brethren, I am brought ofttimes solemnly to a stand, and in the midst of my reflections I exclaim to my God, "Lord didst thou make us to be slaves to our brethren, the whites?" But when I reflect that God is just, and that millions of my wretched brethren would meet death with glory . . . in preference to a mean submission to the lash of tyrants, I am with streaming

49. *Appeal,* 1, 54.

50. *Appeal,* 71n.

51. For example, early in the text he asked: "If God gives you [i.e., white slaveholders] peace and tranquility, and suffers you thus to go on afflicting us, and our children, who have never given you the least provocation—would he be to us *a God of justice?"* (*Appeal,* 5).

eyes, compelled to shrink back into nothingness before my Maker, and exclaim again, thy will be done, O Lord God Almighty.[52]

The apparent resolution of Walker's doubt here is not wholly convincing. He founded it on precisely the quality of individual character—the refusal to submit to slavishness and apathy—the existence of which he had just expressed grave uncertainty in the immediately preceding sentence, among other places.[53]

But this explanation worked splendidly to save God and banish doubt. At no point after the question was proposed were God's existence or God's promises mistrusted. The question of doubt and fulfillment was instead made to hinge solely on whether blacks accepted the character with which God had endowed them and were ready to act accordingly. Walker indicated here that they were ready, but even if he had concluded they were not, God was still safe. The mere fact that blacks were capable of acting in such a way that proved them the equal of whites verified God's presence and promise.

Faith had to be inseparable from action in the world: faith must yield works.

> We believe that, for thy glory's sake,
> Thou wilt deliver us;
> But that thou may'st effect these things,
> Thy glory must be sought.[54]

Nothing God promised would come to pass without an unprecedented exertion of African American wills. Walker circumvented the doubt that even he had about God's promises by making their fulfillment totally contingent on human action. The problem was not proving God's existence, but rather motivating blacks to use the powers God had given them— thus the great need to awaken in them, to shock them into recognition of, their "unconquerable disposition."

The structure of the *Appeal* and its motivational strategy bore significant resemblance to the forms and plans of white revivalists contemporary with Walker. Indeed, Walker's thinking on how to move individuals to make profound transformations in conceptions of self was strikingly similar on some important points to that of Charles Grandison Finney, especially as articulated in Finney's famous *Lectures on Revivals of Reli-*

---

52. *Appeal*, 28.
53. The sentence reads: "For how can they [i.e., how can the whites respect us], when we are confirming him [i.e., Jefferson] every day, by our *groveling submissions* and *treachery?*"
54. *Appeal*, 74.

gion. Finney believed that selfishness, materialism, and sensualism had such a strong grip on the individual and was so sanctioned by contemporary society that the only way the individual could be roused from this slothful malaise and brought to recognize his true self and relationship to God was to elicit intense countervailing emotions in that person:

> Almost all the religion in the world has been produced by revivals. God has found it necessary to take advantage of the excitability there is in mankind, to produce powerful excitements among them, before he can lead them to obey. Men are so spiritually sluggish, there are so many things to lead their minds off from religion, and to oppose the influence of the Gospel, that it is necessary to raise an excitement among them, till the tide rises so high as to sweep away the opposing obstacles. They must be so excited that they will break over these counteracting influences, before they will obey God. Not that excited feeling is religion, for it is not; but it is excited desire, appetite and feeling that prevents religion. The will is, in a sense, enslaved by the carnal and worldly desires. Hence it is necessary to awaken men to a sense of guilt and danger, and thus produce an excitement of counter feeling and desire which will break the power of carnal and worldly desire and leave the will free to obey God.[55]

While Finney obviously did not speak of slavery, he did refer to the pervasiveness of the chains of carnal desire and the need to excite the individual to find the strength to break them. The world without God was a total institution of depravity where God must literally force his way in violently.

Walker understood the slave system similarly as so near a total institution controlled by the slavers that the virtues of personal worth and liberty they had sought to banish from the slaves' purview had to be brought with shocking force into the consciousness of blacks so they could not fail to acknowledge that they were entitled to them. Unlike the mandates of the contemporary white revivalists, the great sin for antebellum blacks was not a self-absorption leading one to pursue worldly ends and pleasures to the exclusion of God; for all intents and purposes, pursuing such worldly mobility was not even an option that was open to blacks at that time. If anything, they had too little of the things of the world. Rather their great sin was in the failure to exert themselves to the fullest to

55. Charles Grandison Finney, *Lectures on Revivals of Religion,* ed. William G. McLoughlin (Cambridge: Harvard University Press, 1960), 9–10.

overcome slavishness and secure the autonomy and integrity that God had promised them.

> O my God!—in sorrow I must say it, that my colour, all over the world, have a mean, servile spirit. . . . When shall we arise from this death-like apathy?—And be men!! You will notice, if ever we become men, (I mean *respectable* men, such as other people are,) we must exert ourselves to the full.[56]

Exertion was faith, for it was the destruction of "this death-like apathy" that sustained ungodly servility.

But deliverance from slavery and the realization of salvation were by no means complete with the accomplishment of inner transformation. While realizing this new conception of self enabled the individual to act more effectively, his or her inner freedom remained imperfect and un-fulfilled so long as the structures that could mute it continued to dominate the society and threaten blacks. Renewed individuals then had to join together to extend their ranks by stirring still others to change and by devising whatever plan might be necessary to secure eventual emancipation. God mandated that outer, social conditions somehow had to be brought into ever closer correspondence with inner, private conditions. The following passage is key to understanding the simultaneously political and Christian/millennialist thrust of Walker's thinking and how those ends were to be effected by a concert of regenerated African American individuals:

> I advanced it therefore to you, not as a *problematical*, but as an unshaken and for ever immovable *fact*, that your full glory and happiness, as well as all other coloured people under Heaven, shall never be fully consummated, but with the *entire emancipation of your enslaved brethren all over the world.* You may therefore, go to work and do what you can to rescue, or join in with tyrants to oppress them and yourselves, until the Lord shall come upon you all like a thief in the night. For I believe it is the will of the Lord that our greatest happiness shall consist in working for the salvation of our whole body. When this is accomplished a burst of glory will shine upon you, which will indeed astonish you and the world. Do any of you say this never will be done? I assure you that God will accomplish it—if nothing else will answer, he will hurl tyrants and devils into *atoms* and make way for his peo-

56. *Appeal,* 62.

ple. But my brethren! I say unto you again, you must go to work
and prepare the way of the Lord.[57]

The tremendous emphasis placed here on exertion is significant. Not only
is the realization of an ultimate objective through deliberate effort celebrated, but the experience of a happiness, and even joy by way of united
exertion is upheld almost as much.

Walker followed an African American tradition, evolving since the late
eighteenth century, of employing evangelical religion not only for individual regeneration but also for radical social transformation. Influenced in
part by the egalitarianism and support for rebellion espoused by many
white evangelicals during the era of the American Revolution, Gabriel, the
rebels of 1802, Vesey, Walker, and Turner crafted a doctrine of religion
and rebellion that by 1831 was well established and gaining momentum
as revivals and abolitionism converged in the social enthusiasms of the
early 1830s. This momentum would be decisively checked in the aftermath of Turner's Rebellion when new restrictions on black preachers
were rigorously enforced and white missionaries labored to gain greater
control over the religious life of blacks through the mission to the slaves.

But contemporary historians have tended to downplay this significant
strain in the African American religious tradition. While acknowledging
the critical role of religion in the thought of these black leaders, such
historians of African American religion as Timothy Smith, Mechal Sobel,
Paul Radin, Albert Raboteau, and—with some significant qualifications—
Eugene Genovese explain this use as merely incidental to the principal
function of evangelical religion for antebellum blacks: the maintenance
of individual psychological integrity and of community coherence and
meaning. The experience of conversion, learning about the Bible, and
group worship allowed the slaves not only to endow their sufferings
and struggles with meaning and significance, but also to endure them and
perhaps even be elevated by them. Mechal Sobel especially emphasizes
how the Baptist faith and its rituals allowed African Americans the opportunity to restore the African spiritual dimension to their lives and to realize inner wholeness. Smith remains an agnostic on the role of African
religion on African American faith, while certain that "evangelical Protestantism became the folk religion of black people in the United States."
Despite some variations in focus, all would concur with Timothy Smith's
appraisal that Christianity enabled antebellum slaves to overcome the
brutal contradictions pervading their lives, "to reconcile suffering and
hope, guilt and forgiveness, tyranny and spiritual freedom, self-hate and

57. *Appeal,* 29–30.

divine acceptance." Evangelicalism brought them the empowering gifts of love, patience, personal integrity, and community.[58]

It did not, however, propel them into a premillennial activism of the sort Gabriel, Vesey, Walker, and Turner all clearly sought to spark. Save for Genovese, all these historians have lost sight of how this impulse endured and at times prospered, up until the crushing reaction against black preachers and black religious autonomy following Turner's uprising. They tend to read back from the post-1831 era, or simply ignore the strength of this tradition in the early nineteenth century, and concentrate instead on the individual and communitarian functionalism of religion. While aid to psychic and community stability was undeniably a critical service religion rendered African Americans, in the early decades of the United States these functions conjoined with a fierce religious impulse to destroy the social structures upholding degradation and submission and replace them with institutions based on Christian love and justice.

Unflagging, common, constructive effort was everything. It was fulfillment of covenant with God and the dawning of the millennium; it was individual regeneration and righteous community; it was denial of non-humanness; and it was the beginning of the destruction of the society that actively kept blacks from all this. The overwhelming burden of the *Appeal* was to move African Americans so to act. It was a work over which tremendous control had been exercised, a work that had been crafted to make inescapable for blacks not only the possibility of individual reconstruction and positive social action, but also the mandate for such action. The fulfillment of self came only through religiously righteous collective action, to which each individual assented, that banished alienation from self and from others. Individual wholeness was impossible without moral, social community. What made the *Appeal* such a humane work was the degree to which it described the system of American slavery and made its criminality clear, and, more important, the way it so sympathetically revealed how the system prevented blacks from realizing individual and social integrity. In a manner unique to him in the antebellum era, Walker grappled with how to motivate a people who were burdened with these obstacles to want freedom and power.

In an equally famous call for slave empowerment and activism—Henry

58. See Timothy Smith, "Slavery and Theology: The Emergence of Black Christian Consciousness in Nineteenth Century America," *Church History* 41 (December 1972), 497–512; Mechal Sobel, *Trabelin' On: The Slave Journey to an Afro-Baptist Faith* (Westport, Conn.: Greenwood Press, 1979); Paul Radin, "Status, Phantasy, and the Christian Dogma," in George P. Rawick, ed., *The American Slave: A Composite Autobiography,* Series 2, vol. 19: *God Struck Me Dead* (Westport, Conn.: Greenwood Press, 1972), iv–xi; Raboteau, *Slave Religion;* Genovese, *Roll, Jordan, Roll,* 159–284.

Highland Garnet's 1843 "Address to the Slaves of the United States of America"—the author fell far short of Walker's impressive effort to speak directly to the slaves through simple and concrete language, powerful emotional liaisons, and emphatic cadences yoked to religious yearning. Garnet often sounded formal, distant, and even admonishing of the slaves, even though he was unquestionably animated by understandings and aspirations similar to Walker's. In greeting the slaves, he abstractly observed:

> Many of you are bound to us, not only by the tie of a common humanity, but we are connected by the more tender relations of parents, wives, husbands, children, brothers, and sisters, and friends. As such we most affectionately address you.

The immediacy of connectedness that is so vital to Walker's structure is absent here. A similar condition exists in Garnet's highly formulaic description of the horrors the slaves were subjected to under slavery:

> Look around you, and behold the bosoms of your loving wives heaving with untold agonies! Hear the cries of your poor children! Remember the stripes your fathers bore. Think of the torture and disgrace of your noble mothers. Think of your wretched sisters, loving virtue and purity, as they are driven into concubinage and are exposed to the unbridled lusts of incarnate devils.

As a motivational device addressed to slaves, this fares poorly against Walker's less antiseptic but evidently pained recollection:

> They brand us with hot iron—they cram bolts of fire down our throats—they cut us as they do horses, bulls, or hogs—they crop our ears and sometimes cut off bits of our tongues—they chain and handcuff us, and while in that miserable condition, beat us with cow-hides and clubs—they keep us half naked and starve us sometimes nearly to death. . . . They put on us fifty-sixes and chains, and make us work in that cruel situation, and in sickness. . . .[59]

The most glaring dissonance between the two, however, occurred at the critical point where Garnet called for a cessation of submission to enslavement:

> TO SUCH DEGRADATION [i.e., slavery] IT IS SINFUL IN THE EXTREME FOR YOU TO MAKE VOLUNTARY SUBMISSION. The divine

59. *Appeal,* 65.

commandments you are in duty bound to reverence and obey. If you do not obey them, you will surely meet with the displeasure of the Almighty. He requires you to love him supremely and your neighbor as yourself—to keep the Sabbath day holy—to search the Scriptures—and bring up your children with respect for his laws, and to worship no other God but him. But slavery sets all these at nought, and hurls defiance in the face of Jehovah. The forlorn condition in which you are placed, does not destroy your moral obligation to God. You are not certain of heaven, because you suffer yourselves to remain in a state of slavery, where you cannot obey the commandments of the Sovereign of the universe. If the ignorance of slavery is a passport to heaven, then it is a blessing, and no curse, and you should rather desire its perpetuity than its abolition. God will not receive slavery, nor ignorance, nor any other state of mind, for love and obedience to him. Your condition does not absolve you from your moral obligation. The diabolical injustice by which your liberties are cloven down, NEITHER GOD, NOR ANGELS, OR JUST MEN, COMMAND YOU TO SUFFER FOR A SINGLE MOMENT. THEREFORE IT IS YOUR SOLEMN AND IMPERATIVE DUTY TO USE EVERY MEANS, BOTH MORAL, INTELLECTUAL, AND PHYSICAL, THAT PROMISES SUCCESS.[60]

Here he sounds almost like an admonishing schoolmaster advising his class of their moral duties rather than a sympathetic compatriot sensitive to the problems in marshaling individual responsibility and to the grievous dangers in resistance. He does not use the language and images of slave culture. He fails to project a knowledge of the daily life, morality, beliefs, and aspirations informing the slave's world. Indeed, this address was much more oriented toward an educated, decorous, reform-minded white and black Northern audience than a very localized, illiterate slave population somewhere in the rural South. My point here is not to disparage the noble intentions of Garnet, but rather to show through a brief examination of an important antislavery document, to which the *Appeal* is often found analogous, how far they were separate from each other in terms of sensibility, structure, and strategy, and thereby to highlight both the unique insight of Walker into the predicament of blacks in the United States and the far greater viability—albeit one not also without difficulty and dangerousness—this understanding lent to his unprecedented effort to rally the black populace.

60. The three passages of Henry Highland Garnet's above are all from "An Address to the Slaves of the United States of America," in John Bracey et al., eds., *The Afro-Americans: Selected Documents* (Boston: Allyn & Bacon, 1972), 192, 194–95.

David Walker's *Appeal to the Colored Citizens of the World* was one of the single most important works to issue from an African American in the antebellum era. Founding his work on a demonstration of African Americans as "the most wretched, degraded and abject set of beings that ever lived since the world began," Walker proceeded to categorize that situation in all its lurid details and to live vividly through his words the pain, doubt, and self-contempt it fostered in its subjects. It is not that David Walker uttered things that were not said by others before him or after him, but rather that he had a unique ability for compressing and articulating in one work the totality of the experience for blacks of existing under that system and communicating it in a form accessible to the mass of blacks. Drawing deeply from his knowledge of the world of enslaved blacks in the South, and combining that with his acute awareness of Northern free black life, Walker used his education, facility with words, and tremendous sympathetic powers to craft an archetype of black life in antebellum America. No other black commentator reached the scope or depth of this composite. No one else so fully wrestled with the complexities of the psychology of the slaves and sought to bring them to a greater sense of personal empowerment. No other African Americans from this era—to the best of our knowledge—not only took on themselves the task of conceiving so grand a strategy of individual and social transformation but also took such innovative and courageous steps to put it into motion.

8

"Why are the Americans so very fearfully terrified respecting my book?"

The Appeal *and the Problem of Antebellum Black Resistance*

In February 1830 a writer for *Niles' Register* reported: "There has been another meeting of persons of 'Colleton district,' South Carolina. The worst days of the 'Hartford convention' presented us with no paper so disreputable as that which appears under the sanction of this meeting—and some of the journals of that state talk very coldly about 'blood-letting!' And all this, when the legislatures of two states have been frightened by a few dozen *pamphlets*, written by a negro, who deals in old clothes!"[1]

What exactly was all this commotion about "a negro, who deals in old clothes"? How could so seemingly insignificant a figure prompt citizens from one of South Carolina's wealthiest and politically most powerful districts not only to carry on but even to surpass the secessionist impulse of

1. *Niles' Register*, February 27, 1830.

the Hartford Convention? Why all this fear and trembling about Walker in the South?

Arriving in Richmond, Savannah, New Orleans, Charleston, and Wilmington at the same time the crisis over nullification of the Tariff of 1828 was escalating and, in the case of the three latter ports, on the heels of the volatile Webster-Hayne debates of late January 1830, the *Appeal* on the one hand seemed only to highlight the threat the Southern way of life faced from a distant federal government supposedly dominated by Northern commercial interests and a rising antislavery sentiment. Indeed, the immediate occasion for the citizens' meeting in Colleton District, the seat of arch-nullificationist Robert Barnwell Rhett, was to chastise their merchant neighbors in Charleston for daring to approach the federal government to purchase bonds for a railroad to Hamburg. Yet such a suspicion-ridden local convention was well disposed to confirm fears about the significance of the recent arrival of the *Appeal* in Virginia and Georgia.[2] Colleton's notables could only have agreed with the assessment of Governor George Gilmer of Georgia, who wrote about the *Appeal*'s broader meaning: "The slave holding states are a minority in the Union. The strongest prejudices are continually excited against us."[3] The pamphlet seemed only to evince further the existence of a distant enemy menacing the South.

Yet the arrival of this work elicited even more immediate and deep-seated fears in the authorities about their problematic black population and the unusual threat the *Appeal* seemed to pose for mobilizing them. Within days after being alerted to the pamphlet's presence in Savannah, the town's mayor, William Thorne Williams, wrote to Governor Gilmer:

> Attempts to introduce into the ports of the South similar dangerous publications will no doubt be made, and there is every probability that their dissemination through the State may be effected. I have deemed it my duty to communicate to you the facts in my possession that you may adopt such measures as you may deem necessary to detect or defeat these destructive efforts.[4]

Williams had aptly discerned the national thrust of Walker's objectives and saw they were dependent on the assistance of a covert distribution

2. For further discussion of these matters in South Carolina, see William Freehling, *Prelude to Civil War: The Nullification Controversy in South Carolina, 1816–1836* (New York: Harper & Row, 1966), esp. 177–218.

3. Governor Gilmer to Mayor Williams, March 13, 1830, Governor's Letter Books, 1829–33, Drawer 62, Box 64, Georgia Department of Archives and History.

4. Williams to Gilmer, December 26, 1829, Records of Chatham County, Mayor's Letter Book, 1821–44, Georgia Historical Society, Savannah.

network, the potential effectiveness of which he did not seem to doubt. What the authorities quickly focused on with the pamphlet was not only its potential to destabilize the local social situation, but also its author's unprecedented intention of circulating it throughout the South. Thus Williams quickly alerted Charleston's Intendant, Henry L. Pinckney, to the work's imminent arrival there, and Governor Gilmer wrote to Governor Giles of Virginia, and both of them wrote to Mayor Harrison Gray Otis of Boston. Measures were quickly taken to apply the Negro Seaman's Act to Savannah and Wilmington, and new laws curtailing contact between free blacks and slaves were enacted in these two towns and New Orleans.[5] The south-wide response to the *Appeal* made clear the authorities were aware that they were up against a strategy the likes of which they had never seen before. Despite claims that Gabriel Prosser had ties with the French, and that Denmark Vesey had ties with the Haitians, all previous conspiracies had been overwhelmingly local, with a few spreading over a handful of counties. Now authorities were confronted with a plan that not only hoped to embrace the entire South but was actually being orchestrated from a distant Northern city. Placed in this context, the extraordinary, secret convening of the Virginia and Georgia legislatures immediately on discovery of the pamphlet makes considerably more sense. They believed with some reason that they were confronted with an unusually menacing threat.

Moreover, they recognized that Walker was most likely aware of underground communication networks existing among blacks—and whites—in port towns, and that these could readily be linked up with those extending into the interior by way of the large number of mobile black laborers who regularly came into these towns from the hinterlands delivering products to the wharfs. Thus Mayor Williams's observation: "There is every probability that their [the pamphlet's] dissemination through the State may be effected." Similar anxieties were voiced in North Carolina in late 1830 when it was discovered that a black courier from Wilmington had "brought some of those pamphlets" to New Bern and possibly as far north as Elizabeth City. An investigative committee in North Carolina concluded in December 1830:

> The actual detection of the circulation of the incendiary publication, . . . and the accidental but partial discovery of design, perhaps not fully developed or digested, which have been entertained by some slaves at points of the State remote from each other, . . . leave no doubt in the minds of your Committee, that the time has arrived . . . to act with firmness and decision.[6]

5. For a fuller discussion of these actions, see Chapter 5.
6. Coon, *Beginnings of Public Education in North Carolina,* 1:478.

In Virginia, the *Richmond Enquirer* emphasized: "We should have taken no further notice of this matter, if we had not reason to believe that a systematic design has been formed for circulating these pamphlets clandestinely among our coloured population."[7] If these various regional networks could even be loosely intertwined, as Walker clearly hoped to have happen, they could form a powerfully subversive amalgam that authorities rightfully feared.

This was by no means the first time that Southern authorities had been confronted with the blacks' facility at communicating information among themselves and over some distance. The perspicacious commentator on Gabriel's conspiracy, George Tucker, wrote in 1801:

> We have hitherto placed much reliance on the difficulty of their acting in concert. Late experience has shewn us, that the difficulty is not insurmountable. Ignorant and illiterate as they yet are, they have maintained a correspondence, which, whether we consider its extent or duration, is truly astonishing.[8]

As reports of conspiracies among the slaves escalated in early 1802 in Virginia and in northeast North Carolina, authorities increasingly noted how blacks seemed to be communicating among themselves. In a letter to Virginia Governor James Monroe, Thomas Matthews of Norfolk reported the widespread belief that "frequent meetings [of slaves] are held in the neighborhood of this place; that those meetings have consisted of from one to three and four hundred; that a correspondence is held by these meetings with similar ones in North Carolina; that an emissary is now in this town shortly to take his leave to that state with communications." While Matthews doubted the credibility of these reports, John Cowper, another local correspondent with Governor Monroe, and others of Norfolk's "most reputable citizens" placed much weight on them and had their anxieties exacerbated by the arrival in the port of hundreds of Haitian émigrés fleeing the insurrection in that island with their slaves. They worried that these Haitian slaves only furthered the opportunities for rebellious communications among the blacks.[9] In the aftermath of the Vesey conspiracy, the Intendant of Charleston, James Hamilton, had little doubt about the scale of the communications network the conspirators had secretly forged. While Governor Thomas Bennett dismissed it, he had not had the benefit of directly interrogating and observing the prisoners as Hamilton had. Southern officials clearly recognized that Walker was draw-

7. *Richmond Enquirer*, January 28, 1830.
8. Tucker, *Letter to a Member*, 11.
9. Palmer, *Calendar of Virginia State Papers*, 9:286–87, 293–94.

ing on these sorts of existing structures, but with a geographical scope and innovativeness that was unprecedented.

The big fear of the authorities in the South was that the arrival of the *Appeal* would not only introduce subversive ideas into their communities, but also stimulate increased efforts of the slaves to communicate among themselves and extend their networks—that its impact would be organizational as well as ideological. Thus their overwhelming preoccupation throughout 1830 with preventing contact between free blacks in the North and local blacks, as well as proscribing teaching any slave to read and write through elaborate legislation.[10] A committee convened in 1830 to determine new regulations for slaves in North Carolina wrote:

> One source of great evil . . . from which the most serious danger may be apprehended, is, the teaching slaves to read and write; thereby affording them facilities of intelligence and communication, inconsistent with their condition, destructive of their contentment and happiness, and dangerous to the community.[11]

The state enacted comprehensive legislation outlawing slave literacy and education.

While Southern authorities rarely commented specifically on the content of the *Appeal,* beyond making the requisite reference to "the seditious pamphlet," Walker's tremendous emphasis on fostering the moral and intellectual uplift of blacks, on forging Southern and national connections among African Americans, and on using evangelicalism to buttress these appeals ideologically could only have fueled officials' anxieties about the work energizing the slaves' covert efforts to extend the breadth of correspondence among themselves. A nationalistic and millennialist impulse pervades the *Appeal.* The pamphlet was infused with a spirit identical to that embodied in the following passage from a key speech Walker gave in Boston in December 1828:

> The primary object of this institution, is, to unite the colored population, so far, through the United States of America, as may be practicable and expedient; forming societies, opening, extending,

10. In February 1830 Mayor Williams of Savannah had passed in council a lengthy law on quarantining Northern free blacks that included the provision that it was the duty of the police to arrest any local "negro or person of color, who shall have any communication whatever with any free negro or person of color, so arriving in any ship or vessel and bring him, her or them before the Mayor who shall sentence the said negro to be whipped, not exceeding thirty-nine lashes" (Charles S. Henry, ed., *A Digest of All the Ordinances of the City of Savannah, which were of force on the 1st July 1854* [Savannah, 1854], 349–50).

11. Coon, *Beginnings of Public Education in North Carolina,* 1:479.

and keeping up correspondences, and not withholding anything which may have the least tendency to meliorate our miserable condition.[12]

While regenerating individuals was crucial to Walker's strategy, of equal concern to him was building a sense of national identity and collective mission among blacks founded on their special relationship to God. In effect, Walker sought to make this expanding network of connectedness a spiritual necessity, to endow it with the moral imperative of racial pride and Christian mission and thereby mandate its further extension:

> Your full glory and happiness, as well as all other coloured people under Heaven, shall never be fully consummated, but with the *entire emancipation of your enslaved brethren all over the world.* . . . For I believe it is the will of the Lord that our greatest happiness shall consist in working for the salvation of our whole body. When this is accomplished a burst of glory will shine upon you, which will indeed astonish you and the world. . . . I say unto you again, you must go to work and prepare the way of the Lord.[13]

Eugene Genovese neatly articulated the problem Walker was attempting to overcome in mobilizing the slave population and why he would appear so unusually threatening to white authorities:

> Without a sense of being God's Chosen People—chosen, that is, to bring His Kingdom, not merely to be delivered by Him—the slaves could not easily develop that sense of national mission which has been so efficacious in the formation of revolutionary ideology—which has so marvelously sparked the liberation of nations and classes and simultaneously brought so much imperialist gangsterism into the world.[14]

Walker was not making some glib gesture to African American bravado when he spoke of his "solemn belief, that if ever the world becomes Christianized, (which must certainly take place before long) it will be through the means, under God of the *Blacks* . . ." or when he said:

> The day of our redemption from abject wretchedness draweth near, when we shall be enabled, in the most extended sense of the word, to stretch forth our hands to the LORD our GOD, but there

12. *Freedom's Journal,* December 19, 1828.
13. *Appeal,* 29–30.
14. Genovese, *Roll, Jordan, Roll,* 279.

must be a willingness on our part, for God to do these things for us, for we may be assured that he will not take us by the hairs of our head against our will and desire, and drag us from our very, mean, low and abject condition.[15]

Instead, he was struggling to inspire what was still a feeble popular movement with his deeply held conviction of the unique spiritual righteousness of African Americans and of their calling to be principal agents in events of vast historical significance. Walker sought to fire such a religious fervor in blacks that the regeneration of their individual souls was seen as only the beginning of a bold and irresistible resolve to remake the world in the image of this newly won inner righteousness. He championed beginning immediately to build this national Christian identity among blacks by extending correspondences and to set it to its millenarian purpose of liberating all from worldly thralldom of whatever form.

If this message could be carried over such a network, and especially if delivered by black preachers, both Walker and Southern authorities believed that it could have a tremendous impact on the black populace. Fear about the power of this merger of African American religious zeal with an underground network of communication among them was best expressed by Governor John Floyd of Virginia. While Floyd reflected on these matters after the Nat Turner rebellion he believed that, right or wrong, the work of Walker had played an important role in laying the ground for Turner's action. Floyd argued that behind the creation of the insurrectionary spirit in Virginia were malevolent Yankees, especially Yankee peddlers and traders, whom he claimed circulated false and inflammatory religious teachings. While whites were supposed to be the only ones introducing these teachings, what Floyd conjectured they taught was in fact identical to what Walker was actually dispensing to the slaves:

> They began first, by making them [i.e., their approaches] religious—their conversations were of that character—telling blacks God was no respecter of persons—the black man was as good as the white—that all men were born free and equal—that they cannot serve two masters—that the white people rebelled against England to obtain freedom, so have the blacks a right to do.

But then he asserted that black preachers soon took over the task of dissemination and had their words invigorated by the fiery prose of Walker:

15. *Appeal,* i, 18.

> At this point, more active operations commenced—our magis-
> trates and laws became more inactive—large assemblages of ne-
> groes were suffered to take place for religious purposes—Then
> commenced the efforts of the black preachers, often from the
> pulpits these pamphlets [i.e., religious tracts] and papers were
> read—followed by the incendiary publications of Walker, Garrison
> and Knapp of Boston, these too with songs and hymns of a similar
> character were circulated, read and commented upon—We resting
> in apathetic security until the Southampton affair.

And by the time of the Turner uprising, Floyd believed the black
preachers were fully in charge of preparing the black populace and that
they orchestrated their actions through a secret system of correspondence:

> From all that has come to my knowledge during and since this
> affair—I am fully convinced that every black preacher in the whole
> country east of the Blue Ridge was in the secret, that the plans as
> published by those Northern presses were adopted and acted upon
> by them—that their congregations, as they were called knew noth-
> ing of this intended rebellion, except a few leading and intelligent
> men, who may have been head men in the Church—*the mass* were
> prepared by making them aspire to an equal station by such con-
> versations as I have related as the first step.[16]

Central to this preparation of "*the mass*," according to Floyd, was the
ability of the leaders to organize themselves over great distances and to
uplift black aspirations through religious conviction. In essence, this
varies not at all from Walker's strategy. Indeed, this dangerous subversive
method described by the governor is one that is much more clearly at-
tributable to Walker than to Turner, given that we will probably never be
certain to what extent—if at all—orchestration over a wide area figured
into Turner's plans.[17] Despite his flawed claim that before Turner the authorities rested "in apathetic security," Floyd gave a retrospective voice
to fears similar to those animating other Southern authorities when the
Appeal arrived in their communities. That so eminent a figure as the Virginia governor would endorse these anxieties only lent further legitimacy
to their suspicions of their slaves' subversive potential.

David Walker's conception of black resistance was by far the most sophisticated and extensive form such plans attained in antebellum Amer-

16. Governor Floyd to Governor Hamilton, November 19, 1831, in Tragle, *The Southampton Slave Revolt,* 275–76.

17. See my discussion of this matter in Chapter 5.

ica. No one throughout the era understood better than he what needed to be accomplished psychologically and organizationally among blacks in order to raise an opposition capable of truly challenging the system of slavery and white supremacy in the United States. Southern authorities quickly recognized this fact and acted decisively to prevent the vehicle for this challenge from being introduced and circulated. What especially disturbed them was Walker's effort to create a national movement by disseminating the pamphlet throughout the South and by beginning to organize through some viable channels to achieve the ideal of collective racial unity. It is important to remember that nothing like this had ever been seen before in the South and that this action predated William Lloyd Garrison's efforts to spread the *Liberator* in the South in 1831 and the Postal Campaign of 1835, which generated an extreme reaction from the South. In a sense, Walker was the progenitor of all these efforts, and if the Southern response to Walker is assessed in terms of their response to these other actions, we can understand better why they reacted as they did to the *Appeal.* The rapid response of Southern authorities to the presence of the *Appeal* was not as much a sign of their tendency to ascribe unwarranted power to some passing antislavery gesture or plot as it was their realistic appraisal of the subversive potential of Walker's plan.

Yet one could pose Walker's query with a very different tone, asking what precisely it was that merited being "so very fearfully terrified" by the pamphlet? After all, the very swiftness, concertedness, and *success* of the officials' actions against it show how difficult it was for African Americans to implement programs that sought to empower blacks and forge the solidarity requisite for effective resistance. Even though signs of stress were appearing in the slaveholding regime in the late 1820s and early 1830s—especially in the upper South—the various members still maintained a cohesiveness and strength that was all but impossible for Walker to overcome. The demographic and military superiority of the white South certainly demanded that some note of doubt be blended into the posing of Walker's question.

Indeed, Walker grappled in muted but significant ways with the reality of the ultimately overpowering might of white Southern forces. Despite his numerous assertions that blacks had far greater strength compared with whites, and that God would lead blacks invariably to victory, Walker made several gestures of conciliation to whites and expressed fear about the consequences of violent confrontation:

> Remember Americans, that we must and shall be free and enlightened as you are, will you wait until we shall, under God, obtain our liberty by the crushing arm of power? Will it not be dreadful for

you? I speak Americans for your good. We must and shall be free I
say, in spite of you. You may do your best to keep us in wretchedness and misery, to enrich you and your children; but God will
deliver us from under you. And wo, wo, will be to you if we have to
obtain our freedom by fighting.[18]

Despite his apparent confidence that African American triumph was fore-
ordained, Walker feared the consequences of open racial warfare. If nothing else, violent resistance would yield profound civil turbulence and an
uncertain outcome for African Americans. Furthermore, as discussed in
Chapter 7, Walker had doubts at several points that God would lead
blacks inevitably to victory, and he actually hung the fulfillment of these
prophecies exclusively on the effective and righteous mobilization of the
black populace—a solidarity he knew full well would be difficult to
achieve.

He was emphatic about the far greater benefits to be realized by a
peaceful reconciliation:

Throw away your fears and prejudices then, and enlighten us and
treat us like men, and we will like you more than we do now hate
you. . . . Treat us like men, and there is no danger but we will all
live in peace and happiness together. For we are not like you, hard
hearted, unmerciful, and unforgiving. What a happy country this
will be, if the whites will listen. What nation under heaven, will be
able to do any thing with us, unless God gives us up into its hand?
. . . Treat us then like men, and we will be your friends. And there
is not a doubt in my mind, but that the whole of the past will be
sunk into oblivion, and we yet, under God, will become a united
and happy people.[19]

While the overwhelming majority of the text was addressed directly to
blacks and given over to rallying them to a recognition of personal entitlement and collective strength in order to solidify them for the seemingly
inevitable racial struggle, crucial passages like the above appeared briefly
and made starkly clear that Walker was quite willing to follow courses of
action that were very different from those he usually proposed. It was
largely his deep-seated belief that whites would not eliminate slavery
without a fight that led him to devote so much of his energies to calling
for militant preparations.

But he was clearly willing to forgo those provisions—especially the

18. *Appeal,* 69–70.
19. *Appeal,* 70.

creation of the sort of collective racial identity he proposed, if whites would only treat with them respectfully and benevolently. What Walker principally sought for African Americans was their admission into full participation in republican and free labor America. Indeed, his drive to regenerate black identity was all about forging stronger individuals who were more confidently autonomous and thus able to compete more effectively in market society. Walker perceived slavery as an abominable aberration in a society that was otherwise healthy and even morally righteous. He found nothing wrong with the individual freedom and equality promised by the Declaration of Independence, except that blacks were savagely excluded from it. Rather than indicting the fundamental values and principles of American society for endorsing a pursuit of individual liberty and profit which could be so immoral that it legitimized such a gross exploitation of labor as slavery, Walker believed that unchristian hypocrites had flourished in America's historically unique freedom and perverted to their own cruel, avaricious, and selfish ends the values of liberty and equality that actually formed the hope that was America. They would either be weeded out by God or made useful, virtuous citizens through Christian regeneration. Indeed, Walker's failure to indict American society should not be seen as a serious lapse in his political vision. He frankly admired revolutionary America, whose commitment to unleashing constructive and righteous individual energies was unprecedented and held for him the key to realizing the growth of individual blacks which would lead inevitably to universal emancipation. He was confronted with the conundrum of attempting to build an opposition to a society he basically endorsed.

It is significant that the most compelling vision of a regenerated America Walker presented was not one in which the collective racial identity of blacks would become more institutionalized as a guarantee of protection against a historically racist society taking renewed steps to exclude them from social, political, and economic advance. Instead, he held up a vision of "what a happy country this will be, if the whites will listen. What nation under heaven, will be able to do anything with us, unless God gives us up into its hand?" Here racial differences are muted, and blacks and whites have suddenly learned how to live together harmoniously. A transformation of individuals that both made them right with God and brought them to cultivate a morality and inner regulation in accord with the culture of moral improvement would obviate any need to protect discrete social groups, because the mass of individuals would not tolerate perverse and avaricious behavior of the sort that so grossly exploited blacks in the past. Walker's abiding faith in the power of individual transformation led him to understand that social problems were not the result of systemic flaws but the result of powerful collections of unregenerate individuals impeding citizens from full expression of republican virtue and Christian grace. Revolutionary change was perceived as occurring first at the individual level, not by way of institutional transformation, especially in antebellum America, where institutional presence—be it economic, religious, political, or social—was much weaker than it was in other Western societies. What was needed was a dramatic change of individuals' hearts.

Nowhere does Walker more forcefully evince this belief that such righteous individual regeneration could occur than when he openly addressed slaveholders and indicated the willingness of blacks to submit to their tutelage if they would only change their hearts:

> I say, let us reason; had you not better take our body, while you have it in your power, and while we are yet ignorant and wretched, not knowing but a little, give us education, and teach us the pure religion of our Lord and Master, which is calculated to make the lion lay down in peace with the lamb, and which millions of you have beaten us nearly to death for trying to obtain since we have been among you, and thus at once, gain our affection while we are ignorant.[20]

Indeed, here he strangely endows the very slaveholders he has excoriated throughout with a much greater knowledge of things secular and divine than blacks have. Those he has proclaimed the most corrupt slaveholders in the history of the world are suddenly to teach the ordained agents of Christian world conversion about that faith, and those agents will "at once" be receptive to them—despite centuries of their having "beaten us nearly to death."

Despite his keen awareness of the slaveholders' integral role in articulating an ideology of the innate inferiority of blacks, Walker did not understand slaveholders ultimately as hopelessly at variance with the black population. He saw them always as potential brothers in Christ, and this possible liaison kept him tied to them and hurt his ability to delineate a fully evolved opposition to them. Walker in large part was able to continue to hope for reconciliation because at bottom he believed whites and blacks were identical—that racial differences were incidental and that black and white Americans could seek the same ends. It is important to recognize that Walker's use of Christianity as a revolutionary tool was a sword that could cut both ways. While it was the key to forging a sense of collective nationhood and mission among African Americans, evangelical teaching also held out hope that the slaveholders would be regenerated

20. *Appeal,* 69.

and reunited with blacks. Walker endorsed both points of view, despite, in terms of building effective resistance, their dangerous divergence: "Throw away your fears and prejudices then, and enlighten us and treat us like men, and we will like you more than we do now hate you."[21]

Walker here compressed both his deep faith in the ability of individuals to change themselves quickly and profoundly and his awareness that blacks will be dependent on whites to help them out of their ignorance and degradation. This was the crux of the problem for him. Despite his claims that blacks had the greater strength, he recognized that African Americans had nowhere else to go and that they must learn how to live with a people who, although they had grossly exploited them, currently possessed far broader knowledge of how to function in the sort of economic and political world Walker wanted blacks to join as equal partners. Blacks had to determine how to work with these realities while maintaining individual autonomy and pride. Warfare against the whites would only generate destruction, bitterness, and distance for blacks from those whose assistance they would need.

Nowhere was Walker's commitment to the culture of moral improvement more evident than in his plea to those who had so cruelly abused them to change their hearts and allow blacks and whites in America to realize through benevolent interaction the social harmony that was the highest ideal of that culture. Walker was certain that the best hope blacks had for their healthy and happy participation in an interracial, republican America lay in peace and conciliatory gestures toward whites, not in aggressive denunciation and warfare. This far less apparent undercurrent of necessary conciliation in the *Appeal* was nevertheless quite important in dissipating the ardor for resistance by holding out not only the possibility but also the requirement of—and even the yearning for—reunion with repentant malefactors.

David Walker's stature as an architect of black nationalism has been overstated, and his commitment to a racially integrated society in which racial distinctiveness would play little role has been relatively ignored. Walker certainly encouraged African Americans to believe in their strength and accomplishments as a people, and to this extent he bore some nationalist impulse. He upheld racial pride and self-help, the vital role of Egypt/Africa in the development of Western civilization, separate religious, political, and reform organizations for blacks, and the special relationship African Americans had to God as unique sufferers of injustice. All of these cultivated positive group identity and differed little from positions held by the vast preponderance of black reformers in the ante-

21. *Appeal,* 70.

bellum era. But they were promoted as tools for uplifting a people whom Walker and others believed were deeply demoralized by racism and who had to be organized in separate associations because they were denied access to the dominant ones. They were not promoted as a way to establish the essential difference of African Americans from white Americans and their consequent need to separate themselves from them.

Sterling Stuckey has been the most influential proponent of the *Appeal* as a pivotal black nationalist document. He argues that it was "the most all-embracing black nationalist formulation to appear in America during the nineteenth century" and that it established "the need for African peoples to rule themselves."[22] Yet Walker clearly intended a mutual white-black rule of the United States: "This country is as much ours as it is the whites, whether they will admit it now or not, they will see and believe it by and by."[23] He adopted separate black organizations as only a temporary expedient. Nowhere does Walker evince the much more definitive nationalistic and separatist impulse of Martin Delany, who wrote in 1852:

> We have, then, inherent traits, attributes, so to speak, and native characteristics, peculiar to our race, whether pure or mixed blood; and all that is required of us is to cultivate these, and develop them in their purity, to make them desirable and emulated by the rest of the world.[24]

Walker made his contributions to black nationalism broadly understood. But unlike Delany, who reflected his era's increasing concern to attribute distinctive traits to various racial and ethnic groups and to establish a hierarchy among them, Walker was filled with a radical egalitarian evangelicalism that postulated a universal equality and connectedness among all humans and races through God.

Yet the great emphasis on collective effort and on resistance is in the *Appeal* because Walker deeply doubted the willingness of whites to change. He was confronted with the probability that, despite offers of peace to the dominant white society, their hearts were already so hardened that they would reject his overtures and that the difficult task of rallying an oppressed people to initiate their liberation would have to begin. Thus the burden of his text is addressed to blacks and intended to inspire them to embrace their anger and power. For Walker, resistance,

22. Sterling Stuckey, *The Ideological Origins of Black Nationalism* (Boston: Beacon Press, 1972), 9. See also Sterling Stuckey, *Slave Culture: Nationalist Theory and the Foundations of Black America* (New York: Oxford University Press, 1987), 98–137.

23. *Appeal,* 55.

24. Martin Delany, "The Political Destiny of the Colored Race," in Stuckey, *Ideological Origins,* 203.

even against overwhelming odds, was preferable to a further miring of blacks in "servile deceit." African Americans had received word from God that they must no longer submit to this, and the apocalyptic destruction of a redeemable society was preferred to further black disobedience of this divine mandate.

Yet this effort too would be severely hampered. Moving the mass of blacks to reject "servile deceit" decisively and to begin organizing this collectivity to throw off submission was profoundly difficult. No scene better encapsulated the difficulties than Walker's encounter with a Boston bootblack on Beacon Hill:

> I met a coloured man in the street a short time since, with a string of boots on his shoulders; we fell into conversation, and in course of which, I said to him, what a miserable set of people we are! He asked, why?—Said I, we are so subjected under the whites, that we cannot obtain the comforts of life, but by cleaning their boots and shoes, old clothes, waiting on them, shaving them &c. Said he, (with the boots on his shoulders) "I am completely happy!!! I never want to live any better or happier than when I can get a plenty of boots and shoes to clean!!!" Oh! how can those who are actuated by avarice only, but think, that our Creator made us to be an inheritance to them for ever, when they see that our greatest glory is centered in such mean and low objects? Understand me, brethren, I do not mean to speak against the occupations by which we acquire enough and sometimes scarcely that, to render ourselves and families comfortable through life. I am subjected to the same inconvenience, as you all. My objections are, to our *glorying* and being *happy* in such low employments; for if we are men, we ought to be thankful to the Lord for the past, and for the future. Be looking forward with thankful hearts to higher attainments than *wielding the razor* and *cleaning boots and shoes.* The man whose aspirations are not *above,* and even *below* these, is indeed, ignorant and wretched enough.[25]

As with the slave woman who aided the slave traders, Walker is infuriated by the ready willingness of the bootblack to accept a lowly station all but forced on him by gross racial injustice. But it was not only the man's comfort with his occupation that enraged Walker. His implicit ease with white dominance and the extensive proscription of blacks galled him equally.

25. *Appeal*, 29.

This encounter elicited one of Walker's deepest fears and frustrations about African Americans: they would not choose full freedom, equality, and self-improvement and would thereby confirm white doubts about their character. Why did the bootblack not rush to endorse Walker's analysis and vision? Was it that they were demoralized from having spent a lifetime under the boot of racism? Was it simply personal preference? Was it a reaction against the perceived judgmental tone of Walker's query and pronouncement? Was it some combination of all or part of these? Unfortunately we will never know. But that Walker judged anyone harshly who veered from his program is far more discernible.

Walker had an enormous enemy to engage if collective resistance was mandated and required nothing less than zealous troops. He had no time for quibbling over the viability of some marginalized niche an individual may have carved out for himself within the structure of exploitation. He sought individuals who thoroughly rejected slavery and submissiveness and who would settle only for full equality with whites. It appears that the bootblack was far from such a position.

Walker needed to prompt change not only within this individual but within tens of thousands of others just like him who had out of necessity accommodated themselves to varying degrees to a society in which the full self-determination of African Americans was either proscribed or severely discouraged. Was Walker's method, as embodied here, the one best calculated to initiate such change in the bootblack and the innumerable others? We are given no evidence of his movement—only of Walker's persisting doubt, anger, and contempt. Intimidation and disdain have been used as tactics for organizing slave resistance: Denmark Vesey employed them to enlist the hesitant and silence the uncommitted. But he used them to hold his forces together at the latter stages of an imminent act of resistance, not as a means for transforming individuals and building group consensus over a much longer period of time.

If we view Walker's method in his exchange with the laborer as a model for how he sought to elevate the awareness of and to change individuals who had not grappled with these matters as deeply as he had, we may well see the germ of reasons for his possible difficulties in gaining adherents of the sort he sought. While Walker credits the man with finding any employment in racist Boston and claims that he does "not mean to speak against the occupations" with which African Americans scrape by, he does finally disdain the work and the individual. If one must do this work, one must be restless and dissatisfied with it. If one has greater opportunity, then one must "be looking forward with thankful hearts to higher attainments than *wielding the razor* and *cleaning boots and shoes.*" To be settled under any circumstance with such a lowly station exposes one as "ignorant and wretched enough."

Walker used the bootblack to represent the average black—North and South—who had common menial employment, little education, a low level of political understanding, and a certain settlement with their social and economic condition. Walker used him to expose the problems of transforming the consciousness of the mass of African Americans. But how could his method readily gain the favorable attention of the populace if he was so swift to indict their labor and outlook? Walker had to reckon in a respectful way with the reality of the bootblack's contentment, false consciousness or not. Rather than gaining the man's confidence by crediting him with having employment and contributing to his community, and then returning to challenge him to think more critically about his social environment, Walker persists in questioning the man's character and clearly ran the risk of alienating him from an opportunity to change. Such disquieting commentary as perhaps "our Creator made us to be an inheritance to them for ever, when they see that our greatest glory is centered in such mean and low objects" should find no place in an exchange whose centerpiece should be the advance of camaraderie and enlightenment. Walker exacerbates his frustrations with the individual by refusing to adapt his measurement of him on the scale of economic and moral improvement to the man's own level of political understanding. For the sort of work Walker undertook, he could not have too much patience and charity.

Walker was an educated individual who had gained broad geographical knowledge through extensive travel in the United States, had wide exposure to the forms of white supremacy there, and reflected deeply on its system. He was also steeped in the early nineteenth century's revolutionary fervor for democracy and faith in a millennial momentum fueled by an interlocking national gridwork of revivals and reform associations. This understanding and experience would have been shared by numerous reform-minded colleagues of his in Boston, New York, Philadelphia, and other cities in the North. Indeed, it was usually Northern free blacks who were best situated to envision and implement the broad geographical organization that would be so essential to effective resistance. The vast majority of blacks, however, had not been brought to appreciate this or embrace it.

This was not a problem just for Walker; other black reformers held this view as well. Maria Stewart, a contemporary admirer of Walker and local Boston activist, significantly echoed his contempt for lowly ambitions in blacks and anxiety over the reactions whites might have to them. She exclaimed in 1832:

> Few white persons of either sex, who are calculated for anything else, are willing to spend their lives and bury their talents in performing mean, servile labor. And such is the horrible idea that I entertain respecting a life of servitude, that if I conceived of their [sic] being no possibility of my rising above the condition of servant, I would gladly hail death as a welcome messenger. O, horrible idea, indeed! to possess noble souls aspiring after high and honorable acquirements, yet confined by the chains of ignorance and poverty to lives of continual drudgery and toil. Neither do I know of any who have enriched themselves by spending their lives as house-domestics, washing windows, shaking carpets, brushing boots, or tending upon gentlemen's tables. I can but die for expressing my sentiments: and I am as willing to die by the sword as the pestilence; for I am a true born American; your blood flows in my veins, and your spirit fires my breast.[26]

Stewart regarded with a chilling disdain the labor practiced by a significant number of blacks in Boston and elsewhere, and whose support for her vision of reform was absolutely critical. Her haughtiness—an appropriate term here—led her to proclaim a preference for death over a life like that of the vast majority of blacks in America. Such a tactic—not unlike Walker's in spirit—damaged far more than it helped the effort to unite and rally the mass of African Americans.

For Walker, it was not sufficient for one to be free and simply satisfied with sustaining oneself. For one's freedom to be merited, one had to have internalized values and expectations that demanded constant improvement of one's life, a steady extension of one's control over personal and public space. Freedom employed in less individually assertive manners was freedom used irresponsibly and pointed to the real possibility that the possessor might have a degraded and even slavish character. Walker found his values in the moral universalism of evangelical Christianity, democratic theory, and the evolving free-labor ideology of the North. With those aspirations, he looked around and could see only degradation and restricted opportunity for himself and his people, and thought to do nothing else but rail and organize against this savage injustice.

Yet the bootblack did not immediately share in this enthusiasm, and if ever he was to do so, leaders like Walker and Stewart would have to bring

26. Maria W. Stewart, "Lecture Delivered at Franklin Hall," in Richardson, *Maria W. Stewart*, 46.

him to it by means of the persuasion and internal assent on which their
system of moral improvement placed so much weight. This process
would be long and not aided by swift judgments of character.

Nowhere during the early decades of the nineteenth century did hopes
for general black emancipation and uplift receive more forceful public
voice than they did from reform-minded antislavery free blacks in the
North. As explored in depth in Chapters 3 and 4, David Walker's *Appeal*
was simply a more prominent and vehement expression of the values,
expectations, and strategies held by most members of this educated
group of community leaders, who by the late 1820s were coalescing into a
North-wide reform association best but by no means solely embodied in
the Negro Convention Movement of the 1830s:

> We have selected four valuable subjects for rallying points, viz.:
> Education, Temperance, Economy, and Universal Liberty. We hope
> to make our people, in theory and practice, thoroughly acquainted
> with these subjects, as a method of future action. . . . We hope to
> unite the colored population in those principles of Moral Re-
> form. . . . In order to [sic] this, we will appoint agents to dissemi-
> nate these truths among our people, and establish auxiliaries
> wherever practicable, that the same leaven of righteousness and
> justice may animate the body politic.[27]

These were a people who not only glorified moral improvement but also
easily thought of forging with others connections that transcended localities and reached over vast geographical distances. They were right
that such far-reaching solidarity of effort and communication could be
vital to achieving black advance nationally.

Yet their commitment to unity among blacks went beyond promoting
an organizational interconnectedness and upholding freedom to expect-
ing "the colored population [to unite] in those principles of moral reform." In the first issue of *The Rights of All,* Samuel Cornish urged a relentless national effort for

> forming associations communicating with our people and the pub-
> lic generally, on all subjects of interest, collecting monies, and de-
> livering stated lectures on industry, frugality, enterprise &c.,
> thereby [linking] together, by one solid chain, the whole free popu-

---

27. "Minutes of the Fifth Annual Convention" (1835), in Bell, ed., *Minutes of the National Negro Conventions,* 26–27.

lation, so as to make them think and feel, and act, as one solid body, devoted to education and improvement.[28]

Here the vision of an associational dynamo generating ideological conformity vividly represents the conviction of black reformers that change for the race could not occur unless all held to these values. The success of organizational unity had to be weighed in terms of the degree to which it reinforced ideological uniformity. They believed that one's freedom was not properly regulated unless disciplined by this virtuous management, and they doubted whether one could truly even know what freedom was, or desire it, unless they subscribed to this culture. The struggle for emancipation was thus not secure unless all endorsed this vision of improvement and education and believed themselves moving toward a fuller participation in the dominant white middle-class culture of the North.

In 1940, W. E. B. Du Bois upheld Walker as the first to formulate a "program of organized opposition to the action and attitude of the dominant white group" and to require of African Americans "ceaseless agitation and insistent demand for equality." Such a program was essential to any black advance in America, yet for Du Bois it was fraught with "manifest difficulties." Perhaps the greatest, according to Du Bois, was that "the effective organization of this plan of protest and agitation involves a large degree of inner union and agreement among Negroes." He continued: "Now for obvious reasons of ignorance and poverty, and the natural envy and bickering of any disadvantaged group, this unity is difficult to achieve. In fact the efforts to achieve it through the Negro conventions of 1833 and thereafter during the fifties . . . were only partly successful."[29] Ideological solidarity must undergird any challenge to as fearsome an opponent as African Americans confronted. Yet critical fissures separated the mass of African Americans from the cadre of black reformers. The reformers often responded to this rift with chastisement of the black folk, which usually only exacerbated rather than healed the differences.

The African American cause for freedom in the antebellum era was hindered by the painful paradox that those who often proved themselves the most capable of envisioning and acting for the sort of national organization required to effectively challenge slavery and the doctrine of white supremacy were also the ones who had great difficulty rallying the black populace to that vision because of their disdain for the foibles and curtailed worldview of the littler folk. Inspiring African Americans to challenge white authority required more than rousing them from the psychologically demoralizing effects of enslavement and discrimination; it also

28. *The Rights of All,* September 18, 1829.
29. Du Bois, *Dusk of Dawn,* 193.

required affirming their integrity and somehow respecting the worlds they had made, however flawed and in need of change. This qualified affirmation the reformers often found difficult.

The tensions and contradictions manifest in the *Appeal* painfully reveal the tremendous pressures under which any antebellum black political thinker would labor who dared to conceive a plan of organized slave resistance. While on the one hand some dignified gesture of conciliation had to be made to the overwhelmingly superior might of the white authorities, they also had the task of presenting a viable vision of black integrity and strength around which they could effectively rally themselves to defy this unjust machine if need be. The problems of forging the essential organizational unity among an oppressed people spread out over a vast geographical range were immense. Moreover, Northern black reformers' exclusion from a culture in which they wanted to participate deeply informed their will to resist and led them to attempt to rally a people with visions of fuller participation in something to which the vast majority of them had had only marginal exposure. Given these daunting difficulties, the possibility that African Americans would mount a threat that would yield the sort of broad social fruits Walker hoped for were slim.

David Walker's *Appeal to the Colored Citizens of the World* stands, however, as the most imaginative and courageous effort to marshal this force ever conceived during the 250 years when slavery haunted America. Few depicted the barbarity of slavery as vividly as Walker and summoned up such righteous outrage against it. No one empathized more dramatically with the painful ambivalence and strong emotions the individual slave could be caught up in, or offered more hope for channeling these emotional realities toward health and strength. The cadences and idioms that infuse Walker's work bespoke an appreciation for the distinctive oral culture of the slaves and an embrace of them through his use of it. And of course the slaves' inseparable intertwining of deliverance with religious imagery and hopes formed the bedrock on which the *Appeal* was built. Walker's effort to deliver an alternative vision of African American identity and heritage to a region where the ideology of black racial inferiority sought increasingly to exclude all other characterizations was bold and unprecedented. His plan to build on existing communication networks emanating from Southern ports was evidence of his familiarity with coastal slave society and his commitment to circulating his work.

Yet if assessed precisely in terms of the sort of machinery he designated as essential to threaten American slavery and racism, Walker's revolutionary endeavor fell short. Although the *Appeal* was a dazzling analysis and narrative that inspired the thousands of African Americans who read or heard it, the very pervasive monstrosity it struggled to expose and overcome proved far too powerful, even for David Walker's brilliant illumination. While always admiring the numerous brave examples of antebellum black resistance and how they kept Southern authorities on edge, we must also be careful not to lose sight—as David Walker never did—of what was required to threaten this deeply entrenched system of slavery and white supremacy.

APPENDIXES

Appendix A

Analysis of Names on the Charleston AME Petition

Blacks				
		In City Directory for		
Name	Trade	1816	1819	1822
Maloom Brown				
Marcus Brown				
Morris Brown	Shoemaker	X	X	X
Samuel Brown				
Harry Bull			X	X
Samuel Cochran	Tailor	X	X	X
Charles Corr	Tailor	X	X	X
Amos Cruckshanks	Painter (1819 & 1822); porter (1816)	X	X	X
Charles Drayton				
Henry Drayton		X		X
John Drayton				
James Eden				
James Haig	Shoemaker			X
Alexander Harleston	Drayman			X
Quash A. Harleston				
Cato Mack				
James Mack				
Henry Mathews	Shoemaker (1822)		X	X
Isaac A. Mathews				
John B. Mathews	Tailor			X
Peter Mathews	Shoemaker (1819 & 1822)	X	X	X
Robert Milner				
Charles Rogers				
James Sagguge (?)				
Smart Simpson	Carpenter			X
London Turpin				X

Whites				
		In City Directory for		
Name	Trade	1816	1819	1822
David Bell	Accountant	X	X	X
Thomas Blackwood	President of Planters' & Mechanics' Bank	X	X	?
A. J. Browne (?)				X
Henry Bryce	Merchant	X	X	X
John Buchan	Pastor, St. Andrew's Presbyterian Church	X	X	X
Dodridge Crocker	Merchant	X	X	?
Daniel Cruckshanks	Shoemaker (1816 & 1822); tanyard (1819)	X	X	X
John Dawson Jr.	Cashier, state bank	X	X	X
James Evans				
Philip Gadsden	Factor	X	X	
Robert R. Gibbs	Planter	X	X	X
John Hoff	Bookseller or grocer	X	X	X
Robert Howard	Collector of excise (1816) or newspaper editor (1819)	X	X	?
J. A. Johnson	Several possibilities	X	X	X
Thomas Jones	Either grocer, merchant, or president of Bank of S.C.		X	X
Daniel Latham	Distiller	X	X	?
Rev. A. W. Leland	Pastor, First Presbyterian Church at Mount Pleasant	X	X	X
John Lukens	Bank cashier	X	X	?
John McKee	Bricklayer	X		
John H. Mitchell	Merchant?	X	X	X
Rev. Israel Munds	Minister & teacher	X	X	X
Rev. Benjamin M. Palmer D.D.	Pastor, Congregational church	X	X	X
Thomas Payne	Harbormaster	X	X	?
Charles Prince	Lamplighter & tinman	X		
George Reid	Pastor, First Presbyterian Church & Clerk, Bank of S.C.	X	X	X
William Thompson	Ship chandler	X	X	X
Isham Williams	Planter	X	X	X
Joseph Yates	Cooper	X	X	X
Joseph Young	Ship chandler	X	X	X

SOURCE: General Assembly Papers, Petitions, n.d., no. 1893, pp. 4, 5, 7, 9, South Carolina Department of Archives and History, Columbia.

Appendix B

Slave and Free Black Members of the African Church Who Were Associated with the Vesey Affair

Member		Sentence
Smart Anderson		Death
Paris Ball		Transportation
George Bampfield		Transportation
Batteau Bennett		Death
Ned Bennett	Class leader	Death
Jesse Blackwood		Death
Jemmy Clement		Death
John Enslow		Workhouse
Polydore Faber		Death
Lot Forrester		Death
Monday Gell		Transportation
Butcher Gibbs		Acquitted but transported
Jack Glenn	Class leader/preacher	Death
Prince Graham (FN)		Transportation
Quash Harleston (FN)		Acquitted but transported
Mingo Harth		Death
Joseph Jore		Death
Jack McNeil		Death
Denbow Martin		Workhouse
Dean Mitchell		Death
Dublin Morris		Transportation
Abraham Poyas		Acquitted but transported
Peter Poyas	Class leader	Death
"Gullah Jack" Pritchard		Death
Adam Robertson		Death
John Robertson		Death
Robert Robertson		Death
Tom Scott		Death
Charles Shubrick	Class leader	Discharged

Scipio Simms		Workhouse
Caesar Smith		Death
Denmark Vesey (FN)	Class leader	Death
Sandy Vesey		Transportation
John Vincent		Transportation
Peter Ward	Class leader	Discharged
Bellisle Yates		Death

SOURCE: John Oliver Killens, ed., *The Trial Record of Denmark Vesey* (Boston: Beacon Press, 1970), 102.
NOTE: FN = Free Negro.

Appendix C

David Walker's Associates in Boston

All of the following men were associates of David Walker. Those who are listed as probable Masons are so indicated because of their presence with Walker at a banquet held for Prince Abduhl Rahhaman at the African Lodge in September 1828. At the banquet they all made short addresses and acted as prominent members. They were also all politically active in the community.

Members of African Lodge #459

From 1828 list of members:

Aaron, William	?
Barbadoes, James	Hairdresser
Bell, Henry	?
Brown, John	Cook
Brown, William	Clothes cleaner
Courreaux, John	?
Dalton, Thomas	Bootblack
De Randamie, Cornelius	Hairdresser
Gaul, Aaron	Sawyer
Hilton, John T.	Hairdresser
Holmes, George	Hairdresser/musician
Howe, James H.	Renovator of human hair
Kerr, William	Hairdresser
Lewis, Walker	Hairdresser
Moody, Sampson	Hairdresser
Paul, Thomas	Minister
Pero, John	Hairdresser
Revalian, Thomas	?
Vassal, William	Tender
Villeneuve, Victor	Hairdresser
Walker, David	Clothes dealer

From 1829 list of members:

Brown, Thomas	Waiter
Francis, Thomas	?
Hauw (?), T. H.	?
Henry, William	Hairdresser
Larlent, Joseph	?
May (?), John	?
Patterson (?), James	Waiter
Potter, Richard	?
Rand, William F.	Bootblack
Rich, William	Hairdresser
Standing, Francis	?
Tidd, Dudley (?)	Laborer
Tidd, Porter	Musician

Probable members of Masons but not on lists:

Blancard, Louis M.	Hairdresser
Eli (Ely), John	Clothier
Freeman, Cato	Bootblack
Nash, Oliver	Barber
Williams, Domingo	Waiter

Involved with Massachusetts General Colored Association (MGCA) or *Freedom's Journal* (FJ)

Brimsley, Frederick (MGCA)	Clothes dealer
Cole, Thomas (MGCA)	Hairdresser
Easton, Hosea (MGCA; FJ)	Blacksmith
Easton, Joshua (MGCA)	?
Gould, James (FJ)	Bootblack
Lee, James (FJ)	Minister
Nell, William G. (MGCA)	Tailor
Pitts, Coffin (MGCA)	Clothier
Scarlett, John E. (MGCA)	Clothes dealer
Snowden, Samuel (AME)	Minister
Tyler, Henry (FJ)	Bootblack

SOURCES: *Boston City Directory*, 1825–30; James & Lois Horton, *Black Bostonians*; John Daniels, *In Freedom's Birthplace*; William Cooper Nell, *The Colored Patriots of the American Revolution*, 345; *Freedom's Journal*, March 16, 1827, and April 25, 1828. My most critical source, however, was the membership rolls of the Prince Hall Masons for the early decades of the nineteenth century contained in the following collection: Prince Hall Records, Minutes of African Lodge, Boston, 1807–46, compiled by H. V. B. Voorhis and housed at the Grand Masonic Lodge of Massachusetts, Boston.

Distribution of Occupations in Black Boston, 1826

Group A employment
(unskilled and semi-skilled workers)

Laborer	126
Mariner	30
Bootblack	17
Laundress	11
Wood sawyer	1
Grain measurer	1
Chimney sweep	1
Stevedore	1
Shipper	1
Tender	1
Window cleaner	1
Total	191

Group B employment
(workers in transportation, food service, personal service)

Hairdresser/barber	40
Waiter	8
Handcartman	2
Clothes cleaner	1
Teamster	1
Cook	1
Cake baker	1
Mariner/cook	1
Servant	1
Total	56

Group C employment
(artisan, entrepreneurial, and professional workers)

Musician	3
Boarding house operator	2
Brewer	2
Hairdresser & musician	2
Grocer	2
Tailor	2
Minister	2
Mason	2
Clothes dealer	1
Rope maker	1
Cordwainer	1
Brass founder	1
Trader	1
Clothing/fruit shop	1
Housewright	1
Soup shop	1
Oyster shop	1
Total	26
Total listed in directory	356
Total with jobs listed	273
Total men listed	282
Total women listed	74

SOURCE: Boston City Directory, 1826.

Appendix E

David Walker's Death and the History of His Family

David Walker married Eliza Butler on February 23, 1826, in Boston.[1] Only one issue of this union is recorded in Boston City Records: Lydia Ann Walker, aged one year and nine months, died on July 31, 1830, of lung fever.[2] Her birth record does not exist.

A great body of lore has embellished the death of David Walker. Some have claimed he was stalked by bounty hunters from Georgia after outraged planters had placed a price on his head. Perhaps their victim, he was supposed to have been found slumped over and dead in a doorway on Boston's North Slope. There seems to be a consensus that he met some violent and untimely death.[3]

No one, however, has checked their claims against municipal death records. The Boston Index of Deaths lists Walker as dying on August 6, 1830, of consumption at the age of thirty-three.[4] The date and cause are repeated in the *Boston Daily Courier*. Nowhere is foul play suggested. He died a week after his daughter, at a time when pulmonary afflictions were numerous in the city. At least seven people had died of lung complications in the last week, lending credibility to that cause.[5] If Walker's death had been suspicious, a coroner's report might have ensued, yet there is none in the Boston City Records. Certainly there were numerous Southerners who wanted Walker dead, and neither the possibility of murder nor

1. Register of Marriages in Boston, 1800–1849, Boston City Hall.

2. Index of Deaths, 1801–48, p. 300, Boston City Hall.

3. The key printed source for these tales of murder is Henry Highland Garnet's brief biography of David Walker in his 1848 work, *Walker's Appeal, with a Brief Sketch of His Life*. But oral sources in Boston's black community played an important role as well, as "A Colored Bostonian" made clear to his readers in *The Liberator*, January 22, 1831. Various modern historians have upheld these claims. Two of the most important are Herbert Aptheker, *"One Continual Cry": David Walker's Appeal to the Colored Citizens of the World (1829–1830)—Its Setting and Its Meaning* (New York: Humanities Press for AIMS, 1965), and Sterling Stuckey, *Slave Culture: Nationalist Theory and the Foundations of Black America* (New York: Oxford University Press, 1987), 137.

4. Index of Deaths, 1801–48, 300, Boston City Hall.

5. *Boston Daily Courier*, August 10, 1830.

the possibility that he was stalked can be discounted. Yet available sources shed no light on the shadowing of Walker, while they strongly support a natural death from a common and virulent urban disease of the nineteenth century.

After David's death, Eliza remarried on September 19, 1833, to a man named Alexander Dewson, or Duson.[6] Dewson appeared in the Boston City Directory for the first time in 1837 and never appeared again after 1839. He was listed as a laborer.

That Eliza had at least one child with Dewson is certain, but when exactly and if more than one is not as evident. City records indicate that they lost a five-month-old baby girl, Margareta, to lung fever on April 11, 1837.[7]

The larger question is who fathered Eliza's son, Edwin Garrison Walker. Edwin would become one of Boston's most famous African Americans in the post–Civil war era. Obviously the surname identifies David as his father, and Edwin is repeatedly referred to as his son. Yet all of Edwin's obituaries, while designating David as his father, place his birth on February 28, or September 28, 1835.[8] While no birth record exists for Edwin, his death record lists February 28, 1835, as his birthdate.[9] But if the birthdate is correct, the selection of "Walker" as surname would have been a great affront to Dewson, even if he had deep regard for Eliza's first husband, and it would have been completely out of step with contemporary conventions.

There is a strong possibility that David was Edwin's father, but confusion persists in determining exactly just who was in Walker's family. Henry Highland Garnet wrote in the 1848 biography that David had had only one child, a son who was then eighteen years old. This individual could well have been Edwin. Yet the federal census of 1830 listed two boys under the age of ten in Walker's household.[10] While these boys could have been the children of boarders in the house, they might also have been the offspring of Eliza and David. Yet Garnet said he had only one child, a son. But this does not accord with the presence of Lydia, or with the son named "David M.," whom *The Liberator* noted as dying on July 16, 1832, at the age of five.[11] If both David and Edwin were alive in 1830, they would have been the two boys under ten in the household. Garnet, who made significant errors in Walker's biography, such as claiming a 1785 birthdate while stating his age at death as thirty-four, may have been wrong as well on the family composition yet right about the eighteen-year-old son. David probably was the father of Edwin Garrison Walker, and many sources point to that provenance. Moreover, the fact of the surname is difficult to explain any other way.

Alexander Dewson died on May 2, 1851, of consumption at the age of forty-six,

6. Register of Marriages in Boston, 1800–1849, Boston City Hall.

7. Boston Alphabetical Death Records, 1801–48, Boston City Hall.

8. *Boston Daily Globe*, January 14, 1901, and *Boston Evening Transcript*, January 14, 1901.

9. Register of Deaths, 1901. The varying reliability of death and birth records is once again indicated in this document because Edwin's mother and father are listed as "unknown."

10. 1830 Federal Census, Massachusetts, Suffolk County, Boston, Ward 5, 197.

11. *The Liberator*, July 28, 1832.

and Eliza apparently never married again.[12] She lived with Edwin in Charlestown for the balance of her life. She was not idle, however, for at some point she helped found the United Daughters of Zion, one of the first black women's organizations in the nation. She died on April 29, 1883, and was buried on Bunker Hill.[13]

Edwin achieved a fame that rivaled David's.[14] After finishing public school in Boston, he learned the leather trade and by 1857 had a shop with fifteen men working for him. Quietly studying law on the side, he passed the bar in 1861 and became only the third black attorney in the history of Suffolk County. He soon entered politics and was initially elected to the Massachusetts General Court in 1866 as a Republican, but by 1867 he had switched to the Democrats and allied himself with popular Civil War general Benjamin Butler. While governor in 1883, Butler rewarded Walker with a nomination as judge to the municipal court of Charlestown, but Republicans foiled the effort three different times. Nevertheless, Walker became a highly regarded local attorney who "was especially friendly to the Irish people." He was also involved with numerous black organizations and benevolent societies, including the Colored National League, of which he was president in the 1890s. Edwin Walker died of pneumonia on January 13, 1901.

---

12. Deaths Registered in the City of Boston, 1851, Boston City Hall.
13. Registry of Deaths in Boston, 1883, Boston City Hall.
14. All the following information comes from the obituaries in note 8 above.

Bibliography

Primary Sources

Manuscripts

Beinecke Rare Book Library, Yale University, New Haven, Connecticut
    Amos G. Beman Papers in James Weldon Johnson Collection
Boston City Hall, Boston, Massachusetts
    Registry of Births, Marriages, and Deaths
    Suffolk County Registry of Deeds
    Suffolk County Registry of Probate
Boston Public Library, Boston, Massachusetts
    City of Boston, Valuation Book, 1825, 1826, 1827, 1829, 1830, 1831
Georgia Department of Archives and History, Atlanta, Georgia
    Record Group 4, File II—Names
    Governor's Letter Books, November 1809–October 1829, 1829–1833
Georgia Historical Society, Savannah, Georgia
    Records of Chatham County, Mayor's Letter Book, 1821–1844
    Chatham County Registers of Free Persons of Color, 1817–1864
Grand Masonic Lodge of Massachusetts, Boston, Massachusetts
    Prince Hall Records, Minutes of African Lodge, Boston, 1807–1846
Historical Society of Pennsylvania, Philadelphia, Pennsylvania
    Minute and Trial Book, Bethel African Methodist Episcopal Church
Library Company of Philadelphia, Philadelphia, Pennsylvania
    Broadside Collection, vol. 54
Lower Cape Fear Historical Society, Wilmington, North Carolina
    Sallie McLaurin, "Walker Family" (typescript)
New Hanover County Public Library, Wilmington, North Carolina
    Nada R. McDonald Cotton, "The Walker-Howe Family of Wilmington, North Carolina in New Hanover County" (typescript)
    "Minutes of the 4th Quarterly Conference, 31 December 1831," Grace Methodist Episcopal Church, Quarterly Reports, 1807–1852

North Carolina State Archives, Raleigh, North Carolina
    Brunswick County, Real Estate Conveyances
    General Assembly Session Records, 1795, 1802, 1825, 1826, November
        1830–January 1831
    Governor John Owen, Letterbook, 1828–1830
    Governors' Papers, Montfort Stokes, State Series
    New Hanover County, Deed Book
    New Hanover County Tax Lists, 1815–1819, 1816, 1836, 1838
    New Hanover County Tax Records, 1779–1869
    Slave Collection, 1787–1856
    John Walker Papers, 1735–1909
Philadelphia City Hall, Philadelphia, Pennsylvania
    City Tax (Real and Personal) Records, 1820–1825
    Poor Tax Register
South Carolina Department of Archives and History, Columbia, South Carolina
    General Assembly Session Records
South Caroliniana Library, University of South Carolina, Columbia, South Carolina
    Richard Furman Papers
Southern Historical Collection, University of North Carolina, Chapel Hill, North
Carolina
    Curtis Papers—Moses Ashley Curtis, Personal Diary, 1830–1836
    John De Berniere Hooper Papers
Virginia State Library, Richmond, Virginia
    Executive Letter Book, Reel 14
    Slave and Free Negro Letterbook, Executive Papers of Governor John Floyd
Yale University, Manuscripts and Archives, New Haven, Connecticut
    Bunnell Family Papers
    Ulrich Bonnell Phillips Papers

Printed Primary Sources

Allen, Richard. *The Life Experience and Gospel Labors of the Rt. Rev. Richard Allen*, with an Introduction by George A. Singleton. Nashville, Tenn.: Abingdon Press, 1960.

Andrew, James O. "Rise and Progress of Methodism in Charleston, South Carolina." *Methodist Magazine and Quarterly Review* 12 (1830), 17–28.

Aptheker, Herbert. *"One Continual Cry": David Walker's Appeal to the Colored Citizens of the World (1829–1830)—Its Setting and Its Meaning.* New York: Humanities Press for AIMS, 1965.

Asher, Jeremiah. *Incidents in the Life of the Rev. J. Asher. . . .* London, 1850.

Beare, Austin. *Reminiscences of Fugitive-Slave Law Days in Boston.* Boston, 1880.

Bell, Howard H., ed. *Minutes of the Proceedings of the National Negro Conventions, 1830–1864.* New York: Arno Press, 1969.

Bentley, William. *The Diary of William Bentley, D.D.,* 4 vols. Salem, Mass.: Essex Institute, 1905–1914.

Berlin, Ira, ed. "After Nat Turner: A Letter from the North." *Journal of Negro History* 55 (April 1970), 144–51.

The Boston Directory Containing Names of the Inhabitants . . . , published by
    Charles Stimpson Jr. et al. [for the years 1825–1830].

Boyd, William K., ed. *Some Eighteenth Century Tracts Concerning North Carolina.*
    Raleigh, N.C.: Edwards & Broughton Co., 1927.

Bracey, John, et al., eds. *The Afro-Americans: Selected Documents.* Boston: Allyn
    & Bacon, 1972.

———. *Black Nationalism in America.* Indianapolis: Bobbs-Merril, 1970.

Brawley, Benjamin. *Early American Negro Writers.* Chapel Hill: University of North
    Carolina Press, 1935.

Brickell, John. *The Natural History of North Carolina.* Dublin, 1737. Reprint
    Raleigh, 1910.

Brown, William Wells. *The Rising Son; or, The Antecedents and Advancement of
    the Colored Race.* Boston, 1876.

Burkitt, Lemuel, and Jesse Read. *A Concise History of the Kehukee Baptist Associa-
    tion from Its Original Rise Down to 1803.* Halifax, N.C., 1803.

Carson, James Petigru, ed. *Life, Letters, and Speeches of James Louis Petigru: The
    Union Man of South Carolina.* Washington, D.C.: W. H. Lowdermilk & Co.,
    1920.

Charleston Directory and Stranger's Guide for the Year 1816.

Clark, Elmer T., ed. *The Journal and Letters of Francis Asbury,* 3 vols. London:
    Epworth Press, 1958.

Clark, Walter, ed. *The State Records of North Carolina,* 20 vols, numbered 11–30.
    Goldsboro, N.C.: Nash Bros., 1895–1914.

Davis, Harry E. "Documents Relating to Negro Masonry in America." *Journal of
    Negro History* 21 (1936), 425–26.

The Directory and Stranger's Guide for the City of Charleston . . . for the Year 1819.

The Directory and Stranger's Guide for the City of Charleston . . . for the Year 1822.

[Earle, Thomas]. *The Life, Travels and Opinions of Benjamin Lundy.* Philadelphia,
    1847.

Easton, Hosea. *A Treatise on the Intellectual Character, and Civil and Political
    Condition of the Colored People of the United States.* Boston, 1837. Re-
    printed in Dorothy Porter, ed., *Negro Protest Pamphlets: A Compendium.*
    New York: Arno Press, 1969.

Evarts, Jeremiah. *Cherokee Removal: The "William Penn" Essays and Other Writ-
    ings.* Ed. Francis Paul Prucha. Knoxville: University of Tennessee Press,
    1981.

Everett, Alexander Hill. *America: or A General Survey of the Political Situation of
    the Several Powers of the Western Continent, with Conjectures on Their
    Future Prospects.* London, 1828.

Finney, Charles Grandison. *Lectures on Revivals of Religion.* Ed. William G.
    McLoughlin. Cambridge: Harvard University Press, 1960.

Foote, William Henry. *Sketches of North Carolina.* New York, 1846.

Fries, Adelaide Lisetta, ed. *Records of the Moravians in North Carolina,* 7 vols.
    Raleigh, N.C.: Edwards & Broughton Co., 1922–70.

[Garnet, Henry Highland]. *Walker's Appeal, With a Brief Sketch of His Life. By
    Henry Highland Garnet. And Also Garnet's Address to the Slaves of the
    United States of America.* New York, 1848.

Hamilton, Stanislaus Murray, ed. *The Writings of James Monroe,* 7 vols. New York: AMS Press, 1898–1903.

Henry, Charles S., ed. *A Digest of All the Ordinances of the City of Savannah, which were of force on the 1st July 1854.* Savannah, Ga., 1854.

[Hilton, John T.]. *An Address, Delivered Before the African Grand Lodge of Boston, No. 459, June 24th, 1828, By John T. Hilton: On the Annual Festival, of St. John the Baptist.* Boston, 1828.

[Holland, Edwin Clifford]. *A Refutation of the Calumnies Circulated Against the Southern and Western States, Respecting the Institution and Existence of Slavery Among Them. . . .* Charleston, S.C., 1822.

Holland, Patricia G., and Milton Meltzer, eds. *The Collected Correspondence of Lydia Maria Child, 1817–1880.* Millwood, N.Y.: Kraus-Thomson Organization, 1979.

Horsmanden, Daniel. *The New York Conspiracy.* Ed. with an introduction by Thomas J. Davis. Boston: Beacon Press, 1971.

Hunter, Clark, ed. *The Life and Letters of Alexander Wilson.* Philadelphia: American Philosophical Society, 1983.

Jefferson, Thomas. *Notes on the State of Virginia.* Ed. William Peden. New York: W. W. Norton & Co., 1972.

Jenkins, James. *Experience, Labours, and Sufferings of Rev. James Jenkins.* N.p., 1842.

Johnson, Oliver. *William Lloyd Garrison and His Times.* Boston, 1879.

Journal of the House of Delegates of the Commonwealth of Virginia. Richmond, Va., 1831.

Journal of the House of Representatives of the State of Georgia, 1829–1830. Milledgeville, Ga., 1830.

Killens, John Oliver, ed. *The Trial Record of Denmark Vesey.* Boston: Beacon Press, 1970.

Klingberg, Frank J., ed. *The Carolina Chronicle of Dr. Francis Le Jau, 1706–1717.* Berkeley and Los Angeles: University of California Press, 1956.

Lee, Jesse. *A Short History of the Methodists in the United States.* Baltimore, 1810.

Lennon, Donald R., and Ida Brooks Kellam, eds. *The Wilmington Town Book, 1743–1778.* Raleigh: North Carolina Division of Archives and History, 1973.

"The Letters of Hon. James Habersham, 1756–1775." *Collections of the Georgia Historical Society,* vol. 6. Savannah: Georgia Historical Society, 1904.

Love, E. K. *History of the First African Baptist Church, from Its Organization, January 20th, 1788, to July 1st, 1888.* Savannah, Ga., 1888.

McLean, Robert C., ed. "A Yankee Tutor in the Old South." *North Carolina Historical Review* 47 (January 1970), 51–85.

May, Samuel J. *Some Recollections of Our Antislavery Conflict.* Boston, 1869.

Minutes of the Annual Conferences of the Methodist Episcopal Church for the Years 1773–1828. New York, 1840.

Mood, F. A. *Methodism in Charleston.* Nashville, Tenn., 1856.

Morgan, David T., ed. *The John Gray Blount Papers,* 4 vols. Raleigh: North Carolina Department of Cultural Resources, 1982.

Nell, William Cooper. *The Colored Patriots of the American Revolution.* Boston, 1855.

Nelson, Truman. *Documents of Upheaval: Selections from William Lloyd Garrison's the Liberator, 1831–1865.* New York: Hill & Wang, 1966.

Nott, Josiah. "Two Lectures on the Natural History of the Caucasian and Negro Races." In Drew Gilpin Faust, ed., *The Ideology of Slavery: Proslavery Thought in the Antebellum South, 1830–1860.* Baton Rouge: Louisiana State University Press, 1981, 206–38.

Palmer, William, ed. *Calendar of Virginia State Papers,* 11 vols. Richmond, Va., 1875–93.

Payson, Edward, D.D. *An Address to Seamen, Delivered at Portland, October 28, 1821; At the request of the Portland Auxiliary Marine Bible Society.* (Copy available at the Rare Book Room of the Boston Public Library.)

Pease, William H., and Jane H. Pease. "Walker's *Appeal* Comes to Charleston: A Note and Documents." *Journal of Negro History* 59 (July 1974), 287–92.

Phillips, Ulrich B., ed. *Plantation and Frontier,* vol. 2 of John R. Commons et al., eds., *A Documentary History of American Industrial Society,* 10 vols. Cleveland, Ohio: Arthur H. Clark Co., 1910.

Porter, Dorothy, ed. *Early Negro Writing, 1760–1837.* Boston: Beacon Press, 1971.

Proceedings of the Grand Lodge of the Most Ancient and Honorable Fraternity of Free and Accepted Masons of the Commonwealth of Massachusetts . . . Quarterly Communication, March 8, 1876. Boston, 1876.

Rachleff, Marshall. "Document: David Walker's Southern Agent." *Journal of Negro History* 62 (January 1977), 100–103.

Richardson, Marilyn, ed. *Maria W. Stewart, America's First Black Political Writer: Essays and Speeches.* Bloomington: Indiana University Press, 1987.

Robinson, William H., ed. *The Proceedings of the Free African Union Society and the African Benevolent Society, Newport, Rhode Island 1780–1824.* Providence: Urban League of Rhode Island, 1976.

Saunders, William, ed. *Colonial Records of North Carolina,* 10 vols. Raleigh, N.C., 1886–1890.

Schaw, Janet. *Journal of a Lady of Quality.* Ed. Evangeline Walker Andrews and Charles McLean Andrews. New Haven: Yale University Press, 1939.

Semple, Robert B. *A History of the Rise and Progress of the Baptists in Virginia.* Richmond, Va., 1810.

Simms, James M. *The First Colored Baptist Church in North America. Constituted at Savannah, Georgia, January 20, A.D. 1788.* Philadelphia, 1888.

Snow, Caleb H. *A History of Boston,* 2nd ed. Boston, 1828.

Stevens, William Bacon. *A History of Georgia,* 2 vols. 1859. Reprint, Savannah, Ga.: Beehive Press, 1972.

Summers, Thomas O., ed. *Autobiography of the Rev. Joseph Travis, A.M.* Nashville, Tenn., 1856.

Third Annual Report of the Board of Directors of the Boston Seamen's Friend Society. Boston, 1831.

Tiffany, Nina M., ed. *Letters of James Murray, Loyalist.* Boston, 1901.

Tragle, Henry Irving. *The Southampton Slave Revolt of 1831: A Compilation of Source Material.* Amherst: University of Massachusetts Press, 1971.

[Tucker, George]. *Letter to a Member of the General Assembly of Virginia on the Subject of the Late Conspiracy of the Slaves, with a Proposal for Their Colonization.* Richmond, Va., 1801.

United States. *Heads of Families at the First Census, 1790: North Carolina.* Wash-
    ington, D.C.: Government Printing Office, 1908.
————. *1800 Federal Census, North Carolina, New Hanover County.*
————. *1810 Federal Census, North Carolina, New Hanover County.*
————. *1830 Federal Census, Massachusetts, Suffolk County.*
Valentin, Pompée, Baron de Vastey. *Réflexions sur une lettre de Mazeres, ex-colon
    français, adressé à M.J.C.L. Sismonde de Sismondi, sur les Noirs et les
    Blancs, la Civilisation de l'Afrique, le Royaume d'Hayti, etc.* Cap-Henri,
    1816.
Van Horne, John C., ed. *Religious Philanthropy and Colonial Slavery: The Ameri-
    can Correspondence of the Associates of Dr. Bray, 1717–1777.* Urbana: Uni-
    versity of Illinois Press, 1985.
Walker, David. *Appeal to the Colored Citizens of the World, But in Particular, and
    Very Expressly, to Those of the United States of America.* Rev. ed. Sean
    Wilentz. New York: Hill & Wang, 1965.
Wightman, William M. *Life of William Capers, . . . Including an Autobiography.*
    Nashville, Tenn., 1858.
Woodson, Carter G., ed. *Negro Orators and Their Orations.* 1925. Reprint, New
    York: Russell & Russell, 1969.
Young, Robert Alexander. *The Ethiopian Manifesto, Issued in Defence of the Black
    Man's Rights in the Scale of Universal Freedom.* New York, 1829.

Slave Narratives

Ball, Charles. *Fifty Years in Chains; or, The Life of an American Slave.* New York,
    1858.
[Clark, Lewis, and Milton Clark]. *Narratives of the Suffering of Lewis and Milton
    Clarke, Sons of a Soldier of the Revolution, During a Captivity of More than
    Twenty Years Among the Slaveholders of Kentucky. . . .* Boston, 1846.
Clinkscales, J. G. *On the Old Plantation: Reminiscences of His Childhood.* 1916.
    Reprint, New York: Negro Universities Press, 1969.
Douglass, Frederick. *Narrative of the Life of Frederick Douglass, An American
    Slave.* Ed. Benjamin Quarles. Cambridge: Belknap Press, 1960.
Grimes, William. *Life of William Grimes, the Runaway Slave.* New York, 1825.
Katz, William, ed. *Five Slave Narratives: A Compendium.* New York: Arno Press,
    1968.
Stroyer, Jacob. *My Life in the South.* Salem, Mass., 1898.
[Veney, Bethany]. *The Narrative of Bethany Veney, a Slave Woman.* Worcester,
    Mass., 1889.
Williams, Sally. *Aunt Sally; or, The Cross the Way to Freedom.* Cincinnati, 1858.

Travel Accounts

Abdy, Edward S. *Journal of a Residence and Tour in the United States of North
    America from April, 1833, to October, 1834.* 3 vols. London, 1835.
Buckingham, J. S. *The Slave States of America.* 2 vols. London, 1842.

Ezell, John S., ed. *The New Democracy in America: Travels of Francisco de Miranda in the United States, 1783–1784*. Norman: University of Oklahoma Press, 1963.

Hall, Basil. *Travels in North America in the Years 1827 & 1828*. 2 vols. Philadelphia, 1829.

Hamilton, T. *Men and Manners in America*. 2 vols. 2nd American ed. Philadelphia, 1833.

Hodgson, Adam. *Remarks During a Journey Through North America in the Years 1819, 1820, and 1821, in a Series of Letters*. New York, 1823.

Janson, Charles William. *The Stranger in America, 1793–1806*. Ed. Carl S. Driver. New York: Press of the Pioneers, 1935.

O'Ferrall, S. A. *A Ramble of Six Thousand Miles Through the United States of America*. London, 1832.

Smyth, J. F. D. *Tour in the United States of America*. 2 vols. London, 1784.

Stuart, James. *Three Years in North America*. 3rd ed. 2 vols. Edinburgh, 1833.

Van Doren, Mark, ed. *Travels of William Bartram*. New York: Dover Publications, 1955.

Newspapers

The African Repository and Colonial Journal
Baton Rouge Gazette
Boston Courier
Boston Daily Courier
Boston Daily Evening Transcript
Cape Fear Recorder
Charleston City Gazette
Charleston City Gazette & Commercial Daily Advertiser
Charleston Courier
Columbian Centinel (Boston)
Freedom's Journal (New York City)
The Genius of Universal Emancipation (Baltimore)
Liberator (Boston)
Liberty Bell (New York)
Milledgeville Federal Union
Milledgeville Southern Recorder
Milledgeville Statesman & Patriot
New York Evening Post
Niles' Register (Washington, D.C.)
Raleigh Register
Richmond Daily Whig
Richmond Enquirer
Rights of All (New York City)
Washington, D.C., Daily National Intelligencer
Wilmington Centinel
Wilmington Chronicle
Wilmington Gazette

Secondary Sources

Books and Articles

Alford, Terry. *Prince Among Slaves*. New York: Harcourt Brace Jovanovich, 1977.

Aptheker, Herbert. *American Negro Slave Revolts*. 5th ed. New York: International Publishers, 1983, 335.

———. "Maroons Within the Present Limits of the United States." *Journal of Negro History* 24 (1939), 167–84.

Baldwin, Lewis V. *"Invisible" Strands in African Methodism: A History of the African Union Methodist Protestant and Union American Methodist Episcopal Churches, 1805–1980*. Metuchen, N.J.: Scarecrow Press, 1983.

Bassett, J. S. "North Carolina Methodism and Slavery." *Historical Society of Trinity College*. 4th ser. Durham, N.C., 1900, 1–11.

Berlin, Ira. *Slaves Without Masters: The Free Negro in the Antebellum South*. New York: Pantheon Books, 1974.

Bernal, Martin. *Black Athena: The Afroasiatic Roots of Classical Civilization,* vol. 1: *The Fabrication of Ancient Greece, 1785–1985*. New Brunswick, N.J., Rutgers University Press, 1987.

Betts, Albert Deems. *History of South Carolina Methodism*. Columbia, S.C.: Advocate Press, 1952.

Bishir, Catherine W. "Black Builders in Antebellum North Carolina." *North Carolina Historical Review* 61 (October 1984), 422–61.

Bolster, W. Jeffrey. "'To Feel Like a Man': Black Seamen in the Northern States, 1800–1860." *Journal of American History* 76 (March 1990), 1173–99.

Brewer, James Howard. "Legislation Designed to Control Slavery in Wilmington and Fayetteville." *North Carolina Historical Review* 30 (April 1953), 155–66.

Browning, James B. "The Beginnings of Insurance Enterprise Among Negroes." *Journal of Negro History* 22 (October 1937), 417–33.

Bucke, Emory Stevens, ed. *The History of American Methodism*. 3 vols. Nashville, Tenn.: Abingdon Press, 1964.

Calhoon, Robert M. *Religion and the American Revolution in North Carolina*. Raleigh: North Carolina Department of Cultural Resources, 1976.

Cecelski, David S. "The Shores of Freedom: The Maritime Underground Railroad in North Carolina, 1800–1861." *North Carolina Historical Review* 71 (April 1994), 174–206.

Chreitzberg, Abel McKee. *Early Methodism in the Carolinas*. Nashville, Tenn., 1897.

Clifton, James M. "Golden Grains of White: Rice Planting on the Lower Cape Fear." *North Carolina Historical Review* 50 (October 1973), 365–93.

Coon, Charles L. *The Beginnings of Public Education in North Carolina: A Documentary History, 1790–1840*. 2 vols. Raleigh, N.C.: Edwards & Broughton Co., 1908.

Cooper, Frederick. "Elevating the Race: The Social Thought of Black Leaders, 1827–1850." *American Quarterly* 24 (December 1972), 604–25.

Cornelius, Janet Duitsman. *"When I Can Read My Title Clear": Literacy, Slavery, and Religion in the Antebellum South*. Columbia: University of South Carolina Press, 1991.

Cottrol, Robert. *The Afro-Yankees: Providence's Black Community in the Ante-bellum Era.* Westport, Conn.: Greenwood Press, 1982.

Craton, Michael. "Slave Culture, Resistance, and the Achievement of Emancipation in the British West Indies, 1783–1838." In James Walvin, ed., *Slavery and British Society, 1776–1846.* Baton Rouge: Louisiana State University Press, 1982, 100–122.

———. *Testing the Chains: Resistance to Slavery in the British West Indies.* Ithaca, N.Y.: Cornell University Press, 1982.

Creative Survival: The Providence Black Community in the 19th Century. Providence: Rhode Island Black Heritage Society, 1984.

Crow, Jeffrey J. *The Black Experience in Revolutionary North Carolina.* Raleigh, N.C: Department of Cultural Resources, 1977.

———. "Slave Rebelliousness and Social Conflict in North Carolina, 1775–1802." *William and Mary Quarterly,* 3rd ser., 37 (1980), 79–102.

Curry, Leonard P. *The Free Black in Urban America, 1800–1850: The Shadow of the Dreams.* Chicago: University of Chicago Press, 1981.

Dain, Bruce. "Haiti and Egypt in Early Black Racial Discourse in the United States." *Slavery and Abolition* 14 (December 1993), 139–61.

Daniel, W. Harrison. "Virginia Baptists and the Negro in the Early Republic." *Virginia Magazine of History and Biography* 80 (January 1972), 60–69.

Daniels, John. *In Freedom's Birthplace.* Boston: Houghton Mifflin, 1914.

Davis, David B. *The Problem of Slavery in the Age of Revolution, 1770–1823.* Ithaca, N.Y.: Cornell University Press, 1975.

———. *The Problem of Slavery in Western Culture.* Ithaca, N.Y.: Cornell University Press, 1966.

Davis, Harry E. *A History of Freemasonry Among Negroes in America.* Cleveland, Ohio: United Supreme Council, 1946.

Degler, Carl. *Neither Black Nor White: Slavery and Race Relations in Brazil and the United States.* New York: Macmillan, 1971.

Dillon, Merton. *Slavery Attacked: Southern Slaves and Their Allies, 1619–1865.* Baton Rouge: Louisiana State University Press, 1990.

Drewry, William Sidney. *The Southampton Insurrection.* 1900. Reprint, Murfreesboro, N.C.: Johnson Publishing Co., 1968.

Du Bois, W. E. B. *Dusk of Dawn: An Essay Toward an Autobiography of a Race Concept.* New York: Harcourt, Brace & Co., 1940.

Eaton, Clement. "A Dangerous Pamphlet in the Old South." *Journal of Southern History* 2 (August 1936), 323–34.

Egerton, Douglas R. "'Fly Across the River': The Easter Slave Conspiracy of 1802." *North Carolina Historical Review* 68 (April 1991), 87–110.

———. "Gabriel's Conspiracy and the Election of 1800." *Journal of Southern History* 56 (May 1990), 191–214.

———. *Gabriel's Rebellion: The Virginia Slave Conspiracies of 1800 and 1802.* Chapel Hill: University of North Carolina Press, 1993.

———. "'Its Origin Is Not a Little Curious': A New Look at the American Colonization Society." *Journal of the Early Republic* 5 (Winter 1985), 463–80.

———. "A Rejoinder." *North Carolina Historical Review* 68 (April 1991), 122–24.

Elkins, Stanley M. *Slavery: A Problem in American Institutional and Intellectual Life.* 3rd ed. Chicago: University of Chicago Press, 1976.

Essig, James, "'A Very Wintry Season': Virginia Baptists and Slavery." *Virginia Magazine of History and Biography* 88 (April 1980), 170–85.

Faler, Paul. "Cultural Aspects of the Industrial Revolution: Lynn, Massachusetts, Shoemakers and Industrial Morality, 1826–1860." *Labor History* 15 (Summer 1974), 367–94.

Faust, Drew Gilpin. "Culture, Conflict, and Community: The Meaning of Power on an Ante-Bellum Plantation." *Journal of Social History* 14 (Fall 1980), 83–97.

Fenn, Elizabeth. "'A Perfect Equality Seemed to Reign': Slave Society and Jonkonnu." *North Carolina Historical Review* 65 (April 1988), 127–53.

Finkenbine, Roy. "Boston's Black Churches: Institutional Centers of the Antislavery Movement." In Donald M. Jacobs, ed., *Courage and Conscience: Black and White Abolitionists in Boston.* Bloomington: Indiana University Press, 1993, 169–89.

Fitchett, E. Horace. "The Traditions of the Free Negro in Charleston, South Carolina." *Journal of Negro History* 25 (April 1940), 139–52.

Foner, Philip S. "William P. Powell: Militant Champion of Black Seamen." In Philip S. Foner, *Essays in Afro-American History.* Philadelphia: Temple University Press, 1978, 83–97.

Fordham, Monroe. *Major Themes in Northern Black Religious Thought, 1800–1860.* Hicksville, N.Y.: Exposition Press, 1975.

Franklin, John Hope. *The Free Negro in North Carolina, 1790–1860.* Chapel Hill: University of North Carolina Press, 1943.

Fredrickson, George. *The Black Image in the White Mind: The Debate on Afro-American Character and Destiny, 1817–1914.* New York: Harper & Row, 1971.

Freehling, Alison Goodyear. *Drift Toward Dissolution: The Virginia Slavery Debate of 1831–1832.* Baton Rouge: Louisiana State University Press, 1982.

Freehling, William. *Prelude to Civil War: The Nullification Controversy in South Carolina, 1816–1836.* New York: Harper & Row, 1966.

Frey, Sylvia. *Water from the Rock: Black Resistance in a Revolutionary Age.* Princeton: Princeton University Press, 1991.

Genovese, Eugene D. *From Rebellion to Revolution: Afro-American Slave Revolts in the Making of the Modern World.* Baton Rouge: Louisiana State University Press, 1979.

———. *Roll, Jordan, Roll: The World the Slaves Made.* New York: Random House, 1974.

George, Carol V. R. *Segregated Sabbaths: Richard Allen and the Rise of Independent Black Churches, 1760–1840.* New York: Oxford University Press, 1973.

Gravely, William B. "The Dialectic of Double-Consciousness in Black American Freedom Celebrations, 1808–1863." *Journal of Negro History* 62 (Winter 1982), 302–17.

———. "The Rise of African Churches in America (1786–1822): Re-examining the Contexts." *Journal of Religious Thought* 41 (1984), 58–73.

Greene, Lorenzo. "Prince Hall: Massachusetts Leader in Crisis." *Freedomways* 1 (Fall 1961), 238–58.

Grimshaw, William H. *Official History of Freemasonry Among the Colored People in North America.* 1903. Reprint, New York: Negro Universities Press, 1969.

Grissom, W. L. *History of Methodism in North Carolina from 1772 to the Present Time.* 2 vols. Nashville, Tenn.: Smith and Lamar, 1905.

Gross, Bella. "*Freedom's Journal* and the *Rights of All.*" *Journal of Negro History* 17 (1932), 241–86.

Halliburton, R., Jr. *Red over Black: Black Slavery Among the Cherokee Indians.* Westport, Conn.: Greenwood Press, 1977.

Harding, Vincent. *There Is a River: The Black Struggle for Freedom in America.* New York: Vintage Books, 1983.

Hart, Albert B. *Slavery and Abolition, 1831–1841.* New York, 1906.

Hayden, Robert. *Faith, Culture, and Leadership: A History of the Black Church in Boston.* Boston: Boston NAACP, 1983.

Horton, James and Lois. *Black Bostonians: Family Life and Community Struggle in the Antebellum North.* New York: Holmes & Meier, 1979.

Irving, John B. *A Day on the Cooper River.* Reprint with notes by Samuel Gaillard Stoney. 3rd ed. Columbia, S.C.: R. L. Bryan, 1969.

Isaac, Rhys. "Evangelical Revolt: The Nature of the Baptists' Challenge to the Traditional Order in Virginia, 1765 to 1775." *William and Mary Quarterly,* 3rd ser., 31 (1974), 345–68.

Jackson, Luther P. "Free Negroes of Petersburg, Virginia." *Journal of Negro History* 12 (July 1927), 365–98.

———. "Religious Development of the Negro in Virginia from 1760 to 1860." *Journal of Negro History* 16 (April 1931), 168–239.

Jacobs, Donald M. "David Walker: Boston Race Leader, 1825–1830." *Essex Institute Historical Collections* 107 (1971), 94–107.

———. "David Walker and William Lloyd Garrison: Racial Cooperation and the Shaping of Boston Abolition." In Donald M. Jacobs, ed., *Courage and Conscience: Black and White Abolitionists in Boston.* Bloomington: Indiana University Press, 1993, 9–17.

Johnson, F. Roy. *The Nat Turner Slave Insurrection.* Murfreesboro, N.C.: Johnson Publishing Co., 1966.

———. *The Nat Turner Story.* Murfreesboro, N.C.: Johnson Publishing Co., 1970.

Johnson, Guion Griffis. *Ante-Bellum North Carolina: A Social History.* Chapel Hill: University of North Carolina Press, 1937.

Johnson, Michael, and James Roark. "'A Middle Ground': Free Mulattoes and the Friendly Moralist Society of Antebellum Charleston." *Southern Studies* 21 (Fall 1982), 246–65.

Jordan, Winthrop D. *White Over Black: American Attitudes Toward the Negro, 1550–1812.* Baltimore: Penguin Books, 1969.

Kaplan, Sidney. *The Black Presence in the Era of the American Revolution, 1770–1800.* New York: New York Graphic Society, 1973.

Kirkland, Thomas J., and Robert M. Kennedy, *Historic Camden,* part two: *Nineteenth Century.* Columbia, S.C.: State Company, 1926.

Lee, Lawrence. *The Lower Cape Fear in Colonial Days.* Chapel Hill: University of North Carolina Press, 1965.

Levesque, George A. *Black Boston: African American Life and Culture in Urban America, 1750–1860.* New York: Garland Publishing, 1994.

———. "Inherent Reformers—Inherited Orthodoxy: Black Baptists in Boston, 1800–1873." *Journal of Negro History* 60 (1975), 491–525.

Levy, Leonard. "The Abolition Riot: Boston's First Slave Rescue." *New England Quarterly* 25 (March 1952), 85–92.

Linebaugh, Peter, and Marcus Rediker. "The Many-Headed Hydra: Sailors, Slaves, and the Atlantic Working Class in the Eighteenth Century." *Journal of Historical Sociology* 3 (September 1990), 225–52.

Litwack, Leon. *Been in the Storm So Long: The Aftermath of Slavery.* New York: Random House, 1979.

———. *North of Slavery: The Negro in the Free States, 1790–1860.* Chicago: University of Chicago Press, 1961.

McLoughlin, William G. *Cherokees and Missionaries, 1789–1839.* New Haven: Yale University Press, 1984.

Mathews, Donald G. *Religion in the Old South.* Chicago: University of Chicago Press, 1977.

———. *Slavery and Methodism: A Chapter in American Morality, 1780–1845.* Princeton: Princeton University Press, 1965.

Miller, Floyd. *The Search for a Black Nationality: Black Colonization and Emigration, 1787–1863.* Urbana: University of Illinois Press, 1975.

Mitchell, J. Marcus. "The Paul Family." *Old Time New England* 63 (Winter 1973), 73–77.

Mohr, Clarence. *On the Threshold of Freedom: Masters and Slaves in Civil War Georgia.* Athens: University of Georgia Press, 1986.

Morgan, Philip. "Black Life in Eighteenth-Century Charleston." *Perspectives in American History,* new ser., 1 (1984), 185–222.

———. "Black Society in the Lowcountry, 1760–1810." In Ira Berlin and Ronald Hoffman, *Slavery and Freedom in the Age of the American Revolution.* Charlottesville, Va.: U.S. Capitol Historical Society, 1983, 83–141.

———. "Work and Culture: The Task System and the World of Lowcountry Blacks, 1700 to 1880." *William and Mary Quarterly,* 3rd ser., 39 (July 1982), 563–99.

Morris, Charles Edward. "Panic and Reprisal: Reaction in North Carolina to the Nat Turner Insurrection, 1831." *North Carolina Historical Review* 62 (January 1985), 29–52.

Moses, Wilson Jeremiah. *Black Messiahs and Uncle Toms: Social and Literary Manipulations of a Religious Myth.* University Park: The Pennsylvania State University Press, 1982.

Mullin, Gerald W. *Flight and Rebellion: Slave Resistance in Eighteenth-Century Virginia.* New York: Oxford University Press, 1972.

Nash, Gary. *Forging Freedom: The Formation of Philadelphia's Black Community, 1720–1840.* Cambridge: Harvard University Press, 1988.

Oates, Stephen B. *The Fires of Jubilee: Nat Turner's Fierce Rebellion.* New York: Harper & Row, 1975.

Parker, Freddie L., ed. *Stealing a Little Freedom: Advertisements for Slave Runaways in North Carolina, 1791–1840.* New York: Garland Publishing, 1994.

Parramore, Thomas C. "Aborted Takeoff: A Critique of 'Fly Across the River.'" *North Carolina Historical Review* 67 (April 1991), 111–21.

———. *Southampton County Virginia.* Charlottesville: University Press of Virginia, 1978.

Payne, Daniel A. *History of the African Methodist Episcopal Church.* Ed. C. S. Smith. Nashville, Tenn., 1891.

Pease, Jane H. and William H. *They Who Would Be Free: Blacks' Search for Freedom, 1830–1861.* New York: Atheneum Press, 1974.

Perdue, Theda. *Slavery and the Evolution of Cherokee Society, 1540–1866.* Knoxville: University of Tennessee Press, 1979.

Perlman, Daniel. "Organizations of the Free Negro in New York City, 1800–1860." *Journal of Negro History* 56 (July 1971), 181–97.

Phillips, Ulrich Bonnell. *American Negro Slavery.* New York: D. Appleton & Co., 1918.

———. *The History of Transportation in the Eastern Cotton Belt to 1860.* New York: Columbia University Press, 1908.

———. "The Slave Labor Problem in the Charleston District." *Political Science Quarterly* 22 (September 1907), 416–39.

Prucha, Francis Paul. *American Indian Policy in the Formative Years: The Indian Trade and Intercourse Acts, 1790–1834.* Cambridge: Harvard University Press, 1962.

Quarles, Benjamin. *The Negro in the American Revolution.* Chapel Hill: University of North Carolina Press, 1961.

Raboteau, Albert. *Slave Religion: The "Invisible Institution" in the Antebellum South.* New York: Oxford University Press, 1978.

Radin, Paul. "Status, Phantasy, and the Christian Dogma." In George P. Rawick, ed., *The American Slave: A Composite Autobiography,* ser. 2, vol. 19: *God Struck Me Dead.* Westport, Conn.: Greenwood Press, 1972, iv–xi.

Rammelkamp, Julian. "The Providence Negro Community, 1820–1842." *Rhode Island History* 7 (January 1948), 20–33.

Rediker, Marcus. *Between the Devil and the Deep Blue Sea: Merchant Seamen, Pirates, and the Anglo-American Maritime World, 1700–1750.* Cambridge: Cambridge University Press, 1987.

Reily, D. A., "William Hammett: Missionary and Founder of the Primitive Methodist Connection." *Methodist History* 10 (October 1971), 30–43.

Schwarz, Philip J. "Gabriel's Challenge: Slaves and Crime in Late Eighteenth-Century Virginia." *The Virginia Magazine of History and Biography* 90 (July 1982), 283–309.

Sherer, Robert G. "Negro Churches in Rhode Island Before 1860." *Rhode Island History* 25 (January 1966), 9–25.

Smith, Charles Spencer. *A History of the African Methodist Episcopal Church.* Philadelphia, 1922.

Smith, Timothy. "Slavery and Theology: The Emergence of Black Christian Consciousness in Nineteenth Century America." *Church History* 41 (December 1972), 497–512.

Sobel, Robert, and John Raimo, eds. *Biographical Directory of the Governors of the United States, 1789–1978.* 4 vols. Westport, Conn.: Meckler Books, 1978.

Sprunt, James. *Chronicles of the Cape Fear River, 1660–1916.* 2nd ed. Raleigh, N.C.: Edwards & Broughton Co., 1916.

Staudenraus, Philip. *The African Colonization Movement, 1816–1865.* New York: Columbia University Press, 1961.

Strickland, John Scott. "The Great Revival and Insurrectionary Fears in North Carolina: An Examination of Antebellum Southern Society and Slave Revolt Panics." In Orville Vernon Burton and Robert C. McMath Jr., eds., *Class, Conflict, and Consensus: Antebellum Southern Community Studies.* Westport, Conn.: Greenwood Press, 1982, 55–95.

Stuckey, Sterling. *The Ideological Origins of Black Nationalism.* Boston: Beacon Press, 1972.

———. *Slave Culture: Nationalist Theory and the Foundations of Black America.* New York: Oxford University Press, 1987.

Swift, David E. "Black Presbyterian Attacks on Racism: Samuel Cornish, Theodore Wright, and Their Contemporaries." In David W. Wills and Richard Newman, eds., *Black Apostles at Home and Abroad: Afro-Americans and the Christian Mission from the Revolution to Reconstruction.* Boston: G. K. Hall & Co., 1982, 39–53.

Talmadge, John E. "The Burritt Mystery: Partisan Journalism in Antebellum Georgia." *Georgia Review* 8 (Fall 1954), 332–41.

Tannenbaum, Frank. *Slave and Citizen: The Negro in the Americas.* New York: Alfred A. Knopf, 1946.

Taylor, R. H. "Slave Conspiracies in North Carolina." *North Carolina Historical Review* 5 (January 1928), 20–34.

Thomas, Lamont D. *Rise to Be a People: A Biography of Paul Cuffe.* Urbana: University of Illinois Press, 1986.

Tolis, Peter. *Elihu Burritt: Crusader for Brotherhood.* Hamden, Conn.: Archon Books, 1968.

Warner, Robert A. "Amos Gerry Beman—1812–1874, A Memoir on a Forgotten Leader." *Journal of Negro History* 22 (January 1937), 200–221.

———. *New Haven Negroes: A Social History.* New Haven: Yale University Press, 1940. Reprint, New York: Arno Press, 1969.

Watson, Alan D. "Impulse Toward Independence: Resistance and Rebellion Among North Carolina Slaves, 1750–1775." *Journal of Negro History* 63 (1978), 317–28.

White, Arthur O. "Prince Saunders: An Instance of Social Mobility Among Antebellum New England Blacks." *Journal of Negro History* 60 (1975), 526–35.

White, David O. "The Fugitive Blacksmith of Hartford: James W. C. Pennington." *The Connecticut Historical Society Bulletin* 49 (Winter 1984), 4–29.

Wikramanayake, Marina. *A World in Shadow: The Free Black in Antebellum South Carolina.* Columbia: University of South Carolina Press, 1973.

Winch, Julie. "American Free Blacks and Emigration to Haiti, 1804–26." *Documentos de Trabajo,* Centro de Investigaciones del Caribe y America Latina, Universidad Interamericana de Puerto Rico, 33 (August 1988), 1–22.

————. *Philadelphia's Black Elite: Activism, Accommodation, and the Struggle for Autonomy, 1787–1848.* Philadelphia: Temple University Press, 1988.

Wood, Peter. *Black Majority: Negroes in Colonial South Carolina from 1670 Through the Stono Rebellion.* New York: Alfred A. Knopf, 1974.

————. "'The Dream Deferred': Black Freedom Struggles on the Eve of Independence." In Gary Y. Okihiro, ed., *In Resistance: Studies in African, Caribbean, and Afro-American History.* Amherst: University of Massachusetts Press, 1986, 166–87.

————. "Nat Turner: The Unknown Slave as Visionary Leader." In Leon Litwack and August Meier, *Black Leaders of the Nineteenth Century.* Urbana: University of Illinois Press, 1988, 21–40.

Woodson, Carter G. *The History of the Negro Church.* Washington, D.C.: Associated Publishers, 1921.

Wyatt-Brown, Bertram. *Southern Honor: Ethics and Behavior in the Old South.* New York: Oxford University Press, 1982.

Theses and Dissertations

Bogger, Tommy L. "The Slave and Free Black Community in Norfolk, 1775–1865." Ph.D. diss., University of Virginia, 1976.

Brewer, James H. "An Account of Negro Slavery in the Cape Fear Region Prior to 1860." Ph.D. diss., University of Pittsburgh, 1949.

Freeman, Rhoda G. "The Free Negro in New York City in the Era Before the Civil War." Ph.D. diss., Columbia University, 1966.

Howard, Cary. "The Georgia Reaction to David Walker's *Appeal.*" M.A. thesis, University of Georgia, 1967.

Jacobs, Donald. "A History of the Boston Negro from the Revolution to the Civil War." Ph.D. diss., Boston University, 1968.

Jelen, Ronald. "Camp-Meetings and Circuits: Elements of the Frontier Religious Landscape of South Carolina." M.A. thesis, University of South Carolina, 1978.

Scott, Julius S. "The Common Wind: Currents of Afro-American Communication in the Era of the Haitian Revolution." Ph.D. diss., Duke University, 1986.

Index